ASP.NET 3.5 Enterprise Application Development with Visual Studio 2008 Problem – Design – Solution

ASP.NET 3.5 Enterprise Application Development with Visual Studio® 2008

Problem – Design – Solution

ASP.NET 3.5 Enterprise Application Development with Visual Studio® 2008

Problem – Design – Solution

Vince Varallo

WILEY

Wiley Publishing, Inc.

ASP.NET 3.5 Application Development with Visual Studio® 2008 Problem – Design - Solution

Published by
Wiley Publishing, Inc.
10475 Crosspoint Boulevard
Indianapolis, IN 46256
www.wiley.com

Copyright © 2009 by Wiley Publishing, Inc., Indianapolis, Indiana
Published by Wiley Publishing, Inc., Indianapolis, Indiana
Published simultaneously in Canada
ISBN: 978-0-470-39686-5
Manufactured in the United States of America

10 9 8 7 6 5 4 3 2 1

Library of Congress Cataloging-in-Publication Data

Varallo, Vince, 1973-
 ASP.NET 3.5 enterprise application development with Visual studio 2008 : problem design solution / Vince Varallo.
    p. cm.
 Includes index.
 ISBN 978-0-470-39686-5 (paper/website)
 1. Application software--Development. 2. Active server pages. 3. Microsoft .NET. 4. Microsoft Visual studio. I. Title.
 QA76.76.A65V36 2009
 006.7'882--dc22
                        2008046999

I must dedicate this book to my true heart and soul, my two daughters, Madison and Courtney. If it weren't for the fact that I have to pay for their college tuition, this book would have never happened. I also must thank the team of developers that I work with: Jack, Joe, Craig, Shaya, Chi, and Tony. These are the guys who work hard every day to produce great software and who have proven that the patterns shown in this book really work. I also would like to thank my boss, Rob, who has given me this team of great developers to work with and the opportunity to explore new technologies. I also thank Brenna Garay, who designed the logo for the sample application in this book and is an amazing artist. Lastly, I have to thank Dr. Bob, but for what I don't know.

About the Author

Vince Varallo has been developing applications for over twelve years using Microsoft technologies and is currently the Director of Application Development for MTI Information Technologies. He develops marketing applications for the pharmaceutical industry using ASP.NET and SQL Server. Prior to working at MTI, he worked in the clinical and the financial industries on a wide array of projects such as clinical data management systems, internal portals, and treasury workstation software.

Vince enjoys exploring new technologies but always finds time for golf, biking, and watching the Phillies. He previously co-authored *Professional Visual Basic 6: The 2003 Programmer's Resource*.

Credits

Acquisitions Editor
Katie Mohr

Development Editor
Rosanne Koneval

Technical Editor
Robert Fayman

Production Editor
Daniel Scribner

Copy Editor
Luann Rouff

Editorial Manager
Mary Beth Wakefield

Production Manager
Tim Tate

Vice President and Executive Group Publisher
Richard Swadley

Vice President and Executive Publisher
Joseph B. Wikert

Project Coordinator, Cover
Lynsey Stanford

Compositor
James D. Kramer, Happenstance Type-O-Rama

Proofreader
Scott A. Clamp, Word One
Josh Chase, Word One

Indexer
Robert Swanson

Acknowledgments

Foremost, I would like to thank Katie Mohr, who entrusted me to write this book. She has been a pleasure to work with and a joy to hang out with. I also thank Rosanne Koneval for all her hard work editing this book and keeping me on schedule, or at least close to it. Thanks also to Bob Fayman, the technical editor on this book. His editing and comments are greatly appreciated. Finally I want to thank the entire team at Wrox for being a continuous source of information about new technologies. They truly stick to their mission of writing books for developers by developers. I have always enjoyed reading their books and it was an honor to write for them again.

Contents

Contents

Contents

Contents

Introduction

This book provides a step-by-step guide for developing an ASP.NET 3.5 application using the latest features in Visual Studio 2008. The Problem Design Solution series by Wrox is unique because it describes a large case study and builds an entire solution chapter by chapter for each incremental step. This book uses a wide variety of new features in Visual Studio 2008, explains each in detail, and produces a solution that you can use as a starting point for your own applications.

If you are responsible for designing or developing enterprise-wide applications, departmental applications, portals, or any line of business application, then this book is for you. Many applications have a similar set of features, and this book builds an application with some of the most common features of enterprise applications. Let's face it: Every application has the same general set of features, but implemented in a different way. A database sits in the back end and you, as the developer, are responsible for enabling users to add, update, select, and delete records. If only it were that simple, no?

The real development work starts when you sit with users and try to understand the business process and why they need a new or improved system in the first place. A lot of companies have departments that use Excel and Access wizards to create small systems that eventually become a lifeline for some part of the business. Usually something bad happens because of the nature of the tool they are using. Senior-level management is called in, project managers are hired, programmers are contracted, and the Project Management Office (PMO) is called to save the world. Suddenly this loosely defined process is high priority and people want documented standard operating procedures, audit reports, more productivity, less people, and of course a system that can do it all, which is where you come in. When you think about it, it's a pretty daunting task. You're expected to become an expert in someone else's business process, flaws and all, and create a system that the company will rely on as the backbone for their existence. OK, maybe I'm exaggerating just a little bit, but when you go looking for that raise you might want to phrase it that way.

This book will give you the tools necessary to build a framework that can be extended to create a solution to solve your company's problems. The design pattern uses the normal three layers, the user interface (UI), the business logic layer (BLL), and the data access layer (DAL), but also builds the classes in each layer that encapsulate common business rules such as role-based security, workflow, reporting, dynamic menus, data entry, dynamic querying, notifications, exception handling, and auditing. As the book guides you through the complete solution, each business requirement is thoroughly examined and some of the latest enhancements in ASP.NET 3.5 and Visual Studio 2008 are used to implement them in a reusable framework.

Enterprise applications are typically complex, and the teams that build enterprise applications come in all shapes and sizes. Some of the roles include a project sponsor, a project manager, business analysts, an architect, UI developers, middle-tier developers, database developers, and, if you're really lucky, testers. Just a side note: Users are not testers. If you ever have the pleasure of working with professional testers, you'll realize how important they are in the process, and how they truly are "quality" assurance engineers. Unfortunately, a lot of companies aren't willing to invest in professional testers, so the users and/or developers end up assuming that role. This book is mainly focused on the architect and developers, but testers may find it valuable as well to help them understand the plumbing that goes into developing and architecting an enterprise application.

I am fortunate enough in my career to be in a position where I am constantly talking with users or business owners about requirements and am responsible for developing solutions to meet their needs. Whether I'm talking to HR about a department-level application or a VP who needs an enterprise application across an entire company, when I break down their requirements into workable entities they are all asking for more or less the same thing. They collect different data points, but they have their own workflow, need e-mail notifications, need to print reports, and require role-based security. That is why the application framework built in this book provides a foundation that can be extended to meet the specific business needs of your organization.

Who This Book Is For

This book is for the intermediate to senior level developer or system architect. It would be helpful if you have experience with Visual Studio, the .NET Framework, ASP.NET, and C# because that is what the samples are written in, but the design pattern could be used in any language. The book is focused on enterprise applications, but the pattern could be used for any type of application that has a web front end and connects to a database.

What This Book Covers

The sample application in this book is built using Visual Studio 2008, ASP.NET 3.5, C#, and SQL Server 2005. Each chapter goes into great detail, with plenty of code samples, and uses some of the new features in Visual Studio 2008 and the language enhancements in the .NET Framework 3.5. The solution includes examples for technologies such as LINQ to SQL, master pages, custom controls, `GridViews`, business objects, data objects, and Crystal Reports. Some of the language enhancements discussed include LINQ, extension methods, partial methods, automatic properties, anonymous types, lambda expressions, and object initializers.

Of course, I realize that the code is what most developers are interested in, and each chapter provides numerous examples.

How This Book Is Structured

The Problem Design Solution series is just that. Each chapter has three sections with a description of the problem to be addressed, the design considerations for choosing a solution for the problem, and the solution that ultimately addresses the problem. The solution includes the bulk of the code. Each chapter builds upon the previous chapter, and it is recommended that you read them in order. The base classes that are described in the first few chapters are critical to an understanding of the rest of the book. Later chapters build upon the base classes and extend their functionality in all three layers of the application.

What You Need to Use This Book

- ❑ Visual Studio 2008 Standard or Professional
- ❑ SQL Server 2005 or SQL Server 2005 Express
- ❑ Windows Vista, Windows XP, Windows 2003, or Windows 2000

Conventions

To help you get the most from the text and keep track of what's happening, we've used a number of conventions throughout the book.

> **Source**
>
> This section includes the source code:
>
>   Source code
>   Source code
>   Source code

> **Output**
>
> This section lists the output:
>
>   Example output
>   Example output
>   Example output

> **Boxes like this one hold important, not-to-be forgotten information that is directly relevant to the surrounding text.**

Notes, tips, hints, tricks, and asides to the current discussion are offset and placed in italics like this.

As for styles in the text:

- ❑ New terms and important words are in *italics* when we introduce them.
- ❑ Filenames, URLs, and code appear within the text like so: `persistence.properties`.
- ❑ Code is presented in two different ways:

      We use a monofont type with no highlighting for most code examples.

      We use gray highlighting to emphasize code that's particularly important
      in the present context.

Source Code

As you work through the examples in this book, you may choose either to type in all the code manually or to use the source code files that accompany the book. All of the source code used in this book is available for download at www.wrox.com. Once at the site, simply locate the book's title (either by using the Search box or by using one of the title lists) and click the Download Code link on the book's detail page to obtain all the source code for the book.

> *Because many books have similar titles, you may find it easiest to search by ISBN; this book's ISBN is 978-0-470-39686-5.*

Once you download the code, just decompress it with your favorite compression tool. Alternately, you can go to the main Wrox code download page at www.wrox.com/dynamic/books/download.aspx to see the code available for this book and all other Wrox books.

Errata

We make every effort to ensure that there are no errors in the text or in the code. However, no one is perfect, and mistakes do occur. If you find an error in one of our books, such as a spelling mistake or faulty piece of code, we would be very grateful for your feedback. By sending in errata, you may save another reader hours of frustration; and at the same time you will be helping us provide even higher quality information.

To find the errata page for this book, go to www.wrox.com and locate the title using the Search box or one of the title lists. Then, on the book details page, click the Book Errata link. On this page you can view all errata that has been submitted for this book and posted by Wrox editors. A complete book list, including links to each book's errata, is also available at www.wrox.com/misc-pages/booklist.shtml.

If you don't spot "your" error on the Book Errata page, go to www.wrox.com/contact/techsupport.shtml and complete the form there to send us the error you have found. We'll check the information and, if appropriate, post a message to the book's errata page and fix the problem in subsequent editions of the book.

p2p.wrox.com

For author and peer discussion, join the P2P forums at p2p.wrox.com. The forums are a Web-based system for you to post messages relating to Wrox books and related technologies and interact with other readers and technology users. The forums offer a subscription feature to e-mail you topics of interest of your choosing when new posts are made to the forums. Wrox authors, editors, other industry experts, and your fellow readers are present on these forums.

At http://p2p.wrox.com you will find a number of different forums that will help you not only as you read this book, but also as you develop your own applications. To join the forums, just follow these steps:

1. Go to p2p.wrox.com and click the Register link.
2. Read the terms of use and click Agree.

3. Complete the required information to join as well as any optional information you wish to provide and click Submit.

4. You will receive an e-mail with information describing how to verify your account and complete the joining process.

> *You can read messages in the forums without joining P2P but in order to post your own messages, you must join.*

Once you join, you can post new messages and respond to messages other users post. You can read messages at any time on the Web. If you would like to have new messages from a particular forum e-mailed to you, click the Subscribe to this Forum icon by the forum name in the forum listing.

For more information about how to use the Wrox P2P, be sure to read the P2P FAQs for answers to questions about how the forum software works, as well as many common questions specific to P2P and Wrox books. To read the FAQs, click the FAQ link on any P2P page.

1

A Framework for Enterprise Applications

The solution you will develop throughout this book is for a fictitious company whose human resources department needs to approve, deny, and report on vacation or holiday time requests by their employees. The solution will be developed using Visual Studio 2008 and implemented as an ASP.NET 3.5 application written in C# with SQL Server 2005 as the back end.

The concept is simple, and the solution is designed to be flexible enough that you can extend it for your own business needs. This chapter defines the requirements for the project and introduces how the solution will be architected. Each chapter details specific requirements and implements a solution in a three-layer architecture: the user interface (UI), the business logic layer (BLL), and the data access layer (DAL).

Problem

Sue is the vice president of human resources and is currently using a combination of Excel and Word templates to manage employee vacation and personal time requests. It has come to her attention that many requests are not accounted for and are difficult to track down. She has received approval to build a system for the entire organization that will replace her current templates with an enterprise-wide application. As the project's sponsor, Sue has designated Mary as the main point of contact for the IT department in order to gather requirements. The following is an initial conversation that might occur when starting on this project, although you could find similarities with almost any project.

Mary: "My manager put me on this project but I really don't know anything about computers or building systems. They tried to build something a few years ago but it never went anywhere and the developer was fired. Let me explain a little bit about what we do. We have a Word template on the Z drive that everyone must fill out for vacation or holidays requests. When we sent our Excel spreadsheet that keeps track of everyone's vacation balance to the managers last December, a lot of discrepancies came up. We were missing days that some managers forgot to send to us or requests had been cancelled and we were never notified. We need a database to replace the Word template."

Me: "So you want to automate the process of requesting vacation. I've used that template, so I know a little bit about the process, but I don't know what happens after my manager signs it. Can you tell me how the process is supposed to work?"

Mary: "When employees want to take a vacation or holiday, they are supposed to fill out the form, print it, sign it, and then hand it to their manager for approval and signature. The manager is then supposed to sign it and inter-office mail it to HR, where I check it against my Excel spreadsheet to ensure that the employee has enough days to cover the request. I then subtract the days in my spreadsheet. Also, people who want to take more than two weeks off at a time need to have their manager and a vice president sign off on the request. This really causes problems because the VPs are so busy they rarely send us the form."

Me: "Then you need a system that allows a user to request time off and then have a workflow built into the system for the manager, vice president, and you to approve or deny the request. What the user enters will determine how many levels of approval are needed."

Mary: "Well, yes. I guess we would need to be able to deny the request too, but we usually just throw them out. It probably would be a good idea to keep them around so we could refer to them."

Me: "You mentioned that one problem is that people cancel vacations and don't tell you, so would you like the system to allow users to cancel a request too? If so, I can have the application send you an e-mail notification that the request was cancelled. I could also send any approvers an e-mail when a request is in their queue for approval."

Mary: "Yes, that would be great. I could then adjust the balance in my Excel spreadsheet."

Me: "Could you send me that spreadsheet? I can likely recreate the spreadsheet as a report in the system that you could then export to Excel. This way, any requests or cancellations are tracked in the system and you won't have to maintain the Excel spreadsheet anymore."

Mary: "Yes, I can send it to you, but if I get rid of the Excel spreadsheet, then I need to keep track of the balances somewhere. I guess that would be in the database. Can you do that?"

Me: "I'm sure we can. You need to be able to enter a starting balance and then subtract any request from that balance and add back in any cancellations, correct?"

Mary: "Yes, but we also allow employees to roll over up to five days to the next year. Everything starts over on January first."

Me: "We can do that. Now, what about security? Do you need some people to have access to the reports, and others such as yourself to have access to everything?"

Mary: "I never thought about that but I definitely don't want Bob to be able to enter the starting balances. He should only be able to print reports and nothing else."

Me: "OK, so you need role-based security that allows groups to have either no access, read-only access, or edit access to screens and execute access to reports."

Mary: "I don't know what role-based security is but that sounds right."

Me: "What about an audit trail? Would you like to see any changes to a request or to security in the system? For example, if someone went into the application and gave someone access to a report, the system would capture that and you can print a report of all those changes. Would you like to track that?"

Mary: "I suppose so. I really didn't think about it but my manager would probably like it and those folks from QA that periodically audit our process would probably like to see that too. Could you do that?"

Me: "Yes, that can be done. What about viewing the requests? Do you need different views such as outstanding requests, cancelled requests, requests by manager, or requests by department? You don't have to know all the different variations now, but I could build the system to enable you to view the data in different ways without having to log a support ticket for a custom report. I could even put these views on a home page so you can see right away what needs action."

Mary: "A home page? Yes, I like that idea."

Me: "OK, I have enough information for now. I'll come back to you later to flush out the rest of the requirements. Can we agree that you need a system that has a workflow for processing requests, reporting capabilities, role-based security, a home page, e-mail notifications, querying capabilities, and an audit trail?"

Mary: "I'm not sure what querying capabilities are, but I trust you. Also, it must be easy to use and consistent. I don't want some screens that are green and others that are blue, with all different fonts."

Me: "We'll take care of it. I'll be back soon with more questions about your process but I have enough for now. I look forward to working with you."

Mary: "Thanks for taking the time. I hope you fare better than the last guy did."

In addition to the preceding requirements that came out of the discussion with Mary, there are also a few IT requirements for all applications within the organization. The IT department requires that nothing can be installed on any user's desktop, and all in-house built applications require the use of single sign on. IT should not be involved in administering the application except from the standpoint of supplying a server and providing an SLA for uptime.

Now that Mary has given us a general idea of her requirements, I'll show you how you can transform this into an application — from concept to design to development. I hope you stick around for the rest of the conversation with Mary; it will get fun.

Design

As stated earlier, the solution consists of an ASP.NET 3.5 web application using the three-layer architecture. The following chapters expand on the general requirements and develop a fully functioning robust enterprise application. The following sections provide a brief outline of each chapter to give you a brief introduction to each topic.

Chapters 2 through 5 review the overall architecture of the framework, and these are the most crucial chapters to read before proceeding. Each chapter is detailed and uses new features in Visual Studio 2008. Chapter 6 and subsequent chapters demonstrate how Mary's requirements are implemented in the application and give you plenty of code you can use in your own applications. The final solution is available for download on the Wrox website, `www.wrox.com`.

Chapter 2: The Data Access Layer

Conceptually, the data access layer is the simplest layer of the traditional three-tiered architecture. Simply put, the data access layer calls stored procedures that reside in the database or executes dynamic SQL against the database. In prior versions of the .NET Framework, as the developer you were responsible for making sure that you knew which type of ADO.NET object should execute a stored procedure and what type of object should be passed back to the business layer. The debate about which object to pass back to the business layer is always heated, but the .NET Framework has given us a tool that could calm those debates.

This chapter introduces the new LINQ to SQL features and utilizes the built-in ORM Designer tool to create a set of entity classes that communicate with the database and are passed back to the business layer. Don't worry, stored procedures still work with LINQ to SQL, and I'll show you how.

Chapter 3: The Business Logic Layer

The business logic layer, aka the middle tier, is where you apply the business rules against any data that should be saved to or deleted from the database. Simply creating a class that mimics the fields in a table is not enough. The business logic layer must protect the integrity of the data in the application by implementing business rules such as required fields, unique fields, limits, and calculations. If rules are broken, then the business logic layer must communicate them back to the caller and not bother the data access layer. This chapter describes the pattern for a set of base classes that encapsulate the business rules for all business objects in the middle tier. It also reviews options for creating lists of business objects and the base classes that are the building blocks for all lists in the application.

Chapter 4: The User Interface Layer

The user interface is the only part of an application that the user sees, so it is important to keep it consistent and easy to navigate. Style sheets and ASP.NET themes can be used to control the fonts and colors of your application, but the developer has complete responsibility for the overall navigation of the system. If you have a Save button on the bottom-left corner in one screen and on the upper-right corner in another, the style sheet won't help you. This chapter reviews style sheets, master pages, nested master pages, and the UI framework that will be used throughout the application. This chapter also builds two custom server-side controls for a dynamic menu that will eventually be integrated with the role-based security built in Chapter 6.

Chapter 5: Exception Handling

This is one area that is often overlooked when building an application, but it's one of the most important. I often see new developers completely forget to add exception handling to an application; or when they do handle exceptions, they aren't handled correctly or don't notify anyone when they occur. It is always better to rely on the application to let you know when an exception occurs, rather than the user. This not only helps in the debugging process, but also makes you look like a more proactive developer. This chapter reviews the Microsoft Exception Handling Application Block, which I use in all my applications for exception handling. The set of classes it provides include logging and e-mailing capabilities, depending on the type of exception, and it is completely configurable.

Chapter 6: Role-Based Security

Most business applications require role-based security. The business owner of an application usually wants certain groups to have full control of all screens, other groups to have full control of a few screens, and another group to have read-only access to a few screens. This chapter demonstrates a pattern for creating roles in a system and associating capabilities with those roles. Access can be categorized as "none," "read only," or "edit," and can optionally be associated with an item on a menu that should or should not be shown to the user. Users are then associated with one or many roles. This pattern enables business owners to administer their own applications and not rely on IT or you to set up users and roles after you release your application to production.

Chapter 7: The Workflow Engine

Simple workflows such as a request for vacation and a manager's approval make up a large percentage of corporate applications. Microsoft developed the Windows Workflow Foundation (WWF) to specifically address this issue in order to give developers a foundation they can build upon in their own applications. Learning the WWF would require much more than a chapter in a book, but in this chapter you will learn a pattern you can use in your own applications, one that is simple to incorporate with a few tables and classes. You could use this pattern for applications that have any type of workflow with multiple states. Examples of such applications are approvals for vacation time, travel, network access, or even an issue-tracking system.

Chapter 8: Notifications

Automated notifications can make a big difference in the value of an application, especially in a workflow-driven application. Systems should proactively notify users when a request is sent for their approval or their request is approved, denied, or unattended to for a certain length of time. In this chapter you will learn to build a Windows service application that monitors activity and sends e-mails to appropriate users based on events within the system. This not only exposes users to a notification service pattern, but also introduces building, debugging, and installing Windows services.

Chapter 9: Reporting

The free Crystal Reports for .NET objects that come with Visual Studio are very powerful and can add a professional look and feel to your application. This chapter explains how to incorporate the Crystal Report objects for .NET to display your data in HTML, PDF, Excel, or Word. Again, a middle-tier pattern serves as the "brains" for fetching and manipulating the data before passing it to the user interface, where a Crystal Report object simply takes the data that was delivered and formats it as appropriate. This pattern enables you to reuse middle-tier objects for multiple report views and shows you how to dynamically set groups, or display headers, footers, or detail lines in the report.

Chapter 10: The Query Builder Control

As soon as you give users access to reports or views of data, they are going to want to filter it based on a date, a user, status, and so on. Most of the time users want the same data but filtered in a different way. This chapter explains how to build a query builder server-side control that uses AJAX to enable users to dynamically create their own filters, which can be applied to views or any report that was designed in Chapter 9. This empowers users to extract the data they are interested in and manipulate it in Excel or simply display it in a PDF file.

Chapter 11: The Dashboard

Dashboards are becoming standard in web applications, and the intrinsic web part controls that come with Visual Studio make it simple to create a useful home page that can display graphs, alerts, documents, and more — and put the most important data right in front of the user. This chapter reviews the web part controls and how they work, and builds a home page with a dashboard for the Paid Time Off application, including alerts for users when requests are pending approval.

Chapter 12: Auditing

Auditing is important, if not mandatory, in most corporate applications. With the introduction of the Sarbanes-Oxley Act in 2002 and increasing government regulations in the pharmaceutical industry, auditing is an important feature that you will likely be asked to implement in your own applications. This chapter demonstrates a design pattern for developing a field-by-field audit trail with before and after values and a date\time stamp, and one that captures the user name for any changes to our vacation request application. You could easily adopt this pattern into your own application and save weeks of programming time needed to comply with the strict guidelines required by the government or your own organization.

Chapter 13: Code Generation

A code-generation tool can automatically write the majority of the patterns used in this book. This custom code-generation tool is written in Visual Studio 2008 and enables the user to point to a database and a table to generate the stored procedures, data layer classes, and business classes. This will save developers a tremendous amount of time, as they won't be stuck coding the tedious pieces of the application and can concentrate on the business rules given to them by the user.

Solution

As stated earlier, this solution uses a three-layered architecture: the user interface (UI), the business logic layer (BLL), and the data access layer (DAL). When building a solution in Visual Studio, you can include multiple project types in the same solution, making it easy to manage all three layers in one place. The UI layer consists of a web application and server-side controls. Essentially, anything that the user interacts with directly is considered part of the UI layer. UI developers or designers control the overall look and feel of the site, and typically excel at design, rather than programming. They focus on fonts, colors, and making sure the application meets the company's branding requirements.

The BLL contains all the business and validation rules that are the real "brains" of the application. For example, suppose you have a screen that allows the user to create a user in the system. The user's name is required and must be unique when adding a new user. You could put logic in the web form that enforces these two rules. Now suppose a new requirement comes along: The application must import a comma-separated file of user names. The user name is still required and must be unique, so that logic would have to be duplicated in the import logic. If you were to put the logic in a class, then the web form and the import program could call the same code. Anytime new rules are added to the application, you would simply change the logic in the shared class. This makes code maintenance much easier.

The third layer is the DAL, which contains the logic to connect to the database, to call stored procedures, or to execute SQL statements. The DAL developer usually understands the intricacies of SQL and can optimize queries. One reason to create a DAL is that it is easier to migrate from one database type to another without affecting the rest of the application. Suppose you started out using an Access database for a small company. As the company grows, you realize that Access isn't scalable enough and you need to migrate to SQL Server. If all of your database logic is in the DAL, then all you should need to change is the DAL. Another reason to separate logic into a DAL is because your application may need to support more than one database type. This is a common occurrence for third-party applications that need to support SQL Server and Oracle, depending on their client's requirements.

Conceptually, the three-layer architecture looks like the diagram shown in Figure 1-1.

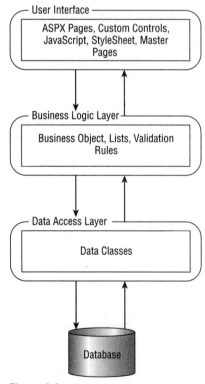

Figure 1-1

The Visual Studio solution for the application created in this book consists of an ASP.NET web application, a class library application for the business logic layer, a class library application for the data layer, and a control library for the custom controls. I also include the Microsoft Exception Handling Application Block, but you could just reference the dlls, rather than the project files.

The fictitious company's name is "Powered By V2." It is a good idea to create all your projects with a namespace that designates your company name in the beginning of the namespace. For this solution, all namespaces will begin with "V2." Follow these steps to build the Visual Studio solution that will be used throughout the rest of this book:

1.   Start Visual Studio 2008 and select File ⇨ New Project from the menu.

2.   Expand the Other Project Types item and click Visual Studio Solutions.

3.   Enter **PaidTimeOffSolution** for the solution name.

4.   Enter the location where you want the solution folder to be created in the Location box and click the OK button. By default, this is under the My Documents\Visual Studio 2008\Projects folder. An empty solution is created.

This solution will contain the ASP.NET web application and the class libraries that will be used to implement the Paid Time Off application. Visual Studio 2008 enables you to create a file-based website that uses its own built-in web server, but I used IIS for development because that is the environment where the application will be deployed. I want my development environment to mimic production as much as possible. If you were to add a website project to your solution at this point using http for the location, you would end up with a folder under the `Inetpub/wwwroot` folder. What you really want is for the folder and virtual directory to be created in the solution folder. To do this you first have to create the folder using Windows Explorer:

1.   Navigate to the solution folder and create a folder called `PaidTimeOffUI`.

2.   Launch IIS and create a virtual directory that points to this new folder and name it the same. In Visual Studio 2008, right-click on the `PaidTimeOff` solution in the Solution Explorer and select Add New WebSite, select ASP.NET Web Site, and change the location to http.

3.   Click the Browse button and select Local IIS from the Choose Location dialog box. The virtual directory you just added should appear in the list.

4.   Select the `PaidTimeOffUI` virtual directory and click the Open button. Make sure Visual C# is selected for the language and then click the OK button. This will add the `Default.aspx`, `Default.aspx.cs`, and `web.config` files and the `AppData` folder to the `PaidTimeOffUI` folder.

Now you can add the business logic layer project and the data access layer project to the solution just created:

1.   Right-click on the `PaidTimeOffSolution` solution again and select Add New Project.

2.   Select Class Library from the C# project types.

3.   Enter `V2.PaidTimeOffBLL` for the project name. The location should be pointed to the solution folder.

4.   Click OK. This will create a folder in the `PaidTimeOffSolution` folder for the BLL project and add the default project files to that folder.

Now repeat the same steps for the data access layer and name the project V2.PaidTimeOffDAL.

Next, add the control library by right-clicking on the solution file again and select Add New Project. In the left-hand side of the dialog, click the Web folder under the Visual C# node. Select ASP.NET Server Control as the project type and enter **V2.FrameworkControls** for the name. The location should still be the solution folder. Click the OK button.

Now, add a reference to V2.PaidTimeOffBLL to the website. To do this, right-click on the PaidTime OffUI project and select Add Reference from the menu. Click on the Projects tab and choose the V2 .PaidTimeOffBLL project. Then add a reference to the V2.PaidTimeOffDAL to the V2.PaidTime OffBLL project using the same instructions. Finally, add a reference to V2.FrameworkControls to the PaidTimeOffUI project.

Congratulations! You have successfully created a three-layered solution in Visual Studio 2008.

Summary

This chapter focused on presenting the business problem that will be solved by the application developed throughout this book. Each chapter dissects a part of the problem and discusses the design and the code in great detail, ultimately solving the problem. The goal is to give you a framework that you can use and enhance in your own applications to meet the requirements for your next application. Imagine how nice it would be to be able to start your next project with a complete set of controls, classes, stored procedures, and a data model for role-based security, reporting, dynamic queries, auditing, dynamic menus, and workflow — especially workflow! How many applications out there have approval processes? The workflow pattern defined in this book could be used by many applications for a variety of departments in your company. HR could have a hiring workflow, application development could have an issue-tracking workflow, finance could have a capital expenditure workflow, and the list goes on and on. I am excited to share my experience with you and I look forward to the feedback readers provide about how they have used this framework and improved upon it.

The adventure begins in the next chapter with an exploration of a new feature in Visual Studio 2008 called LINQ to SQL. You'll learn all about how you can incorporate LINQ in your data access layer to avoid a tremendous amount of repetitive code for making calls to the database. In addition, you'll never have to write another custom entity class again to pass data back to the business logic layer. It's all built into LINQ to SQL. Happy coding, my friend!

2

The Data Access Layer

Before starting to develop the functionality of the application that is specific to Mary's requirements, the focus will be on building the overall architecture for the three layers in the application.
The architecture is independent of the requirements and provides all developers working on the
project with a standard way of presenting data to the user, validating data, and saving data to the
database. The first layer to be discussed is the *data access layer* (DAL). This layer manages communication between the database and the business logic layer.

One of my favorite new features in Visual Studio 2008 is LINQ to SQL. You can find plenty of mate-
rial on the web covering this topic. www.asp.net has some great videos covering this topic, showing you how to quickly create classes that mimic your tables and then bind them to the `GridView`
control to display them to the user. You can also enable insert, update, and delete in a `GridView`
with little or no code. The demos are great, and LINQ to SQL truly helps with rapid application
development. I have found that there aren't as many articles about integrating LINQ to SQL into
a three-layered architecture. The samples usually have the user interface directly communicate
with the entity classes created by the ORM Designer. This chapter covers the following:

❑   Exploring options for creating a data layer

❑   Walking through the traditional approach

❑   Implementing a similar design pattern using LINQ to SQL

If this book has one chapter that is a "must read," it is this one.

Problem

The goal of the DAL is to create classes that expose methods that enable the business layer to
retrieve or persist data to the database. The DAL should not communicate directly with the user
interface, although it is tempting when you can easily bind `DataSets` and `DataReaders` to a
`GridView` or other bound controls. The diagram shown in Figure 2-1 demonstrates a typical

three-layered architecture. The user interface layer is the layer that interacts with the user. This could be via a web browser, a Windows Forms application, a mobile application, and so on.

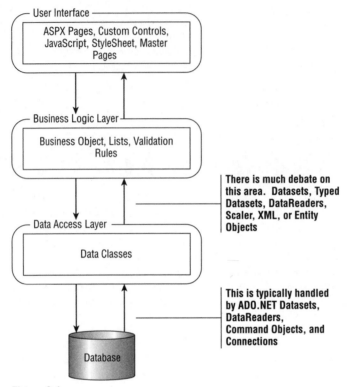

Figure 2-1

This book concentrates on building a web application. The user interface will be comprised of Web Forms, custom controls, server controls, and JavaScript. Chapter 4 goes into more detail about the user interface, but the key concept here is understanding that one of the goals of a three-layered architecture is to separate the logic from the presentation so that you can divide development in each layer to draw on a particular developer's strengths. UI developers have a keen sense for colors, fonts, layout, and the overall user experience. Correctly structured, an application can transform its appearance depending on the browser or device being used to display the application. The only layer the UI interacts with is the business logic layer.

The *business logic layer* (BLL) contains the brains of the application and interacts with the UI and the data access layer. Business processes are represented by business entity objects that encapsulate the business rules. The BLL removes the complexity of the database from the UI developer and presents data in a more business-modeled fashion. It also serves to protect the integrity of the data that it passes to the data layer. The BLL doesn't really care whether an ASP.NET website or Windows Forms application is using it — it will act the same way. Separating rules into the business layer and removing them from the UI avoids duplicate code.

Rapid application development (RAD) tools typically have business rules wrapped in a particular screen. When you want to manage the same records in a second screen, you have to repeat the code that is buried in the first screen. When the business logic is separated into a different layer, you can be assured that each screen or process is processing the data the same way, provided that you advertise your nifty classes. Many applications have screens that enable users to enter records one at a time in the database, and import programs that enable users to upload a file to enter the same types of records. By separating the logic into a BLL, the screen and the import process could create the same business object, set the object's properties, and try to save the data to the database. This guarantees that the same validation rules and database calls are made for each process.

The data access layer communicates with the business layer and the database. How the DAL communicates with both layers is a matter of great debate. Many people have differing opinions on whether one should pass data back to the business layer as `DataSets`, typed `DataSets`, `DataReaders`, scalar values, or entity objects. However, with the introduction of LINQ to SQL, you now have options regarding how the DAL communicates with the database too. Historically, ADO.NET was the preferred way to communicate with the database and it didn't matter how the data was passed back to the business layer — developers always used ADO.NET to communicate with the database. With LINQ to SQL, communication with the database is hidden from the developer, and you interface with a `DataContext` object and entity objects, although behind the scenes it is making the ADO.NET calls for you.

The data layer must also address the issue of transactions. A transaction ensures that when you are updating two or more tables at the same time, they are all committed to the database if all statements succeed. If one call to a table fails, then none of the statements should be committed to the database. Some design patterns have all transactions in stored procedures, others manage them in the data layer, while others manage them in the business layer. There are advantages and disadvantages to each option; what matters is that your choice works for your application and that the design pattern is implemented consistently throughout the entire application. I do not recommend that some aspects of the application use transactions in the middle layer while others use stored procedures. This can make it difficult to track down defects, as well as to justify when to use either option for each module.

Design

The data access layer performs CRUD operations against the database. CRUD stands for create, read, update, and delete. The object model that the .NET Framework provides for performing these operations is ADO.NET. Several .NET data provider namespaces contain implementations of the ADO.NET object model; the most common are `System.Data.SqlClient`, `System.Data.OracleClient`, `System.Data.OleDb`, and `System.Data.Odbc`. Each namespace has `Connection`, `Command`, `DataReader`, `DataAdapter`, `Parameter`, and `Transaction` objects. The name of the object is prefixed by `Sql`, `Oracle`, `OleDb`, or `Odbc`, respectively. For example, the `SqlClient Connection` object is called `SqlConnection`. Each object implements an interface that is defined by ADO.NET.

For example, all the connection objects implement the `IDBConnection` interface, which has a standard set of methods for opening, closing, and executing commands against a database. This provides consistency across all data providers and makes it easier to switch between providers. If you had an application that needed to support both SQL Server and Oracle, you could implement your classes with generics and specify the name of the class you want to create when creating the object. This would ensure that the `open` method for each performs the same action, as they implement the same interface.

ADO.NET Connections

Before passing data to or from the database, you must first connect to the database. This is accomplished by using a Connection object and is as simple as the following statement:

```
using (SqlConnection cn = new SqlConnection(connectionString))
{
    cn.Open();
}
```

The connectionString is an optional parameter that can be passed into the constructor or set as a property after the object has been created. The open method opens a connection to the database and remains open until you close it. It is very important that you close your database connections in order for them to be placed back in the connection pool. Failing to close database connections can degrade application performance, so be sure to take care when opening connections. You can check the State property of a connection to determine whether it is opened or closed. The preceding example uses a using statement, which automatically closes the connection once it goes out of scope.

After you have a connection, you can execute SQL statements against the database to either perform action queries or queries that return data from the database. You can use either dynamic SQL or stored procedures to execute queries, but either way you need the assistance of a Command object.

Action Queries

An *action query* is a query that performs an action such as an insert, update, or delete against one or many tables. The ExecuteNonQuery method of a Command object is used to execute action queries. To execute an update statement using dynamic SQL, you would write the following, assuming you have already opened the connection:

```
SqlCommand cmd = new SqlCommand();
cmd.Connection = cn;
cmd.CommandType = CommandType.Text;
cmd.CommandText = "UPDATE UserAccount " +
                  "SET Name = 'John Smith' " +
              "WHERE UserAccountId = 1 " +
                  "AND Version = 2";
int recordsAffected = cmd.ExecuteNonQuery();
```

Notice that the ExecuteNonQuery method returns the number of rows affected. This can be helpful when executing an update statement and you need to know whether the record was actually updated. Many design patterns use a version field on each record and pass the original version as part of the where clause. If the version were changed, the update statement would not fail but it would return zero records affected.

If you prefer to use a stored procedure, then you would convert the preceding dynamic SQL statement as follows:

```
CREATE PROCEDURE UserAccountUpdate(
    @Name varchar(50),
    @UserAccountId int,
    @Version int
```

```
    )
    AS
        SET NOCOUNT ON
        UPDATE UserAccount
            SET Name = @Name
          WHERE UserAccountId = @UserAccountId
            AND Version = @Version
```

Following is the code to execute the stored procedure:

```
    SqlCommand cmd = new SqlCommand();
    cmd.Connection = cn;
    cmd.CommandType = CommandType.StoredProcedure;
    cmd.CommandText = "UserAccountUpdate";

    //Add parameters
    cmd.Parameters.Add("@Name", SqlDbType.VarChar, 50);
    cmd.Parameters[0].Value = "John Smith";

    cmd.Parameters.Add("@UserAccountId", SqlDbType.Int);
    cmd.Parameters[1].Value = 1;

    cmd.Parameters.Add("@Version", SqlDbType.Int);
    cmd.Parameters[2].Value = 2;

    int recordsAffected = cmd.ExecuteNonQuery();
```

Notice that the CommandType property is now StoredProcedure, the Parameters collection has three parameter objects added, and their values are set on separate lines. An advantage of using stored procedures is that they help prevent SQL injection attacks, whereas in dynamic SQL you are exposed to an attack if the developers do not handle the parameters correctly.

Row Returning Queries

Row Returning Queries are Select queries. Again, you can implement these as either dynamic SQL or stored procedures. You also have the option to return the records either in a disconnected object, which is a DataSet, or in a connected object, which is a DataReader. The decision is solely based on what you plan to do with the data.

A simple dynamic SQL Select query that returns all records from the UserAccount table would look like this:

```
    SqlCommand cmd = new SqlCommand();
    cmd.Connection = cn;
    cmd.CommandType = CommandType.Text;
    cmd.CommandText = "SELECT Name FROM UserAccount";
```

Before executing this query, you can choose whether to return a DataReader or a DataSet. To return a DataReader, do the following:

```
    SqlDataReader reader = cmd.ExecuteReader();
```

A `DataReader` is the fastest type of object to return multiple records and is a forward-only, connected cursor to the database. These are particularly useful when you need to do a one-time pass of the data to load an object. Very little about the underlying structure is returned from the `DataReader` and you must specifically cast each field. In order to read the value returned from this query, use the following code:

```
if (reader.HasRows)
{
    reader.Read();
    string name = Convert.ToString(reader["Name"]);
}
```

The `HasRows` property is used to determine whether any records were returned. The `Read()` method moves the cursor to the next record; if there is not another record, it returns false. To reference a field in the `reader` object, you can specify the name as a string to the indexer or you can reference it by index. I recommend using the name as shown in the example. Because this field's value is a string, it must be explicitly cast to a string. The developer is responsible for casting the field's value each time it is used. That's one reason why it is good practice to copy the data to an entity object — so the casting occurs only once.

You could easily convert the preceding code to use a stored procedure by changing the `CommandType` to `StoredProcedure` and the `CommandText` to the name of the stored procedure.

Another option besides the `DataReader` is the `DataSet`. A `DataSet` is a generic object in ADO.NET that isn't specific to any data provider. In fact, the `DataSet` does not appear in any data provider's namespace — it is in the `System.Data` namespace and all providers know how to populate it. If you needed the flexibility to traverse back and forth in a cursor, you would have to use a `DataSet`. To do that, use the following code:

```
DataSet ds = new DataSet();
using (SqlDataAdapter da = new SqlDataAdapter(cmd))
{
    da.Fill(ds, "UserAccount");
}
```

Notice that another object called the `SqlDataAdapter` is used to fill the `DataSet` with records. The second parameter to the `fill` method is the name of the `DataTable` you want to create in the `DataSet`. The `DataAdapter` object is provided by each provider, and it knows how to populate a `DataSet`. It also knows how to add, update, and delete records when you send a `DataSet` back to the database. A `DataSet` is disconnected from the database and contains one or more `DataTables` depending on your query. It can also contain the relationships between the tables, so you can return less data and query the `DataSet` as if it were a mini database. The code to access the data for the preceding query is as follows:

```
string name =
    Convert.ToString(ds.Tables["UserAccount"].Rows[0]["Name"]);
```

Because a `DataSet` can contain more than one table, you must reference the `Tables` collection and retrieve the table by name or index. This returns a `DataTable` object, which has a `Rows` collection property. To retrieve the value of a field, pass in either a name or an index to its indexer. Again, you are responsible for casting the value to the right type.

Scalar Queries

Scalar queries are queries that are supposed to return only one row with one field. A typical example of a scalar query is when you want to return a count of records in a table. Scalar queries perform better than `DataReaders` and `DataSets` because they return less data. The following example shows how to execute a scalar query against a database:

```
SqlCommand cmd = new SqlCommand();
cmd.Connection = cn;
cmd.CommandType = CommandType.Text;
cmd.CommandText = "SELECT COUNT(*) FROM UserAccount";
int countOfUsers = Convert.ToInt32(cmd.ExecuteScalar());
```

The trusty `Command` object is still used but the `ExecuteScalar` method is called, which returns an object. You have to cast the object to the expected type. Be aware that if the query you execute returns more than one column or row, you will not get an exception. They will be ignored and you will be none the wiser, so be sure to write your queries correctly.

SqlHelper

The syntax for connecting to a database and executing queries can become quite repetitive. A good practice is to wrap these calls into a single class that the DAL can easily call with typed parameters. Luckily, Microsoft already did this. From their website, you can download the Microsoft Data Access Application Block, which contains a class called `SqlHelper` that is a wrapper for all of the aforementioned methods but contains overloaded methods of each depending on how you implement the DAL. Numerous progressive versions of the Data Access Application Block are available on Microsoft's site, but I like to stick with version 2.0 (before Enterprise Library) because it is simple to use and easy to understand. Later versions use generics and can be used against different databases such as SQL Server and Oracle, but the code is much more complex. To download the code, visit http://msdn2.microsoft.com/en-us/library/aa480458.aspx. The `SqlHelper` class is a static class that sits between the DAL and the database. The most common public methods to use are as follows:

- ❑ `ExecuteNonQuery`
- ❑ `ExecuteDataset`
- ❑ `ExecuteReader`
- ❑ `ExecuteScalar`
- ❑ `FillDataset`

It is important to look at the pattern of overloading each method, as it provides a good OO pattern of design. This chapter reviews only the `ExecuteNonQuery` overloaded methods, but all of the methods have the exact same overload pattern:

```
public static int ExecuteNonQuery(string connectionString, CommandType commandType,
    string commandText)
{    ...    }

public static int ExecuteNonQuery(string connectionString, CommandType commandType,
    string commandText, params SqlParameter[] commandParameters)
```

```
{    ...    }

public static int ExecuteNonQuery(string connectionString, string spName, params
    object[] parameterValues)
{    ...    }

public static int ExecuteNonQuery(SqlConnection connection, CommandType
    commandType, string commandText)
{    ...    }

public static int ExecuteNonQuery(SqlConnection connection, CommandType
    commandType, string commandText, params SqlParameter[] commandParameters)
{    ...    }

public static int ExecuteNonQuery(SqlConnection connection, string spName, params
    object[] parameterValues)
{    ...    }

public static int ExecuteNonQuery(SqlTransaction transaction, CommandType
    commandType, string commandText)
{    ...    }

public static int ExecuteNonQuery(SqlTransaction transaction, CommandType
    commandType, string commandText, params SqlParameter[] commandParameters)
{    ...    }

public static int ExecuteNonQuery(SqlTransaction transaction, string spName, params
    object[] parameterValues)
{    ...    }
```

The first three methods take a connection string argument, the next three take an open connection object as an argument, and the last three take a transaction as an argument. This provides the calling procedure with greater flexibility because you may need to execute the same stored procedure but it may be part of a transaction in one call and by itself in another call. The first, fourth, and seventh methods call the second, fifth, and eighth methods, respectively. The only difference is that it passes in null for the SqlParameters argument. When calling the second, fifth, or eighth method, you need to know the parameters for the stored procedure and create them before calling the method. If you call the third, sixth, or ninth method, you don't need to create the SqlParameter object — the method will actually query the database to figure out the parameters and then assign the value to each parameter passed in the parameterValues array. This involves an extra hit to the database because it queries the database, but the SqlHelper class caches the parameter list the first time the procedure is called and then uses the cached parameters for all subsequent calls. After the SqlParameters have been resolved, they call the second, fifth, and eighth methods, which take a SqlParameters array, so all calls eventually make it to either the second, fifth, or eighth methods.

I've used the SqlHelper class for almost all my projects and I usually call the method that takes the SqlParameter object as a parameter. This way, I avoid the extra hit to the database, I can explicitly create the parameter and assign its value, unlike when calling the methods with the object[] array, and I can use output parameters and retrieve their values. The call to the UserAccountUpdate procedure would look like the following when using the SqlHelper class:

```
SqlParameter[] parameters =
{
```

```
        new SqlParameter( "@Name", SqlDbType.VarChar, 50),
        new SqlParameter( "@UserAccountId", SqlDbType.Int),
        new SqlParameter( "@Version", SqlDbType.Int)
    } ;

    parameters[0].Value = name;

    int rowsAffected = SqlHelper.ExecuteNonQuery(connectionString,
            CommandType.StoredProcedure, "UserAccountUpdate", parameters);
```

In your DAL classes you could implement the same design pattern as the `SqlHelper` class and create three signatures for each method: one that passes in a connection string, one that passes in a connection object, and one that passes in a transaction. This would give you flexibility in the BLL when calling the DAL.

When adding records, you normally return the ID of the newly added record. To do this you would create the following stored procedure:

```
CREATE PROCEDURE UserAccountInsert(
    @Name varchar(50),
    @UserAccountId int OUTPUT
)
AS
    SET NOCOUNT ON
    INSERT INTO UserAccount (Name)
        VALUES (@Name)

    SET @UserAccountId = Scope_Identity()
```

Now change the calling procedure to this:

```
public int InsertUserAccount(string connectionString, string name)
{
    SqlParameter[] parameters =
    {
        new SqlParameter( "@Name", SqlDbType.VarChar, 50),
        new SqlParameter( "@UserAccountId", SqlDbType.Int)
    };

    parameters[0].Value = name;
    parameters[1].Direction = ParameterDirection.Output;

    SqlHelper.ExecuteNonQuery(connectionString,
        CommandType.StoredProcedure, "UserAccountInsert", parameters);

    return Convert.ToInt32(parameters[1].Value);
}
```

Another issue that comes up when updating records is concurrency. If a user pulls up a record on the screen, looks at it for a minute and makes a change and saves the record back to the database, the system should only update the record if it was the same as when the user started looking at it. To accomplish this, you can add a `datetime` field or an `int` field that is incremented each time a record is updated. When you retrieve the record from the database, you need to persist this value somewhere on the page and pass it back to the database when saving the record. The update procedure would include this value in the `where` clause and only update the record if the value matches what it was when the record was retrieved. You could also use the `TimeStamp` type field in SQL Server to keep track of versions that SQL Server manages itself, but you are still responsible for checking when updating the record. The `TimeStamp` field is discussed in more detail later in this chapter.

Use the `UserAccount` sample shown earlier as an example. If you added a field called `LastUpdateDate` as a `datetime` field to track the version, you would then write the `update` stored procedure as follows:

```
CREATE PROCEDURE UserAccountUpdate(
    @Name varchar(50),
    @UserAccountId int,
    @LastUpdateDate datetime
)
AS
    UPDATE UserAccount
        SET Name = @Name,
            LastUpdateDate = GetDate()
    WHERE UserAccountId = @UserAccountId
        AND LastUpdateDate = @LastUpdateDate
```

The calling procedure would look like this:

```
public bool UpdateUserAccount(string connectionString, string name, int
        userAccountId, DateTime lastUpdateDate)
{
    SqlParameter[] parameters =
    {
        new SqlParameter( "@Name", SqlDbType.VarChar, 50),
        new SqlParameter( "@UserAccountId", SqlDbType.Int),
        new SqlParameter( "@LastUpdateDate", SqlDbType.DateTime)
    };

    parameters[0].Value = name;
    parameters[1].Value = userAccountId;
    parameters[2].Value = lastUpdateDate;

    int rowsAffected =
        Convert.ToInt32(SqlHelper.ExecuteNonQuery(connectionString,
        CommandType.StoredProcedure, "UserAccountUpdate", parameters));

    return rowsAffected == 1;
}
```

Because the `ExecuteNonQuery` method returns the number of rows affected, you can confirm that this value is equal to 1, as you expect to update one record. If the rows affected do not equal 1, then the method returns false and the business layer can handle it appropriately. I typically do not throw exceptions here because this is a special case that I expect to handle. Exceptions can be expensive and they should be used only for an unknown condition.

Up until now, ADO.NET and ADO.NET data providers were the objects used to pass data between the DAL and the database. This is still true in Visual Studio 2008, but there is also another option with LINQ to SQL, which further abstracts the details about the ADO.NET objects from the developer and makes it even easier to communicate with the database. Before that, however, let's tackle the next topic in the DAL that should be agreed upon before starting a project: how data is passed back from the DAL to the BLL.

Passing Data between the BLL and the DAL

You have several options for passing data between the business logic layer and the data access layer. As noted in Figure 2-1, this is an area of much debate. After explaining the options most people have been debating about, the solution proposes a model that uses LINQ to SQL, which is a good compromise between the options. You'll want to make this decision early in your design discussions because it is one of the basic building blocks for your architecture. The method for getting data to and from your business objects is irrelevant to the user interface, but your choice can affect how the data gets to and from your database. This section discusses the options you have for passing data back and forth between the BLL and the DAL:

- ❏   DataReaders
- ❏   DataSets
- ❏   Typed DataSets
- ❏   Custom entity objects
- ❏   Scalar values

The first option is the DataReader. DataReaders are extremely quick and are great for a one-time pass of the data for loading objects. If you have written three-layered components before, then you've probably written plenty of code that maps the fields from the database to the properties of a business object. DataReaders are connected to the database and are forward-only. They have properties that tell you if the cursor "HasRows," and they have a Read method that moves the cursor to the next record.

A disadvantage of the DataReader is that it is connected to the database and the caller is responsible for closing and releasing the connection back to the connection pool. This might not be a problem for small application teams, but on larger teams where different people work on different layers, you need to trust that everyone knows to close the connection. (All developers know that, so it shouldn't be a problem, right?) Another disadvantage of the DataReader is that it is only a one-way communication vehicle for passing data back to the caller. You cannot use a DataReader to pass data into the DAL to update the database. By definition, a DataReader is read-only, so if you choose the DataReader as the vehicle for passing data back to the caller, you need a different vehicle for passing data into the DAL.

Another disadvantage to the DataReader is that it is not strongly typed and each field must be cast to its correct type by the user of the DataReader. This can make maintenance a pain if you change a field's type from a tinyint to an int and then you have to change your code to cast this field to the correct type. You can't rely on the compiler to tell you where you need to make this change because the DataReader is unaware of the type.

The second option is the DataSet. The DataSet is an in-memory representation of the tables in the database. The DataSet is completely disconnected from the data source, which could be a database or any other source such as an XML document. Because DataSets are disconnected, you don't have to worry about the caller closing the connection. DataSets also have built-in support for adding, updating, and deleting records in the database. They also handle optimistic concurrency control and enable the caller to manage issues accordingly. You can also represent complex data structures in a DataSet and represent relational data between DataTables with DataRelation objects. This helps limit the data passed through the layers.

As with the `DataReader`, a disadvantage of the `DataSet` is that it is not strongly typed, so you have to cast each field to its correct type when using a `DataSet`. Maintenance can then become an issue. `DataSets` are also more expensive than `DataReaders` because they return more information about the underlying `DataTables`. This can be an issue if you are marshaling objects across tiers.

The third option is the typed `DataSet`. Typed `DataSets` were all the rage when the .NET Framework was first released. I can remember watching demo after demo demonstrating how easy it was to create a typed `DataSet` and bind it to the `DataGrid`. (By the way, whatever happened to the `DataGrid`? That was the `DataSet`'s best friend.) Anyway, a typed `DataSet` uses a `DataSet` for its underlying data but uses strongly typed properties to access the fields, which makes it easier for the caller to access the data. This makes reading code much easier and it enables you to use IntelliSense when developing your application. Typed `DataSets` also provide compile-time checking, rather than runtime checking, for their properties. Anytime you can use the compiler to find an exception, rather than the runtime, it is usually worth it. Microsoft provides tools for generating the code for a typed `DataSet` but I'm not going to cover it here. Just keep reading — there's a much cooler tool for representing tables.

A disadvantage of typed `DataSets` is that they are difficult to maintain. The tool that is used to generate a typed `DataSet` creates a class that you add to your project. You can then customize that class to add business rules or calculated fields, but if you change the underlying table you need to either regenerate the class, which causes you to lose all your custom code, or manually update the class yourself.

The fourth option is custom entity objects. Custom entity objects are custom-built classes that mimic the relational structure of the database. You usually create properties for each field in the underlying table and represent more than one record using a generic `List` object or an `ArrayList`. An entity object can be populated in the DAL by using a `DataReader` and then the entity object can be passed back to the BLL. This enables the DAL to remain in control of the connection, which is a good thing. You could also use structs, rather than classes, to represent the data, as structs are lighter than classes because they are value types, whereas classes are reference types. Entity objects are also easier to read, and they support IntelliSense because the properties are strongly typed.

A disadvantage of entity objects is that you have to create them manually. Tools are available that will do this or you can roll your own tool to create entity classes, but it still adds another level of complexity to your project. You are also responsible for maintaining these objects when a change is made to the underlying table. In addition, you still have to cast the fields to properties, just as you do for `DataReaders` and `DataSets`; and these types of exceptions are only caught at runtime, not design time. For those of you familiar with LINQ to SQL, please hang on, I know what you're thinking. I evangelize about the wonders of LINQ to SQL later in the chapter.

The last option is scalar values. Scalar values are good when you want to insert, update, or delete a single record. You can pass in the individual fields to a method in your DAL object and the method knows how to map them to a stored procedure or dynamic SQL statement. Scalar values also offer greater performance than the other options because of the simplistic nature of the types.

A disadvantage of scalar values it that they don't make it easy to represent sets of data, so these have the reverse issue that `DataReaders` have: You can get data in but it is difficult to get the data out. There is also tight coupling because the method signatures contain all the fields that are used by a method. If you add a new field, you need to change the method signatures. This could be good or bad depending on how you look at it. If you add a field, you have to change all the code that called that method to pass the field in, but that makes people think about what they should do with that field now that it exists. Making people think is a good thing.

LINQ to SQL

Now that I've reviewed what many people may already know about a data access layer, I'm ready to reveal one of the best new features in Visual Studio 2008, one that could revolutionize the way you write your next DAL: LINQ to SQL. LINQ is a major enhancement in the .NET Framework 3.5, and it can be applied to objects, ADO.NET objects, XML, and a SQL Server database. LINQ stands for Language Integrated Query. It is a uniform programming model for implementing any kind of data access. Visual Studio 2008 has an Object Relational Model (ORM) Designer that automatically generates the classes to handle the calls to ADO.NET; it also creates entity classes that can be passed back to the middle tier. The `DataContext` class that is created is similar to the `SqlHelper` class, and the entity classes created by the ORM Designer can be used to replace `DataReaders`, `DataSets`, and custom entity objects for passing data back to the middle tier.

We'll start by taking a simple database table and using LINQ to SQL to model the entity classes in the DAL:

1. Create a new SQL Server 2005 database. You could use either the SQL Server Express edition or the Standard edition. I prefer to use the Standard edition because I find the SQL Server Management Studio interface easier to use, and it has more capabilities than the Visual Studio Environment.

2. Name the database `HRPaidTimeOff`.

3. Create a table called `ENTUserAccount` with the fields shown in Figure 2-2.

ENTUserAccount

Column Name	Data Type	Allow Nulls	Identity	Default Value
ENTUserAccountId	int	☐	☑	
WindowsAccountName	varchar(50)	☐	☐	
FirstName	varchar(50)	☐	☐	
LastName	varchar(50)	☐	☐	
Email	varchar(100)	☐	☐	
IsActive	bit	☐	☐	
InsertDate	datetime	☐	☐	(getdate())
InsertENTUserAccountId	int	☐	☐	
UpdateDate	datetime	☐	☐	(getdate())
UpdateENTUserAccountId	int	☐	☐	
		☐	☐	

Figure 2-2

This table will be used in Chapter 6 when you build the application's role-based security model. The table is prefixed by `ENT`, which denotes that this table is part of the reusable Enterprise framework being built in this book and can therefore be used for any application, not just the sample HR application being built.

Before moving on, let's look at the standard fields in each table. Each table has a primary key called `TABLENAMEId`, which is an identity field and the primary key of the record. Also present are four fields that help with auditing: `InsertDate`, `InsertENTUserAccountId`, `UpdateDate`, and `UpdateENTUserAccountId`. These fields contain the date and time the record was added, the ID of the user who added the record, the date and time the record was last updated, and the ID of the user who updated the record. The two user fields refer to the `ENTUserAccount` table, so for this table it is self-referencing. I use this pattern in all my applications, as it is helpful when users ask about data issues. This doesn't serve as a complete audit trail, but it does help. The pattern for the full audit trail is discussed in Chapter 12.

The `UpdateDate` field can also be used for concurrency. The other fields in the table are specific to the role-based security pattern, so I won't explain them here. Understand that these five fields will exist in every table, and the specific fields for the business entity will be different in each table. Because every record needs to have a `ENTUserAccountId` associated with it, you need to create a seed record before you can add new records to this table. The seed record will reference itself for the inserted and updated `ENTUserAccountId`. Add the following record to the `ENTUserAccount` table:

```
ENTUserAccountId = 1
WindowsAccountName = VARALLO1\VinceVarallo
FirstName = Vince
LastName = Varallo
Email = vince.varallo@v2.com
IsActive = True
InsertDate = Today
InsertENTUserAccountId = 1
UpdateDate = Today
UpdateENTUserAccountId = 1
```

Now that the table is created, fire up your solution again in Visual Studio and create a data connection to this database in the Server Explorer:

1. Select View ➪ Server Explorer from the menu in Visual Studio.

2. Click the Connect to Database button in the Server Explorer window. The Add Connection window will appear. The data source should be set to Microsoft SQL Server (SqlClient). If you are using SQL Server Express, change this to Microsoft SQL Server Database File (SqlClient) by clicking the Change button.

3. Select the server from the Server Name drop-down list where you created your database. Use Windows Authentication to connect to the database.

4. Select the `HRPaidTimeOff` database from the list of databases.

5. Click the Test Connection button to verify that you set things up correctly. If you get an error message, check your settings and try again.

6. After you successfully test your connection, click the OK button.

The database will now appear in the Server Explorer window under the Data Connections node.

Creating a DataContext

A `DataContext` is similar to a connection and the `SqlHelper` class. It is used to communicate to the database and execute commands against it. To create a `DataContext`, right-click on the `V2.PaidTimeOffDAL` project and select Add New Item. The Add New Item dialog should appear. Click the Data node under the Visual C# items. Select LINQ to SQL Classes from the right-hand pane. Rename the file to `HRPaidTimeOff.dbml` and click the Add button (see Figure 2-3).

Visual Studio automatically adds references to the `System.Data.Linq` namespace. It also adds three files: `HRPaidTimeOff.dbml`, `HRPaidTimeOff.dbml.layout`, and `HRPaidTimeOff.designer.cs`. The dbml and dbml.layout files are used by the graphical ORM Designer tool in Visual Studio. The .cs file contains all the classes that are automatically created for you.

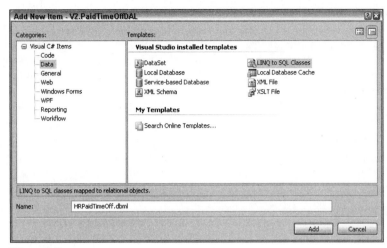

Figure 2-3

The ORM Designer should appear and be the active window. Double-clicking on the HRPaidTimeOff .designer.cs file will open it and you can see that Visual Studio created a partial class called HRPaid TimeOffDataContext that inherits from the System.Data.Linq.DataContext object. Think of a DataContext object as a connection object on steroids. You'll use the DataContext object every time you want to interact with the database. It has one member variable called MappingSource and numerous constructors. The constructor optionally takes a connection string or a connection object that supports the IDBConnection interface. This enables you to save your connection string in your web.config file and pass it into the DataContext. All the constructors call a method called OnCreated. There is also a collapsed region called "Extensibility Method Definitions." If you expand the region you will see the following.

```
partial void OnCreated();
```

This is new to the .NET Framework 3.5. It is called a partial method. A partial method enables you to implement code similarly to how partial classes work. For example, you could create a separate partial class called HRPaidTimeOffDataContext and implement a partial method called OnCreated that will be executed any time the OnCreated method is called in this class. A partial method is similar to an event in that the designer of the base class can introduce hooks into their code and let implementers of their class choose to catch the event and fire off custom code in that method. The signature of the partial methods in both classes must match, the method must return void, and no modifiers or attributes are allowed. In this instance, you could "catch" the OnCreated event in a separate partial class and log an event to the event log every time a DataContext object is created, although I wouldn't recommend it. Nonetheless, partial methods are useful, as you'll see later in this chapter.

Close the HRPaidTimeOff.designer.cs file and double-click the HRPaidTimeOff.dbml file. This will open the ORM Designer if it is not already open. This graphical tool will map tables to entity classes, and stored procedures to methods, in the DataContext object. Drag and drop the ENTUserAccount table from the Server Explorer onto the left side of the design surface. If you are using SQL Authentication, you will get a message about the connection string containing credentials with a clear-text password and not using integrated security. Click Yes to the message. If you use Windows Authentication, the message does not appear.

The table and all the fields should appear on the design surface (see Figure 2-4).

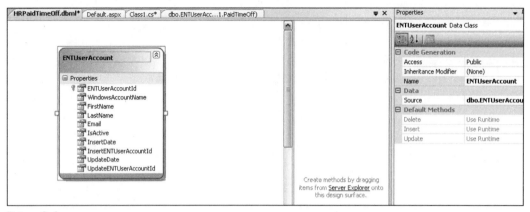

Figure 2-4

Visual Studio created an entity class for you that mimics the ENTUserAccount table. Open the HRPaidTimeOff.designer.cs file again and take a look at what changed. The first thing you'll notice is that an attribute was added to the top of the class:

```
[System.Data.Linq.Mapping.DatabaseAttribute(Name="HRPaidTimeOff")]
```

Three new partial methods were added to the Extensibility Method Definitions:

```
partial void InsertENTUserAccount(ENTUserAccount instance);
partial void UpdateENTUserAccount(ENTUserAccount instance);
partial void DeleteENTUserAccount(ENTUserAccount instance);
```

A new constructor was added that takes no parameters but calls the base constructor, which takes a connection string and a mapping source:

```
public HRPaidTimeOffDataContext() :
        base(global::V2.PaidTimeOffDAL.Properties.Settings.Default
            HRPaidTimeOffConnectionString, mappingSource)
{
    OnCreated();
}
```

The global:: syntax is used to specifically access this member in the global namespace, just in case this class was hidden by another class of the same name. Unbeknownst to you, another file was added to the project. Look at your Solution Explorer and you'll see a Settings.settings file and a Settings.Designer.cs file. If you open the .cs file, you'll see a new class was created, Settings, that inherits from global::System.Configuration.ApplicationSettingsBase. A property was added to this class called HRPaidTimeOffConnectionString, which returns the connection string that is passed into the parameterless constructor above. Essentially, the connection string is in the Settings file.

Click back to the `HRPaidTimeOffDataContext` class. There is also a new property in the
`HRPaidTimeOffDataContext` class:

```
public System.Data.Linq.Table<ENTUserAccount> ENTUserAccounts
{
    get
    {
        return this.GetTable<ENTUserAccount>();
    }
}
```

This property will return a generic `Table` object that contains objects of type `ENTUserAccount`.
The `Table` object is a new object in the `Linq` namespace. It represents a table in the underlying data
source. `ENTUserAccount` is a new class that Visual Studio just created for you. Scroll down a bit in the
code pane and you will see this new class. The `ENTUserAccount` class has a `table` attribute that sets
the name of the table this object represents. This class implements the `INotifyPropertyChanging`
and `INotifyPropertyChanged` interfaces. A `PropertyChangingEvenArgs` object is declared as
a member, and there are private member variables for each field in the table. There is also a default
constructor, a property for each field, with a whole lot of code in it, two events, and two methods.
The events and methods are required because the class implements the `INotifyProperyChanging`
and `INotifyPropertyChanged` interfaces. There is also another region called Extensibility Method
Definitions. If you expand this region, you will see a bunch of partial methods. The `OnLoaded` method
can be used to run code after the object's data has been loaded from the database. The `OnValidate`
method is called before the object's data is saved to the database, and `OnCreated` is called when the
object is instantiated. There is also a `Changing` and `Changed` partial method for every property. You
can use these methods to inject code when a user changes any properties in this object.

Take a look at each property declaration. The attributes from the field in the database are translated into
something that LINQ to SQL can understand. The `ENTUserAccountId` field has the following attributes:

```
[Column(Storage="_ENTUserAccountId", AutoSync=AutoSync.OnInsert, DbType="Int NOT
NULL IDENTITY", IsPrimaryKey=true, IsDbGenerated=true)]
```

The `Storage` attribute states the name of the member variable that holds the data. `AutoSync.OnInsert`
tells the framework to retrieve this value automatically when a record is added. This replaces returning the newly added ID in the stored procedure demonstrated previously. The rest are self-explanatory.
Notice that each property has its specific attributes defined for you automatically, and some have more
than others.

In each property set you see code

```
this.OnFIELDNAMEChanging(value);
this.SendPropertyChanging();
this._FIELDNAME = value;
this.SendPropertyChanged("FIELDNAME");
this.OnFIELDNAMEChanged();
```

where FIELDNAME is the property being changed. The `OnFIELDNAMEChanging` and
`OnFIELDNAMEChanged` methods were defined earlier as partial methods. You could validate the
data as it is passed into the property and throw an exception if someone tried to enter bad data.

The `SendPropertyChanging` and `SendPropertyChanged` methods are called as part of the implemented interfaces for this class. These methods will raise an event back to any object subscribed to it. The `FIELDNAME` = `value` reflects how the member variable is set, and is what you are used to doing in a regular class.

Adding a Record

For demonstration purposes only, in the website project, add a reference to the `V2.PaidTimeOffDAL` project. You will remove this reference when actually creating the site, but temporarily reference the DAL to make it easy to test the entity objects. You also need to add a reference to the `System.Data.Linq` namespace:

1. Add a button to the `Default.aspx` page and set the ID to `btnInsert` and the Text to `Insert`.

2. Add a `using` directive to the code-behind page to reference `V2.PaidTimeOffDAL`.

3. Add the following code to the `btnInsert_Click` event:

```
protected void btnInsert_Click(object sender, EventArgs e)
{
    //Create an instance of the data context
    HRPaidTimeOffDataContext db = new HRPaidTimeOffDataContext();

    //Create a new ENTUserAccount object and set the properties
    ENTUserAccount userAccount = new ENTUserAccount
    {
        WindowsAccountName = @"VARALLO1\VaralloMadison",
        FirstName = "Madison",
        LastName = "Varallo",
        Email = "madison.varallo@v2.com",
        IsActive = true,
        InsertDate = DateTime.Now,
        InsertENTUserAccountId = 1,
        UpdateDate = DateTime.Now,
        UpdateENTUserAccountId = 1
    };

    //Signal the context to insert this record
    db.ENTUserAccounts.InsertOnSubmit(userAccount);
    //Save the changes to the database
    db.SubmitChanges();
}
```

The first line of code creates an instance of the `HRPaidTimeOffDataContext`. This is similar to creating a connection object in ADO.NET. The next line creates an instance of the `ENTUserAccount` object and uses the new object initializer syntax, which enables you to set the properties of your objects in the constructor without having to create overridden constructors in your class. The next line adds the `userAccount` object to the `ENTUserAccounts` property of the data context. Recall that this property was created for you when you dragged the table onto the ORM Designer. This line tells the data context to add the record to the table. The `db.SubmitChanges()` line saves the changes to the database.

Test this code by setting the website as the startup project and make the `Default.aspx` page the start page. Run the project and click the Insert button on the `Default.aspx` page. If you step through the code, you will see all the property set methods get called when the `userAccount` object is initialized.

Even more interesting is when you step through the db.SubmitChanges()line: The system will step through each property set and then call the ENTUserAccountId property set and return the newly added ID to the object. All that without writing a single SQL statement! Pretty cool stuff, isn't it?

Updating a Record

Add a second button to the Default.aspx page and set the ID to btnUpdate and the Text to Update. In the btnUpdate_Click procedure, enter the following code:

```
protected void btnUpdate_Click(object sender, EventArgs e)
{
    HRPaidTimeOffDataContext db = new HRPaidTimeOffDataContext();

    ENTUserAccount userAccount = db.ENTUserAccounts.Single(u =>
        u.WindowsAccountName == @"VARALLO1\VaralloMadison");

    userAccount.IsActive = false;

    db.SubmitChanges();
}
```

The first line creates an instance of the HRPaidTimeOffDataContext. The next line retrieves the record from the ENTUserAccounts table, where the WindowsAccountName equals VARALLO1\ VaralloMadison. The Single method enables you to tell Linq to return one record with the criteria; and if no records are found, to throw an error. Behind the scenes, Linq is actually creating a SELECT SQL statement for you. The syntax for querying the database in this sample uses a Lambda expression. This expression is referred to as a *predicate*. A predicate is a Boolean expression that is intended to indicate membership in a group. You can also put and and or conditions in the Lambda expression. The next line changes the value of the IsActive field to false, and db.SubmitChanges() saves the changes to the database. Again, all that without writing a single SQL statement!

As you might have noticed in this example, the record was first retrieved from the database, changed, and then saved back to the database. This pattern will not work for web applications because you typically retrieve a record from the database, display it on the screen, wait for the user to click a button to submit the changes back to the server, and then pass the data to your DAL to execute an UPDATE SQL statement. For this reason, the developers of LINQ created the Attach method. The Attach method enables you to attach an object that wasn't originally created from the data context. Change the code in the btnUpdate_Click to the following:

```
protected void btnUpdate_Click(object sender, EventArgs e)
{
    //Create an ENTUserAccount object and set the properties
    ENTUserAccount userAccount = new ENTUserAccount
    {
        ENTUserAccountId = 2,
        WindowsAccountName = @"VARALLO1\VaralloMadison",
        FirstName = "Madison",
        LastName = "Varallo",
        Email = "madison.varallo@v2.com",
        IsActive = false,
        UpdateDate = DateTime.Now,
        UpdateENTUserAccountId = 1
```

```
            };

            HRPaidTimeOffDataContext db = new HRPaidTimeOffDataContext();
            db.ENTUserAccounts.Attach(userAccount, true);
            db.SubmitChanges();
    }
```

This example sets the IsActive switch back to true. Looks easy enough, right? If you run this code it will not work. You will get the following error message:

```
An entity can only be attached as modified without original state if it declares
a version member or does not have an update check policy.
```

If you want to "disconnect" an object and then update it later, you must have a timestamp field in your underlying table, so add a field to the ENTUserAccount table called Version and make its data type timestamp. Because you changed the structure of the table, you need to update your ENTUserAccount class. You can either manually update the class or open the Object Relational Designer and delete and drag the table onto the design surface. I prefer to use the Object Relational Designer.

After the Version field is added in your ENTUserAccount class, try the example again. This time you get the following error:

```
SqlDateTime overflow. Must be between 1/1/1753 12:00:00 AM and 12/31/9999 11:59:59 PM.
```

You get this error because the InsertDate is not set. Change the code to fix the object initializer to set the InsertDate and the InsertENTUserAccountId and run the code again. You will get this error:

```
Row not found or changed.
```

You get this error because you need to set the Version field's value to the original value of the record when it was first retrieved. This means you need to come up with a caching mechanism or find some place to persist the version information while the user is viewing the record. You would need to do this for the InsertDate and InserENTUserAccountId fields too because you wouldn't want them to ever change. An easy place to store this information is in the ViewState. It would be ideal to store the entire object in the ViewState so you could keep all the fields' old and new values, but the ENTUserAccount class is not marked as serializable when it is automatically generated; and even if you did put the serializable attribute above the class declaration, you would get an error stating "Type 'System.Data.Linq.ChangeTracker+StandardChangeTracker' in Assemble . . . is not marked as serializable." Therefore, just save the InsertDate, InsertUserId, Version, and the ENTUserAccountId to the page's view state in the Page_Load event:

```
    protected void Page_Load(object sender, EventArgs e)
    {
        HRPaidTimeOffDataContext db = new HRPaidTimeOffDataContext();

        ENTUserAccount userAccount = db.ENTUserAccounts.Single(ua =>
            ua.WindowsAccountName == @"VARALLO1\VaralloMadison");

        ViewState["ENTUserAccountId"] = userAccount.ENTUserAccountId;
        ViewState["InsertENTUserAccountId"] =
            userAccount.InsertENTUserAccountId;
```

```
            ViewState["InsertDate"] = userAccount.InsertDate;
            ViewState["Version"] = userAccount.Version;
    }
```

Add a using directive in the code-behind to reference System.Data.Linq because the Version field must be cast back to a Binary field, which is in the System.Data.Linq namespace. Now change the btnUpdate_Click to the following:

```
protected void btnUpdate_Click(object sender, EventArgs e)
{
    //Create an ENTUserAccount object and set the properties
    ENTUserAccount userAccount = new ENTUserAccount
    {
        WindowsAccountName = @"VARALLO1\VaralloMadison",
        FirstName = "Madison",
        LastName = "Varallo",
        Email = "madison.varallo@v2.com",
        IsActive = false,
        UpdateDate = DateTime.Now,
        UpdateENTUserAccountId = 1
    };

    userAccount.ENTUserAccountId =
        Convert.ToInt32(ViewState["ENTUserAccountId"]);
    userAccount.InsertENTUserAccountId =
        Convert.ToInt32(ViewState["InsertENTUserAccountId"]);
    userAccount.InsertDate =
        Convert.ToDateTime(ViewState["InsertDate"]);
    userAccount.Version = (Binary)ViewState["Version"];

    HRPaidTimeOffDataContext db = new HRPaidTimeOffDataContext();
    db.ENTUserAccounts.Attach(userAccount, true);
    db.SubmitChanges();
}
```

Run the code again and it will update the record correctly now.

OK, so we've found a couple of gotchas so far, but nothing that's a showstopper yet. Let's keep exploring.

Deleting a Record

Add a third button to the Default.aspx page and specify btnDelete for the ID, and Delete for the text. In the btnDelete_Click procedure, enter the following code:.

```
protected void btnDelete_Click(object sender, EventArgs e)
{
    HRPaidTimeOffDataContext db = new HRPaidTimeOffDataContext();

    //Create an ENTUserAccount object
    ENTUserAccount userAccount = new ENTUserAccount();

    userAccount.ENTUserAccountId =
        Convert.ToInt32(ViewState["ENTUserAccountId"]);
```

```
        userAccount.Version = (Binary)ViewState["Version"];

        db.ENTUserAccounts.Attach(userAccount);
        db.ENTUserAccounts.DeleteOnSubmit(userAccount);
        db.SubmitChanges();
}
```

Only two properties need to be set for the data context in order to determine which record to delete: ENTUserAccountId and Version. If you don't set the ENTUserAccountId, then the system will not throw an error or delete the record. Notice that you have to attach the object to the data context before being able to delete it. If you don't attach the object, then you'll get a runtime exception stating that the object was not attached. The DeleteOnSubmit method tells the data context to delete this record when SubmitChanges() is called. If you run this code and click the Delete button, the record will be deleted from the database.

Selecting Records

Add a fourth button to the Default.aspx page, specifying an ID of btnSelect, and Select for the text. Now add a GridView object to the page. In the btnSelect_Click procedure, enter the following code:

```
protected void btnSelect_Click(object sender, EventArgs e)
{
    HRPaidTimeOffDataContext db = new HRPaidTimeOffDataContext();

    var userAccounts =
        from u in db.ENTUserAccounts
        select u;

    GridView1.DataSource = userAccounts;
    GridView1.DataBind();
}
```

This is the syntax for querying data using Linq. The var keyword implicitly types a variable. This means the compiler will figure out what the type should be based on its use. These two statements act the same:

```
int x = 10;
var x = 10;
```

Because we are using Linq syntax on the right side of the equals sign, the userAccounts becomes a collection of anonymous types. The from clause tells the data context what objects to query. This is similar to SQL syntax, and you can use join and out join syntax. The select clause is last and states what fields should be returned. In this instance, all fields would be returned. Behind the scenes, a SELECT SQL statement is being created. You can view this statement by putting a breakpoint on the line that sets the DataSource of the GridView1 control. If you run the project, click the Select button, and wave your mouse over the userAccounts variable, you will see the SQL statement that was created:

```
{SELECT [t0].[ENTUserAccountId], [t0].[WindowsAccountName], [t0].[FirstName],
        [t0].[LastName], [t0].[Email], [t0].[IsActive], [t0].[InsertDate],
        [t0].[InsertENTUserAccountId], [t0].[UpdateDate],
        [t0] [UpdateENTUserAccountId],
        [t0].[Version]
    FROM [dbo].[ENTUserAccount] AS [t0]
}
```

Be aware that the statement isn't executed until you actually bind the data to the grid. If you continue execution, the GridView will be populated with all the records and fields from the ENTUserAccount table.

If you don't want to select all the fields, the syntax would be as follows:

```
var userAccounts =
        from u in db.ENTUserAccounts
        select new { u.WindowsAccountName, u.FirstName, u.LastName };
```

This code creates a new anonymous type with just three properties. The userAccounts variable no longer contains a collection of ENTUserAccount objects. You can still iterate through the collection using the following code:

```
foreach (var userAccount in userAccounts)
{
    string windowsAccount = userAccount.WindowsAccountName;
    string firstName = userAccount.FirstName;
    string lastName = userAccount.LastName;
}
```

If you want to add a where clause, the syntax would be as follows:

```
var userAccounts =
        from u in db.ENTUserAccounts
        where u.ENTUserAccountId == 1
        select new { u.WindowsAccountName, u.FirstName, u.LastName };
```

Notice the == sign. Because this is C# code, the equality operator must be used. You can also use functions such as StartsWith or Contains in your where clauses.

Pretty cool stuff, no? When I first saw the demos on LINQ to SQL I was very impressed, and as I started using it I was even more impressed.

Stored Procedures

If you are in a shop that requires you to use stored procedures, you might think you're out of luck if you're using LINQ to SQL, but you're not. In fact, working with stored procedures is made even easier with LINQ to SQL. Open the Object Relational Designer again. On the right-hand side there should be a pane that says "Create methods by dragging items from Server Explorer onto this design surface." If it does not appear, then right-click on the designer surface and select the Show Methods Pane item. You can add support for stored procedures by dragging a stored procedure object from the Server Explorer onto the Methods pane. In this section I'll show you how to use stored procedures to add, update, and delete records, rather than rely on LINQ to SQL to create the SQL dynamically for you.

Adding a Record with a Stored Procedure

Create a stored procedure in the database to add a record to the ENTUserAccount table:

```
CREATE PROCEDURE ENTUserAccountInsert
(
    @WindowsAccountName varchar(50),
```

```
    @FirstName varchar(50),
    @LastName varchar(50),
    @Email varchar(100),
    @IsActive bit,
    @InsertENTUserAccountId int
)
AS

    SET NOCOUNT ON

    INSERT INTO ENTUserAccount(WindowsAccountName, FirstName, LastName,
            Email, IsActive, InsertENTUserAccountId, InsertDate,
            UpdateENTUserAccountId, UpdateDate)
    VALUES (@WindowsAccountName, @FirstName, @LastName, @Email,
            @IsActive, @InsertENTUserAccountId, GetDate(),
            @InsertENTUserAccountId, GetDate())


    RETURN
```

1. Drag the stored procedure object from the Server Explorer to the Methods pane.

2. Click the ENTUserAccount table in the designer and bring up its properties, which include a property called Insert.

3. Click the button with the ellipse on it. This brings up the Configure Behavior dialog, shown in Figure 2-5.

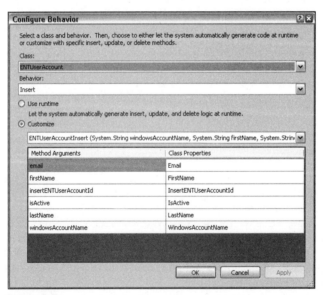

Figure 2-5

4. Select the Customize option and choose the ENTUserAccountInsert procedure from the drop-down list. Visual Studio will automatically map the properties of the class to the parameters of the stored procedure.

5. Click the OK button.

6. Run the project again and click the Delete button on the `Default.aspx` page to get rid of the second record.

7. Click the Insert button to insert the record.

This time, the data context called the stored procedure to add the record, instead of the dynamic SQL that was generated before. If you step into the code when the `SubmitChanges()` method is called, you will see that two new methods where added to the `HRPaidTimeOffDataContext` class:

```
private void InsertENTUserAccount(ENTUserAccount obj)
{
    this.ENTUserAccountInsert(obj.WindowsAccountName, obj.FirstName,
    obj.LastName, obj.Email, ((System.Nullable<bool>)(obj.IsActive)),
    ((System.Nullable<int>)(obj.InsertENTUserAccountId)));
}

[Function(Name="dbo.ENTUserAccountInsert")]
public int ENTUserAccountInsert([Parameter(Name="WindowsAccountName",
    DbType="VarChar(50)")] string windowsAccountName,
    [Parameter(Name="FirstName", DbType="VarChar(50)")] string
    firstName, [Parameter(Name="LastName", DbType="VarChar(50)")] string
    lastName, [Parameter(Name="Email", DbType="VarChar(100)")] string
    email, [Parameter(Name="IsActive", DbType="Bit")]
    System.Nullable<bool> isActive,
    [Parameter(Name="InsertENTUserAccountId", DbType="Int")]
    System.Nullable<int> insertENTUserAccountId)
{
    IExecuteResult result = this.ExecuteMethodCall(this,
        ((MethodInfo)(MethodInfo.GetCurrentMethod())),
        windowsAccountName, firstName, lastName, email, isActive,
        insertENTUserAccountId);
    return ((int)(result.ReturnValue));
}
```

The first method takes an `ENTUserAccount` object as a parameter and calls the second method, passing the properties as parameters. The second method takes a parameter for each parameter of the stored procedure. It then calls the `ExecuteMethodCall` of the `DataContext` object. The `ExecuteMethodCall` method knows how to call a stored procedure and return its result.

Two problems are caused by what we just changed. First, every time we make a change to the `ENTUserAccount` table we have to regenerate the class using the Designer and remember to change the `Insert` property to call the stored procedure. This makes you vulnerable to mistakes, because if you forget to change the `insert` property to the stored procedure you won't get an error — the object will generate the `insert` statement dynamically.

Second, we are no longer returning the ID of the newly added record. If you change the stored procedure to return `Scope_Identity()`, then the `ENTUserAccountInsert` method that takes all the parameters will return the ID of the newly added record. The problem is that it doesn't automatically set this to the `ENTUserAccountId` property of the entity object. We'll take care of this issue later during the discussion of the design pattern for the DAL classes.

Updating a Record with a Stored Procedure

Updating a record with a stored procedure is very similar to adding a record with a stored procedure:

1. Create the procedure in SQL Server and drag it onto the Methods pane:

```sql
CREATE PROCEDURE ENTUserAccountUpdate
(
    @ENTUserAccountId int,
    @WindowsAccountName varchar(50),
    @FirstName varchar(50),
    @LastName varchar(50),
    @Email varchar(100),
    @IsActive bit,
    @UpdateENTUserAccountId int,
    @Version timestamp
)
AS
        SET NOCOUNT ON

    UPDATE ENTUserAccount
        SET WindowsAccountName = @WindowsAccountName,
            FirstName = @FirstName,
            LastName = @LastName,
            Email = @Email,
            IsActive = @IsActive,
            UpdateENTUserAccountId = @UpdateENTUserAccountId,
            UpdateDate = GetDate()
      WHERE ENTUserAccountId = @ENTUserAccountId
        AND Version = @Version

    RETURN @@ROWCOUNT
```

2. Click the `ENTUserAccount` table in the Object Relational Designer and change the `Update` property to point to the new stored procedure.

3. Change the code in the `btnUpdate_Click` event to the following:

```csharp
//Create a ENTUserAccount object and set the properties
ENTUserAccount userAccount = new ENTUserAccount{
    WindowsAccountName = @"VARALLO1\VaralloMadison",
    FirstName = "Madison",
    LastName = "Varallo",
    Email = "madison.varallo@v2.com",
    IsActive = false,
    UpdateENTUserAccountId = 1};

userAccount.ENTUserAccountId =
    Convert.ToInt32(ViewState["ENTUserAccountId"]);
userAccount.Version = (Binary)ViewState["Version"];

HRPaidTimeOffDataContext db = new HRPaidTimeOffDataContext();
db.ENTUserAccounts.Attach(userAccount, true);
db.SubmitChanges();
```

A few things changed here. First, you no longer set the `UpdateDate` property here; it is taken care of in the stored procedure. Second, you no longer have to set the `InsertDate` and `InsertENTUserAccountId` because they are not updated in the stored procedure. Third, when you attach the `userAccount` object, you pass in a second parameter with a value of true, which tells the data context that this object should be treated as a changed object, and call its `update` method. If you don't pass in true, nothing happens when you call `SubmitChanges()`. If you step through the code, you will see that two methods were added to the `HRPaidTimeOffDataContext` object that call the `ENTUserAccountUpdate` stored procedure.

Note that you can get rid of the Version column if you like, as you are using a stored procedure to update the column. I still prefer to use this column to handle concurrency. I always put a check for this column in the `WHERE` clause of the `update` statement. I can tell whether the record was updated by examining the return value of the stored procedure with `@@ROWCOUNT`. There is no way to examine this number unless you call the `ENTUserAccountUpdate` method on the `HRPaidTimeOffDataContext` object, but that isn't such a bad thing.

Deleting a Record with a Stored Procedure

Deleting a record follows the same pattern: drag the stored procedure to the Methods pane and set the `Delete` property of the `ENTUserAccount` entity. I omit that code for sake of brevity.

Selecting Records with a Stored Procedure

Selecting a record is a little different from adding, updating, and deleting. There isn't a `Select` property of the `ENTUserAccount` entity to associate a stored procedure with. Instead, the stored procedure is created as a method of the `DataContext` object and it returns a collection of `ENTUserAccount` entities:

1. Create a stored procedure that selects all the fields and all the records from the `ENTUserAccount` table:

```
CREATE PROCEDURE ENTUserAccountSelectAll
AS
  SET NOCOUNT ON

  SELECT ENTUserAccountId, WindowsAccountName, FirstName, LastName,
         Email, IsActive, InsertDate, InsertENTUserAccountId,
         UpdateDate, UpdateENTUserAccountId, Version
    FROM ENTUserAccount

  RETURN
```

2. Drag the store procedure to the Methods pane in the ORM Designer and save the file.

3. Open the code-behind page of the `HRPaidTimeOffDataContext` and you will notice that a new method has been added to the `HRPaidTimeOffDataContext` class:

```
[Function(Name="dbo.ENTUserAccountSelectAll")]
public ISingleResult<ENTUserAccountSelectAllResult>
           ENTUserAccountSelectAll()
{
    IExecuteResult result = this.ExecuteMethodCall(this,
        ((MethodInfo)(MethodInfo.GetCurrentMethod())));
    return ((ISingleResult<ENTUserAccountSelectAllResult>)(result.ReturnValue));
}
```

4. Also added was a new class called `ENTUserAccountSelectAllResult`, which has member variables and properties for all the return fields from the stored procedure. Change the `Default.aspx` page to load the grid from this method:

```
protected void btnSelect_Click(object sender, EventArgs e)
{
    HRPaidTimeOffDataContext db = new HRPaidTimeOffDataContext();

    GridView1.DataSource = db.ENTUserAccountSelectAll();
    GridView1.DataBind();
}
```

5. Run the project again and click the Select button. The grid is populated correctly with all the fields and all the records from the `ENTUserAccount` table.

The `ENTUserAccountSelectAll` method returns a generic type called `ISingleResult`. This type is defined in the `System.Data.Linq` namespace and enables you to represent the results of a mapped function that has a single return sequence. This can be helpful when you build custom queries that do not return all the fields, but an `ENTUserAccount` entity is already defined in our Designer and that is what we would like to work with. To change the method to return the `ENTUserAccount` entity, you have to remove the stored procedure from the Methods pane of the ORM Designer. Drag the `ENTUserAccount SelectAll` stored procedure from the Server Explorer onto the `ENTUserAccount` table instead of the Methods pane. The procedure will appear in the Methods pane again but now look at the code that was generated. The `ENTUserAccountSelectAll` method now returns `ISingleResult<ENTUserAccount>` entities, and the `ENTUserAccountSelectAll` class was removed:

```
public ISingleResult<ENTUserAccount> ENTUserAccountSelectAll()
```

Run the project again and click the Select button. You will get the same results in the grid.

Now let's see what happens when the stored procedure is changed and it doesn't return all the fields. Change the SQL in the `ENTUserAccountSelectAll` stored procedure to the following:

```
SELECT ENTUserAccountId, WindowsAccountName, FirstName, LastName, Email,
       IsActive
  FROM ENTUserAccount
```

Run the project again and click the Select button. You will not get an error and the grid will still be populated with all the properties in the `ENTUserAccount` entity. The fields that were not returned from the query have their default value set in the object.

Solution

Now that you have some background on options for creating a data access layer, this section describes the design pattern for using LINQ to SQL in a three-layered architecture. The pattern uses the `DataContext` to handle communication with the database, and the entity objects created from the ORM Designer to handle communication with the BLL.

Conceptually, the design pattern is shown in Figure 2-6.

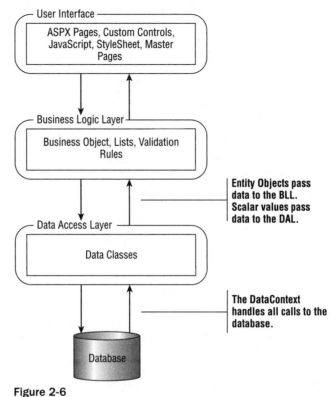

Figure 2-6

In keeping with the three-layered design, this pattern has a DAL class library that uses the `DataContext` object created by the ORM Designer to handle all communication with the database, and uses stored procedures to access the data. Prior to Visual Studio 2008, this would have been handled by the `SqlHelper` class. The method of communication between the BLL and the DAL will be a mix of entity objects created by the ORM Designer and scalar values. Entity objects are used to pass data back to the BLL, and scalar values are used to pass data into the DAL for `insert`, `update`, and `delete` commands.

All tables will have six standard fields. The first field is the primary key, and the naming convention is *TableName*Id. The other five fields are `InsertDate`, `InsertENTUserAccountId`, `UpdateDate`, `UpdateENTUserAccountId`, and the `Version`. The `Version` field is a timestamp field. None of the fields allow nulls.

All tables will have five standard stored procedures. The first is the `Insert` procedure:

```
CREATE PROCEDURE [dbo].[ENTUserAccountInsert]
(
    @ENTUserAccountId int OUTPUT,
    @WindowsAccountName varchar(50),
    @FirstName varchar(50),
    @LastName varchar(50),
    @Email varchar(100),
```

```
    @IsActive bit,
    @InsertENTUserAccountId int
)
AS
    SET NOCOUNT ON
    INSERT INTO ENTUserAccount (WindowsAccountName, FirstName,
                    LastName, Email, IsActive, InsertDate,
                    InsertENTUserAccountId, UpdateDate,
                    UpdateENTUserAccountId)
            VALUES (@WindowsAccountName, @FirstName, @LastName,
                    @Email, @IsActive, GetDate(),
                    @InsertENTUserAccountId, GetDate(),
                    @InsertENTUserAccountId)

    SET @ENTUserAccountId = Scope_Identity()
    RETURN
```

The name is always *TableName*Insert, and the first parameter is always an OUTPUT parameter that returns the ID of the newly added record. The stored procedure will only receive the InsertENTUserAccountId and set the InsertENTUserAccountId and Update ENTUserAccountId based on the value passed in. The InsertDate and UpdateDate are set by calling the GetDate() function and are not passed in.

The second standard procedure is the Update procedure:

```
CREATE PROCEDURE [dbo].[ENTUserAccountUpdate]
(
    @ENTUserAccountId int,
    @WindowsAccountName varchar(50),
    @FirstName varchar(50),
    @LastName varchar(50),
    @Email varchar(100),
    @IsActive bit,
    @UpdateENTUserAccountId int,
    @Version timestamp
)
AS
    SET NOCOUNT ON

    UPDATE ENTUserAccount
            SET WindowsAccountName = @WindowsAccountName
            , FirstName = @FirstName
            , LastName = @LastName
            , Email = @Email
            , IsActive = @IsActive
            , UpdateDate = GetDate()
            , UpdateENTUserAccountId = @UpdateENTUserAccountId
        WHERE ENTUserAccountId = @ENTUserAccountId
          AND Version = @Version

    RETURN @@ROWCOUNT
```

The name is always *TableName*Update. The id and Version fields are always in the WHERE clause to handle concurrency issues, and the procedure always returns the @@ROWCOUNT, which indicates the number of rows updated. If the record is successfully updated, it should return 1.

The third standard procedure is the `Delete` procedure:

```
CREATE PROCEDURE [dbo].[ENTUserAccountDelete]
(
  @ENTUserAccountId int
)
AS
  SET NOCOUNT ON

  DELETE
    FROM ENTUserAccount
   WHERE ENTUserAccountId = @ENTUserAccountId

  RETURN
```

The name is always *TableName*Delete. id is the only parameter and is used in the WHERE clause to delete only one record.

The fourth standard procedure is a `Select` procedure that returns all fields and all records:

```
CREATE PROCEDURE ENTUserAccountSelectAll
AS
  SET NOCOUNT ON

  SELECT ENTUserAccountId, WindowsAccountName, FirstName, LastName,
          Email, IsActive, InsertDate, InsertENTUserAccountid,
          UpdateDate, UpdateENTUserAccountId, Version
    FROM ENTUserAccount

  RETURN
```

The name of the procedure is always *TableName*SelectAll. This takes no parameters.

The fifth standard stored procedure is another `Select` procedure, which returns all fields but only one record based on the id:

```
CREATE PROCEDURE ENTUserAccountSelectById
(
   @ENTUserAccountId int
)
AS
  SET NOCOUNT ON

  SELECT ENTUserAccountId, WindowsAccountName, FirstName, LastName,
          Email, IsActive, InsertDate, InsertENTUserAccountid,
          UpdateDate, UpdateENTUserAccountId, Version
    FROM ENTUserAccount
   WHERE ENTUserAccountId = @ENTUserAccountId

  RETURN
```

The name of the procedure is always *TableName*SelectById, and it takes the id as the only parameter.

After creating all the stored procedures just described, delete the `HRPaidTimeOff.dbml` file that was previously added to the DAL project. Add the `DataContext` file again by following the same procedure as before, but when you drag the `ENTUserAccount` table from the Server Explorer to the ORM Designer do not save the password information to the configuration file. When the ORM Designer prompts you to save this information, click the No button. Instead of using the `Settings` file to save the connection string, we'll use the `web.config` file's ConnectionStrings section and pass this into the constructor of the `HRPaidTimeOffDataContext` whenever we use it.

Drag the `ENTUserAccountInsert`, `ENTUserAccountUpdate`, and `ENTUserAccountDelete` stored procedures to the Methods pane. Drag the `ENTUserAccountSelectAll` and `ENTUserAccountSelectById` procedures on top of the `ENTUserAccount` table. You'll end up with the five procedures in the Methods pane, and the `select` procedures will return the `ENTUserAccount` generic `ISingleResult` object. Save the file. The `HRPaidTimeOffDataContext` class and `ENTUserAccount` entity class will be created and the stored procedure methods will be created in the `HRPaidTimeOffDataContext` class.

This project has tables that are reusable and considered part of the framework, and other tables that are specific to the HR Paid Time Off application. To distinguish between the two, I prefix the tables with "ENT" and create a folder in the DAL called `Framework`. All data classes that are part of the framework will go in this folder, while all other classes will go in the root folder. Note that I consider the classes created by the ORM Designer "entity objects" and the classes that manage these objects "data objects."

Because all entity objects contain five fields with the same exact name, in every table I created an interface called `IENTBaseEntity`. Create a folder in the DAL project called `Framework` and save the interface file in this folder.

```
namespace V2.PaidTimeOffDAL.Framework
{
    public interface IENTBaseEntity
    {
        DateTime InsertDate { get; set; }
        int InsertENTUserAccountId { get; set; }
        DateTime UpdateDate { get; set; }
        int UpdateENTUserAccountId { get; set; }
        Binary Version { get; set; }
    }
}
```

In the preceding code you must add a `using` statement to the `System.Data.Linq` namespace in order for the `Binary` data type to be recognized. The sample code shows you a shortcut syntax for creating properties in Visual Studio 2008. You only need to declare the properties with `get` and `set` and the member variable will be automatically created for you behind the scenes. You won't see the variables declared in the file, but when you reference the class or interface they will appear in IntelliSense. This is a great time saver.

We want all of our entity classes that are created by the ORM Designer to implement this interface. You could open the file that contains all the entity objects and modify the class declaration to inherit from this interface, but the next time you regenerate a table's class from the ORM Designer you would have to remember to modify the result. This is where partial classes come in handy. You can create another file and then create a partial class that is named the same as the entity class and have that inherit the correct interface. That way, you can regenerate the entity class as often as you want and not have to worry about customizing its code. The goal is to never have to customize the auto-generated code because you will find yourself doing this a lot.

The partial classes all go into one class file called `CustomizedEntities` in the root folder. Right-click on the DAL project and select Add New Item to add this class to the root folder. You need to add a `using` statement to reference the `V2.PaidTimeOffDAL.Framework` namespace and replace the default code with this:

```
using V2.PaidTimeOffDAL.Framework;

namespace V2.PaidTimeOffDAL
{
    public partial class ENTUserAccount : IENTBaseEntity { }
}
```

The next step is to create the `Data` class that will manage the entity objects. Ideally, these would be static classes with all static methods, but we want to ensure that they all implement certain abstract methods so we're limited to creating an abstract class with instance methods. To accomplish this, right-click on the `Framework` folder and select Add New Item. Add a new class module and name it `ENTBaseData`. It looks like this:

```
public abstract class ENTBaseData<T> where T : IENTBaseEntity
{
    public abstract List<T> Select();

    public abstract T Select(int id);

    public abstract void Delete(HRPaidTimeOffDataContext db, int id);

    public void Delete(string connectionString, int id)
    {
        using (HRPaidTimeOffDataContext db = new
            HRPaidTimeOffDataContext(connectionString))
        {
            Delete(db, id);
        }
    }
}
```

This class is declared with the generic type `T` and it has a constraint that `T` is always of type `IENTBaseEntity`. The `Select` method, with no parameters, returns a list of these objects; and the `Select` method, with the `id` parameter, returns a single instance of this type of object. I didn't add abstract methods for the `Insert` and `Update` methods because they will be different for each class (because I use the pattern of passing in each field, rather than the object, to insert or update a method). I use this pattern so that if I add a field, I can change the signature of the `Insert` and `Update` methods and let the compiler tell me where to fix the calling code. If I were to pass in an object, I could forget to set the new field's value in all classes that call this method, and bad data would get into the database.

These are the only two base classes in the DAL. Now create the `Data` class that handles the `ENTUserAccount` entity object. Add a class to the `Framework` folder called `ENTUserAccountData`. The class should be made public and it should inherit from `ENTBaseData`. The first code to add for the class is as follows:

```
public class ENTUserAccountData : ENTBaseData<ENTUserAccount>
{
    public override List<ENTUserAccount> Select()
```

```
    {
        using (HRPaidTimeOffDataContext db = new
                HRPaidTimeOffDataContext())
        {
            return db.ENTUserAccountSelectAll().ToList();
        }
    }

    public override ENTUserAccount Select(int id)
    {
        using (HRPaidTimeOffDataContext db = new
                HRPaidTimeOffDataContext())
        {
            return db.ENTUserAccountSelectById(id).SingleOrDefault();
        }
    }
}
```

The Select method returns a list of ENTUserAccount objects by using the ToList method. The second Select method returns a single record from the database and passes it back to the BLL as an ENTUserAccount object. If no record is found with that ID, then null is passed back to the caller.

The next method handles the delete. The only code needed is the code to call the method on the DataContext object. The Delete in the base class that takes a connection string parameter calls this procedure to actually delete the record:

```
public override void Delete(HRPaidTimeOffDataContext db, int id)
{
    db.ENTUserAccountDelete(id);
}
```

The next two methods handle the adding of a record. They both have the same signature except the first method takes a connection string and the second takes a DataContext. The first calls the second to insert the record. This is similar to the pattern in the SqlHelper class and is useful when you want the methods to be wrapped in a transaction. The first method would be called when there is no transaction, whereas the second would be called to enlist in a transaction. I use the TransactionScope object to manage transactions and have found that if you do not pass the same DataContext object for all your database updates, you will sometimes get an exception thrown from the DataContext. This is more evident in the next chapter covering the BLL and transaction management.

```
public int Insert(string connectionString, string
        windowsAccountName, string firstName, string lastName, string
        email, bool isActive, int insertUserAccountId)
{
    using (HRPaidTimeOffDataContext db = new
        HRPaidTimeOffDataContext(connectionString))
    {
        return Insert(db, windowsAccountName, firstName, lastName,
            email, isActive, insertUserAccountId);
```

```
        }
    }

    public int Insert(HRPaidTimeOffDataContext db, string
        windowsAccountName, string firstName,
        string lastName, string email, bool isActive, int
        insertUserAccountId)
    {
        Nullable<int> entUserAccountId = 0;

        db.ENTUserAccountInsert(ref entUserAccountId,
            windowsAccountName, firstName, lastName,
            email, isActive, insertUserAccountId);

        return Convert.ToInt32(entUserAccountId);
    }
```

The next two methods handle the update of a record and follow the same overloaded pattern as the insert methods:

```
    public bool Update(string connectionString, int userAccountId,
        string windowsAccountName, string firstName, string lastName,
        string email, bool isActive, int updateUserAccountId,
        Binary version)
    {
        using (HRPaidTimeOffDataContext db = new
            HRPaidTimeOffDataContext(connectionString))
        {
            return Update(db, userAccountId, windowsAccountName,
                firstName, lastName, email, isActive,
                updateUserAccountId, version);
        }
    }

    public bool Update(HRPaidTimeOffDataContext db, int userAccountId,
        string windowsAccountName, string firstName, string lastName,
        string email, bool isActive, int updateUserAccountId,
        Binary version)
    {
        int rowsAffected = db.ENTUserAccountUpdate(userAccountId,
                windowsAccountName, firstName,
                lastName, email, isActive, updateUserAccountId,
                version);
        return rowsAffected == 1;
    }
}
```

That's it. Each and every table will have an entity class generated by the ORM Designer, and a Data class to handle communication to the database and the BLL.

Summary

The main points of this chapter reflect the main functions of the data access layer:

❑ The model used to communicate between the DAL and the database

❑ The model used to communicate between the BLL and the database

❑ The most frequently used objects in ADO.NET

❑ The pattern exposed by the `SqlHelper` class, which overloads each method with connection strings, connection objects, or transaction objects

❑ The new LINQ to SQL objects and the ORM Designer

❑ The differences between the default functionality in LINQ to SQL and using stored procedures

❑ The base classes and standard structure for all DAL classes in the application going forward

The example in this book uses LINQ to SQL for this application, but if you are not ready to make the move to Visual Studio 2008 or you're hesitant to use such a new technology, then you could follow the exact same design pattern using custom entity objects to pass data back to the BLL and use the `SqlHelper` class to communicate using ADO.NET objects with the database.

3

Designing the Business Logic Layer

The *business logic layer* (BLL) in the three-layered architecture is really the brains of your application. It is here that you model the business process defined by the user and enforce validation rules to protect the integrity of the data. The BLL sits between the user interface and the DAL. Technology is constantly changing and there are always new ways of presenting data to the user, such as with AJAX, Silverlight, or even your phone, but the business rules for your application remain the same regardless of the user interface. The design of the BLL should be flexible enough that any type of front end can use it, even a Windows service.

Depending on the size and budget of your application, the database could start out as Access but eventually migrate to SQL Server or Oracle. Again, the business rules do not change based on the database, so all the business rules should be separated from the data access code. If you were to put your business rules in stored procedures or Oracle packages, then you would be married to that database. Changing databases becomes quite a daunting task. If a database is used simply as a place to store the data, then changing databases is much easier.

To successfully develop an application that can easily work with multiple user interfaces or multiple databases, you should model your business process and place all your validation rules in the business logic layer. A BLL typically consists of classes that represent a single entity or lists of entities. Users can select, add, update, or delete data through these entity objects. Selecting data simply retrieves the records from the DAL and maps the fields to an appropriate property of the object. Adding, updating, and deleting data is where the validation rules come into play. Usually the validation rules for adding and updating are the same, such as required fields, boundary checks, and uniqueness. When deleting, you need to check referential integrity issues or other rules that would prevent a user from deleting a record.

Communicating the broken rules back to the UI is also the responsibility of the BLL. Some schools of thought put this logic in the UI with validation controls, but this marries you to a specific type of UI. If you switch the UI, you have to rewrite all that code in the new UI. By keeping the validation rules in the BLL, you gain code reuse and consistency between user interfaces.

This chapter focuses on creating the base classes for all objects in the BLL. Future chapters build upon this pattern when creating the functionality for requesting vacation, viewing data, and querying data. It is important to understand the concept of the *base classes*, especially the abstract methods that you must implement when inheriting from these classes.

Problem

This chapter develops a design pattern for static business objects and editable business objects. It also explains where to code validation rules to allow for the flexibility to work with any user interface or database. The distinction between business requirements and validation rules may be confusing because many terms are used interchangeably in different companies. Terms such as user requirements, business requirements, business logic, functional requirements, and usability requirements are just a few.

Think of business requirements as a definition of the business process or workflow. These requirements help define your object model. A business requirement for the example in this book would be "the system must allow for three levels of approval for every request and track the date when the request was approved." That requirement could be designed it two different ways. One way would be to have three different approval properties called first, second, and third, which store the date the request was approved. A second way would be to create an array of approvals on a request object, which store the level and date of approval. This is totally up to you; the goal is to meet the business requirement.

Validation rules are for data integrity checks such as required or unique fields. These rules are still defined as business requirements by the user but they don't affect the object model. For example, another requirement is "the user's name is required and must be unique." This doesn't affect the object model; it is a validation rule that should be applied to any data trying to be saved to the database. If the user says "I need to be able to do this task with one button," that isn't a business requirement, it is a usability requirement, which should be considered in the user interface. The data isn't affected by this statement either. It takes some time to figure out which business requirements affect the object model, which are validation rules, and which do not affect the BLL at all. It is hoped that the pattern introduced in this chapter will help to both clarify the difference and make that decision for your own applications easier.

Conceptually, the goals of the business logic layer are as follows:

❑ Model business processes into business objects that exhibit behaviors of the process being implemented.

❑ Protect the integrity of the data by implementing validation rules against any data the consumer is trying to persist to the database. A consumer is any UI that references the BLL and uses the exposed objects.

❑ Create an object model that hides the complexity of the database from the consumer of the object.

❑ Represent single business objects and lists of business objects.

❑ Communicate validation errors to the consumer.

❑ Ensure that data is persisted as a whole and cancelled if any part of the whole fails.

Design

The role of the BLL is to model your classes according to the business rules and processes, not necessarily the tables in the database. There is often a one-to-one relationship between a business object and a table, but the flexibility needs to be present to break from the table design and represent relationships between objects other than primary/foreign key relationships. Chapter 2 explained how the ORM Designer is used to create the entity objects that the DAL will pass back to the BLL for retrieval of data. Once you receive the entity object from the DAL, it is up to you to correctly map it to your business object. Chapter 2 also explained how to pass data to the DAL as parameters to save or delete the data from the database. Your business object may call one or more methods in the DAL depending on the business rules, and it should wrap multiple calls within a transaction. To make these ideas concrete, let's look at our example.

Create a folder called `Framework` in the `PaidTimeOffBLL` project to hold all of the classes defined in this section. The class diagram shown in Figure 3-1 displays the four base classes that you will develop in this section.

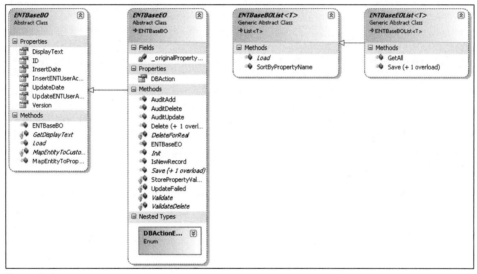

Figure 3-1

ENTBaseBO

The most generic type of business object is one that cannot be changed by the user. An example is a "status" object that has predefined values and specific code to handle each status. Users of the application should not be able to create a new status because the system would need to implement it. Usually these types of objects are displayed to the user in a drop-down list. From a database perspective they are usually one table, and a foreign key is added to other tables to reference the data. In the design pattern being developed in this book, these types of object inherit from the `ENTBaseBO` class. The BO suffix stands for "business object."

```
[Serializable()]
public abstract class ENTBaseBO
{ ... }
```

The class is declared with the `Serializable` attribute so that any object that inherits from this object can be serialized. Serialization is required in many applications, so always put it in the base class because it doesn't hurt performance. The class is declared as abstract because there are numerous abstract methods that every inheriting class must implement.

Properties

As a standard, every table has `ID`, `InsertDate`, `InsertENTUserAccountId`, `UpdateDate`, `UpdateENTUserAccountID`, and `Version` fields. These are defined as properties in the `ENTBaseBO` class:

```
public int ID { get; set; }
public DateTime InsertDate { get; private set; }
public int InsertENTUserAccountId { get; private set; }
public DateTime UpdateDate { get; private set; }
public int UpdateENTUserAccountId { get; private set; }
public Binary Version { get; set; }
```

The properties are defined with the new C# property syntax in Visual Studio 2008 and have a member variable generated automatically behind the scenes. The set accessors for the `InsertDate` and `UpdateDate` properties are declared as private because they should be controlled by the business object and not the consumer of the object. This is how to implement read-only properties with the new shorthand property syntax in Visual Studio 2008. If you were not using the shorthand syntax, you would not include the set accessor method to make a property read-only. Note that the `Binary` type used for the `Version` property is found in the `System.Data.Linq` namespace and is needed because the `Version` field is defined as a timestamp in the database. You need to add a reference to this namespace, and add a `using` statement at the top of the class module for this to work correctly. The generic property `ID` is used so that the consumer can always rely on one property to get the object's identity field, rather than a custom ID property on each object.

Another useful read-only property added to this class is `DisplayText`, which goes hand in hand with an abstract method:

```
public string DisplayText
{
    get { return GetDisplayText(); }
}

protected abstract string GetDisplayText();
```

This property calls `GetDisplayText`, which you must implement in the inheriting class. This property is used when you want to display the object to the user on the screen or in a bound control such as a drop-down list. Because this is a property, you can bind a list of these objects to any data-bound control and set the `DataTextField` property to "DisplayText." It must be defined as a property for this to work. Setting the `DataTextField` to a method does not work. For example, if a `person` class inherits from `ENTBaseBO` and has `FirstName` and `LastName` properties and the user requested that all users be displayed as last name and then first name, then the `GetDisplayText` method would return `LastName` + ", " + `FirstName`. Every drop-down list would display the data consistently. If later the requirements changed and a maturity suffix property were added, only the `GetDisplayText` method would have to be changed to modify all the drop-down lists.

Methods

The only public method for this class is the Load method. These objects only need to be retrieved from the database — never added, updated, or deleted:

```
public abstract bool Load(int id);

protected abstract void MapEntityToCustomProperties(IENTBaseEntity entity);

public void MapEntityToProperties(IENTBaseEntity entity)
{
    if (entity != null)
    {
        InsertDate = entity.InsertDate;
        InsertENTUserAccountId = entity.InsertENTUserAccountId;
        UpdateDate = entity.UpdateDate;
        UpdateENTUserAccountId = entity.UpdateENTUserAccountId;
        Version = entity.Version;
        this.MapEntityToCustomProperties(entity);
    }
}
```

Any class that inherits from ENTBaseBO must implement the Load and MapEntityToCustomProperties methods. When implementing the Load method, it should retrieve a single entity from the DAL and call the MapEntityToProperties method. The MapEntityToProperties method is the method that maps the five common fields to the current instance and then calls the MapEntityToCustomProperties method. The MapEntityToCustomProperties method should copy the properties from the entity object to the business object's properties. The reason why it has CustomProperties in the name is because the business object will have properties that are not the standard properties defined in the base. This method should map only the custom properties; the base can handle itself in the MapEntityToProperties method. A typical implementation of the Load method looks like this:

```
public override bool Load(int id)
{
    MyRecord myRecord = new MyRecordData().Select(id);
    if (myRecord != null)
    {
        MapEntityToProperties(myRecord);
        return true;
    }
    else
    {
        return false;
    }
}
```

Note that the MapEntityToCustomProperties method takes an IENTBaseEntity object as a parameter, which is defined in the DAL. A generic could be used here as the parameter to the MapEntityToCustomProperties method but that would cause the user interface to reference the DAL because the types are defined in the DAL. This is a no-no, so it is implemented with the IENTBaseEntity interface and then cast up in the implemented method.

ENTBaseBOList

Most applications need to represent single records and multiple records back to the user. Generic list objects are great for this type of functionality. The ENTBaseBOList object serves as the base for all lists of business objects. The ENTBaseBOList class contains the following code:

```
[Serializable()]
public abstract class ENTBaseBOList<T> : List<T> where T:ENTBaseBO,new()
{
    public abstract void Load();
}
```

The class inherits from the generic List class in the System.Collections.Generic namespace and there is a constraint on the type of class the generic can represent. This guarantees that the generic object is of the type ENTBaseBO. Notice the new() keyword at the end of the declaration. This allows any class that inherits from this class to create a new instance of the T class without knowing the type, as shown here:

```
T myType = new T();
```

Methods

There is only one abstract method in this class, Load, which must be implemented. This method will load the current instance with all the records from the database. You can overload the Load method if you need to add a filter to the records, but by default all records are loaded. An implementation of Load looks like this:

```
public override void Load()
{
    List<MyObject> myObjects = new MyObjectData().Select();

    if (myObjects.Count > 0)
    {
        foreach (MyObject myObject in myObjects)
        {
            MyObjectBO newMyObjectBO = new MyObjectBO();
            newMyObjectBO.MapEntityToProperties(myObject);
            this.Add(newMyObjectBO);
        }
    }
}
```

Notice that the data is retrieved from the DAL using the Select method, which takes no parameters. This always returns all records. The DAL returns a list of MyObject objects that is defined by the ORM Designer. Once the data is returned as a list, you can enumerate through the list and create a new instance of your custom business object, call the MapEntityToProperties method, and then add it to the current list. This is the simplest implementation of the Load method, but you could add code to load child records in the Load as well.

ENTBaseEO

Another base class is the ENTBaseEO class. The EO stands for "edit object" and represents a single instance of a special business object. What makes this different from the ENTBaseBO is that it allows the object's consumer to add, update, and delete records in the database. It inherits from the ENTBaseBO class and is also marked as Serializable. Because this class inherits from ENTBaseBO, it already has a mechanism for loading itself:

```
[Serializable()]
public abstract class ENTBaseEO : ENTBaseBO
{ ... }
```

Properties

There is an enumeration called DBActionEnum and a new property declared as DBAction:

```
public enum DBActionEnum
{
    Save,
    Delete
}

//Property declaration
public DBActionEnum DBAction { get; set; }

/// <summary>
/// Default constructor
/// </summary>
public ENTBaseEO() : base()
{
    //Default the action to save.
    DBAction = DBActionEnum.Save;
}
```

The enumeration controls what should happen to the data when the user tries to add, update, or delete records. Save will either add or update a record depending on the value of the ID property. An ID with a value of 0 indicates a new record. The default constructor sets the default action to Save. The other enumerated value is Delete. This will delete the record from the database based on the ID property of the object. This property comes in handy when you have a one-to-many relationship and the user has decided to remove some items and add others. You can use this flag to mark which items should be added or deleted when the entire object is saved, and wrap everything in a single transaction. You'll see an example of this in the ENTBaseEOList class later in this chapter.

Methods

The next section in this class is the Save methods:

```
public bool Save(ref ENTValidationErrors validationErrors, int userAccountId)
{
    if (DBAction == DBActionEnum.Save)
    {
        // Begin database transaction
        using (TransactionScope ts = new TransactionScope())
```

```
            {
                // Create the data context
                using (HRPaidTimeOffDataContext db = new HRPaidTimeOffDataContext())
                {
                    //Now save the record
                    if (this.Save(db, ref validationErrors, userAccountId))
                    {
                        // Commit transaction if update was successful
                        ts.Complete();
                        return true;
                    }
                    else
                    {
                        return false;
                    }
                }
            }
        }
        else
        {
            throw new Exception("DBAction not Save.");
        }
    }
}

public abstract bool Save(HRPaidTimeOffDataContext db, ref ENTValidationErrors
    validationErrors, int userAccountId);
```

The Save methods return true or false depending on whether the object passed all the validation rules. The first Save method is implemented in the base class and starts a transaction, creates a HRPaidTimeOff DataContext object, and calls the second Save method, which takes a HRPaidTimeOffDataContext as a parameter. In the design pattern developed in this book, if a DataContext object is passed to a method, it is assumed that the transaction has already been started. This enables you to either save one record at a time or have the object partake in a separate transaction that saves more than one record.

The second Save method is declared as abstract. The class that inherits from this object must implement the save logic, which saves one or more records depending on the business rules. An implementation of the Save method looks like this:

```
public override bool Save(HRPaidTimeOffDataContext db, ref ENTValidationErrors
    validationErrors, int userAccountId)
{
    if (DBAction == DBActionEnum.Save)
    {
        //Validate the object
        Validate(db, ref validationErrors);

        //Check if there were any validation errors
        if (validationErrors.Count == 0)
        {
            if (IsNewRecord())
            {
                //Add
                ID = new MyObjectData().Insert(db, Field1, Field2, userAccountId);
            }
```

```
            else
            {
                //Update
                if (!new MyObjectData().Update(db, ID, Field1, Field2,
                        userAccountId, Version))
                {
                    UpdateFailed(ref validationErrors);
                    return false;
                }
            }

            return true;
        }
        else
        {
            //Didn't pass validation.
            return false;
        }
    }
    else
    {
        throw new Exception("DBAction not save.");
    }
}
```

Notice the parameter called ENTValidationErrors. This is a list of a custom class that contains error messages for validation errors. A list is used so the user can receive multiple messages for all validation errors, rather than one at a time. The Save method must validate the data before passing it to the DAL, and any validation errors are added to this list and passed back to the consumer. If there are validation errors, the data won't even make it to the DAL to be saved.

The ENTValidationError and ENTValdationErrors classes are quite simple. These classes should be added to a new class file called ENTValidationError.cs:

```
#region ENTValidationError
/// <summary>
/// This class contains the error message when a validation rule is broken
/// A validation error object should be created when validating input from the user
/// and you want to display a message back to the user.
/// </summary>
public class ENTValidationError
{
    public ENTValidationError() { }

    public string ErrorMessage { get; set;}
}

#endregion ENTValidationError

#region ENTValidationErrors

/// <summary>
/// This class contains a list of validation errors.  This allows you to
/// report back multiple errors.
```

```
///   </summary>
public class ENTValidationErrors : List<ENTValidationError>
{
    public void Add(string errorMessage)
    {
        base.Add(new ENTValidationError { ErrorMessage = errorMessage });
    }
}

#endregion ENTValidationErrors
```

The ENTValidationError class has only one property called ErrorMessage. You could expand on this object to denote severity levels, but for this book I'll keep it simple. The ENTValidationErrors list allows the consumer to add an ENTValidationError object by simply passing in an error message string. Notice the syntax for creating the ENTValidationError object. This is new to Visual Studio 2008. You can instantiate an object and set any properties without creating overloaded constructors. Instead of instantiating an object with (), you simply use {} and set the property values between the brackets. Visual Studio 2008 will even list the properties for you using IntelliSense. The Validate and ValidateDelete methods populate the ENTValidationErrors list with any validation errors.

Validate

The Validate method is where you put all the validation rules when adding or updating a record for your edit object:

```
protected abstract void Validate(HRPaidTimeOffDataContext db, ref
    ENTValidationErrors validationErrors);
```

For example, if a field is required you would write the following code:

```
if (myValue == null)
{
    validationErrors.Add("The My Value field is required.");
}
```

The Save method calls the Validate method and checks the validationErrors.Count to determine whether it can save the record to the database. Wrapping all the validation rules in the Validate routine makes it much easier to determine where your rules should go and where other developers have put their validation logic. The Validate method is where most of the custom code appears in the edit object. Almost all other code can be generated automatically by a code generator by looking at a table's fields. Later in the book you will see how this code generator is created.

Init

The next abstract method is called Init:

```
public abstract void Init();
```

This method should contain the code to set default values for new records. An Init method is used, rather than a constructor, because you only want to run through this code for new records, not every time an instance of the object is created.

Delete

The last two abstract methods deal with deleting a record:

```
protected abstract void DeleteForReal(HRPaidTimeOffDataContext db);

protected abstract void ValidateDelete(HRPaidTimeOffDataContext db, ref
    ENTValidationErrors validationErrors);
```

The DeleteForReal method calls the Delete method in the DAL. The ValidateDelete method is similar to the Validate method in that it is the method that enforces validation rules. This is where you would put referential integrity checks and other rules that prevent users from deleting a record. It is much nicer to give users a friendly message that they cannot delete a record, rather than rely on the database message, which could be confusing to users and display information about the database's structure that a hacker could exploit.

The Delete method is implemented in the base and calls the DeleteForReal method. It is similar to Save in that it is overloaded to take a HRPaidTimeOffDataContext parameter. The first Delete method starts the transaction and calls the second Delete method, passing in the HRPaidTimeOffDataContext object. The second Delete method calls the ValidateDelete method before calling the DeleteForReal method. The Delete method does not have to be implemented in the inheriting class:

```
public bool Delete(ref ENTValidationErrors validationErrors, int userAccountId)
{
    if (DBAction == DBActionEnum.Delete)
    {
        // Begin database transaction
        using (TransactionScope ts = new TransactionScope())
        {
            // Create data context
            using (HRPaidTimeOffDataContext db = new HRPaidTimeOffDataContext())
            {
                this.Delete(db, ref validationErrors, userAccountId);

                if (validationErrors.Count == 0)
                {
                    //Commit transaction since the delete was successful
                    ts.Complete();
                    return true;
                }
                else
                {
                    return false;
                }
            }
        }
    }
    else
    {
        throw new Exception("DBAction not delete.");
    }
}
```

```
    }

    internal virtual bool Delete(HRPaidTimeOffDataContext db, ref
        ENTValidationErrors validationErrors, int userAccountId)
    {
        if (DBAction == DBActionEnum.Delete)
        {
            //Check if this record can be deleted.  There may be referential
            //integrity rules preventing it from being deleted
            ValidateDelete(db, ref validationErrors);

            if (validationErrors.Count == 0)
            {
                this.DeleteForReal(db);
                return true;
            }
            else
            {
                //The record can not be deleted.
                return false;
            }
        }
        else
        {
            throw new Exception("DBAction not delete.");
        }
    }
```

IsNewRecord

The IsNewRecord method returns true if the object is new. This is used in the Save method to determine whether the object is supposed to be inserted or updated. Because this class inherits from the ENTBaseBO class, it is guaranteed to have an ID property:

```
public bool IsNewRecord()
{
    return ID == 0;
}
```

UpdateFailed

The last method, UpdateFailed, is called when a user tries to edit a record while another user is updating it, which causes a concurrency issue. The UpdateFailed method adds a message to the validationErrors list, which will be bubbled up to the user. This provides a consistent message for all concurrency issues.

```
protected void UpdateFailed(ref ENTValidationErrors validationErrors)
{
    validationErrors.Add("This record was updated by someone else while you were
        editing it.  Your changes were not saved.");
}
```

ENTBaseEOList

The last base class is ENTBaseEOList, which represents a list of edit objects. This class inherits from the ENTBaseBOList class and constrains the type to be an ENTBaseEO object. This class is also declared as Serializable:

```
[Serializable()]
public abstract class ENTBaseEOList<T> : ENTBaseBOList<T>
    where T : ENTBaseEO, new()
{ … }
```

Methods

The ENTBaseEOList class has two methods, both called Save. The Save methods will add or delete any objects in the list from the database. The same pattern holds true: The first Save does not take the DataContext parameter and it calls the second, which has the parameter. The code for the Save methods is as follows:

```
public bool Save(ref ENTValidationErrors validationErrors, int userAccountId)
{
    // Check if this object has any items
    if (this.Count > 0)
    {
        using (TransactionScope ts = new TransactionScope())
        {
            using (HRPaidTimeOffDataContext db = new HRPaidTimeOffDataContext())
            {
                if (this.Save(db, ref validationErrors, userAccountId))
                {
                    // Commit transaction if update was successful
                    ts.Complete();
                    return true;
                }
                else
                {
                    return false;
                }
            }
        }
    }
    else
    {
        //No items in the list so return true.
        return true;
    }
}

public bool Save(HRPaidTimeOffDataContext db, ref ENTValidationErrors
    validationErrors, int userAccountId)
{
    foreach (ENTBaseEO genericEO in this)
    {
```

```
            if (genericEO.DBAction == ENTBaseEO.DBActionEnum.Save)
            {
                if (!genericEO.Save(db, ref validationErrors, userAccountId))
                {
                    return false;
                }
                else
                {
                    if (genericEO.DBAction == ENTBaseEO.DBActionEnum.Delete)
                    {
                        if (!genericEO.Delete(db, ref validationErrors, userAccountId))
                        {
                            return false;
                        }
                    }
                    else
                    {
                        throw new Exception("Unknown DBAction");
                    }
                }
            }
        }
        return true;
}
```

The first method starts a transaction and creates an instance of the HRPaidTimeOffDataContext and then calls the second method. The second Save method loops through all the edit objects in the current instance and calls either the Save or the Delete method based on the DBAction property of the object.

Solution

Now that all the base classes are defined, we can create an edit object that uses the ENTUserAccount classes built in the DAL to manage ENTUserAccount records in our application. This object is considered an edit object because the application will allow users to add and update users. If there were no need for adding or updating, then the base class would be the ENTBaseBO class, rather than the ENTBaseEO class.

Here are the business requirements that apply to "users" in the system:

❑ Users can be added and updated in the system. (Business rule)

❑ Users cannot be deleted. (Validation rule)

❑ Users must be identified by their Windows Logon ID for single sign-on. (Business rule)

❑ User account names are required and must be unique. (Validation rule)

❑ User first name, last name, and e-mail are required. (Validation rule)

❑ E-mail addresses must be unique. (Validation rule)

❑ E-mail addresses must contain the @ sign, end in V2.com, and have at least two letters to the left of the @ sign. (Validation rule)

The First Edit Object Class

Add a class to the V2.PaidTimeOffBLL project in the Framework folder called ENTUserAccountEO. Add using directives to reference the V2.PaidTimeOffDAL and V2.PaidTimeOffDAL.Framework namespaces. Add the Serializable attribute to the class and change the scope to public. The class should inherit from the ENTBaseEO class because the user will be able to add and update users. If you press Shift+Alt+F10 while on the ENTBaseEO name, you will get a menu to implement the abstract members of the base class. Automatically implement the inherited abstract methods by clicking on the pop-up menu. The resulting code should look like the following:

```
[Serializable()]
public class ENTUserAccountEO : ENTBaseEO
{
    public override bool Save(HRPaidTimeOffDataContext db, ref ENTValidationErrors
        validationErrors, int userAccountId)
    {
        throw new NotImplementedException();
    }

    protected override void Validate(HRPaidTimeOffDataContext db, ref
        ENTValidationErrors validationErrors)
    {
        throw new NotImplementedException();
    }

    protected override void DeleteForReal(HRPaidTimeOffDataContext db)
    {
        throw new NotImplementedException();
    }

    protected override void ValidateDelete(HRPaidTimeOffDataContext db,
        ref ENTValidationErrors validationErrors)
    {
        throw new NotImplementedException();
    }

    public override void Init()
    {
        throw new NotImplementedException();
    }

    public override bool Load(int id)
    {
        throw new NotImplementedException();
    }

    protected override void MapEntityToCustomProperties(IENTBaseEntity entity)
    {
        throw new NotImplementedException();
    }

    protected override string GetDisplayText()
```

```
        {
            throw new NotImplementedException();
        }
    }
}
```

Properties

Before implementing any of the abstract methods, the custom properties that are specific to this class need to be added:

```
public string WindowsAccountName { get; set; }
public string FirstName { get; set; }
public string LastName { get; set; }
public string Email { get; set; }
public bool IsActive { get; set; }
```

The first four properties are self-explanatory. The IsActive property is added because the business requirements state that a user cannot be deleted. The IsActive flag is used to hide users who are no longer with the company. It is good practice to name Boolean values with the prefix "Is" to make them easier to read.

Save Method

The first method to implement is the Save method:

```
public override bool Save(HRPaidTimeOffDataContext db, ref ENTValidationErrors
        validationErrors, int userAccountId)
{
    if (DBAction == DBActionEnum.Save)
    {
        //Validate the object
        Validate(db, ref validationErrors);

        //Check if there were any validation errors
        if (validationErrors.Count == 0)
        {
            if (IsNewRecord())
            {
                //Add
                ID = new ENTUserAccountData().Insert(db, WindowsAccountName,
                    FirstName, LastName, Email, IsActive, userAccountId);
            }
            else
            {
                //Update
                if (!new ENTUserAccountData().Update(db, ID,WindowsAccountName,
                    FirstName, LastName, Email, IsActive, userAccountId, Version))
                {
                    UpdateFailed(ref validationErrors);
                    return false;
                }
            }
        }

        return true;
```

```
            }
            else
            {
                //Didn't pass validation.
                return false;
            }
        }
        else
        {
            throw new Exception("DBAction not save.");
        }
    }
```

The first line checks whether the DBAction property was set to Save. Remember that the DBAction property is in the ENTBaseEO class and defaults to Save. This check is in place in case a user sets this to Delete but calls the Save method instead of the Delete method. The method throws an exception if the wrong DBAction is set in the class. The next line calls the Validate method to execute the validation rules against the object's data. The Validate method is another abstract method in the base that you need to customize in the inheriting class. If any validation rules fail, then a message is added to the validationErrors list.

After the Validate method is called, the Count property is checked and the record is saved if there are no validation errors. The next line checks the IsNewRecord method, which is in the base, to see if the ID is equal to 0. The Insert method on the ENTUserAccountData class is called for new records, returning the ID of the newly added record and setting this to the ID property in the edit object. The Update method of the ENTUserAccountData class is called for existing records. The Version property is passed into this method to check for concurrency issues, and the method returns false if the record wasn't updated. If so, the UpdateFailed method is called in the base, which adds a message to the validationErrors list and the Save function returns false. If the record is inserted or updated successfully, then the Save method returns true. This pattern is the same for most edit objects. It varies if an object has child objects and needs to save more than one record in a transaction. An example of this appears in Chapter 6, when a "role" object is saved that has multiple users.

Validate Method

The next method to implement is the Validate method. Because the code is repetitive for each field, only the important parts are shown here:

```
protected override void Validate(HRPaidTimeOffDataContext db, ref
    ENTValidationErrors validationErrors)
{
    //Windows Account Name is required.
    if (WindowsAccountName.Trim().Length == 0)
    {
        validationErrors.Add("The windows account name is required.");
    }

    //The windows account name must be unique.
    ENTUserAccountData entUserAccountData = new ENTUserAccountData();
    if (entUserAccountData.IsDuplicateWindowsAccountName(db, ID,
            WindowsAccountName))
    {
```

```
                    validationErrors.Add("The windows account name must be unique.");
            }
    }
```

Because there is a business requirement for the Windows account name, the first check adds an error message to the `validationErrors` list if the `WindowsAccountName` is blank. The second business requirement implemented is that the Windows account name must be unique. An `IsDuplicate WindowsAccountName` method is added to the `ENTUserAccountData` class in the DAL to check this. It's important to dig under the covers of this method:

```
public bool IsDuplicateWindowsAccountName(HRPaidTimeOffDataContext db,
        int userAccountId, string windowsAccountName)
{
    return IsDuplicate(db, "ENTUserAccount", "WindowsAccountName",
        "ENTUserAccountId", windowsAccountName, userAccountId);
}
```

This method calls another method that was added to the `ENTBaseData` class, a generic method that can check any table for a duplicate field value. The `IsDuplicate` method parameters are the table name to check, the field name whose value must be unique, the field name for the ID, the value to be checked, which in this instance is the `windowsAccountName`, and the value for the ID. The ID is passed in because when updating you want to exclude the record being updated for the duplicate value check. Here is the `IsDuplicate` code:

```
protected static bool IsDuplicate(HRPaidTimeOffDataContext db, string tableName,
        string fieldName, string fieldNameId, string value, int id)
{
    string sql = "SELECT COUNT(" + fieldNameId + ") AS DuplicateCount " +
                    "FROM " + tableName +
                " WHERE " + fieldName + " = {0}" +
                    " AND " + fieldNameId + " <> {1}";

    var result = db.ExecuteQuery<DuplicateCheck>(sql, new object[] { value, id });

    List<DuplicateCheck> list = result.ToList();

    return (list[0].DuplicateCount > 0);
}
```

This is where it gets interesting. The code builds a dynamic query based on the table name and fields passed into this method. The `DataContext` object has an `ExecuteQuery` method that can execute dynamic SQL statements, enabling you to pass parameters to the SQL statement using an array of objects. `ExecuteQuery` is a generic method that takes a type as a parameter. The `DuplicateCheck` type is a new custom class in the DAL that has one field, `DuplicateCount`. The `ExecuteQuery` method returns an object that can convert the results to a list of `DuplicateCheck` objects. The `result.ToList()` line converts the result to the `List` object. Now you have a strongly typed object to reference the results of the query. Add the `DuplicateCheck` class to the `PaidTimeOffDAL` project:

```
internal class DuplicateCheck
{
    public int DuplicateCount { get; set; }
}
```

Note that the field name in the query must match the property in the class; if it doesn't you won't get an error, but the value will be the default value for the type the property is declared as. This is some pretty slick functionality in LINQ to SQL that you can use if you don't want to use stored procedures for some reason. The `IsDuplicate` method is called in many different `Data` classes anytime a field must be checked for uniqueness.

DeleteForReal and ValidateDelete Methods

The requirements state that users cannot delete a user, so this class leaves the default implementation of the `DeleteForReal` and `ValidateDelete` methods, which throw exceptions if a user calls these methods. For most other classes you would add code that calls the `Delete` method of the `Data` class in the `DeleteForReal` method. The `ValidateDelete` method would be implemented similarly to the `Validate` method by checking any business rules on delete or referential integrity rules, and adding a message to the `validationErrors` list if any rules are broken.

Init Method

The `Init` method is used for defaulting values in the object for new records. The only code for the `ENTUserAccountEO` object is `IsActive = true`. Users shouldn't have to default a new user to active because they wouldn't be adding them if they weren't active:

```
public override void Init()
{
    IsActive = true;
}
```

Load Method

The `Load` method loads the current instance with the data from the record ID passed in as a parameter. The code for `Load` is as follows:

```
public override bool Load(int id)
{
    ENTUserAccount userAccount = new ENTUserAccountData().Select(id);
    if (userAccount != null)
    {
        MapEntityToProperties(userAccount);
        return true;
    }
    else
    {
        return false;
    }
}
```

The `Load` method first calls the `Select` method in the DAL, which returns a single entity object. If the record is not in the database, then the DAL returns a `null` object reference. If the record is found, then the `MapEntityToProperties` method is called and the entity object is passed in to this method. If the record isn't found, then the `Load` method returns false.

MapEntityToCustomProperties Method

The `MapEntityToCustomProperties` method maps the `ENTUserAccount` entity object to the properties of the edit object. In this example, there is a one-to-one relationship between the two classes, but classes that have children will be more complicated. The code for `MapEntityToCustomProperties` is as follows:

```
protected override void MapEntityToCustomProperties(IENTBaseEntity entity)
{
    ENTUserAccount userAccount = (ENTUserAccount)entity;

    ID = userAccount.ENTUserAccountId;
    WindowsAccountName = userAccount.WindowsAccountName;
    FirstName = userAccount.FirstName;
    LastName = userAccount.LastName;
    Email = userAccount.Email;
    IsActive = userAccount.IsActive;
}
```

The `entity` parameter is an `IENTBaseEntity` object so it must be cast up to the actual entity object for this class. What's nice here is that once the object is cast to the correct entity, you don't need to cast any of the properties. If you were using `DataSets` or `DataReaders` to retrieve the record, you would have to cast each field to each property.

GetDisplayText Method

The `GetDisplayText` method is called to determine what should be displayed in drop-down lists or list boxes when this object is used as the data source. For user accounts, always display the last name first, then the first name, separated by a comma:

```
protected override string GetDisplayText()
{
    return LastName + ", " + FirstName;
}
```

That's it for the edit object. You now can serve this object back to the consumer to allow them to add and update users in the system.

The First Edit Object List Object

Every edit object has a list object that can be passed back to the user interface to be displayed in a grid or html table. This object is very simple to create and implement. It inherits from the `ENTBaseEOList` object and must implement one abstract method called `Load`. The `list` class is added to the same file as the edit object class. This reduces the number of files in the project by half and makes it easier to manage.

```
[Serializable()]
public class ENTUserAccountEOList : ENTBaseEOList<ENTUserAccountEO>
{
    public override void Load()
```

```
        {
            LoadFromList(new ENTUserAccountData().Select());
        }

        protected void LoadFromList(List<ENTUserAccount> users)
        {
            foreach (ENTUserAccount user in users)
            {
                ENTUserAccountEO newUserAccountEO = new ENTUserAccountEO();
                newUserAccountEO.MapEntityToProperties(user);
                this.Add(newUserAccountEO);
            }
        }
    }
```

The Load method calls the Select method in the DAL, which returns all the records in the table. This method then calls the LoadFromList method, which takes a list of ENTUserAccount objects as a parameter and loads the list with edit objects. Notice that the LoadFromList object enumerates through the users object, creates an instance of the edit object, and then calls the MapEntitytoProperties method, which copies the entity object to the edit object's properties. If you need to filter the records returned from the database, then overload the Load method, call a specialized Select method in the DAL that contains your where condition, and then call the LoadFromList method. This pattern makes it simple to retrieve lists from the database and ensures that all developers are following the same pattern.

Summary

This chapter focused on the business logic layer and created the base classes used throughout the rest of the book. There are two types of business objects in the BLL: static business objects, which cannot have their data changed by the user, and edit objects, which include functionality for adding, updating, deleting, and selecting records from the DAL. Transactions are started and committed in the BLL and objects can either enlist in an existing transaction or start a new one.

Keep in mind two key points regarding communication between the BLL and the DAL:

❑ Data retrieved from the DAL is passed back to the BLL as a single entity object, a list of entity objects, or scalar values.

❑ Data passed to the DAL is passed as scalar values.

The key points to remember for communicating between the BLL and the user interface are as follows:

❑ The user interface creates instances of business objects and calls the Load method to retrieve the data.

❑ The user interface creates instances of business objects, sets their properties, and calls either Save to add or update a record, or Delete to delete a record.

❑ Broken validation rules are passed back to the user interface in the ENTValidationErrors list.

The key points to remember when creating a class that inherits from the ENTBaseBO class are as follows:

- ❑ Declare the class as Serializable.
- ❑ Create the custom properties for the business object.
- ❑ Implement the GetDisplayText method to return the text that should be displayed to the user when viewing this object in a drop-down list or list box.
- ❑ Implement the Load method to retrieve a single entity object from the DAL.
- ❑ Implement the MapEntityToCustomProperties method to map the properties of the entity object to the properties of the business object.

The key points to remember when creating a class that inherits from the ENTBaseBOList class are as follows:

- ❑ Declare the class as Serializable.
- ❑ Implement the Load method to retrieve all the entity objects from the DAL.
- ❑ Overload the Load method to filter entity objects that should be returned from the DAL.

The key points to remember when creating a class that inherits from the ENTBaseEO class are these:

- ❑ Follow all the steps defined above for implementing the ENTBaseBO class.
- ❑ Implement the Save method, which calls the Validate method and determines whether to add or update a record. Pass the data to the appropriate method in the DAL as scalar values.
- ❑ Implement the Validate method by enforcing the validation rules for your object. Any broken rules should be added to the validationErrors list.
- ❑ Implement the DeleteForReal method, which calls the Delete method in the data class in the DAL.
- ❑ Implement the ValidateDelete method, which enforces any validation rules for your object when deleting, usually referential integrity checks.
- ❑ Implement the Init method, which sets the default properties of the object when the user is creating a new record.

The key points to remember when creating a class that inherits from the ENTBaseEOList class are as follows:

- ❑ Follow all the steps defined above for implementing the ENTBaseBOList class.

Functionality for saving and deleting is automatically implemented in the base class, and all objects in the list will be added, updated, or deleted if the user calls the Save method.

4

The User Interface Layer

Have you ever built an application with a tremendous amount of functionality, one on which you've spent a great deal of time meeting all of the user's requirements, designing the perfect database, and creating a slick object model to handle the business rules, yet the user's first comment after your demo is "the font is too small"? Users don't care how great everything works behind the scenes and how much time and effort you expended considering multiple scenarios and confirming that the application's functionality works as expected. All they have to say is that the font is too small. What a way to take the wind out of your sails. I've met a lot of developers in my time and most think very similarly. Developers are very logical and possess the skills to dissect a problem into manageable pieces. They can translate requirements into a data model or object model without blinking an eye, but when it comes to building the user interface, things start to fall apart. The tools used to develop slick interfaces aren't the same tools used to design code or databases, and developers have to come out of their comfort zone to become a Picasso. Lining up text boxes on a screen isn't typically the programmer's primary focus. That's what junior developers are supposed to do, right? It's like being a percussionist in a band. You are responsible for keeping the beat, but the lead singer gets all the glory while you are buried behind the drums where no one can see you.

Of course, there is some merit in what the user is expressing. The look and feel of an application can make or break a system regardless of whether the application meets the user's requirements. A simple and easy-to-use application that covers 75% of the requirements will win hands down every time over an application that is hard to use and covers 100% of the requirements. You are responsible for making the overall user experience pleasant and intuitive. Intuitive is the key, as most users don't read documentation even if it exists. They just want to dive right in and start using the system. If they can't figure it out, they are unlikely to continue to buy into the system.

Problem

This chapter focuses on developing a user interface that is consistent, intuitive, visually pleasing, and meets the company's branding guidelines. This is accomplished using a variety of technologies in Visual Studio 2008. The main goals are as follows:

❑ Creating a style sheet that is used across all pages

❑ Creating a master page that contains the company logo, the application name, the user's information, a menu, a footer, and a content region

❑ Creating a nested master page for displaying lists of data in a `GridView`

❑ Creating a nested master page for all pages that enables the user to edit records

❑ Creating a tablike control for the menu, positioned horizontally across the top of the page

❑ Creating a tree control for the menu, positioned on the left side of the page

❑ Creating a custom `GridView` control that supports custom columns, paging, and sorting using objects at runtime

❑ Creating a control to display validation error messages passed back from the business logic layer

❑ Creating a base class for all pages to inherit that contains common functionality across all pages

❑ Creating a base page for all pages that enables users to edit records

❑ Creating the business classes, the data classes, and the table to bind to the menu

The main master page is designed to look like Figure 4-1.

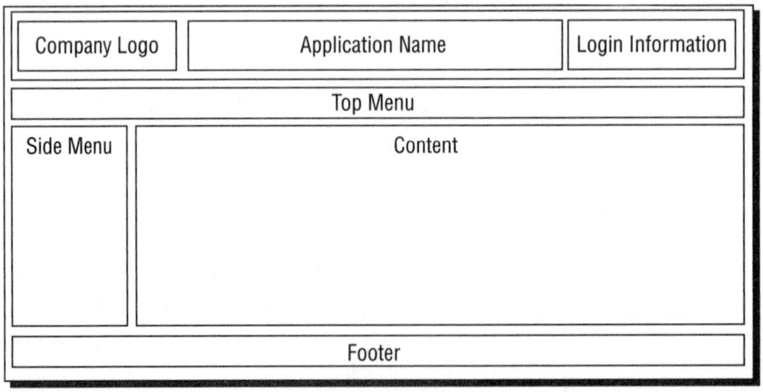

Figure 4-1

The application has a header that contains the company logo, the application name, and the current user's information. Below the main header is a horizontal menu that looks like tabs. Clicking on a tab changes the side menu and content page. The side menu contains hyperlinks, which when clicked load pages with custom content regions. The footer contains copyright information and the version of the application. The Administration tab within the application will look like Figure 4-2.

Figure 4-2

Design

This section explains how to create the style sheet mentioned earlier, master pages, controls, and classes. The solution section walks through an example demonstrating how to use these features to create both the page that displays the list of users defined in the system and the page that enables users to add or update existing users. The following table describes all the master pages, controls, style sheets, and classes that will be built in this chapter.

File	Description
PaidTimeOffUI: PaidTimeOff.css	This style sheet contains the company brand colors and is used by all other pages to consistently display the correct fonts and colors across all pages.
PaidTimeOffUI: PaidTimeOff.master	This is the main master page that contains the layout shown in Figure 4-1. All pages should use this master page or a master page that is nested in this master page.
PaidTimeOffUI: PaidTimeOffEditGrid.master	This is a nested master page that is used for all pages that display lists of records to the user in a `GridView`.
PaidTimeOffUI: PaidTimeOffEditPage.master	This nested master page is used for all pages to enable users to edit a record. A Save and Cancel button are placed on this page so every page is consistent.

File	Description
PaidTimeOffUI: App_Code\ BasePage	This class is the base for all pages in the application and contains common logic for encrypting and decrypting query strings, setting menus, etc. This class is built in this chapter and extended in future chapters.
PaidTimeOffUI: App_Code\ BaseEditPage	This class inherits from the `BasePage` class. All pages that allow users to edit a record should inherit from this class. This class defines numerous abstract methods that enforce consistent coding conventions in all pages that inherit from this class.
PaidTimeOffUI: Administration\ Administration.aspx	This page is displayed when the user selects the Administration tab from the menu. It lists all the pages to which a user has access and provides a brief description of the page.
PaidTimeOffUI: Administration\Users.aspx	This page displays all the users defined in the application.
PaidTimeOffUI: Administration\User.aspx	This page enables users to add or edit an existing user.
V2.FrameworkControls: MenuTabs.cs	This control is placed at the top of the `PaidTimeOff.master` page and displays the tabs that enable users to navigate between the home page, the administration pages, and the reports pages.
V2.FrameworkControls: MenuTree.cs	This control is placed on the left side of the `PaidTimeOff.master` page and displays the list of pages to which a user has access in a tree control.
V2.FrameworkControls: ValidationErrorMessages.cs	This control displays messages back to users when they try to save a record but a business rule is broken.
V2.FrameworkControls: CustomGridView.cs	This control inherits from the `GridView` control and displays lists of objects to users. The functionality of sorting and paging is turned on by default in this control.

The PaidTimeOff Style Sheet

A cascading style sheet (CSS) is used to obtain consistency of fonts, colors, text sizes, and many other visual aspects of a page. It is a good idea to always place these settings into a separate style sheet file, rather than bury them in the HTML of a particular page. Having them in a separate file enables you to share them across all pages in the project. Visual Studio 2008 has greatly improved its support for cascading style sheets by adding a couple of new windows in the designer called Manage Styles and Apply Styles. The Manage Styles window enables you to attach a style sheet to a page, add new styles to a style sheet, modify styles in a style sheet, and visually see which styles have been applied to a page. The Apply Styles page is similar to the Styles and Formatting window in Microsoft Word. You can see how the style is rendered in HTML and apply it to elements in the page. You can view either of these windows by opening an ASP.NET page in Visual Studio and then selecting View ⇨ Manage Styles or View ⇨ Apply Styles from the menu. The two windows are shown in Figure 4-3.

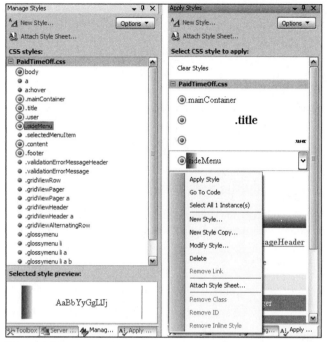

Figure 4-3

In order to add the style sheet to the application built in this book, right-click on the `PaidTimeOffUI` project and select Add New Item from the menu. Select the Style Sheet template from the dialog and name the file `PaidTimeOff.css`. You can apply some common settings to specific elements in a page, such as the body tag or hyperlinks. To attach a style to a specific tag, you simply add the tag name followed by the style, defined in brackets. The following code sets the style for the anchor tag, and the hover action of an anchor tag:

```
a{
    color: #0064FF;
    text-decoration:none;
}

a:hover{
    text-decoration: underline;
}
```

Now each page that uses this style sheet will have a consistent look for all hyperlinks. I won't go into all the tags that can or should be defined in the style sheet, as the syntax is the same. Wrox has a plethora of books covering this topic in more detail, which I recommend buying as a handy reference for your CSS needs.

If you want to apply a style to a specific control, you can create a class within the style sheet and set the control's `class` attribute to the class name. To create a class in the style sheet, simply preface the name with a period. The following code creates a class called `mainContainer` and sets its background color to white:

```
.mainContainer
{
  background-color: #ffffff;
}
```

The Parent Master Page

The parent master page is the main page that contains the header, menu, and footer for all the pages in the application. Other master pages can be nested inside this page either to create a specific look and feel for pages that display lists of data or to enable users to edit records. There will also be a base page class that all pages must inherit from to work in conjunction with the master page. This can get confusing because a lot of people think that if you use a master page, the page is inheriting from the master page. Think of the master page as just another control on a page. The control creates the visual framework for placing other controls to display data to the user. The master page creates a consistent look for all of the pages, whereas the base page creates consistent behavior for the pages. Figure 4-4 shows the `PaidTimeOff` master page in design view.

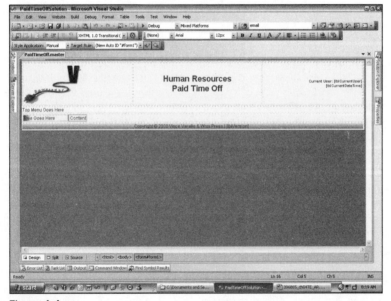

Figure 4-4

Figure 4-5 shows conceptually how the master page and base page are merged to create a content page.

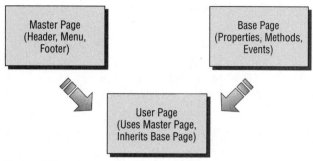

Figure 4-5

The BasePage Class

The `BasePage` class is the lowest-level class that all pages should inherit from in this project. The goals of the `BasePage` class are as follows:

❑ Create a class that all pages inherit from and that contains common logic that can be used across all pages.

❑ Force the developer to set the correct menu for the page being displayed.

❑ Provide functionality for encrypting and decrypting query strings so users cannot manipulate the text in the browser's address bar.

Manipulation of a query string can lead to unexpected security flaws in an application, such as cross-site scripting and SQL injection attacks. Usually business users aren't going to know how to hack into a site like this, but if you leave an ID parameter in a query string, in plain text, they typically are smart enough to change the ID's value and refresh the page to potentially pull up a record they shouldn't.

The base class in this project is an abstract class called `BasePage` and it will be extended as the book progresses. It's always a good idea to have a `BasePage` from which all your pages inherit so you can easily add functionality to all pages. Because this is essential for the rest of the chapter, let's add this to the `PaidTimeOffUI` project now:

1. Add a new class to the `PaidTimeOffUI` project called `BasePage.cs`.

2. Visual Studio will ask you if it should create a folder called `App_Code`. Select Yes.

3. Change the class declaration so it is abstract. It should also inherit from the `System.Web.UI.page` class.

4. Create the default constructor with no parameters. Here is the code for the `BasePage` class:

```
public abstract class BasePage : System.Web.UI.Page
{
    public BasePage() { }
}
```

The next step is to add an abstract method called `MenuItemName`. This method must be implemented by the calling class and return the name of the menu item that belongs to this page. The name of the menu item will drive which top and side menu should appear:

```
public abstract string MenuItemName();
```

Next, add a method that will return the root path for this page. This is a utility function that is useful when you cannot use relative paths for hyperlinks. The root path returns the protocol, the website, and the virtual directory for the application. For example, `http://localhost/PaidTimeOffUI/` is returned for this application:

```
public static string RootPath(HttpContext context)
{
    string urlSuffix = context.Request.Url.Authority +
        context.Request.ApplicationPath;
    return context.Request.Url.Scheme + @"://" + urlSuffix + "/";
}
```

Another common challenge while developing an ASP.NET application is passing data between two pages. You can find a great article that covers the many different options for passing data between pages at `http://steveorr.net/articles/PassData.aspx`. This book uses the tried-and-true QueryString for passing simplistic values to pages. The most common scenario is displaying a record on a page to the user. The ID of the record is passed in the QueryString and read by the called page so it can be displayed to the user. This can be dangerous, however, because users can manipulate the value in the QueryString and potentially view data they are not allowed to see. Therefore, all QueryStrings in the application will be encrypted before being sent to the browser, and decrypted when being read from the `Request` object. There are three methods in the `BasePage` class that handle encrypting and decrypting a query string. The code for these methods is as follows:

```
using System.Collections.Specialized;

public static NameValueCollection DecryptQueryString(string queryString)
{
    return StringHelpers.DecryptQueryString(queryString);
}

public static string EncryptQueryString(NameValueCollection queryString)
{
    return StringHelpers.EncryptQueryString(queryString);
}

public static string EncryptQueryString(string queryString)
{
    return StringHelpers.EncryptQueryString(queryString);
}
```

These three methods call methods in a custom class called `StringHelpers`. The `StringHelper` class contains common logic for manipulating any strings, not just a query string. Add another class to the App_Code folder and call it `StringHelpers`. The code for this class is as follows:

```
using System;
using System.Security.Cryptography;
```

```
using System.IO;
using System.Text;

public class StringHelpers
{
    private static RijndaelManaged _cryptoProvider;

    //128 bit encyption: DO NOT CHANGE
    private static readonly byte[] Key = {18, 19, 8, 24, 36, 22, 4, 22, 17, 5, 11,
        9, 13, 15, 06, 23};
    private static readonly byte[] IV = {14, 2, 16, 7, 5, 9, 17, 8, 4, 47, 16, 12,
        1, 32, 25, 18};

    static StringHelpers()
    {
        _cryptoProvider = new RijndaelManaged();
        _cryptoProvider.Mode = CipherMode.CBC;
        _cryptoProvider.Padding = PaddingMode.PKCS7;
    }

    public static string Encrypt(string unencryptedString)
    {
        byte[] bytIn = ASCIIEncoding.ASCII.GetBytes(unencryptedString);

        // Create a MemoryStream
        MemoryStream ms = new MemoryStream();

        // Create Crypto Stream that encrypts a stream
        CryptoStream cs = new CryptoStream(ms,
            _cryptoProvider.CreateEncryptor(Key,IV),
            CryptoStreamMode.Write);

        // Write content into MemoryStream
        cs.Write(bytIn, 0, bytIn.Length);
        cs.FlushFinalBlock();

        byte[] bytOut = ms.ToArray();
        return Convert.ToBase64String(bytOut);
    }

    public static string Decrypt(string encryptedString)
    {
        if (encryptedString.Trim().Length != 0)
        {
            // Convert from Base64 to binary
            byte[] bytIn = Convert.FromBase64String(encryptedString);

            // Create a MemoryStream
            MemoryStream ms = new MemoryStream(bytIn, 0, bytIn.Length);

            // Create a CryptoStream that decrypts the data
            CryptoStream cs = new CryptoStream(ms,
                _cryptoProvider.CreateDecryptor(Key,IV),
                CryptoStreamMode.Read);
```

```csharp
            // Read the Crypto Stream
            StreamReader sr = new StreamReader(cs);

            return sr.ReadToEnd();
        }
        else
        {
            return "";
        }
    }

    public static NameValueCollection DecryptQueryString(string queryString)
    {
        if (queryString.Length != 0)
        {
            //Decode the string
            string decodedQueryString = HttpUtility.UrlDecode(queryString);

            //Decrypt the string
            string decryptedQueryString =
                StringHelpers.Decrypt(decodedQueryString);

            //Now split the string based on each parameter
            string[] actionQueryString = decryptedQueryString.Split(new char[] {
                QUERY_STRING_DELIMITER });

            NameValueCollection newQueryString = new NameValueCollection();

            //loop around for each name value pair.
            for (int index = 0; index < actionQueryString.Length; index++)
            {
                string[] queryStringItem = actionQueryString[index].Split(new
                    char[] { '=' });
                newQueryString.Add(queryStringItem[0], queryStringItem[1]);
            }

            return newQueryString;
        }
        else
        {
            //No query string was passed in.
            return null;
        }
    }

    public static string EncryptQueryString(NameValueCollection queryString)
    {
        //create a string for each value in the query string passed in.
        string tempQueryString = "";

        for (int index = 0; index < queryString.Count; index++)
        {
            tempQueryString += queryString.GetKey(index) + "=" +
```

```
                    queryString[index];

            if (index != queryString.Count - 1)
            {
                tempQueryString += QUERY_STRING_DELIMITER;
            }
        }

        return EncryptQueryString(tempQueryString);
    }

    public static string EncryptQueryString(string queryString)
    {
        return "?" + HttpUtility.UrlEncode(StringHelpers.Encrypt(queryString));
    }
}
```

The first member variable, _cryptoProvider, is declared as a RijndaelManaged class. The Rijndael Managed class is found in the System.Security.Cryptography namespace. This class inherits from the SymmetricAlgorithm class, which uses a chaining mode called *cipher block chaining* that requires a key and an initialization vector to perform cryptographic transformations. The same key and initialization vector must be used to encrypt and decrypt the data. The two member variables called Key and IV contain the key and initialization vectors. This sample uses 128-bit encryption, but you could use the Rijndael class, which supports 192- and 256-bit encryption, as well. Set these values to your own set of random numbers and do not change them. If you changed them, you wouldn't be able to decrypt any data that was encrypted using the original values.

The constructor for the StringHelpers class instantiates the _cryptoProvider object and sets its mode to CipherMode.CBC. CBC stands for *cipher block chaining,* and if you look in the help file it is defined as follows:

> *"Before each plain text block is encrypted, it is combined with the cipher text of the previous block by a bitwise exclusive OR operation. This ensures that even if the plain text contains many identical blocks, they will each encrypt to a different cipher text block. The initialization vector is combined with the first plain text block by a bitwise exclusive OR operation before the block is encrypted. If a single bit of the cipher text block is mangled, the corresponding plain text block will also be mangled. In addition, a bit in the subsequent block, in the same position as the original mangled bit, will be mangled."*

The algorithm does not encrypt each byte at a time; instead, it encrypts blocks at a time. If a string is passed in that does not contain enough bytes to fill in the last block, the Padding property is used to fill in the remaining bytes. In this instance, the PaddingMode.PKCS7 is used, which fills the bytes in the block with the total number of padding bytes added. For example, if the block length is 8 bytes and the data contained 9 bytes, then the first block would be filled with the first 8 bytes and the second block would contain the ninth byte plus seven bytes, with 07 filled in for the last seven bytes.

The Encrypt method takes an unencrypted string and uses the CryptoStream object to encrypt the data into a memory stream. The CryptoStream then writes the data to a byte array, which is converted back to a string. The Decrypt method does essentially the reverse.

The DecryptQueryString method takes an encrypted string as a parameter and decrypts it, splits the name\value parameters in the QueryString into a string array, and then passes them back in a NameValueCollection object.

The EncryptQueryString method is overloaded, so it can take either a NameValueCollection object or a string. If a NameValueCollection is passed in, it is converted to a string by concatenating the name and the value with an equals (=) sign. This string is then passed into the overloaded EncryptQueryString method, which takes a string. The string is encrypted and URL encoded and then returned from the function.

The Menu Controls

Before creating the master page, the controls to be used on the master pages should be created. Two menu controls will be placed on the master page. One is the top menu, which looks like a tab control (see Figure 4-6).

Figure 4-6

The other is the side menu, which is a customized tree control (see Figure 4-7).

Figure 4-7

Clicking on the tab changes the side menu items. All of this is driven by an ENTMenuItem table in the database. This section discusses the table and the controls.

The first control to be developed is the tab menu control that appears at the top of the screen. I'm not a graphics guy, so I tend to do some searching on the Internet whenever I need fancy graphics. The tab control is an adaptation of the Glossy Horizontal Menu sample shown on www.DynamicDrive.com. This is a great website that offers plenty of free code and examples of menus, calendars, dynamic affects, text animations, and much more. I often look to this site when a user is asking for a special effect or I am looking for a JavaScript function. The gentleman who provides the images and style sheet for the Glossy Horizontal Menu sample is Santosh Setty, http://webdesigninfo.wordpress.com. The HTML behind the scenes is quite simple. Three images create the left, middle, and right side of the tab. The text for each tab is placed in an unordered list. For this project, though, the tabs need to be dynamic because not everyone may have access to every tab. In order to do this, the menu item names will be stored in a table in the database and dynamically built by the server-side control. The table that will store the menu items for both the top menu and the side menu is ENTMenuItem.

ENTMenuItem Table

The `ENTMenuItem` table has the following fields:

Field Name	Type	Required	Description
ENTMenuItemId	int	Yes	The primary key for this table
MenuItemName	varchar(50)	Yes	The name as you would like it to appear on the menu
Description	varchar(MAX)	No	A textual description for this menu item
Url	varchar(MAX)	No	The URL to which the menu item link points
ParentENTMenuItemId	int	No	Enables you to nest menu items under other menu items. If there is no `ParentENTMeniItemName`, then this will be rendered on the tabs across the top of the screen.
DisplaySequence	tinyint	Yes	The order in which you want this item to appear
IsAlwaysEnabled	bit	Yes	Enables the menu regardless of security
InsertDate	datetime	Yes	The date the record was inserted
InsertENTUserAccountId	int	Yes	The user who inserted the record
UpdateDate	datetime	Yes	The date the record was last updated
UpdateENTUserAccountId	int	Yes	The user who last updated the record
Version	timestamp	Yes	The version of the record

This solution has three top-level menu items: Home, Administration, and Reports. These records need to be manually added to the table. Here are the values for the three records:

Field Name	Home	Administration	Reports
ENTMenuItemId	1	2	3
MenuItemName	Home	Administration	Reports
Description	Go back to the home page.	View the list of administrative pages in the application.	View the list of reports in the application.
Url	Default.aspx	Administration/ Administration.aspx	Reports/Reports. aspx
ParentENTMenuItemId	Null	Null	Null

Field Name	Home	Administration	Reports
DisplaySequence	1	2	3
IsAlwaysEnabled	True	False	False
InsertDate	Today's Date	Today's Date	Today's Date
InsertENTUserAccountId	1	1	1
UpdateDate	Today's Date	Today's Date	Today's Date
UpdateENTUserAccountId	1	1	1
Version	This is auto-filled by SQL Server	This is auto-filled by SQL Server	This is auto-filled by SQL Server

You have to set the audit field to the current date and use a valid ID in the `ENTUserAccount` table for the audit fields. Because the `ParentENTMenuItemId` field is null, these will appear in the top menu tabs. More records will be added for the side menu, and they will have parent IDs that point back to the top-level items.

ENTMenuItem Stored Procedures

Next, create the stored procedures that will be used to access this table. Records will never be added, updated, or deleted in this table by a user, so only the `SelectAll` stored procedure needs to be created:

```
CREATE PROCEDURE ENTMenuItemSelectAll
AS
    SET NOCOUNT ON

    SELECT ENTMenuItemId, MenuItemName, Description, Url, ParentENTMenuItemId,
           DisplaySequence, IsAlwaysEnabled, InsertDate, InsertENTUserAccountId,
           UpdateDate, UpdateENTUserAccountId, Version
      FROM ENTMenuItem
    ORDER BY ParentENTMenuItemId, DisplaySequence, MenuItemName

    RETURN
```

This procedure should return all the records ordered by the `ParentENTMenuItemId`, `DisplaySequence`, and then the `MenuItemName`. The class that consumes the result set returned by this procedure expects the data to be ordered this way so it can build a treelike structure for the menu. This is further explained in the `Load` method of the `ENTMenuItemBOList` class.

ENTMenuItem ORM Designer

Now that you have the table and stored procedures created, you can create the entity objects and `DataContext` method for the stored procedure using the ORM Designer:

1. Open the ORM Designer by double-clicking on the `HRPaidTimeOff.dbml` file in your DAL project.

2. Drag the `ENTMenuItem` table from the Server Explorer to the ORM Designer.

3. Drag the `ENTMenuItemSelectAll` procedure to the `ENTMenuItem` table on the ORM Designer surface. Dragging it onto the `ENTMenuItem` table will make the return type an `ENTMenuItem` object. If you were to drag the stored procedure directly to the Methods pane, a new class would be created that contains all the fields returned from the stored procedure as properties of the class.

4. Open the `HRPaidTimeOff.designer.cs` file to see the new `ENTMenuItem` class and the `ENTMenuItemSelectAll` method that was added to the `HRPaidTimeOffDataContext` class. Remember from Chapter 2 that all the entity objects need to inherit from the same base class, so add the following line to the `CustomizedEntities.cs` file:

```
public partial class ENTMenuItem : ENTBaseEntity { }
```

ENTMenuItemData Class

The data classes are next:

1. Add a new class to the `V2.PaidTimeOffDAL` project in the `Framework` folder called `ENTMenuItemData`.

2. Change the class declaration so that it inherits from `ENTBaseData` and pass in `ENTMenuItem` as the `T` parameter. Have Visual Studio automatically implement the abstract methods for the class by right-clicking on `ENTBaseData` and choosing Implement Abstract Class from the menu. The resulting class should look like this:

```
public class ENTMenuItemData : ENTBaseData<ENTMenuItem>
{
    public override List<ENTMenuItem> Select()
    {
        throw new NotImplementedException();
    }

    public override ENTMenuItem Select(int id)
    {
        throw new NotImplementedException();
    }

    public override void Delete(HRPaidTimeOffDataContext db, int id)
    {
        throw new NotImplementedException();
    }
}
```

Because this class does not need support for selecting a single record or deleting, you can leave the default implementation. Change the `Select()` method to the following:

```
public override List<ENTMenuItem> Select()
{
    using (HRPaidTimeOffDataContext db = new HRPaidTimeOffDataContext())
    {
        return db.ENTMenuItemSelectAll().ToList();
    }
}
```

This will call the `ENTMenuItemSelectAll` method just generated by the ORM Designer that calls the `ENTMenuItemSelectAll` stored procedure.

ENTMenuItemBO and ENTMenuItemBOList Business Classes

Add a new class to the `V2.PaidTimeOffBLL` project in the `Framework` folder called `ENTMenuItemBO`. Add two `using` directives to reference the `V2.PaidTimeOffDAL` and `V2.PaidTimeOffDAL.Framework` projects. Because the `ENTMenuItem` records will never be edited by a user, the class should inherit from the `ENTBaseBO` class. Again, use Visual Studio to automatically generate the abstract methods in the base class. You should also change the class declaration to be public and serializable. Next, create the properties that are custom to this class:

```
public string MenuItemName { get; set; }
public string Description { get; set; }
public string Url { get; set; }
public Nullable<int> ParentMenuItemId { get; set; }
public short DisplaySequence { get; set; }
public bool IsAlwaysEnabled { get; set; }
```

Now implement the `MapEntityToCustomProperties` method:

```
protected override void MapEntityToCustomProperties(ENTBaseEntity entity)
{
    ENTMenuItem menuItem = (ENTMenuItem)entity;

    ID = menuItem.ENTMenuItemId;
    MenuItemName = menuItem.MenuItemName;
    Description = menuItem.Description;
    Url = menuItem.Url;
    ParentMenuItemId = menuItem.ParentENTMenuItemId;
    DisplaySequence = menuItem.DisplaySequence;
    IsAlwaysEnabled = menuItem.IsAlwaysEnabled;
}
```

Do not implement the other methods at this point. The next task is to create the `ENTMenuItemBOList` class. Add this class to the `ENTMenuItemBO` file so you have two classes in the same file. I like to keep the lists and base objects for the lists in the same file to reduce the number of files in the project. This class should be changed to public and inherit from `ENTBaseBOList`. The `Load` method is the only method that must be implemented:

```
[Serializable()]
public class ENTMenuItemBOList : ENTBaseBOList<ENTMenuItemBO>
{
    public override void Load()
    {
        throw new NotImplementedException();
    }
}
```

This is where it gets interesting. The concept for the menu is to have top-level menu items that appear across the top of the screen. These top-level items all have children that will be displayed on the side menu. The side menu items can have children as well. The side menu will be implemented with a tree control, and there can be multiple levels of menu items nested in other menu items to form the tree. In reality, you should never create more than two levels on the side menu, but the design allows for an unlimited amount of levels. To represent this in the business layer, a property should be added to the `ENTMenuItemBO` class called `ChildMenuItems`, with the type `ENTMenuItemBOList`. This should be a read-only property because you don't want anyone to be able to set it. The constructor should instantiate an instance of this class for this property:

```
public ENTMenuItemBOList ChildMenuItems { get; private set; }

public ENTMenuItemBO()
{
    ChildMenuItems = new ENTMenuItemBOList();
}
```

The Load method for the ENTMenuItemBOList object can now be implemented. The key point about this method is that it should not just load the list of records as they appear in the table. Instead, it should load the top-level items first, and each of those objects should have their children loaded, and their children should be loaded. It is similar to an XML document that has nodes within nodes. Here is the code for the Load method:

```
public override void Load()
{
    //Load the list from the database.  This will then be traversed to create the
    //parent child relationships in for each menu item.
    List<ENTMenuItem> menuItems = new ENTMenuItemData().Select();

    //Traverse through the list to create the parent child relationships
    foreach (ENTMenuItem menuItem in menuItems)
    {
        ENTMenuItemBO menuItemBO = new ENTMenuItemBO();
        menuItemBO.MapEntityToProperties(menuItem);

        // Check if the menu already exists in this object.
        if (MenuExists(menuItemBO.ID) == false)
        {
            //Doesn't exist so now check if this is a top level item.
            if (menuItemBO.ParentMenuItemId== null)
            {
                //Top level item so just add it.
                this.Add(menuItemBO);
            }
            else
            {
                // Get the parent menu item from this object if it exists.
                ENTMenuItemBO parent =
                    GetByMenuItemId(Convert.ToInt32(menuItemBO.ParentMenuItemId));

                if (parent == null)
                {
                    // If it gets here then the parent isn't in the list yet.
                    // Find the parent in the list.
                    ENTMenuItemBO newParentMenuItem = FindOrLoadParent(menuItems,
                        Convert.ToInt32(menuItemBO.ParentMenuItemId));

                    // Add the current child menu item to the newly added parent
                    newParentMenuItem.ChildMenuItems.Add(menuItemBO);
                }
                else
```

```
                     {
                         // Parent already existed in this object.
                         // Add this menu to the child of the parent
                         parent.ChildMenuItems.Add(menuItemBO);
                     }
                 }
             }
         }
     }
```

The first thing this method does is get all the records from the database. To make it easier to process, the top-level menu items should be the first records returned, followed by all other records ordered by their display sequence. Once the records are returned as entity objects, the method traverses through the list and loads the current instance according to the parent-child relationship between the menu items. Notice the MenuExists call. This method returns true if the menu item exists in the list or in any of the children in any object in the list. Here is the code for the MenuExists method, which calls another method that retrieves an ENTMenuItemBO object by MenuItemId. These methods should be added to the ENTMenuItemBOList class:

```
public bool MenuExists(int menuItemId)
{
    return (GetByMenuItemId(menuItemId) != null);
}


public ENTMenuItemBO GetByMenuItemId(int menuItemId)
{
    foreach (ENTMenuItemBO menuItem in this)
    {
        // Check if this is the item we are looking for
        if (menuItem.ID == menuItemId)
        {
            return menuItem;
        }
        else
        {
            // Check if this menu has children
            if (menuItem.ChildMenuItems.Count > 0)
            {
                // Search the children for this item.
                ENTMenuItemBO childMenuItem =
                    menuItem.ChildMenuItems.GetByMenuItemId(menuItemId);

                // If the menu is found in the children then it won't be null
                if (childMenuItem != null)
                {
                    return childMenuItem;
                }
            }
        }
    }

    //It wasn't found so return null.
    return null;
}
```

MenuExists simply calls the GetByMenuItemId method and returns true if the object returned is not null. The GetByMenuItemId is a recursive method that traverses through the list and any children in the list for the menu item ID being sought.

Going back to the Load method, if the menu item wasn't already in the list, it should be added. If it doesn't have a parent, then it should be added to the top-level list. If it does have a parent, then it should be added to its parent's ChildMenuItems. The problem is that there is no guarantee that the parent was already loaded. This calls another recursive method called FindOrLoadParent. This method searches the list to find the parent. If it doesn't exist in the list already, it will add it. Here is the code for FindOrLoadParent:

```
private ENTMenuItemBO FindOrLoadParent(List<ENTMenuItem> menuItems, int
    parentMenuItemId)
{

    // Find the menu item in the entity list.
    ENTMenuItem parentMenuItem = menuItems.Single(m => m.ENTMenuItemId ==
        parentMenuItemId);

    // Load this into the business object.
    ENTMenuItemBO menuItemBO = new ENTMenuItemBO();
    menuItemBO.MapEntityToProperties(parentMenuItem);

    // Check if it has a parent
    if (parentMenuItem.ParentENTMenuItemId == null)
    {
        this.Add(menuItemBO);
    }
    else
    {
        // Since this has a parent it should be added to its parent's children.
        // Try to find the parent in the list already.
        ENTMenuItemBO parent =
            GetByMenuItemId(Convert.ToInt32(parentMenuItem.ParentENTMenuItemId));

        if (parent == null)
        {
            // This one's parent wasn't found.  So add it.
            ENTMenuItemBO newParent = FindOrLoadParent(menuItems,
                Convert.ToInt32(parentMenuItem.ParentENTMenuItemId));
            newParent.ChildMenuItems.Add(menuItemBO);
        }
        else
        {
            // Add this menu to the child of the parent
            parent.ChildMenuItems.Add(menuItemBO);
        }
    }

    return menuItemBO;
}
```

Notice the line menuItems.Single(m => m.ENTMenuItemId == parentMenuItemId). This is new LINQ syntax that can be used to query lists of objects. The Single method will return a single object from the list being searched based on the criteria passed in. If no object meets the criteria or more than one object exists, an error will be thrown. This is a great shortcut for searching lists in Visual Studio 2008. You won't have to write a `foreach` loop anymore to search through lists. That finishes the `Load` method.

Two more methods need to be added that will be used by the `MenuTabs` control: `GetTopMenuItem` and `GetByMenuItemName`. The `GetTopMenuItem` takes in a `menuItemName` parameter and finds the upper-most parent related to that menu item. The `GetByMenuItemName` is similar to `GetByMenuItemId` in that it traverses through the children of the list to find the menu item with the name passed in. The code for the two methods is as follows:

```
public ENTMenuItemBO GetTopMenuItem(string menuItemName)
{
    //Find the menu item by it name.
    ENTMenuItemBO menuItem = GetByMenuItemName(menuItemName);

    while (menuItem.ParentMenuItemId != null)
    {
        menuItem = GetByMenuItemId(Convert.ToInt32(menuItem.ParentMenuItemId));
    }

    return menuItem;
}

public ENTMenuItemBO GetByMenuItemName(string menuItemName)
{
    foreach (ENTMenuItemBO menuItem in this)
    {
        // Check if this is the item we are looking for
        if (menuItem.MenuItemName == menuItemName)
        {
            return menuItem;
        }
        else
        {
            // Check if this menu has children
            if (menuItem.ChildMenuItems.Count > 0)
            {
                // Search the children for this item.
                ENTMenuItemBO childMenuItem =
                    menuItem.ChildMenuItems.GetByMenuItemName(menuItemName);

                // If the menu is found in the children then it won't be null
                if (childMenuItem != null)
                {
                    return childMenuItem;
                }
            }
        }
    }

    //It wasn't found so return null.
    return null;
}
```

MenuTabs Control

Now that the entity class, the data class, and the business classes are created, you can create the two menu controls. The MenuTabs control is a server-side control that will be added to the V2.FrameworkControls project. It is a server-side control instead of a custom control so it can be reused in other solutions:

1. Add a new server-side control by right-clicking on the V2.FrameworkControls project and selecting Add New Item.

2. Click on the Web node in the left-hand pane and select ASP.NET Server Control in the right-hand pane.

3. Rename the file MenuTabs.cs and click the Add button. The new server-side control class will be added to your project. By default, Visual Studio adds a Text property and creates the signature to override the RenderContents method. You should remove the Text property because it is not relevant for this control. In addition, remove the DefaultProperty attribute for the class, as it is set to the Text property. The RenderContents method can stay and will be built later.

4. Add a reference to V2.PaidtimeOffBLL and add a using directive at the top of the file that references the V2.PaidTimeOffBLL.Framework namespace.

The HTML for the tabs is actually quite simple. It is merely an unordered list that is linked to a style sheet to give the appearance of a tab. The HTML that the control should render, once you write the code below, looks like this:

```
<ul class="glossymenu">
    <li class="current">
        <a href="http://localhost/PaidTimeOff/Default.aspx">
            <b>Home</b>
        </a>
    </li>
    <li>
        <a href="http://localhost/PaidTimeOff/Administration/Administration.aspx">
            <b>Administration</b>
        </a>
    </li>
    <li>
        <a href="http://localhost/PaidTimeOff/Reports.aspx">
            <b>Reports</b>
        </a>
    </li>
</ul>
```

The menu that is currently selected will have a class of "current." The other menu items are just list items in the unordered list.

The control needs to know the list of all menu items and the one that is selected. To accomplish this, add two properties to the MenuTabs control:

```
[Browsable(false)]
public ENTMenuItemBOList MenuItems { get; set; }

[Browsable(false)]
public string CurrentMenuItemName { get; set; }
```

Set the `Browsable` attribute to false, as you don't want users to be able to see these in the Properties window in Visual Studio. Developers that use this control must set these two properties in order for the control to work correctly.

One more property needs to be added: `RootPath`. This control uses absolute references for the links so the `Url` field on the record will be appended to the `RootPath` property. Remember that the `BasePage` class has a method to return this value:

```
[Browsable(true)]
[DefaultValue("Enter Application Root Path")]
[Description("Enter the root path for your application.  This is used to determine
    the path for all items in the menu.")]
public string RootPath { get; set;}
```

The next step is to override the `RenderContents` method. This method creates the necessary HTML to create the unordered list:

```
protected override void RenderContents(HtmlTextWriter writer)
{
    base.RenderContents(writer);

    string html;

    //Check if the menus are there.  In design mode this is null so you don't want
    //to display an error.
    if (MenuItems != null)
    {
        //Get the parent menu item for the current menu item.  The parent will be
        //the one with a null ParentMenuItemId
        ENTMenuItemBO topMenuItem = MenuItems.GetTopMenuItem(CurrentMenuItemName);

        html = "<ul class=\"glossymenu\">";

        //Loop around the top level items
        foreach (ENTMenuItemBO mi in MenuItems)
        {
            //Check if this is the selected menu tab.
            if (mi.MenuItemName == topMenuItem.MenuItemName)
            {
                html += GetActiveTab(mi);
            }
            else
            {
                html += GetInactiveTab(mi);
            }
        }

        html += "</ul>";
    }
    else
    {
        html = "<div>Top Menu Goes Here</div>";
```

```
        }

    writer.Write(html);
}
```

This calls two private methods that return the string for either the selected tab or the unselected tab:

```
private string GetActiveTab(ENTMenuItemBO subMenu)
{
    return "<li class=\"current\"><a href=\"" + RootPath + subMenu.Url + "\"><b>" +
        subMenu.MenuItemName + "</b></a></li>";
}

private string GetInactiveTab(ENTMenuItemBO subMenu)
{
    return "<li><a href=\"" + RootPath + subMenu.Url + "\"><b>" +
        subMenu.MenuItemName + "</b></a></li>";
}
```

This control works as follows: Users can click either the top tab or a link on the side menu. If they click on the top tab, then this is the tab that should be highlighted. If they click on the side menu, then the top-level menu item must be determined and then highlighted. The GetTopMenuItem method traverses up the tree to determine the top-level menu item.

MenuTree Control

The MenuTree control is the control that displays the menu on the left side of the screen. It uses the same business objects as the MenuTabs control:

1. Add another server control to the V2.FrameworkControls project called MenuTree.cs.
2. Remove the default code as you did before.
3. Add a using statement to reference the V2.PaidtimeOffBLL namespace.
4. Add the same three properties for MenuItemsBOList, CurrentMenuItemName, and RootPath.

This control is different from the MenuTabs control because it doesn't render HTML. It creates a tree control and adds nodes to the control based on the menu items that should be displayed on the side menu. To accomplish this, you should override the CreateChildControls method:

```
protected override void CreateChildControls()
{
    TreeView menuControl = new TreeView();
    menuControl.SelectedNodeStyle.CssClass = "selectedMenuItem";
    menuControl.ID = "tvSideMenu";
    menuControl.NodeWrap = true;

    //Find the top most menu item.  This is the tab at the top.
    ENTMenuItemBO topMenuItem = MenuItems.GetTopMenuItem(CurrentMenuItemName);

    CreateChildMenu(menuControl.Nodes, topMenuItem.ChildMenuItems);
```

```
        Controls.Add(menuControl);

        base.CreateChildControls();
}
```

This method creates the tree control and then finds the top menu item. Once the top menu item is found, you want to traverse through all of its children to build the tree:

```
private void CreateChildMenu(TreeNodeCollection nodes, ENTMenuItemBOList menuItems)
{
    foreach (ENTMenuItemBO mi in menuItems)
    {
        //Create an instance of the menu
        TreeNode menuNode = new TreeNode(mi.MenuItemName, mi.ID.ToString(), "",
            (string.IsNullOrEmpty(mi.Url) ? "" : RootPath + mi.Url), "");

        if (string.IsNullOrEmpty(mi.Url))
        {
            menuNode.SelectAction = TreeNodeSelectAction.None;
        }

        //Check if this is the menu item that should be selected.
        if (mi.MenuItemName == CurrentMenuItemName)
        {
            menuNode.Selected = true;
        }

        //Check if this has children.
        if (mi.ChildMenuItems.Count > 0)
        {
            //Create items for the children.
            CreateChildMenu(menuNode.ChildNodes, mi.ChildMenuItems);
        }

        nodes.Add(menuNode);
    }
}
```

Because the `Url` field is optional, the code must check if the field is null. If it is, then the node acts like a label; if it is filled in, it acts like a hyperlink. The code then checks whether this is the current menu item; if it is, then it is displayed in bold font. Now if the menu item has children, it calls itself to create the children for this node. Again, it is unlikely that the control will need to support more than two levels of nesting but it can.

Because this control uses other controls, you still want to override the `RenderContents` method so that you can display text to the user at design time. The `RenderContents` method looks like this:

```
protected override void RenderContents(HtmlTextWriter writer)
{
    base.RenderContents(writer);

    string html = "";
    //Check if the menus are there.  In design mode this is null so you don't want
```

```
        //to display an error.
        if (MenuItems == null)
        {
            html = "<div>Tree Goes Here</div>";
        }

        writer.Write(html);
    }
```

This checks whether the `MenuItems` property is null. If it is, then that means it is either design time or someone forgot to set the `MenuItems` property. Either way, the control renders the text "Tree Goes Here" to the user.

The PaidTimeOff Master Page

Now that the `BasePage` class and the menu controls are created, the master page can be built. The design view of the master page was shown in Figure 4-4. This page contains the company logo, the title of the application, the user information, the top and side menus, and the footer. You can start to create this page by following these steps:

1. Right-click on the `PaidTimeOffUI` project and select Add New Item.

2. Choose the MasterPage template and rename the file to `PaidTimeOff.master`. Be sure to select the language as C# and place a check next to the "Place code in separate file" checkbox.

3. Click Add. The HTML markup for the master page should be displayed.

In previous versions of Visual Studio you had the option to view the HTML markup or the rendered HTML for your page. Visual Studio 2008 has another view called *split,* which enables you to view both at the same time. This makes developing screens much easier if you aren't an HTML wizard. You can see your changes by refreshing the rendered HTML pane without having to switch back and forth. Simply save your changes and the rendered HTML will refresh.

Before starting to build the HTML markup for the master page, add the style sheet to the page using the new Manage Styles window. The Manage Styles window will be used to build the style sheet as you create this page. If you do not see the Manage Styles window in your development environment, select View ⇨ Manage Styles from the menu. Click the Attach Style Sheet link on the Manage Styles window, select the `PaidTimeOff.css` file, and click OK. Notice that the HTML link tag was added to the master page markup, with the `href` attribute pointing to the `PaidTimeOff.css` file.

By default, Visual Studio creates the HEAD, BODY, and FORM sections in your HTML document. It also creates a DIV in the BODY section and places the `ContentPlaceHolder` control inside the DIV. At this point, I'm going to break with many developers and use tables for positioning elements in the master page. The reason to use tables instead of DIVs is because screens that use grids vary in length. If the grid falls outside the width of the DIV, it overlays it and the grid sticks out. You could encase the grid in a separate DIV with a fixed width and allow scrollbars, but then you could potentially get scrollbars on the page and scrollbars on the browser. Scrollbars inside of scrollbars don't lend themselves to ease of use in a web application.

Although using tables may not be considered best practice, it works without the problems you face with the `GridView` control. Therefore, remove the DIV tag and replace it with the TABLE begin and end tags. The table within the master page will contain four rows. The first contains the company logo, the application title, and the user information. The second row contains the tab menu control. The third row contains the side menu and the content control. The fourth row contains the footer and version information. The HTML code should look like this:

```
<table width="100%" id="mainContainer" class="mainContainer">
<tr>
    <td>
        <table width="100%">
            <tr>
                <td>
                    <asp:Image ID="Image1" runat="server"
                        ImageUrl="~/images/V2_Enterprise.gif" />
                </td>
                <td class="title">
                    <asp:Label ID="lblHeader" runat="server" Text="Human
                        Resources"></asp:Label><br />
                    <asp:Label ID="lblSubHeader" runat="server" Text="Paid Time
                        Off"></asp:Label>
                </td>
                <td class="user">
                    <asp:Label ID="Label1" runat="server" Text="Current User: ">
                    </asp:Label>
                    <asp:Label ID="lblCurrentUser" runat="server" Text="">
                    </asp:Label><br />
                    <asp:Label ID="lblCurrentDateTime" runat="server" Text="">
                    </asp:Label>
                </td>
            </tr>
        </table>
    </td>
</tr>
<tr>
    <td>
    </td>
</tr>
<tr>
    <td valign="top">
        <table>
            <tr valign="top">
                <td class="sideMenu">
                </td>
                <td class="content">
                    <asp:ContentPlaceHolder ID="ContentPlaceHolder1"
                        runat="server">
                        Content
                    </asp:ContentPlaceHolder>
                </td>
            </tr>
        </table>
    </td>
</tr>
<tr class="footer">
    <td>
        <asp:Label ID="lblCopyright" runat="server">Copyright &copy 2008 Vince
```

```
                Varallo & Wrox Press | </asp:Label>
          <asp:Label ID="lblVersion" runat="server"></asp:Label>
      </td>
   </tr>
</table>
```

Note that the class names being used are not defined in the style sheet. To add the names, simply click the New Style link in the Manage Styles window. The screen shown in Figure 4-8 will appear.

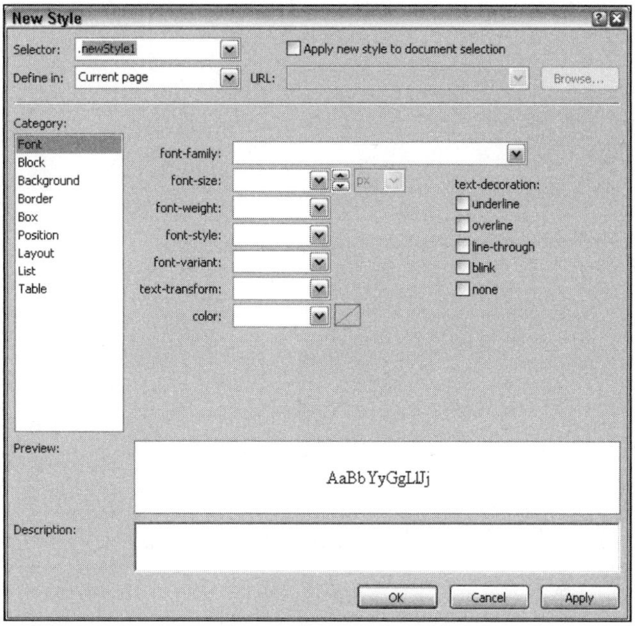

Figure 4-8

Change the Selector drop-down list item to ".mainContainer"; change the Define In drop-down list item to "Existing style sheet"; and select PaidTimeOff.css in the URL drop-down list.

The mainContainer class should have a white background. To do this, simply select the Background item in the Category list and then enter **#ffffff** for the background color. Notice that as you type in the background color, the new color is displayed to indicate what you have entered. Click the OK button. The mainContainer class is added to the CSS Styles list in the Manage Styles window and the class is automatically added to the PaidTimeOff style sheet file.

Now modify the body element's style by following these steps:

1. Right-click the "body" item in the CSS Styles list and select Modify Style.

2. Select Font from the Category list and change the font-family to Arial, the font-size to 12px, and the color to #3A3D84.

3. Select Background in the Category list and change the background-color to #79A9F4.

4. Select Box from the Category list and change Padding to 1px and Margin to 2px. The Same for All checkbox should be checked so you don't have to enter the padding and margin for the top, right, bottom, and left attributes.

5. Click the OK button. The design view of the master page should be automatically updated and the background should be a light blue.

You can create the rest of the styles the "old school" way or use the Manage Styles window, depending on whatever you are comfortable with. The `title`, `user`, `sideMenu`, `content`, and `footer` classes should be defined as follows:

```
.title
{
    text-align:center;
    font-weight:bold;
    font-size:22px;
}

.user
{
  text-align:right;
  font-size:10px;
  font-weight:bold;
}

.sideMenu
{
    width: 125px;
    border-right-style: groove;
    border-right-width: 1px;
    border-right-color: #0064FF;
    background-image:url(images/side_background.jpg);
    background-repeat:repeat-y;
}

.content
{
    padding-left: 3px;
}

.footer
{
    text-align:center;
    background-image:url(images/footer_background.jpg);
}
```

The side menu and footer have background images that need to be added to the images folder of the project. Create this folder and copy the images from the sample code available on the Wrox website. The company logo file should also be added to the images folder. Again, replace the logo with your own company logo, and change the colors to the brand colors defined by your marketing department.

The next step is to add the MenuTabs control to the second row. Drag the MenuTabs control from the toolbox between the <td></td> tags on the second row. If you are in split view, you will see the text "Top Menu Goes Here" in the second row. This was the text that was added in the RenderContents method when no menu items existed. Now add the MenuTree control the same way by dragging it to the first column in the third row. The text "Tree Goes Here" should appear in the column.

Now that the visual elements of the master page are created, you have to add logic to the code-behind page. The menu controls need a menu item list passed to them in order to render the menu correctly. This should be done in the Page_Load event. Because the MenuItems are rarely changed, they will be cached to avoid unnecessary trips to the database. Anytime I cache variables, I like to put them in a class called Globals and create methods to pull items out of and put items into the cache. This centralizes the code for "global" variables. Add a class to the PaidTimeOffUI project called Globals.cs. Change the class to static and remove the constructor. There should never be multiple instances of this class because it is accessing global data.

Now add using directives to reference the System.Web.Caching and V2.PaidTimeOffBLL.Framework namespaces. The Cache object in the .NET Framework is a key/value pair collection, so add a constant at the top of the Globals class to state the string for the MenuItems key:

```
private const string CACHE_KEY_MENU_ITEMS = "MenuItems";
```

Now add methods to retrieve the menu items from the cache and load the menu items in the cache:

```
public static ENTMenuItemBOList GetMenuItems(Cache cache)
{
    //Check if the menus have been cached.
    if (cache[CACHE_KEY_MENU_ITEMS] == null)
    {
        LoadMenuItems(cache);
    }
    return (ENTMenuItemBOList)cache[CACHE_KEY_MENU_ITEMS];
}

private static void LoadMenuItems(Cache cache)
{
    ENTMenuItemBOList menuItems = new ENTMenuItemBOList();
    menuItems.Load();

    cache.Remove(CACHE_KEY_MENU_ITEMS);
    cache[CACHE_KEY_MENU_ITEMS] = menuItems;
}
```

The GetMenuItems method checks the cache for the existence of the menu items. If they are not found, then it will load them into the cache. The LoadMenu method creates an instance of the MenuItemBOList class and adds it to the cache. Notice that the Remove method is called prior to adding the object to the cache. This ensures that you will not get an exception when the object is added and a fresh copy of the data is loaded. Calling the Remove method will not throw an exception if there isn't a value for the key passed into the method.

Now add code to the master page's `Page_Load` event to set the menu properties using the cached data. Double-click on the master page to generate the `Page_Load` event handler and add the following code:

```
//Set the top menu properties
MenuTabs1.MenuItems = Globals.GetMenuItems(this.Cache);

//Set the side menu properties
MenuTree1.MenuItems = Globals.GetMenuItems(this.Cache);
```

The next step is to set the `CurrentMenuItemName` and `RootPath` properties. This presents a problem because this is the master page and you don't know the current menu item name until a page uses this master page. You could rely on the "child" page to set this or you could retrieve it from the "child" in the master page. I prefer setting these properties in the master page so that the page is self-contained. In order to retrieve the current menu name from the child, you somehow have to guarantee that the child knows its current menu name. This is why the `BasePage` class has an abstract method called `MenuItemName` — because the inheriting page must implement this method. Therefore, every page that uses the master page must inherit from `BasePage`. The page load event in the master page can access this property in the `BasePage` class as follows:

```
MenuTabs1.RootPath = BasePage.RootPath(Context);
MenuTabs1.CurrentMenuItemName = ((BasePage)Page).MenuItemName();

MenuTree1.RootPath = BasePage.RootPath(Context);
MenuTree1.CurrentMenuItemName = ((BasePage)Page).MenuItemName();
```

The `CurrentMenuItemName` property is set by casting the `Page` object to a `BasePage` object and calling its `MenuItemName` property. An exception would be thrown if a page used this master page and didn't inherit from the `BasePage` class.

The last step in the master page is to set the current user, the date/time, and the version labels in the header and footer. This code should be placed in the page load as well:

```
lblCurrentUser.Text = Page.User.Identity.Name;
lblCurrentDateTime.Text = DateTime.Now.ToString();
lblVersion.Text = ConfigurationManager.AppSettings["version"].ToString();
```

The virtual directory for this site should have anonymous access turned off, and use Integrated Windows authentication so the `Page.User.Identity.Name` property displays the current user's Windows logon on the screen. This will later be changed to display the user's first and last name, but that happens in Chapter 6 when users and roles are created. The version is stored in an `appSettings` key in the `web.config` file. The `ConfigurationManager` object has built-in methods to retrieve values from the `appSetting` section in the `web.config` file:

```
<appSettings>
    <add key="version" value="1.0.0.0"/>
</appSettings>
```

The Master Edit Grid Page

The pattern developed in this book for screens that allow users to edit data first displays data in a `GridView`. Each row in the grid has an Edit link that navigates to a separate page that enables the user to update the record. When appropriate, each row also contains a Delete link that allows the user to delete the record in the database. If a referential integrity error occurs or a business rule is broken when the user tries to delete a record, a message is displayed on the screen in red. There is also an Add button on the screen to enable the user to add new records. In order to create a consistent interface for all grid pages, a nested master page will be created. The design view of this page is shown in Figure 4-9.

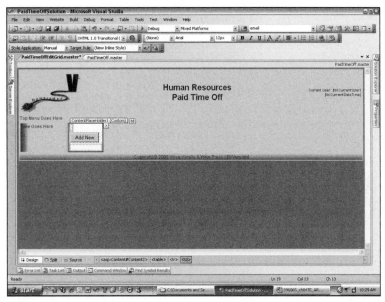

Figure 4-9

The developer can add a `GridView` or other controls to this screen to display the data. Figure 4-2, shown earlier, indicates how this page is displayed at runtime to display the list of users in the system.

ValidationErrorMessages

Before creating the master page, a new server-side control will be created that displays error messages to the user if a validation error is broken when deleting a record. Recall from Chapter 3 that the business logic layer returns an `ENTValidationErrors` list to the user interface to pass back information about validation errors. A control will be created that can consume the `ENTValidationErrors` object and display the list of messages to the user in red:

1. Add another control to the `V2.FrameworkControls` project called `ValidationErrorMessages`.

2. Remove the default code as you did with the other controls.

3. Add a `using` directive to reference the `V2.PaidTimeOffBLL.Framework` namespace. This control will display the error messages in an HTML table, so add a `using` directive to reference the `System.Web.UI.HtmlControls` namespace. The only property for this control is the list of validation error messages. The constructor should instantiate this object in order to avoid null exceptions:

```
[Bindable(false),
Browsable(false)]
public ENTValidationErrors ValidationErrors { get; set; }

public ValidationErrorMessages()
{
    ValidationErrors = new ENTValidationErrors();
}
```

The only method to override is the RenderContents method. This will create an HTML object and loop around the validation errors, adding a row for each error:

```
protected override void RenderContents(HtmlTextWriter output)
{
    //Show all the messages in the ENTValidationErrors

    //Check if there are an items in the array list
    if (ValidationErrors.Count != 0)
    {
        //There are items so create a table with the list of messages.
        HtmlTable table = new HtmlTable();

        HtmlTableRow trHeader = new HtmlTableRow();
        HtmlTableCell tcHeader = new HtmlTableCell();
        tcHeader.InnerText = "Please review the following issues:";
        tcHeader.Attributes.Add("class", "validatioErrorMessageHeader");
        trHeader.Cells.Add(tcHeader);
        table.Rows.Add(trHeader);

        foreach (ENTValidationError ve in ValidationErrors)
        {
            HtmlTableRow tr = new HtmlTableRow();
            HtmlTableCell tc = new HtmlTableCell();
            tc.InnerText = ve.ErrorMessage;
            tc.Attributes.Add("class", "validationErrorMessage");
            tr.Cells.Add(tc);
            table.Rows.Add(tr);
            tc = null;
            tr = null;
        }

        table.RenderControl(output);
        tcHeader = null;
        trHeader = null;
        table = null;
    }
    else
    {
        //Write nothing.
        output.Write("");
    }
}
```

The HTML table object has a `RenderControl` method that takes an `HtmlTextWriter` object, which will correctly render this control to the screen. In addition, two classes need to be added to the style sheet: to make the messages display in red and the make the header underlined:

```
.validationErrorMessageHeader
{
    font-weight: bold;
    color: red;
    text-decoration: underline;
}

.validationErrorMessage
{
    color: red;
}
```

The PaidTimeOffEditGrid Master Page

The `PaidTimeOffEditGrid` page is displayed in Figure 4-9. To create this page, add a new master page called `PaidTimeOffEditGrid.master`. When creating this page, be sure to check the "select master page" check box and choose the `PaidTimeOff` master page. Once you've added the page, open the page's HTML markup. Notice that there are only two ASP content controls in this master page, unlike the other master page containing all the HTML tags for the header and the body. That is because this is a *nested* master page and the tags are rendered in the parent master page:

```
<asp:Content ID="Content1" ContentPlaceHolderID="head" Runat="Server">
</asp:Content>
<asp:Content ID="Content2" ContentPlaceHolderID="ContentPlaceHolder1"
            Runat="Server">
</asp:Content>
```

The `Content2` control will contain the body for our work area. This area contains the `ValidationError Messages` control, the Add button, and another content region where the child pages of this master can add content:

```
<table>
    <tr>
        <td>
        <v2:validationerrormessages ID="ValidationErrorMessages1" runat="server" />
        </td>
    </tr>
</table>
<table>
    <tr>
        <td>
        <asp:Button ID="btnAddNew" runat="server" Text="Add New"
            onclick="btnAddNew_Click" />
        </td>
    </tr>
</table>
<table width="100%">
```

```
        <tr>
            <td>
                <asp:ContentPlaceHolder ID="ContentPlaceHolder3" runat="server">
                </asp:ContentPlaceHolder>
            </td>
        </tr>
    </table>
```

What's interesting here is that there is a button on this form that any child pages must be able to catch in the click event. This is a little tricky for master pages. In order for the child pages to catch this event, you must declare a delegate and an event, and then raise the event in the master page:

```
public delegate void ButtonClickedHandler(object sender, EventArgs e);

public event ButtonClickedHandler AddButton_Click;
```

The delegate is declared with the signature for a button click event because the children need to catch the Add button click event. The event is named `AddButton_Click` and is declared as a `ButtonClicked Handler`. Add the code to raise this event in the Add button's click event:

```
protected void btnAddNew_Click(object sender, EventArgs e)
{
    if (AddButton_Click != null)
    {
        AddButton_Click(sender, e);
    }
}
```

Any child object that uses this master page must add a handler to catch this event. Normally this code would go in the `Page_Load` event for the child page. Here is a sample of how the child page's code should look:

```
protected void Page_Load(object sender, EventArgs e)
{
    Master.AddButton_Click += new
        PaidTimeOffEditGridPage.ButtonClickedHandler(Master_AddButton_Click);
}
```

This attaches the `Master_AddButton_Click` method to the `AddButton_Click` event in the master page. You also need to add the `Master_AddButton_Click` method in the child:

```
void Master_AddButton_Click(object sender, EventArgs e)
{
    //Do something
}
```

There is one more trick to make this work. The `Master` property in the child page does not know about the `AddButton` event by default. You must add the following directive in the HTML markup of the child page for the code-behind to recognize the `AddButton_Click` event:

```
<%@ MasterType virtualPath="~/PaidTimeOffEditGrid.master"%>
```

Now when you use the `Master` property in the code-behind, it will recognize the `AddButton_Click` event in Visual Studio's IntelliSense.

Go back to the `PaidTimeOffEditGrid` master page. A property needs to be added here that allows the child to pass the validation errors to this page. In the code-behind, add a `using` directive that references the `V2.PaidTimeOffBLL.Framework` namespace and add the following property:

```
public ENTValidationErrors ValidationErrors
{
    get
    {
        return ValidationErrorMessages1.ValidationErrors;
    }

    set
    {
        ValidationErrorMessages1.ValidationErrors = value;
    }
}
```

This property sets or gets the `ValidationErrors` property on the `ValidationErrorMessages` control.

You also need to add a method that allows a child page to get a reference to the Add button. This is helpful if the child page needs to hide the Add button or change its text. The code for this method is shown here:

```
public Button btnAddNewRef()
{
    return btnAddNew;
}
```

One last function needs to be added to this master page. Because the children of this page will allow users to delete records, a common method should be added that displays a dialog confirming that the user truly wants to delete the record. The dialog should have both an OK and a Cancel button to enable users to either confirm or cancel the deletion, respectively. This will be implemented as a JavaScript function and placed in the head content holder:

```
<asp:Content ID="Content1" ContentPlaceHolderID="head" Runat="Server">
    <script language="javascript" type="text/javascript">
        function ConfirmDelete()
        {
            return confirm("Do you want to permanently delete this item?");
        }
    </script>
</asp:Content>
```

Any Delete link can call this function, giving users a consistent question whenever they want to delete a record.

The CustomGridView Control

Pages that use the `PaidTimeOffEditGrid` master page are supposed to display the data in an HTML table and be able to support functionality that enables users to click on a link to edit or delete a record. Because the data could contain a lot of records, the table needs to support paging as well as sorting. Sounds like a great place to use a `GridView` control, no? Well, let's take a look at that option. You could add a `GridView` to a page and then add an `ObjectDataSource` that maps to the `ENTUserAccountEOList` object, but sorting doesn't work in the `GridView` when using an object data source, so `ObjectDataSource` is out. You could use the LINQ data source, but then you would be communicating directly with the data layer, so that option is out.

Another option is to manually bind your list object to the `GridView` control. If you do that, then it is up to you to handle the paging and sorting events. The paging is quite simple to implement with a few lines of code, but the sorting is a different story. In order to handle sorting, you must add code in the `GridView` control's `OnSorting` event. This event takes a parameter that indicates the field being sorted and the sort direction. The problem is that the sorting field is passed as a string. You could create a stored procedure that can handle dynamic SQL, but then you would have to add a method to the data layer to call the stored procedure and add a method in the business object to load the data. All that just to handle sorting in a `GridView` control.

Another option, and the one I'll demonstrate, is to use a lambda expression against the list object to sort the objects dynamically. This is new to Visual Studio 2008. By default, list objects support all the functionality to execute lambda expressions. It takes some time to get used to the syntax, but once you have done it a few times it becomes easy.

The other issue that should be tackled here is eliminating redundant code. Any table that allows a user to edit data will have a list page. You don't want to repeat all the code for paging and sorting in every page, so this is a good opportunity to use another custom server-side control. The goals of this control are as follows:

❑ To create a common control to handle displaying lists of data

❑ To centralize the code that handles sorting data

❑ To centralize the code that handles paging data

❑ To ensure that all grids display the header, rows, and pager in the same format

❑ To create a control that is flexible enough that it can be customized to enable developers to add columns based on an object's properties

Start by adding another server-side control to the `V2.FrameworkControls` project and name it `CustomGridView.cs`. Remove the `Text` property as you've done before. Change the class declaration so it inherits from the `GridView` class, rather than the `WebControl` class. You can also remove the `RenderContents` method because we are inheriting from the `GridView` and the base will handle this for us. Add the following code for the constructor:

```
public CustomGridView()
{
    AutoGenerateColumns = false;
    AllowPaging = true;
    AllowSorting = true;
```

```
            PageSize = 25;
            GridLines = GridLines.Both;
            HeaderStyle.CssClass = "gridViewHeader";
            RowStyle.CssClass = "gridViewRow";
            AlternatingRowStyle.CssClass = "gridViewAlternatingRow";
            PagerStyle.CssClass = "gridViewPager";
            CellPadding = 3;
        }
```

Because this control inherits from the `GridView` control, you have access to all the same properties as the `GridView`. The constructor sets the default settings for this control, but you can change these in the page that contains this control. By default, the control should not generate the columns automatically. Later in this chapter, the columns that you want to bind to will be added through code. This gives you great flexibility regarding how the data should appear. Paging and sorting is turned on by default and the default page size is 25. The control will also display both horizontal and vertical grid lines between the cells. The styles for the header, row, alternating row, and pager are defaulted to classes that should be defined in the style sheet. I've omitted the style sheet code here, but you can view these classes in the code available on the Wrox website. The last line adds padding between the text in the cell and the border.

The next step is to write the code that handles the paging. To do this you override the `OnPageIndexChanging` method:

```
        protected override void OnPageIndexChanging(GridViewPageEventArgs e)
        {
            PageIndex = e.NewPageIndex;

            //Use the sorting stored in view state
            BindGridView(SortExpressionLast, SortDirectionLast);
        }
```

This sets the `NewPageIndex` property and calls a custom method to bind the data source to the `GridView`. Because the columns are dynamically created, you need to load the grid each time there is a postback to the server. The `BindGridView` method handles retrieval of the data and binding it to the grid. Here is the `BindGridView` method (before creating this method you need to add a `using` directive to reference the `System.Reflection` namespace):

```
        private void BindGridView(string sortExpression, SortDirection sortDirection)
        {
            //Create an instance of the list object
            Type objectType = Type.GetType(ListClassName);
            object listObject = Activator.CreateInstance(objectType);

            //Call the method to load the object
            objectType.InvokeMember(LoadMethodName, BindingFlags.InvokeMethod, null,
              listObject, _methodParameters.ToArray());

            //Call the SortByPropertyName method.  This is in the ENTBaseBOList class.
            //The object must inherit from this class.
            base.DataSource = objectType.InvokeMember("SortByPropertyName",
                BindingFlags.InvokeMethod, null, listObject, new object[] { sortExpression,
                sortDirection == SortDirection.Ascending});
```

```
        base.DataBind();

        //Save the sortExpression and sortDirection to the view state.
        SortExpressionLast = sortExpression;
        SortDirectionLast = sortDirection;

        objectType = null;
        listObject = null;
    }
```

This requires some explanation. First, notice that this method is using reflection to create an instance of an object, and then it calls a method to load the data in the object. ListClassName, LoadMethodName, and LoadMethodParameters are custom properties that should be added to this class:

```
    private ArrayList _methodParameters = new ArrayList();

    public string ListClassName
    {
        get { return ViewState["ListClassName"].ToString(); }
        set { ViewState["ListClassName"] = value; }
    }

    public string LoadMethodName
    {
        get { return ViewState["LoadMethodName"].ToString(); }
        set { ViewState["LoadMethodName"] = value; }
    }

    public ArrayList LoadMethodParameters
    {
        get
        {
            return _methodParameters;
        }
    }
```

The ListClassName and LoadMethodName properties are strings that store the fully qualified name for the list class that should be created, and the method on that class that should be called to load the object. You can have a list object with multiple Load methods, which filter the data differently based on different parameters. To pass parameters to the Load method, simply add the parameter values to the LoadMethodParameters array list. For example, if you had a Load method that took two parameters, an int and a string, you would need to write the following code:

```
    cgvPTORequests.LoadMethodParameters.Add(10);
    cgvPTORequests.LoadMethodParameters.Add("my string parameter");
```

The parameters are passed to the Load method using reflection in the objectType.InvokeMember (LoadMethodName, BindingFlags.InvokeMethod, null, listObject, _methodParameters .ToArray()); line.

If you are wondering why we didn't use a property of type ENTBaseBOList to act as the data source, the answer is that the ENTBaseBOList would need to be defined with the generic type, such as ENTBase BOList<T>. T would have to be declared in the control's class declaration, but server-side controls cannot use abstract classes as generic types. That is why the object is being created using reflection. Besides, it's fancy!

The next thing to notice about this method is that after it calls the load method, it invokes another method called SortByPropertyName. This is another new method that must be added to the ENTBase BOList class. This method sorts the list by a property name, given the name as a string. Here is the code for the SortByPropertyName method:

```
//Add to top of class
using System.Linq.Expressions;

//Return a sorted list
public List<T> SortByPropertyName(string propertyName, bool ascending)
{
    //Create a Lambda expression to dynamically sort the data.
    var param = Expression.Parameter(typeof(T), "N");

    var sortExpresseion = Expression.Lambda<Func<T, object>>
        (Expression.Convert(Expression.Property(param, propertyName),
        typeof(object)), param);

    if (ascending)
    {
        return this.AsQueryable<T>().OrderBy<T,
            object>(sortExpresseion).ToList<T>();
    }
    else
    {
        return this.AsQueryable<T>().OrderByDescending<T,
            object>(sortExpresseion).ToList<T>();
    }
}
```

This method returns a generic list that can be bound to the GridVIew. It does not sort the current instance. A lambda expression is used to dynamically sort the data in either ascending or descending order. Before explaining the lambda expression, consider what this would look like if it weren't generic. If you wanted to sort an instance of the ENTUserAccountEOList object by the Email property ascending, you could write the following code:

```
var sortedUsers = users.OrderBy(U => U.Email);
```

The users object in this example is an instance of ENTUserAccountEOList. To sort it descending, the code is as follows:

```
var sortedUsers = users.OrderByDescending(U => U.Email);
```

The => is the lambda operator, which is read as "goes to." The left side specifies the input parameter and the right side holds the expression. The type for U is inferred by the compiler based on the type of objects in the list. You can, however, explicitly state the type by passing a generic to the method, like this:

```
var sortedUsers = users.OrderBy<ENTUserAccountEO, string>(U => U.Email);
```

If you look at the IntelliSense for the OrderBy method, you will see the parameters for the method. The method signature is OrderBy <TSource, TKey>(Func<TSource, TKey> keySelector), where TSource represents the type of source elements, TKey represents the type returned by keySelector, and keySelector is a function to extract the key from an element.

In the SortByPropertyName method, the (U => U.Email) statement is created dynamically using an expression. The Expression.Parameter(typeof(T), "N") statement creates the equivalent of the U input parameter, except in this case it is called N. The Expression.Lambda is building the full lambda expression. The <Func<T, object>> statement explicitly states the type of object that N is supposed to represent. The Expression.Property(param, propertyName) statement says to use the property on the object that was passed in as the keySelector. This property needs to be converted to its correct type so that strings and numbers are sorted correctly. If you execute this code and put a breakpoint after the sortExpression variable and then mouse-over the variable to see its value, you would see "N => Convert(N.PropertyName)", where PropertyName is replaced by whatever string parameter you passed in. This expression variable is then passed into the OrderBy or OrderByDescending method of the object to sort the objects in the list. For more information about lambda expressions, see *Introducing Microsoft LINQ* by Paolo Pialorsi and Marco Russo (Microsoft Press, 2007).

Getting back to the BindDataGrid method, after the SortByPropertyName method is called, it sets the base.DataSource and then calls the base.DataBind() to populate the grid. You must explicitly call base.DataSource and base.DataBind because later in this section these methods will be overridden in this control, so the creator of this control cannot call these methods directly.

Because you must use the ListClassName instead of a DataSource for this control, you should throw an exception if a user tries to set the DataSource property:

```
public new object DataSource
{
    set{ throw new NotImplementedException(); }
}
```

This code creates a new method for the DataSource that hides its base implementation. If users try to set this property they will get a NotImplementedException.

To prevent the calling page from using the default functionality of the DataBind method, add the following code:

```
public new void DataBind()
{
    BindGridView(SortExpressionLast, SortDirectionLast);
}
```

When you define a method with the new keyword, you can change the functionality of the base class's implementation of that method. In this instance, the DataBind method will always call the BindGridView method and pass in the latest sort expression and direction.

Two more properties, SortExpressionLast and SortDirectionLast, are needed to set the current sort expression and direction:

```
public string SortExpressionLast
{
    get
    {
        if (ViewState["SortExpressionLast"] == null)
            //Default to displaytext
            return "DisplayText";
        else
            return ViewState["SortExpressionLast"].ToString();
    }

    set { ViewState["SortExpressionLast"] = value; }
}

private SortDirection SortDirectionLast
{
    get
    {
        if (ViewState["SortDirectionLast"] == null)
            //Default to ascending
            return SortDirection.Ascending;
        else
            return (SortDirection)ViewState["SortDirectionLast"];
    }

    set { ViewState["SortDirectionLast"] = value; }
}
```

These properties persist the data to the ViewState because it needs to be saved between postbacks. If the user is paging through the data, the sorting should remain constant through each postback.

To support sorting in the GridView you must override the OnSorting method:

```
protected override void OnSorting(GridViewSortEventArgs e)
{
    //Start at the first page whenever the user sorts.
    PageIndex = 0;

    //Check if the field being sorted is the same as last time.
    if (e.SortExpression == SortExpressionLast)
    {
        //Reverse the direction.
        if (SortDirectionLast == SortDirection.Ascending)
        {
            BindGridView(e.SortExpression, SortDirection.Descending);
        }
        else
        {
            BindGridView(e.SortExpression, SortDirection.Ascending);
        }
    }
```

```
        else
        {
            //Default to Ascending
            BindGridView(e.SortExpression, SortDirection.Ascending);
        }
    }
```

Whenever users sort the data, it will return them to the first page. The method then checks whether the e.SortExpression equals the last sort expression, reversing the direction if they are the same. The reason why it isn't looking at e.SortDirection is because it always returns ascending. The way this grid is implemented, it will sort ascending the first time a user clicks a column header and then sort descending the second time the user clicks the column header.

The last method to add to this control is the AddBoundField method. This control does not auto-generate columns, so you must explicitly state the columns that should be added to the grid. The AddBoundField method is a helper method that enables the caller to add a field using one line of code:

```
public void AddBoundField(string dataField, string headerText, string
    sortExpression)
{
    BoundField bf = new BoundField();
    if (dataField != "")
        bf.DataField = dataField;

    if (headerText != "")
        bf.HeaderText = headerText;

    if (sortExpression != "")
        bf.SortExpression = sortExpression;

    Columns.Add(bf);
}
```

This method enables you to specify the dataField, which is a property of an item in the bound list. The headerText will be displayed in the column header and the sortExpression is passed to the OnSorting method when the user clicks on a column header. The page that contains the custom grid control can add a column using the following code:

```
myGridView.AddColumn("Field1", "My Field", "Field1");
```

The Master Edit Page

The third master page for this project will handle any page that allows users to add or update a record. As stated earlier, users are presented with an Add button or an Edit link to add or update records from the grid page. Clicking the button or the link will navigate to a new screen. This new screen should also have a consistent interface with some common functionality shared among all the pages. These pages use the edit objects that were defined in Chapter 3 to manipulate records in the database. The design view for this page is shown in Figure 4-10.

Before creating the master page, another base page will be created from which all child pages that use this master page must inherit. The name of this base class is BaseEditPage.

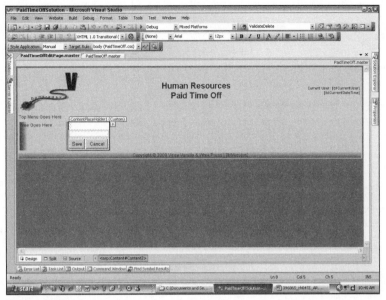

Figure 4-10

The BaseEditPage Class

Here are the goals of this class:

- ❏ Create a common class from which all pages that add or update records inherit.
- ❏ Create a consistent method for loading default values for new records.
- ❏ Create a consistent method for all screens to map an object's properties to the controls on the screen.
- ❏ Create a consistent method for all screens to map the controls on the screen to an object's properties.
- ❏ Create a consistent method for loading controls on the screen, such as drop-down lists or list boxes.
- ❏ Create a consistent method for navigating users back to the grid page.
- ❏ Create a consistent pattern for identifying whether the screen is being used to add a new record or edit an existing one. The pattern in this book uses the same page for adding and editing.

Add a new class to the ASP.NET application and name it BaseEditPage. This class will contain the common logic for all pages that allow users to edit data, and contain some abstract methods that each page must implement. Again, the goal of these base classes is to create placeholders so that certain types of logic always appear in the same routine, regardless of developer. Add a using directive that references the V2.PaidTimeOffBLL.Framework and V2.PaidTimeOffBLL namespaces. This class should be declared as abstract and inherit from the BasePage created earlier. This will give it the functionality needed to set the menu item. Here is the code for the BaseEditPage class:

```
using System.Collections.Specialized;
using V2.PaidTimeOffBLL.Framework;

public abstract class BaseEditPage<T> : BasePage
```

```
        where T : ENTBaseEO, new()
    {
        public BaseEditPage() { }

        /// <summary>
        /// Initializes a new edit object and then calls load object from screen.
        /// </summary>
        protected virtual void LoadNew()
        {
            T baseEO = new T();
            baseEO.Init();
            LoadScreenFromObject(baseEO);
        }

        /// <summary>
        /// Scrapes the screen and loads the edit object.
        /// </summary>
        /// <param name="baseEO"></param>
        protected abstract void LoadObjectFromScreen(T baseEO);

        /// <summary>
        /// Load the controls on the screen from the object's properties.
        /// </summary>
        /// <param name="baseEO"></param>
        protected abstract void LoadScreenFromObject(T baseEO);

        /// <summary>
        /// Preload the controls such as drop down lists and listboxes.
        /// </summary>
        protected abstract void LoadControls();

        /// <summary>
        /// Navigate the user back the list page.  The cancel button and a successful
        /// save should both call this.
        /// </summary>
        protected abstract void GoToGridPage();

        protected override void OnLoad(EventArgs e)
        {
            base.OnLoad(e);

            if (!IsPostBack)
            {
                //Load any list boxes, drop downs, etc.
                LoadControls();

                int id = GetId();

                if (id == 0)
                {
                    LoadNew();
                }
                else
                {
                    T baseEO = new T();
```

```
                        baseEO.Load(Convert.ToInt32(id));
                        LoadScreenFromObject(baseEO);
                    }
                }
            }

        public int GetId()
        {
            //Decrypt the query string
            NameValueCollection queryString =
                DecryptQueryString(Request.QueryString.ToString());

            if (queryString == null)
            {
                return 0;
            }
            else
            {
                //Check if the id was passed in.
                string id = queryString["id"];

                if ((id == null) || (id == "0"))
                {
                    return 0;
                }
                else
                {
                    return Convert.ToInt32(id);
                }
            }
        }
    }
}
```

The first thing to notice is the generic being used by this class. An edit object must be used in conjunction with this page. Because an edit object is being used, you are guaranteed that certain methods exist on that object that you can call. The next line is the default constructor, which at this point does not do anything. The next method is a virtual method called LoadNew. This method is called when the screen is used to add a new record. Because it is virtual, you can override this functionality if you had custom logic for loading a new record to the screen. The method creates an instance of the generic class and calls its Init method. Recall from Chapter 3 that the Init method is used to set default values for new records. It then calls an abstract method called LoadScreenFromObject.

The LoadScreenFromObject method must be implemented by the inheriting class, and this is where the properties of the edit object should be mapped to the controls on the screen. You generally are setting the text for textboxes, setting indexes in drop-down lists, or loading grids.

LoadObjectFromScreen is the counterpart to LoadScreenFromObject. This is where you map the values of the controls on the screen to the properties of the edit object. You typically would do this when the user clicks the Save button.

The LoadControls method is used to populate any controls on the screen before calling the LoadScreen FromObject method. Drop-down lists or list boxes should be filled in this method and the LoadScreen

`FromObject` method should just set the correct index for the control. The `LoadControls` method is only called once in the page load event when it is not a postback.

The `GoToGridPage` method must be implemented in the inheriting class. It navigates the user back to the edit grid page. This is usually called when the user clicks the Cancel button or after a successful save. Typically there is only a `Server.Redirect` call in this method.

The last section overrides the `OnLoad` event and takes action if this is the first time coming to this page. The `LoadControls` method is called to load the drop-down lists or list boxes. The query string is then decrypted to determine the ID of the record being displayed. If the user clicked the Add button, then the ID will be zero. If this is a new record, then the `LoadNew` method is called. If the user is editing an existing record, then the generic class is instantiated, and the edit object is loaded and then mapped to the screen. As you can see, all of the pieces are starting to fit together between the data access layer, the business logic layer, and the user interface.

The PaidTimeOffEdit Master Page

Add a new nested master page to the project called `PaidTimeOffEditPage.master`. The master page should be `PaidTimeOff.master`. The goal of this new page is to provide a consistent interface for all screens that allow users to add or update records. The page will contain a `ValidationErrorMessages` control, a content section, a Save button, and a Cancel button. Any content page that uses this master page must inherit from the `BaseEditPage` class.

Add the following HTML in the `Content2` control:

```
<table>
    <tr>
        <td>
        <V2:ValidationErrorMessages ID="ValidationErrorMessages1" runat="server" />
        </td>
    </tr>
</table>
<table width="100%">
    <tr>
        <td>
            <asp:ContentPlaceHolder ID="ContentPlaceHolder3" runat="server">
            </asp:ContentPlaceHolder>
        </td>
    </tr>
</table>
<table>
    <tr>
        <td>
            <asp:Button ID="btnSave" runat="server" Text="Save"
                onclick="btnSave_Click" />
        </td>
        <td>
            <asp:Button ID="btnCancel" runat="server" Text="Cancel"
                onclick="btnCancel_Click" />
        </td>
    </tr>
</table>
```

This is very similar to the `PaidTimeOffGridPage` master page. The validation errors will appear at the top of the screen. The form for data entry will be placed in the middle section, and the Save and Cancel buttons will appear in the bottom-left corner of the page. The next step is to add the delegates and events to the code-behind page for the buttons. Because the button click events have the same signature, you can use one delegate for both the Save and Cancel button click events:

```
public delegate void ButtonClickedHandler(object sender, EventArgs e);

public event ButtonClickedHandler SaveButton_Click;
public event ButtonClickedHandler CancelButton_Click;

protected void btnSave_Click(object sender, EventArgs e)
{
    if (SaveButton_Click != null)
    {
        SaveButton_Click(sender, e);
    }
}

protected void btnCancel_Click(object sender, EventArgs e)
{
    if (CancelButton_Click != null)
    {
        CancelButton_Click(sender, e);
    }
}
```

The last step is to add the property for the `ValidationErrors` that gets or sets the `ENTValidation Errors` list on the `ValidationErrorMessages1` control. You need to add a `using` directive to the `V2.PaidTimeOffBLL.Framework` namespace so the `ENTValidationErrors` class is recognized:

```
public ENTValidationErrors ValidationErrors
{
    get
    {
        return ValidationErrorMessages1.ValidationErrors;
    }

    set
    {
        ValidationErrorMessages1.ValidationErrors = value;
    }
}
```

Solution

The design section covered the controls, the master pages, and the base classes that will be used to build every page in this project. This section walks through implementing these pages and classes using the `ENTUserAccountEO` object created in the previous chapter.

Managing users is an administrative function, and the link to access the user screens will appear under the Administration top-level menu. Because managing users is a security function, a Security node will be created on the side menu, and the link to the user screens will be a child of this node. Figure 4-2, shown earlier, indicates how the menu is structured for this page. All you need to do is add two records to the ENTMenuItem table to accomplish this structure.

Field Name	Security Record	Users Record
ENTMenuItemId	4	5
MenuItemName	Security	Users
Description		Manage the users who can access the system.
Url		Administration/Users.aspx
ParentENTMenuItemId	2	4
DisplaySequence	1	1
IsAlwaysEnabled	False	False

Notice that the parent for the security menu item is the administration menu item, and the parent for users is the security menu item. Because the Url is null for the security menu item, it will be rendered without the hyperlink.

The Administration Page

Each top-level menu on the MenuTabs control must have a landing page. The administrative landing page will display the description for each menu item in that section. This page is shown in Figure 4-11.

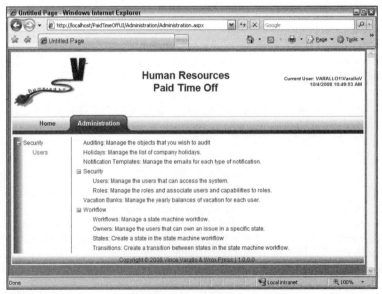

Figure 4-11

Users can click on the specific menu item on the side menu to access the screens. All pages in the administration section will be placed in a subfolder called `Administration` under the root directory. Add this folder to the project before adding the Administration landing page.

Add a page called `Administration.aspx` to the Administration folder. This page uses the `PaidTime Off` master page. Change the page so it inherits from the `BasePage` class. Because this inherits from `BasePage`, you must implement the `MenuItemName` method. Return the string "Administration" in this method. Add a `TreeView` control to the `Content2` control and set its ID to `tvMenuDescriptions`. The `TreeView` control will be dynamically populated with each menu item and its description in the database. You won't need to create any extra business objects or data classes for this page because the `ENTMenuItemBOList` object already contains the data that will be displayed on the screen. Open the code-behind file for this page and add a `using` directive to reference the `V2.PaidTimeOffBLL .Framework` namespace, adding the following code:

```
protected void Page_Load(object sender, EventArgs e)
{
    if (!IsPostBack)
    {
        //Get the Administration menu item from the cache
        ENTMenuItemBO administrationMenuItem =
            Globals.GetMenuItems(Cache).GetByMenuItemName("Administration");

        //Create a node for each child element of the administrative menu.
        CreateChildNodes(tvMenuDescriptions.Nodes,
            administrationMenuItem.ChildMenuItems);
    }
}

private void CreateChildNodes(TreeNodeCollection treeNodeCollection,
    ENTMenuItemBOList childMenuItems)
{
    foreach (ENTMenuItemBO menuItem in childMenuItems)
    {
        TreeNode menuNode = new TreeNode(menuItem.MenuItemName +
            (menuItem.Description == null ? "" : ": " + menuItem.Description));

        menuNode.SelectAction = TreeNodeSelectAction.None;

        if (menuItem.ChildMenuItems.Count > 0)
        {
            CreateChildNodes(menuNode.ChildNodes, menuItem.ChildMenuItems);
        }

        treeNodeCollection.Add(menuNode);
    }
}
```

The page load event will pull the Administration menu object from the cache and then create a node in the `TreeView` control for each child. The `CreateChildNodes` method is another recursive method; it creates the hierarchy of nodes in the tree. If you run the project and click the Administration tab, the page will appear with the description of the User menu item. For now this page is bleak, but don't worry — there will be plenty of screens built into the administrative section and the screen will look better.

The User List Page

The User List page should display the list of all users defined in the system and enable users to add new users or edit existing ones. There is a requirement that users cannot be deleted from the system, so delete functionality will not be built into this page. The page will look like Figure 4-2, shown earlier.

Add another page to the Administration folder called Users.aspx. The master page should be PaidTimeOffEditGrid.master. Change the page so it inherits from BasePage and return "Users" in the MenuItemName method. If you run the project, select Administration ➪ Users. The page should display and the Users menu item should be bold.

The next step is to handle the Add button's click event. Add the following tag in the HTML so your code-behind will recognize the events defined in the master page:

```
<%@ MasterType virtualPath="~/PaidTimeOffEditGrid.master"%>
```

Add the following code to the code-behind page:

```
protected void Page_Load(object sender, EventArgs e)
{
    Master.AddButton_Click += new
        PaidTimeOffEditGrid.ButtonClickedHandler(Master_AddButton_Click);
}

void Master_AddButton_Click(object sender, EventArgs e)
{
    Response.Redirect("User.aspx" + EncryptQueryString("id=0"));
}
```

When users click the Add button, they will be redirected to the User.aspx page, which contains a form that lists the fields in the user table. In order to tell the User.aspx page that a new record is being added, a zero is passed in the query string for the id. This is where encrypting a string comes into play. Recall that EncryptQueryString is a method in the BasePage defined earlier.

Click back to view the HTML markup for this page. Drag a CustomGridView control from the toolbox into the Content control and rename the control cgvUsers. Now switch to the code-behind to define the columns that should be rendered in this control. This code goes in the page load event also:

```
if (!IsPostBack)
{
    //Tell the control what class to create and the load method.
    cgvUsers.ListClassName = typeof(ENTUserAccountEOList).AssemblyQualifiedName;
    cgvUsers.LoadMethodName = "Load";

    //Action column-Contains the Edit link
    cgvUsers.AddBoundField("", "Actions", "");

    //Name
    cgvUsers.AddBoundField("DisplayText", "Name", "DisplayText");
```

```
        //Windows Account Name
        cgvUsers.AddBoundField("WindowsAccountName", "Windows Account",
            "WindowsAccountName");

        //Email
        cgvUsers.AddBoundField("Email", "Email", "Email");

        //Is Active-This will be a checkbox column
        cgvUsers.AddBoundField("", "Active", "IsActive");

        cgvUsers.DataBind();
    }
```

The `ListClassName` is set by calling the `AssemblyQualifiedName` method of the `Type` object. The control uses this name to create an instance of this class. The default `Load` method is used to populate the object with data. The next line creates a column called `Actions`, which will be populated with the Edit link that navigates to the `User.aspx` page where the user can edit this record. The link will be added to this cell in the `RowDataBound` event. The `DisplayText` property is used to display the user's last and first name, and then the `WindowsAccountName` and `Email` columns are added. The `Active` column is added, but instead of binding it to the `IsActive` property of the `ENTUserAccountEO` object, a checkbox is added to the cell in the `RowDataBound` event. The last line calls the `DataBind` method, but remember that this was overridden in the custom `GridView` control, so it really calls the internal `BindGridView` method.

Now add the code for the `RowDataBound` event. Click back to the HTML markup view of the `Users .aspx` page. Put your cursor in the custom `GridView` control and view its properties. In the top of the Properties window you should see a lightning bolt icon. Click the lightning bolt to display all the events of this control in the Properties window. Double-click the `RowDataBound` event. Visual Studio will automatically create the method for the `RowDataBound` event and hook it to the custom `GridView` control. Add the following code in the `RowDataBound` event handler:

```
if (e.Row.RowType == DataControlRowType.DataRow)
{
    //Add the edit link to the action column.
    HyperLink editLink = new HyperLink();
    editLink.Text = "Edit";
    editLink.NavigateUrl = "User.aspx" + EncryptQueryString("id=" +
        ((ENTUserAccountEO)e.Row.DataItem).ID.ToString());

    e.Row.Cells[COL_INDEX_ACTION].Controls.Add(editLink);

    //Add checkbox to display the isactive field.
    CheckBox chkActive = new CheckBox();
    chkActive.Checked = ((ENTUserAccountEO)e.Row.DataItem).IsActive;
    chkActive.Enabled = false;

    e.Row.Cells[COL_INDEX_ACTIVE].Controls.Add(chkActive);
}
```

This code adds a hyperlink to the `Actions` column called "Edit." The Edit link navigates to the `User.aspx` page and passes the ID of the record for this row. The ID is determined by casting the `DataItem` property to an `ENTUserAccountEO` object and grabbing its `ID` property. The link is added to the `Controls` collection in the action cell in the row's `Cells` collection. The cells are referenced by index, so it is a good idea to add constants that represent the index for each cell:

```
private const int COL_INDEX_ACTION = 0;
private const int COL_INDEX_NAME = 1;
private const int COL_INDEX_WINDOWSNAME = 2;
private const int COL_INDEX_EMAIL = 3;
private const int COL_INDEX_ACTIVE = 4;
```

The checkbox is then added to the `Active` column and it will be checked if the user is active.

That's all you need to create this page. If you run the project, navigate to the Users menu, and click the link, your page will appear and the grid should be populated with all the records in the `ENTUserAccount` table. Click the column headers to see how the sorting works. You can test the paging by adding more than five records to the `ENTUserAccount` table and changing the paging size to 5. If you click the paging links at the bottom of the grid, you'll see that the sorting remains consistent.

The User Edit Page

The User edit page is used to add or update records in the `ENTUserAccount` table. The `Users.aspx` page directs users to this page from either the Add button or the Edit link. The user edit page is shown in Figure 4-12.

Figure 4-12

Add a new page to the `Administration` folder in the `PaidTimeOffUI` project. Name the file `User.aspx` and select `PaidTimeOffEditPage.master` as the master page. Open the code-behind page and add a `using` statement to reference the `V2.PaidTimeOffBLL.Framework` namespace. Change the class so that it inherits from `BaseEditPage<ENTUserAccountEO>` and then have Visual Studio automatically

120

generate the abstract methods for this class. Change the `MenuItemName` method to return "Users." Add the following code to the `GoToGridPage` method:

```
Response.Redirect("Users.aspx");
```

This will direct a user back to the User list page when they press the Cancel button or successfully save a record.

The next step is to hook up the Save and Cancel button click events. Switch to the HTML view of the page and add the following page directive:

```
<%@ MasterType virtualPath="~/PaidTimeOffEditPage.master"%>
```

This enables the code-behind to recognize the events defined in the master page. Hook the event handlers into the `AddButtonClick` and `CancelButtonClick` events in the `Page_Load` method. As you type the event handler code, Visual Studio will prompt you to automatically create the event procedure that handles the event after you enter +=. Your code should look like this:

```
protected void Page_Load(object sender, EventArgs e)
{
    Master.SaveButton_Click += new
        PaidTimeOffEditPage.ButtonClickedHandler(Master_SaveButton_Click);
    Master.CancelButton_Click += new
        PaidTimeOffEditPage.ButtonClickedHandler(Master_CancelButton_Click);
}

void Master_CancelButton_Click(object sender, EventArgs e)
{
    throw new NotImplementedException();
}

void Master_SaveButton_Click(object sender, EventArgs e)
{
    throw new NotImplementedException();
}
```

Change the `CancelButton_Click` procedure so it calls the `GoToGridPage()` method. Next, remove the `NotImplementedException` from the `LoadControls` method. Because there are no drop-down lists or list boxes to populate for this screen, this method will be blank, although it is always called in the `Page_Load` event in the base class so you must remove the exception.

The next step is to add the controls to the HTML markup to display the fields for the `ENTUserAccount` record. This will be implemented with a two-column table that has labels in the first column and controls in the second column. Add the following code inside the `Content` control:

```
<table>
    <tr>
        <td>Windows Account Name:</td>
        <td>
            <asp:TextBox ID="txtWindowsAccountName" runat="server"></asp:TextBox>
        </td>
    </tr>
```

```
        <tr>
            <td>First Name:</td>
            <td>
                <asp:TextBox ID="txtFirstName" runat="server"></asp:TextBox>
            </td>
        </tr>
        <tr>
            <td>Last Name:</td>
            <td>
                <asp:TextBox ID="txtLastName" runat="server"></asp:TextBox>
            </td>
        </tr>
        <tr>
            <td>Email Address:</td>
            <td>
                <asp:TextBox ID="txtEmail" runat="server"></asp:TextBox>
            </td>
        </tr>
        <tr>
            <td>Active:</td>
            <td>
                <asp:CheckBox ID="chkActive" runat="server" />
            </td>
        </tr>
</table>
```

Now that the controls are defined, you can add the code to load the screen from the object, and load the object from the controls on the screen. The code for the LoadScreenFromObject method is as follows:

```
txtWindowsAccountName.Text = baseEO.WindowsAccountName;
txtFirstName.Text = baseEO.FirstName;
txtLastName.Text = baseEO.LastName;
txtEmail.Text = baseEO.Email;
chkActive.Checked = baseEO.IsActive;

//Put the object in the view state so it can be attached back to the data context.
ViewState[VIEW_STATE_KEY_USER] = baseEO;
```

This code will map each property of the ENTUserAccountEO object to the controls on the screen. It also serializes the object to the ViewState so the ID and audit fields can be set when saving the record. We add a constant for the ViewState key because this is referenced in multiple methods:

```
private const string VIEW_STATE_KEY_USER = "User";
```

Now add the following code to the LoadObjectFromScreen method:

```
baseEO.WindowsAccountName = txtWindowsAccountName.Text;
baseEO.FirstName = txtFirstName.Text;
baseEO.LastName = txtLastName.Text;
baseEO.Email = txtEmail.Text;
baseEO.IsActive = chkActive.Checked;
```

This simply takes the values from the controls and sets them to the properties on the object.

The last step is to add the code to the `SaveButton_Click` event:

```
ENTValidationErrors validationErrors = new ENTValidationErrors();

ENTUserAccountEO userAccount = (ENTUserAccountEO)ViewState[VIEW_STATE_KEY_USER];
LoadObjectFromScreen(userAccount);

if (!userAccount.Save(ref validationErrors, 1))
{
    Master.ValidationErrors = validationErrors;
}
else
{
    GoToGridPage();
}
```

This method creates an `ENTValidationErrors` object that is passed to the `Save` method by `ref`. If there are any validation errors, then they are populated in the `ValidationErrors` control on the master page. If there are no validation errors, then the record is saved correctly and the user is navigated back to the `Users.aspx` page. Notice that the `Save` method also takes a `userAccountID` parameter, which is passed in as 1 in this code snippet. For now, just make this an ID of any user in your `ENTUserAccount` table. In Chapter 6, this will be changed to dynamically retrieve the ID from a cached list of users, but for simplicity just hard-code this value for now.

That's all you need to do. You can now run the project and add new users or edit existing users using this page. Try adding a new user without any fields filled in. You should see the screen shown in Figure 4-13.

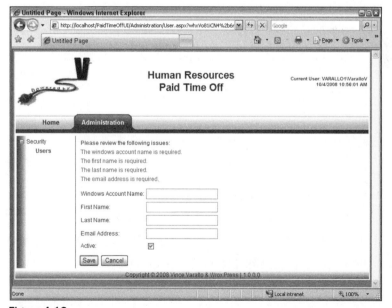

Figure 4-13

Note that the `ValidationError` control is displaying the messages at the top of the screen in red, and the record was not saved. Try entering another record that contains a duplicate Windows account name. If you step through the code you'll see how the dynamic SQL is executed in the `DataContext` that checks for duplicate fields.

Summary

A lot happened in this chapter. The framework for all screens is now developed and linked in with the business logic layer and the data access layer built in the previous two chapters. Most of the code is not in the pages themselves — it is either in the master page or in the business layer, and the pages the user sees become quite trivial to code.

Note the following key points to remember for the menu controls:

❑   Records that do not have a `ParentENTMenuItemId` will appear on the tabs at the top of the screen.

❑   Any record that has a `ParentENTMenuItemId` will appear on the side menu in the `TreeView` control.

❑   The side menu can have nested nodes in the `TreeView` control. This is controlled by the `ParentENTMenuItemId`.

❑   Use the `DisplaySequence` to set the order in which you want the menu item to appear.

❑   If the menu item has a URL, it will appear as a link on the menu; otherwise, it will appear as a label.

❑   The menu is cached in the `Globals` class.

The key points to remember when implementing a grid page are as follows:

❑   Use the `PaidTimeOffEditGrid.master` page.

❑   Add a `MasterType` tag in the HTML markup that points to the `PaidTimeOffEditGrid .master` page.

❑   Inherit from the `BasePage` class.

❑   Hook up the `AddButton_Click` event handler in the `Page_Load` event.

❑   Add a `Response.Redirect` statement in the `AddButton_Click` event that redirects the user to the edit page and pass an ID of zero in the query string. Be sure to encrypt the query string.

❑   Override the `MenuItemName` with the side menu or top menu that belongs to the page.

❑   Add a custom grid control to display the data to the user.

❑   Add code in the `Page_Load` event to set the custom `GridView`'s `ListClassName`.

❑   Add code in the `Page_Load` event to set the custom `GridView`'s `LoadMethodName`.

❑   Add code in the `Page_Load` event to add the columns you want to display in the grid.

❑   Add constants that represent the column index for each column in the grid.

❑   Add code to the `RowDataBound` event to add controls to each row in the `GridView`. Usually, there is at least an Edit link that navigates to the edit page. Any query strings should be encrypted.

Keep in mind the following key points when implementing an edit page:

- ❑ Use the `PaidTimeOffEditPage.master` page.

- ❑ Add a `MasterType` tag in the HTML markup that points to the `PaidTimeOffEditPage` `.master` page.

- ❑ Inherit from the `BaseEditPage` class.

- ❑ Hook up the `SaveButton_Click` and `CancelButton_Click` event handlers in the `Page_Load` event.

- ❑ Add a `Response.Redirect` in the `GoToGridPage` method that redirects the user to the list page.

- ❑ Override the `MenuItemName` with the side menu or top menu that belongs to this page.

- ❑ Add code to the `LoadControls` method to load list boxes or drop-down lists. If there is nothing to load, then remove the `NotImplementedException` from the method.

- ❑ Add a call to the `GoToGridPage` method in the `CancelButton_Click` event.

- ❑ Add a constant for the `ViewState` key that contains the serialized edit object.

- ❑ Add code to the `SaveButton_Click` event that creates an `ENTValidationErrors` object, loads the edit object with the values from the screen, calls the `save` method, and displays any errors or redirects to the list page by calling the `GoToGridPage` method if there are no errors.

- ❑ Add the HTML and ASP.NET controls to display the data on the form.

- ❑ Add code to the `LoadObjectFromScreen` method that maps the values in the controls to the properties on the object.

- ❑ Add code to the `LoadScreenFromObject` method that maps the properties of the object to the controls on the screen.

So far, this book has covered the data layer, the business logic layer, and now the user interface. Only one more chapter is considered part of the core framework before getting into the functionality of the application that uses this pattern. The next chapter discusses exception handling and creates a standard for managing exceptions in this application. Once you've finished the next chapter, you'll be ready to start building the functionality of the application or even take the base classes in the first five chapters and start building your own applications.

5

Exception Handling

Have you ever taken over an application for another developer and been asked to track down a problem only to find that an exception was being thrown by the code but the previous developer was ignoring it? I've seen this happen plenty of times. VB used to make it easy to cover up exceptions with the dreaded `On Error Resume Next` statement. This would tell the application to just keep on executing line after line even if an exception occurred. I've actually heard the excuse, "Well, if the system doesn't show the user the exception, the application will look more professional." Anyone with that type of mentality toward a system should be moved to technical support and they'll change their mind immediately. These are some of the toughest "bugs" to track down.

An exception is an error that occurs during execution. Sometimes there are known exceptions that the developer can handle, while other exceptions are unexpected. An example of a known exception would be when you try to write to a file and it is marked as read-only. You can trap this exception and give the user a friendly message to change the file's attributes. Unexpected exceptions are obviously different because you can't anticipate them, but you still need to make the user aware that something happened and the system didn't perform as expected. You would hope that users call the help desk to let someone know that a problem has occurred so you can fix it, but usually they won't. Even if they do, it is often hard to get a clear explanation of exactly what they were doing in order to give you a clue as to how to fix it.

Wikipedia defines exception handling as "a programming language construct or computer hardware mechanism designed to handle the occurrence of a condition that changes the normal flow of execution." Essentially, this means you need to add code to your application that expects unexpected exceptions to occur. Your strategy for exception handling should be designed early in the development process, and one of the issues that should be addressed is not relying on the user to let you know what happened, but instead letting the system tell you what happened and when. Luckily, Microsoft has given you a few pre-built options when it comes to exception handling, and rather than reinvent the wheel you can just piggyback off of their exception handling strategy and incorporate it into your application.

Problem

This chapter focuses on the exception handling strategy in the PaidTimeOff solution. One of the goals of the pattern is to make it generic so it can be used in any of your ASP.NET projects. Another goal is to make it easy enough that you can set it and forget it. That is, you should only need to follow a few simple steps each time you set up a new solution, and not have to think about unhandled exceptions. The main points of discussion in this chapter are as follows:

- ❏ Understanding the built-in health monitoring capabilities of the .NET Framework
- ❏ The Microsoft Application Block for exception handling
- ❏ The Microsoft Application Block for logging
- ❏ How to log exceptions to the event log
- ❏ How to e-mail exceptions to the appropriate personnel
- ❏ How to set up exception handling in the PaidTimeOff solution

Design

Let's face it — even the most tested software with the most gifted programmers will have exceptions. It's impossible to think of every single scenario that a user may encounter when using your software. The system should be designed to handle unexpected exceptions even if Bill Gates himself is writing the application. Expected exceptions should be caught and handled gracefully. As mentioned in the introduction to this chapter, an example of an expected exception would be if a user tried to write to a read-only file. This kind of exception should be trapped in the specific method that is writing to the file and either try again or give the user a message to try again later.

The main focus of this chapter is unexpected exceptions. What should the application do when this occurs? Before getting on my soapbox about how these should be handled, let me first explain the options that the .NET Framework gives you for handling exceptions. Then I'll get into more specifics about how to use these options in the PaidTimeOff solution.

Application-Level Exception Handling

ASP.NET applications support handling all exceptions in a single event handler in the Global.asax file. When you add a Global.asax file to your application, an Application_Error event handler is automatically added to the file. This handler catches any unhandled exceptions that have been raised throughout the application. The event handler is as follows:

```
void Application_Error(object sender, EventArgs e)
{
    // Code that runs when an unhandled error occurs
}
```

You could catch any unexpected exception in this method, log it to the event log, send an e-mail to a developer, and then redirect the user to a common page with a friendly message:

```
Exception error = Server.GetLastError().GetBaseException();

//Log exception to the event log
if (!EventLog.SourceExists("PaidTimeOff"))
{
    EventLog.CreateEventSource("PaidTimeOff", "Application");
}

EventLog eventLog = new EventLog();
eventLog.Log = "Application";
eventLog.Source = "PaidTimeOff";
eventLog.WriteEntry(error.ToString(), EventLogEntryType.Error);

//Email exception to a developer
MailMessage email = new MailMessage("administrator@PoweredByV2.com",
    "vince.varallo@PoweredByV2.com");
email.Body = error.ToString();
email.Subject = "An error occurred in the PaidTimeOff Application";

SmtpClient smtpClient = new SmtpClient("127.0.0.1", 25);
smtpClient.Send(email);

Response.Redirect("ErrorPage.aspx");
```

In order for the preceding code to work, you must add the following Import directives at the top of the Global.asax page. You also need to replace the IP address with your e-mail server and use a valid e-mail address for the sender and receiver:

```
<%@ Import Namespace="System.Diagnostics" %>
<%@ Import Namespace="System.Net.Mail" %>
```

Adding the Import directive is the same as adding a using directive in a code-behind page. Because the Application_Error handler is written in a server script, you need to use the Import directive. You also need to give the LOCALMACHINE\ASPNET user, or the user who the application pool is running as, access to the Eventlog registry key. If you run this code without giving the proper permissions on the registry key, you will get an error when the EventLog.SourceExists method is executed. In order for you to search the event log for a source and create a source, you need to grant read permission to the HKEY_LOCAL_MACHINE\SYSTEM\CurrentControlSet\Services\Eventlog registry key and all subkeys. You then have to grant full control to the Application key under the Eventlog key. Here are the steps to do that:

1. Click the Start button and select Run from the menu.

2. Enter "**regedit**" and click the OK button. This should open the registry editor.

3. In the left-hand pane, navigate to the HKEY_LOCAL_MACHINE\SYSTEM\CurrentControlSet\Services\Eventlog key.

4. Right-click on this key and select Permissions from the menu. This will bring up the Permissions for EventLog window.

5. Click the Add button. This will bring up the Select Users or Groups window.

6. Enter ASPNET for the object name and click the Check Names button. The system should find the local ASPNET user and display it in the Object Name text box.

7. Click the OK button. This will bring you back to the Permissions for EventLog window.

8. Check the Read permission from the permissions list and click the OK button.

9. Close the registry editor.

This enables you to create "PaidTimeOff" as a source in the event log. If you do not want to grant access to the ASPNET user, then you could impersonate a local user before this code is executed and grant that user permission to the registry. See the following article for information about setting up impersonation for an ASP.NET application: http://support.microsoft.com/kb/306158/en-us.

When the preceding exception handling code is run, it will create an entry in the event log (see Figure 5-1).

Figure 5-1

Assuming you have the permissions set up correctly, the preceding code would log the event to the Application event log and then redirect the user to the ErrorPage.aspx page. Notice that our custom error appears in the event log with a source of PaidTimeOff, and the .NET Framework automatically created another Warning entry with a source of ASP.NET 2.0.50727.0.

If you didn't have the call to the Response.Redirect method in the procedure, the user would get the default error page, which looks like Figure 5-2. For this example, I added a new page and caused a division-by-zero exception in the Page_Load event.

As you can see, this gives the user way too much information and could potentially pose a threat to the application. Even if you did put the call to the Response.Redirect method in the event handler and an exception occurred before the Response.Redirect method is called, the default error page is shown instead of the custom error page — but keep reading, you can fix this.

Server Error in '/PaidTimeOffUI' Application.

Attempted to divide by zero.

Description: An unhandled exception occurred during the execution of the current web request. Please review the stack trace for more information about the error and where it originated in the code.

Exception Details: System.DivideByZeroException: Attempted to divide by zero.

Source Error:

```
Line 98:     {
Line 99:         int x = 0;
Line 100:        int y = 5 / x;
Line 101:    }
Line 102:}
```

Source File: c:\WroxSamples\PaidTimeOffSolution\PaidTimeOffUI\Default.aspx.cs   **Line:** 100

Stack Trace:

```
[DivideByZeroException: Attempted to divide by zero.]
   _Default.btnCreateError_Click(Object sender, EventArgs e) in c:\WroxSamples\PaidTimeOffSolution\PaidTimeOffUI\Default.aspx.cs:100
   System.Web.UI.WebControls.Button.OnClick(EventArgs e) +105
   System.Web.UI.WebControls.Button.RaisePostBackEvent(String eventArgument) +107
   System.Web.UI.WebControls.Button.System.Web.UI.IPostBackEventHandler.RaisePostBackEvent(String eventArgument) +7
   System.Web.UI.Page.RaisePostBackEvent(IPostBackEventHandler sourceControl, String eventArgument) +11
   System.Web.UI.Page.RaisePostBackEvent(NameValueCollection postData) +33
   System.Web.UI.Page.ProcessRequestMain(Boolean includeStagesBeforeAsyncPoint, Boolean includeStagesAfterAsyncPoint) +1746
```

Figure 5-2

Page-Level Exception Handling

You can also implement exception handling on a page-by-page basis. To do so, you create a `Page_Error` event handler in the code-behind page:

```
public void Page_Error(object sender, EventArgs e)
{
    //Insert same code that is in the Application_Error event.
}
```

Whenever an unhandled exception is thrown in the page, it will be caught in this event handler. If you were to copy the same code that is in the `Application_Error` event handler and run code that causes an exception in this page, you would see that the `Page_Error` code is executed but the `Application_Error` code is not executed. If you open the Event Viewer, you should see our custom exception logged with a source of PaidTimeOff, but the ASP.NET exception did not get logged.

Method-Level Handling

If you need to capture certain exceptions at the method level, use a `try-catch` block. To turn exception handling on, you simply wrap the code in the `try` block:

```
try
{
    int x = 0;
    int y = 5 / x;
}
```

You can then catch specific types of exceptions and handle them accordingly. Note that the order in which you catch the exceptions is important. Start with the most specific type of error first, and the last type should be the generic `Exception` type. Once the code finds an exception that matches the type in the `catch` statement, it will execute that block of code and ignore the rest of the `catch` statements. Add the following `catch` statements after the preceding `try` block:

```
catch (DivideByZeroException divByZeroEx)
{
    Response.Write("You attempted to divide by zero.  Try again!");
}
catch (Exception ex)
{
    throw ex;
}
```

When this code is executed, the exception is caught in the first `catch` block and a message is written back to the page. The `Page_Error` and `Application_Error` events would not be fired. If you were to reverse this order and put the generic `Exception` catch block first, you would get a compile-time error: "A previous catch clause already catches all exceptions of this or of a super type ('System.Exception')". The compiler realizes that the `DivideByZeroException` is a sub-exception of the generic `exception` object and it won't let you compile the code because the second `catch` block would never be executed.

In some instances you may want to trap a specific exception and throw a new one with a nicer message. Instead of using the `Response.Write` method to display a message, you can use the following:

```
throw new Exception("You attempted to divide by zero.  Try again!");
```

This will create a new exception with a friendly message, and then the `Page_Error` or `Application_Error` code will be executed to handle the error. It is up to you to determine how you are going to handle specific errors. Sometimes you may want to use the default message, whereas at other times you may want to override the message with your own.

There is one more very important part to a `try-catch` block: the `finally` block. The `finally` block is optional but it is important to understand what it does because it should be used in many situations. This is code that will always be executed regardless of whether an exception occurred or not. This is a great place to put clean-up code such as closing database connections or closing files if an exception occurred while they were open. The `catch` block could handle the exception appropriately, and even if it throws another exception, the `finally` block will be executed. If an exception happens in the `finally` block, it is bubbled up to the first `catch` block in the call stack, the `Page_Error` event handler, or the `Application_Error` event handler if they exist. Also be aware that if you put a `Response` `.Redirect` in the `finally` block and an exception occurs in the `try` block, execution will flow to the `catch` block and then the `finally` block, which redirects the user to the other page, but the exception is lost and not bubbled up to the `Page_Error` or `Application_Error` event handlers.

Web.config

There are also several options to configure exception handling in the `web.config` file. By default, the `customErrors` section is commented out when Visual Studio 2008 adds the `web.config` file to the project. The `customErrors` section is embedded in the `system.web` section in the `web.config` file. Here is an example of the `customErrors` section:

```
<customErrors mode="RemoteOnly" defaultRedirect="ErrorPage.aspx">
    <error statusCode="403" redirect="NoAccess.htm" />
```

```
            <error statusCode="404" redirect="FileNotFound.htm" />
        </customErrors>
```

Notice the `mode` attribute. The available values for mode are `"RemoteOnly"`, `"On"`, and `"Off"`. Setting this to `"RemoteOnly"` tells IIS to redirect to page set in the `defaultRedirect` attribute for unhandled exceptions to remote clients. If you were to run the application on the local host, you would see the generic ASP.NET error page instead of `ErrorPage.aspx`, which is what a client would see. This ensures that unintentional information is never sent back to the user. If an exception were thrown indicating that a SQL login was wrong, and the default exception page were shown to users, they would see the connection string that was used to try to connect — not a good thing. If the value is set to `"On"`, then both the remote clients and the local user would be redirected to the page that is set in the `default-Redirect` attribute. If no `defaultRedirect` page exists, then the generic ASP.NET page is displayed. If the value is set to `"Off"`, then the generic ASP.NET error page is displayed to the clients and the local user.

This sounds great, no? If you were to set the `defaultRedirect` page in the `web.config` file and add event logging and e-mailing code in the `Page_Load` event of the `defaultRedirect` page, then everything should work great, right? Well, it gets tricky. Remove the code in the `Application_Error` and `Page_Error` event handlers and add it to the `Page_Load` event in the code-behind of the page set in the `defaultRedirect` attribute. Then create an exception in your application. `Server.GetLastError()` now returns null, so the exception isn't bubbled up to this page. What you need to do is handle the exception in the `Application_Error` or `Page_Error` event handlers and remove the `Response.Redirect` line. The redirect is handled by the `web.config` settings. If an error occurs when writing to the event log, the user will still be redirected to the `ErrorPage.aspx` page instead of the default ASP.NET error page; but if an error occurred in the `ErrorPage.aspx` page, the user would see the default ASP.NET error page, so it is best to keep this page clean — with only HTML — so the user always sees this page.

You can override the redirect page in each specific page in your application by setting the `Page.ErrorPage` property. This property expects a string of the name of the page that the user should be redirected to in the event of an unhandled exception on the page.

You can also configure specific errors in the `customErrors` section to handle IIS errors such as page not found or no access errors. This is done by adding an error element in the `customErrors` section and setting the `statusCode` and `redirect` attributes. This is similar to how you can trap specific exceptions in the IIS property page on the virtual directory. The `statusCode` attribute is the number for the error that IIS throws, and the `redirect` attribute is the page you want to display.

Health Monitoring

When .NET 2.0 came out, a new feature called *Health Monitoring* was included. It enabled developers to monitor certain events that are fired during the life of an application. Some of the events that can be monitored are application start, application shutdown, ASP.NET authentication failures, successful authentication events, and errors. You can also create your own custom events that can be monitored as well. You can configure your application to log these events to the event log, save them to a SQL server database, pass them to WMI, e-mail them to a user, or pass them to the page's tracing system. The objects that handle the logging, e-mailing, and so on are called *providers*. You can hook more than one provider to an event — for example, an event could be logged to the event log and e-mailed to a user. You associate providers with events by using rules in the `web.config` file.

By default, exceptions are logged to the event log. That is why in the previous section you saw two events logged to the event log when an exception was caught in the `Application_Error` event. If you want to turn the default event logging off, you can add the following section to the `system.web` section of your `web.config` file:

```
<healthMonitoring enabled="false"></healthMonitoring>
```

If you plan to use the health monitoring features in .NET, you simply set the `enabled` attribute to true. To log any unhandled exception to the event log, first add the `healthMonitoring` section to your `web.config` file under the `system.web` tags. Next, define the event that you would like to listen for. In this case, it is anytime an unhandled exception occurs:

```
<eventMappings>
    <clear />
    <add name="Unhandled Exceptions"
        type="System.Web.Management.WebBaseErrorEvent" />
</eventMappings>
```

The `eventMappings` section defines all the events you would like to listen for. You then add these events using the `add` tag. The `name` attribute is just a user-friendly name to associate with the event; it can be anything you choose. The `type` attribute is what is important. In this case, we are telling the health monitoring system to listen for all event-based classes that derive from the `WebBaseErrorEvent` class. Other event classes that can be mapped include the following:

❑ `WebApplicationLifetimeEvent` — Fired for events that occur during the lifetime of an application, such as startup and shutdown

❑ `WebAuthenticationFailureAuditEvent` — Fired when ASP.NET authentication fails

❑ `WebAuthenticationSuccessAuditEvent` — Fired when a successful authentication occurs

❑ `WebFailureAuditEvent` — Fired when security failures occur

❑ `WebRequestErrorEvent` — Fired when a web request error occurs

❑ `WebSuccessAuditEvent` — Fired when successful security events occur

❑ `WebViewStatFailureAuditEvent` — Fired when view state failure occurs

In addition to these events, you can create your own events by deriving from the base classes defined in the `System.Web.Management` namespace. The bases classes are as follows:

❑ `WebAuditEvent` — Base class for all health-monitoring audit events

❑ `WebBaseErrorEvent` — Base class for all health-monitoring error events

❑ `WebBaseEvent` — Base class for all health-monitoring events

❑ `WebManagementEvent` — Base class for application and process health-monitoring events

❑ `WebRequestEvent` — Base class for web request health-monitoring events

The next step is to define the provider that you would like to use for this event. This is defined in the `providers` section:

```
<providers>
    <clear />
    <add name="EventLogProvider"
        type="System.Web.Management.EventLogWebEventProvider" />
</providers>
```

Again, the `name` attribute is just a user-friendly name for the provider. The `type` attribute specifies that this is the `EventLogWebEventProvider`. The providers are in the `System.Web.Management` namespace. Other providers are as follows:

❑   `SqlWebEventProvider` — Used to log events to a SQL Server database

❑   `WmiWebEventProvider` — Used to pass events to the WMI and convert them to WMI events

❑   `SimpleMailEventProvider` — Used to send an e-mail message when an event is fired

❑   `TemplatedMailEventProvider` — Used to send an e-mail that has a template defined to format the e-mail

❑   `TraceWebEventProvider` — Used to pass data to the ASP.NET page-tracing system

You can create your own providers by inheriting from the `WebEventProvider` or `BufferedWebEvent Provider`. An example of a custom provider would be if you wanted to write to a text file.

The next step is to associate the event with the provider by using the `rules` section:

```
<rules>
 <clear />
 <add name="Unhandled Exceptions Rule"
      eventName="Unhandled Exceptions"
      provider="EventLogProvider"
      profile="Default"
      minInstances="1"
      maxLimit="Infinite"
      minInterval="00:00:00" />
</rules>
```

The `eventName` attribute should map to the name that was given to the event. The `provider` attribute should map to the name that was given to the provider. The `minInstances` attribute denotes the number of times this event can occur before a notification is sent. Here it is set to 1, so the first time the event happens it will be logged. The `maxLimit` attribute denotes the maximum number of times the event can happen before notifications stop. Setting this to Infinite will stop at 2,147,483,647. The `minInterval` attribute is the minimum time between two events that will cause a second event to be logged. Setting this to 00:00:00 will cause all events to be fired. If you set this to 00:01:00, the minimum time between two events being logged would be one minute.

That's all you have to do to log exceptions to the event log. It isn't so fancy here because this is turned on by default, but you can see the power in the Health Monitoring framework by the number of options you have for events and providers; and because you can create your own events or providers, the possibilities are limitless.

To mimic what you did in the `Application_Error` event handler, you need to add e-mail support for exceptions. To enable e-mailing capabilities for the exceptions, add another provider tag for the `SimpleMailWebEventProvider` and specify any properties for the message to be sent:

```
<add name="SimpleMailProvider"
     type="System.Web.Management.SimpleMailWebEventProvider"
     from="admin@V2Enterprises.com"
     to="varallov@V2Enterprises.com"
     cc="someone@V2Enterprises.com"
     bcc="someone@V2Enterprises.com"
     bodyHeader="Warning!"
     bodyFooter="Please investigate ASAP."
     subjectPrefix="Action required."
     buffer="true"
     bufferMode="Critical Notification" />
```

Associate this provider by adding a new rule:

```
<add name="Unhandled Exceptions Notifications Rule"
     eventName="Unhandled Exceptions"
     provider="SimpleMailProvider"
     profile="Default"
     minInstances="1"
     maxLimit="Infinite"
     minInterval="00:00:00" />
```

Finally, add a section to the `web.config` that specifies the SMTP server settings. This is its own section under the `configuration` section in the `web.config` file:

```
<system.net>
  <mailSettings>
    <smtp deliveryMethod="PickupDirectoryFromIis">
      <network defaultCredentials="true" host="127.0.0.1" />
    </smtp>
  </mailSettings>
</system.net>
```

Change these settings to your appropriate SMTP server.

If you run the program and cause an exception, the exception will be logged in the event log and an e-mail will be sent. The text of the e-mail is as follows:

```
Warning!
** Summary **
---------------
This message contains events 1 to 1 from the total of 1 events scheduled for this
notification. There were 0 events left in the buffer at the beginning of this
notification.
```

```
** Application Information **
---------------
Application domain: /LM/W3SVC/1/Root/PaidTimeOff-8-128568561945730250
Trust level: Full
Application Virtual Path: /PaidTimeOff
Application Path: C:\Wrox\EnterpriseAppDev\PaidTimeOffUI\
Machine name: VARALLO1


** Events **
---------------
Event code: 3005
Event message: An unhandled exception has occurred.
Event time: 6/2/2008 12:56:38 AM
Event time (UTC): 6/2/2008 4:56:38 AM
Event ID: 45519bda1fdc4c16b9a8ebb64a07f733
Event sequence: 4
Event occurrence: 1
Event detail code: 0

Process information:
    Process ID: 5804
    Process name: aspnet_wp.exe
    Account name: VARALLO1\ASPNET

Exception information:
    Exception type: System.Exception
    Exception message: Test

Request information:
    Request URL: http://localhost/PaidTimeOff/Default.aspx
    Request path: /PaidTimeOff/Default.aspx
    User host address: 127.0.0.1
    User: VARALLO1\VaralloV
    Is authenticated: True
    Authentication Type: Negotiate
    Thread account name: VARALLO1\ASPNET

Thread information:
    Thread ID: 1
    Thread account name: VARALLO1\ASPNET
    Is impersonating: False
    Stack trace:    at _Default.Page_Load(Object sender, EventArgs e) in c:\Wrox
EnterpriseAppDev\PaidTimeOffUI\Default.aspx.cs:line 18
    at System.Web.Util.CalliHelper.EventArgFunctionCaller(IntPtr fp, Object o,
Object t, EventArgs e)
    at System.Web.Util.CalliEventHandlerDelegateProxy.Callback(Object sender,
EventArgs e)
    at System.Web.UI.Control.OnLoad(EventArgs e)
    at System.Web.UI.Control.LoadRecursive()
    at System.Web.UI.Page.ProcessRequestMain(Boolean includeStagesBeforeAsyncPoint,
Boolean includeStagesAfterAsyncPoint)


---------------
Please investigate ASAP.
```

As you can see, this is quite simple to set up and it gives you quite a bit of flexibility, as you can create your own events and providers.

Enterprise Application Blocks

The Enterprise Application Blocks are a set of libraries that Microsoft created to give programmers a head start on common tasks, and to show off some of the latest language enhancements in .NET. Version 4 of the EAB was released in May 2008 and can be found at http://msdn.microsoft.com/en-us/library/cc467894.aspx. Nine applications blocks are included with this release:

❑ **Caching Application Block** — Provides functionality for adding caching to your application.

❑ **Cryptography Application Block** — Provides functionality for adding hashing and symmetric encryption to your application.

❑ **Data Access Application Block** — Wraps common logic for communicating with a database. This is different from the SQLHelper class discussed in Chapter 2 and has much more functionality.

❑ **Exception Handling Application Block** — Provides functionality for handling exceptions by creating policies in configuration files, and interacts with the Logging Application Block to communicate exceptions.

❑ **Logging Application Block** — Provides functionality to log data to the event log, text files, XML files, or e-mail.

❑ **Policy Injection Application Block** — Provides functionality to create interception policies for logging, caching, exception handling, and validation. This block interacts with the other application blocks, and you can create your own custom handlers.

❑ **Security Application Block** — Provides functionality for authorization-related functionality and caching users' authentication data.

❑ **Unity Application Block** — This is a dependency injection container with support for constructor, property, and method call injection.

❑ **Validation Application Block** — A set of classes that provides functionality for validating .NET Framework data types.

An entire book could be written about all nine application blocks, but this book covers only two of them: the exception handling and logging application blocks. Probably the easiest way to learn how these blocks work is to use the Quick Start samples that are installed by the Enterprise Library Source Code Installer. If you choose all the default settings during installation, you'll find all the Quick Start examples in the c:\EntLib4Src\Quick Starts folder. The ExceptionHandling\CS subfolder has two solution files: ExceptionHandlingBasicQuickStart.sln and ExceptionHanldingWithLoggingQuickStart.sln. Open the ExceptionHandlingWithLoggingQuickStart solution. This solution provides a sample demonstrating how to log an exception to the event log, change the message, and display the changed method to the user. There are six projects in this solution. The ExceptionHandlingWithLogging QuickStart is a WinForms application that has one form with buttons that call into the Exception HandlingQuickStart.BusinessLayer, which raises exceptions. The other four projects are the components in the Enterprise Library.

The Exception Handling Application block enables you to define how you want to handle all or specific exceptions by adding entries to the app.config or web.config files, depending on the type of project.

Because the `QuickStart` is a WinForms app, these settings are in the `App.config` file. Open this file and you'll see a lot of entries. When you first start using the Enterprise Blocks, this can seem intimidating, so Microsoft provides a tool that you can use to edit the configuration file with a user interface. Access the tool either by right-clicking on the file and selecting Edit Enterprise Library Configuration or by running the Enterprise Library Configuration program located in the Enterprise Library program group folder. The solution section in this chapter uses the tool to edit the file, but for now walk through the file manually so you get an understanding of what the tool is doing behind the scenes.

The first section to look at is `exceptionHandling`. Notice that the first element in the `exception Handling` section is the `exceptionPolicies`. Policies are what you use to define how to handle exceptions differently. This sample has three policies defined: the Global Policy, the Log Only Policy, and the Notify Policy. Inside each policy is the `exceptionTypes` section, which lists the exception types that the policy should handle. The Global Policy handles the generic exception type:

```
<exceptionTypes>
    <add name="Exception" type="System.Exception, mscorlib, Version=2.0.0.0,
        Culture=neutral, PublicKeyToken=b77a5c561934e089"
        postHandlingAction="None">
```

The Notify Policy handles a specific exception called the `BusinessLayerException`, which is a custom exception defined in the `ExceptionHandlerQuickStart.BusinessLayer` project. The `type` attribute defines the fully qualified name of the exception you are trying to handle. The `postHandlingAction` attribute determines what should be done after the exception is handled. In the Global Policy this is set to none, but in the Notify Policy this is set to `ThrowNewException`, which tells the application block to throw another exception after it has been handled.

Once you define the exceptions to be handled, you can define the classes that should handle the exception. This is done in the `exceptionHandlers` section. The Global Policy states to use the type called `AppMessageExceptionHandler`, which is defined in the `ExceptionHandlingQuickStart` application. This simply displays a message box to the user:

```
<exceptionHandlers>
    <add name="Application Message Handler"
        type="ExceptionHandlingQuickStart.AppMessageExceptionHandler,
            ExceptionHandlingWithLoggingQuickStart"/>
</exceptionHandlers>
```

The Notify Policy has two handlers:

```
<exceptionHandlers>
    <add logCategory="Default Category"
        eventId="100" severity="Error"
        title="Enterprise Library Exception Handling" priority="0"
        formatterType="Microsoft.Practices.EnterpriseLibrary.ExceptionHandling.Tex
            tExceptionFormatter, Microsoft.Practices.EnterpriseLibrary.Exception
            Handling"
        name="Logging Handler"
        type="Microsoft.Practices.EnterpriseLibrary.ExceptionHandling.Logging.Logg
            ingExceptionHandler, Microsoft.Practices.EnterpriseLibrary.Exception
            Handling.Logging"
    />
    <add name="Replace Handler"
```

```
                    type="Microsoft.Practices.EnterpriseLibrary.ExceptionHandling.ReplaceHandl
                        er, Microsoft.Practices.EnterpriseLibrary.ExceptionHandling"
                    exceptionMessage="An error occurred while processing your request. Please
                        contact technical support using the following identifier:
                        {handlingInstanceID}"
                    replaceExceptionType="System.ApplicationException, mscorlib,
                        Version=2.0.0.0, Culture=neutral, PublicKeyToken=b77a5c561934e089"
        />
    </exceptionHandlers>
```

The first handler uses the LoggingExceptionHandler type in the Microsoft.Practices.Enterprise Library.ExceptionHandling namespace. This takes care of logging the message to the event log. You use attributes to define the event ID, severity, title, and other properties associated with the event log entry. The second handler is a ReplaceHandler, which tells the application to replace the original exception with a new exception that has a different message. The new message is defined in the exceptionMessage attribute. The ReplaceHandler is one of the core classes installed with the ExceptionHandling block.

Notice that a type is defined in the configuration file by its fully qualified name. The application dynamically creates instances of these types to handle the exceptions, but you must either use a type that is already defined in the application block or create a custom handler. The real magic happens in the classes that are defined in the type attribute.

The next section in the configuration file defines the logging configuration. There are five subsections in the logging configuration: logFilters, categorySources, specialSources, listeners, and formatters. The order of these subsections doesn't matter in the configuration file, and it is easier to start by explaining what the formatters section does. The formatters define how the message should be displayed in the event log, e-mail message, text file, or whatever output source you create on your own. A TextFormatter type converts the message to a string and uses the template attribute to define what should be placed in the string:

```
<formatters>
    <add name="Default Formatter"
        type="Microsoft.Practices.EnterpriseLibrary.Logging.Formatters.TextFormatter,
            Microsoft.Practices.EnterpriseLibrary.Logging"
        template="Timestamp: {timestamp}
                    Message: {message}
                    Category: {category}
                    Priority: {priority}
                    EventId: {eventid}
                    Severity: {severity}
                    Title:{title}
                    Machine: {machine}
                    Application Domain: {appDomain}
                    Process Id: {processId}
                    Process Name: {processName}
                    Win32 Thread Id: {win32ThreadId}
                    Thread Name: {threadName}
                    Extended Properties: {dictionary({key} - {value}
                    )}"
    />
```

Notice that the template attribute uses a token-based string; the logging block will replace the tokens defined in curly braces ({}) with a dynamic value. If you wanted to add or subtract text from the message, then you would change it here. Other formatters are the `BinaryLogFormatter` and the `XmlLog Formatter`, but you can also create your own formatter.

Once you have a formatter, you can define the "listeners" that are used to actually listen for certain events, and either e-mail, write to a file, or add to the event log:

```
<listeners>
    <add name="Event Log Destination"
        type="Microsoft.Practices.EnterpriseLibrary.Logging.TraceListeners.Formatt
            edEventLogTraceListener, Microsoft.Practices.EnterpriseLibrary
            .Logging"
        listenerDataType="Microsoft.Practices.EnterpriseLibrary.Logging.Configurat
                ion.FormattedEventLogTraceListenerData,
                Microsoft.Practices.EnterpriseLibrary.Logging"
        source ="Enterprise Library Logging"
      formatter="Default Formatter"
    />
    <add name="Flat File Destination"
        type="Microsoft.Practices.EnterpriseLibrary.Logging.TraceListeners.FlatFil
            eTraceListener, Microsoft.Practices.EnterpriseLibrary.Logging"
        listenerDataType="Microsoft.Practices.EnterpriseLibrary.Logging.Configurat
                ion.FlatFileTraceListenerData, Microsoft.Practices.Enter
                priseLibrary.Logging"
        fileName ="trace.log"
    />
</listeners>
```

The two listeners used in this example are the `FormattedEventLogTraceListenerData` and the `Flat FileTraceListenerData` types. Their names are self-explanatory. You use attributes for each listener to define how the listeners behave. For example, the `fileName` attribute for the Flat File Destination listener is set to `trace.log`, which is the name of the file to which the listener should write.

The next step is to define the sources, which can be either a category source or a special source. Notice that the Log Only Policy and Notify Policy specify a `logCategory` attribute when adding a handler. The source is used to hook a listener to the event you are listening for. You can use one or more listeners for any one source. The special sources, predefined by the application block, are "All Events," "Logging Errors & Warnings," and "Unprocessed Category." The Logging Errors & Warnings can be used for exceptions that happen while in the Logging Application block.

The `logFilters` section is used to filter categories or priorities assigned to categories. You can entirely enable or disable logging based on the filters. To see how all of these pieces fit together, run the solution; you should see the screen shown in Figure 5-3.

Put a breakpoint in the `notifyUserButton_Click` event handler and then click the "Notify the user when an exception occurs" button. The first part of the event handler just creates a string that will be displayed to the user in the text box on the screen. The `AppService` is just a dummy class in the business layer that will throw an error:

```
AppService svc = new AppService();
svc.ProcessAndNotify();
```

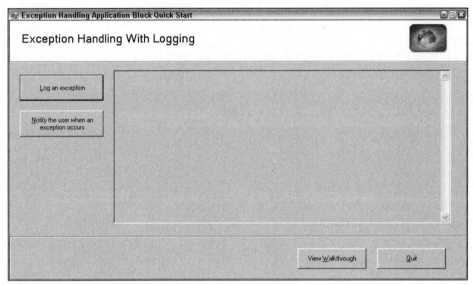

Figure 5-3

The `ProcessAndNotify` method throws a `BusinessLayerException`, which is caught in the try-catch block. Remember that the Notify Policy in the configuration file was set up to handle the `BusinessLayerException` type:

```
public void ProcessAndNotify()
{
    try
    {
        ProcessD();
    }
    catch(Exception ex)
    {
    // Invoke our policy that is responsible for making sure no secure information
    // gets out of our layer.
        bool rethrow = ExceptionPolicy.HandleException(ex, "Notify Policy");

        if (rethrow)
    {
            throw;
        }
    }
}
```

The `catch` block calls the `HandleException` method of the `ExceptionPolicy` object. The `Exception Policy` object is part of the Exception Handling Application block and it knows how to read the configuration file and create the correct instances of the handlers. Stepping through this code might give you a headache, but take some aspirin and keep moving. Once the policy is created, the handlers for the policy are created and executed. The first handler for the Notify Policy is the `LoggingException Handler`, which creates the message that is to be logged in the event log. This is done in the `Create Message` method:

```
private string CreateMessage(Exception exception, Guid handlingInstanceID)
{
    StringWriter writer = null;
    StringBuilder stringBuilder = null;
    try
    {
        writer = CreateStringWriter();
        writer.WriteLine("HandlingInstanceID: {0}", handlingInstanceID.ToString());
        ExceptionFormatter formatter = CreateFormatter(writer, exception);
        formatter.Format();
        stringBuilder = writer.GetStringBuilder();
    }
    finally
    {
        if (writer != null)
        {
        writer.Close();
        }
    }

    return stringBuilder.ToString();
}
```

Notice the code is creating an `ExceptionFormatter` object. In this case, it is creating the `Text ExceptionFormatter` type, which was defined in the `formatterType` for this handler in the configuration file. The formatter has a `Format` method that creates the text string that should be written to the log. This string is then passed back to the `HandleException` method and then passed to the `WriteToLog` method. This method creates a `LogEntry` object that is eventually used to write to the event log:

```
protected virtual void WriteToLog(string logMessage, IDictionary exceptionData)
{
    LogEntry entry = new LogEntry(
        logMessage,
        logCategory,
        minimumPriority,
        eventId,
        severity,
        defaultTitle,
        null);

    foreach (DictionaryEntry dataEntry in exceptionData)
    {
        if (dataEntry.Key is string)
        {
            entry.ExtendedProperties.Add(dataEntry.Key as string, dataEntry.Value);
        }
    }
```

```
        if (useDefaultLogger)
        {
            Logger.Write(entry);
        }
        else
        {
            this.logWriter.Write(entry);
        }
    }
```

The code then loops back around and creates an instance of the `ReplaceHandler` type, as this was defined as the second handler in the configuration file. This will replace the original message with the message defined in the configuration file. Note that the event log has the original message but the user will actually see the message defined in the configuration file. Because the policy has a `postHandling` `Action` set to `ThrowNewException`, this `ExceptionPolicy` object will throw this new error back to the caller, which is the click event; and then this new exception will be handled by the Global Policy defined as the policy for the exceptions that occur in the WinForms application.

The result of all this? The user sees the message shown in Figure 5-4.

Figure 5-4

The event log will contain everything that appears in Figure 5-5.

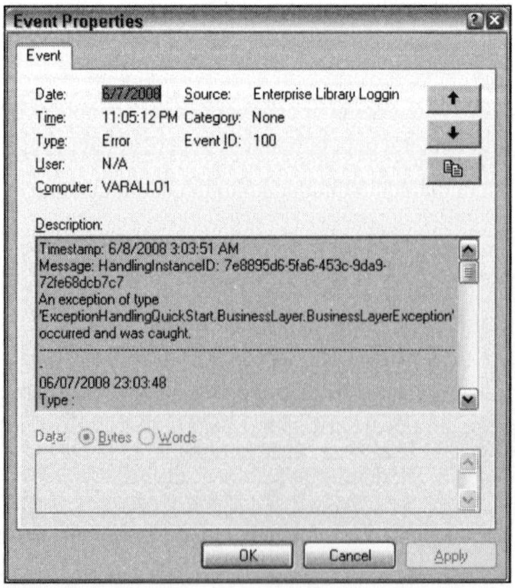

Figure 5-5

The event log contains much more detail about the exception than users need to know about. As the developer, you should be able to trace what happened in the event log, but users don't need to know all the gory details.

In fact, you don't really have to know what is going on behind the scenes if you don't want to. The advantage of the application blocks over the Health Monitoring feature is that you have the source code and can see exactly what is going on. That is why this solution uses the Exception Handling Application block. The next section puts together all the pieces defined so far to set up the exception handling in the `PaidTimeOff` solution.

Solution

The goals of exception handling in this application are quite simple:

- ❑ All exceptions should be caught and displayed to the user in one page. Details about the exception should not be shown to users.

- ❑ The system should automatically send an e-mail with details about the exception that occurred, the user who caused the exception, and the call stack.

- ❑ The system should log the details of the exception to the event log in case the e-mail failed to be sent.

- ❑ The system should allow an administrator to control who receives an e-mail without having to recompile and deploy the application.

Start by defining the common page that will be used to show users a message:

1. Add a new page to the `PaidTimeOffUI` project that uses the `PaidTimeOff` master page and name it `ErrorPage.aspx`. Only text should be displayed to users, so we won't put any code in this page that could potentially cause another error to occur because that would make it difficult to track down the original error. You can add text that says something to the effect that a problem has occurred and that the appropriate personnel have been notified. Since this page uses the `PaidTimeOff` master page, change the code-behind so the partial class inherits from `BasePage`, and then override the `MenuItemName` method. Change this method so it returns "Home." This will display the page with the Home tab highlighted.

2. Turn custom error handling on in the `web.config` file:

```
<customErrors mode="RemoteOnly" defaultRedirect="ErrorPage.aspx">
</customErrors>
```

Since the mode is set to RemoteOnly, you will see the default .NET error page while developing the application; but when you deploy this to a test or production server, users will see the `ErrorPage.aspx` page. If you want to see what the custom error page looks like, you can change the mode to On.

3. Configure the solution to use the Enterprise Application Blocks Version 4. You could include the project source code in the solution for each application block, but it's easier to just reference the DLLs. The correct DLLs to reference are installed in the `Program Files\Microsoft Enterprise Library 4.0 - May 2008\bin` folder. The following DLLs need to be referenced:

   ❑ Microsoft.Practices.EnterpriseLibrary.Common

   ❑ Microsoft.Practices.EnterpriseLibrary.ExceptionHandling

   ❑ Microsoft.Practices.EnterpriseLibrary.ExceptionHandling.Logging

   ❑ Microsoft.Practices.EnterpriseLibrary.Logging

   ❑ Microsoft.Practices.ObjectBuilder2

   The `Common` and `ObjectBuilder2` namespaces contain the common logic that is needed for all application blocks. The `Logging` namespace contains the classes that are needed to turn logging on. In our project, we use the event log to save the exception information, and e-mail to notify the appropriate personnel that an exception occurred. The `ExceptionHandling` and `ExceptionHandling.Logging` namespaces contain the necessary classes to handle the exceptions and log them.

4. Configure the exception handling in the `web.config` file. Right-click on your `web.config` file and select Edit Enterprise Library Configuration from the pop-up menu. This opens the graphical tool that was installed when you installed the Enterprise Application Block (see Figure 5-6).

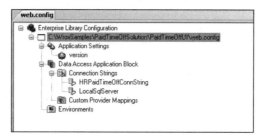

Figure 5-6

Right-click on the `web.config` node and select New ➪ Logging Application Block from the pop-up menu. This will add a Logging Application Block node with numerous child nodes, as shown in Figure 5-7.

By default, an event log trace listener is added to the Trace Listeners. An e-mail trace listener must be added to enable e-mailing. Right-click on the Trace Listeners folder and select New ➪ Email Trace Listener. This will add the Email TraceListener node. Left-click on the Email TraceListener node and then click the Properties window in Visual Studio.

This enables you to specify the correct parameters for the e-mail configuration. Click on the `Formatter` property and then select Text Formatter from the drop-down list. Next, set the `FromAddress` property to an account that you want as the sender. You can change the SmtpPort or SmtpServer to your appropriate e-mail server settings. For SMTP, 25 is the normal port, so check with your network administrators before changing this. By default, the e-mail trace listener will add the word "Error" in the subject line of the e-mail. You can use the `SubjectLineEnder` and `SubjectLineStarter` properties to add text after or before the word "Error" in the subject line. Set the `SubjectLineEnder` property to Paid Time Off, and the `SubjectLineStarter` to Attention Needed. Next, set the ToAddress to your e-mail address. You can leave TraceOutputOptions at None.

Figure 5-7

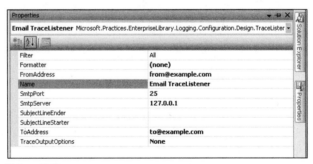

Figure 5-8

Now that you have an e-mail trace listener, you have to set up the exception handling block to use it. Right-click on the `web.config` node again and select New ⇨ Exception Handling Application Block from the pop-up menu. This will add the Exception Handling Application Block node above the Logging Application Block node (see Figure 5-9).

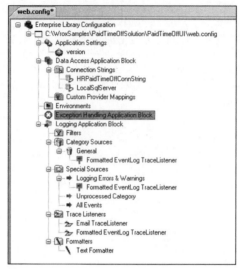

Figure 5-9

Right-click on the Exception Handling Application Block node and select New ⇨ Exception Policy from the pop-up menu. Rename the policy node to "**Global Policy.**" Right-click on this node and select New-Exception Type from the pop-up menu. A window will appear that lists all exception types defined in this project or any referenced projects. This enables you to handle different errors with different handlers (see Figure 5-10).

Because this is the all-purpose exception handler, select the default exception type and click OK. Now you have to associate the logging handler to log the message to the event log. Right-click on the Exception Node and select New ⇨ Logging Handler. Left-click on the Logging Handler node and then open the Properties window. When you click the `FormatterType` property, a button with an ellipse will appear. Click this button, select TextExceptionFormatter, and click the OK button (see Figure 5-11).

Click the `LogCategory` property and select General from the drop-down list. You can leave all the other properties at their default value.

To turn the e-mail notifications on, right-click on the Logging Application Block\Special Source\ All Events node and select New ⇨ Trace Listener Reference from the pop-up menu. Left-click on the newly added Trace Listener Reference node and view its properties. Change the `ReferencedTrace Listener` property to e-mail trace listener and save the `web.config` file. That's all you have to do in the `web.config` file. Now you can add the code to the application to use the new Global Policy.

Add a `Global.asax` file to the application, and then add an `Import` directive to reference the `Exception Handling` namespace:

```
<%@ Import Namespace="Microsoft.Practices.EnterpriseLibrary.ExceptionHandling" %>
```

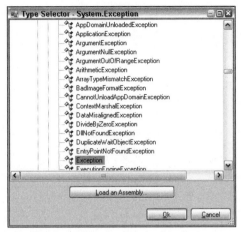

Figure 5-10

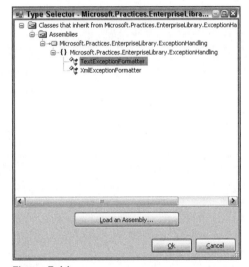

Figure 5-11

In the `Application_Error` event handler, add the following code:

```
void Application_Error(object sender, EventArgs e)
{
    // Code that runs when an unhandled error occurs
    ExceptionPolicy.HandleException(Server.GetLastError(), "Global Policy");
}
```

This will call the static method `HandleException` and pass in the last error, telling the application block to use the "Global Policy" defined in the `web.config` file. This must match the name of the policy that was defined earlier when setting up the `web.config` file.

Test this by throwing a `DivisionByZeroException` in the page load of the `Default.aspx` page:

```
throw new DivideByZeroException();
```

Now run the application and make sure the `Default.aspx` page is the startup page. Since the `web.config` file set the custom errors mode to `RemoteOnly`, you should get the default .NET error page, which looks like Figure 5-12.

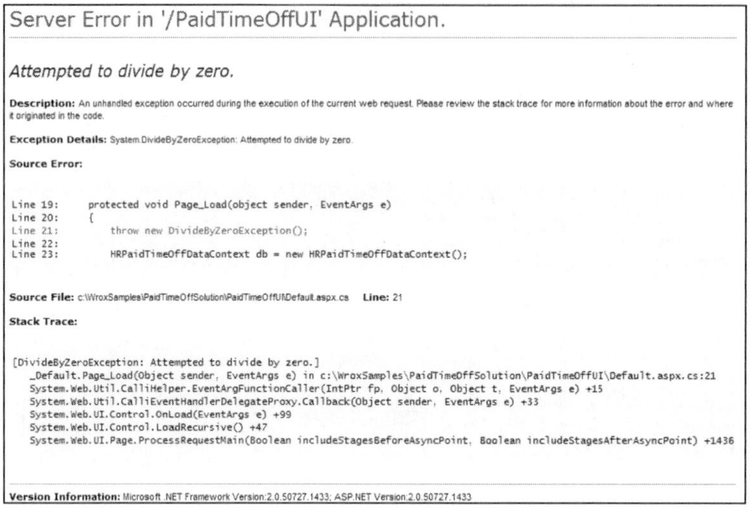

Figure 5-12

Now look at the event log. There should be two new entries in the Application event log. One has a source of ASP.NET 2.0.50727.0 and the other has a source of Enterprise Library Logging. If you double-click on the latter, you will see all the information about the exception (see Figure 5-13).

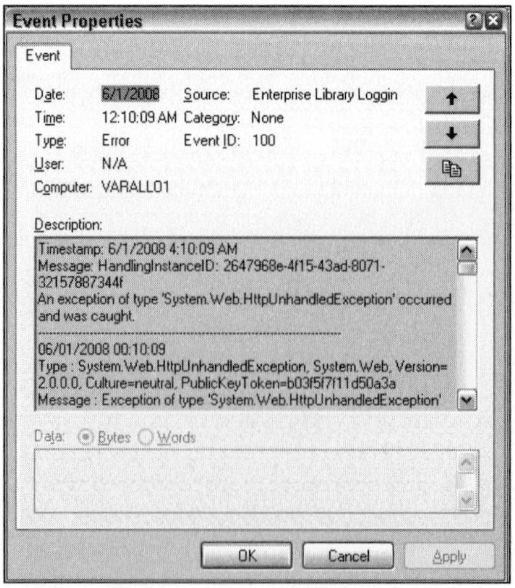

Figure 5-13

You should also receive an e-mail with exception details:

```
Timestamp: 6/1/2008 4:15:29 AM
Message: HandlingInstanceID: f4f49a2f-87d1-4228-8c11-ab6bb5c965a5
An exception of type 'System.Web.HttpUnhandledException' occurred and was caught.
---------------------------------------------------------------------------
06/01/2008 00:15:29
Type : System.Web.HttpUnhandledException, System.Web, Version=2.0.0.0,
Culture=neutral, PublicKeyToken=b03f5f7f11d50a3a
Message : Exception of type 'System.Web.HttpUnhandledException' was thrown.
Source : System.Web
Help link :
ErrorCode : -2147467259
Data : System.Collections.ListDictionaryInternal
TargetSite : Boolean HandleError(System.Exception)
Stack Trace :    at System.Web.UI.Page.HandleError(Exception e)
   at System.Web.UI.Page.ProcessRequestMain(Boolean includeStagesBeforeAsyncPoint,
Boolean includeStagesAfterAsyncPoint)
   at System.Web.UI.Page.ProcessRequest(Boolean includeStagesBeforeAsyncPoint,
Boolean includeStagesAfterAsyncPoint)
   at System.Web.UI.Page.ProcessRequest()
   at System.Web.UI.Page.ProcessRequestWithNoAssert(HttpContext context)
   at System.Web.UI.Page.ProcessRequest(HttpContext context)
   at ASP.default_aspx.ProcessRequest(HttpContext context) in c:\WINDOWS\Microsoft.
NET\Framework\v2.0.50727\Temporary ASP.NET Files\paidtimeoffui\a276ab9f\faf86814\
App_Web_45zvmtcq.2.cs:line 0
   at System.Web.HttpApplication.CallHandlerExecutionStep.System.Web.
HttpApplication.IExecutionStep.Execute()
   at System.Web.HttpApplication.ExecuteStep(IExecutionStep step, Boolean&
completedSynchronously)


Additional Info:

MachineName : VARALLO1
TimeStamp : 6/1/2008 4:15:29 AM
FullName : Microsoft.Practices.EnterpriseLibrary.ExceptionHandling,
Version=4.0.0.0, Culture=neutral, PublicKeyToken=31bf3856ad364e35
AppDomainName : /LM/W3SVC/1/Root/PaidTimeOffUI-35-128567673231771020
ThreadIdentity : VARALLO1\VaralloV
WindowsIdentity : VARALLO1\ASPNET
Inner Exception
---------------
Type : System.DivideByZeroException, mscorlib, Version=2.0.0.0, Culture=neutral,
PublicKeyToken=b77a5c561934e089
Message : Attempted to divide by zero.
Source : App_Web_45zvmtcq
Help link :
Data : System.Collections.ListDictionaryInternal
TargetSite : Void Page_Load(System.Object, System.EventArgs)
Stack Trace :    at _Default.Page_Load(Object sender, EventArgs e) in c:\
WroxSamples\PaidTimeOffSolution\PaidTimeOffUI\Default.aspx.cs:line 21
   at System.Web.Util.CalliHelper.EventArgFunctionCaller(IntPtr fp, Object o,
Object t, EventArgs e)
   at System.Web.Util.CalliEventHandlerDelegateProxy.Callback(Object sender,
EventArgs e)
```

```
    at System.Web.UI.Control.OnLoad(EventArgs e)
    at System.Web.UI.Control.LoadRecursive()
    at System.Web.UI.Page.ProcessRequestMain(Boolean includeStagesBeforeAsyncPoint,
Boolean includeStagesAfterAsyncPoint)


Category: General
Priority: 0
EventId: 100
Severity: Error
Title:Enterprise Library Exception Handling
Machine: VARALLO1
Application Domain: /LM/W3SVC/1/Root/PaidTimeOffUI-35-128567673231771020
Process Id: 1220
Process Name: C:\WINDOWS\Microsoft.NET\Framework\v2.0.50727\aspnet_wp.exe
Win32 Thread Id: 6416
Thread Name:
Extended Properties:
```

By default, this text of the e-mail and the event log is quite verbose. You can control the content of this message by changing the template used by the `TextFormatter`. Open your `web.config` file again with the Enterprise Library Configuration tool. Click the TextFormatter node at the bottom of the tree to view it properties. Select the `Template` property and click the ellipse button. This opens the Template Editor window (see Figure 5-14).

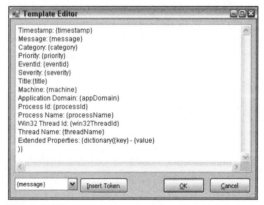

Figure 5-14

The template is token-based, and the application block will search and replace the text of the message based on the tokens defined in the template. If you remove the tokens, they will not be added to the e-mail. You're now ready to capture any exceptions in this application and fill up your e-mail inbox, or some intern's inbox, with every exception that occurred in this application.

Summary

This chapter reviewed the options available for handling exceptions in a .NET application. It used the Microsoft Enterprise Application blocks to implement exception handling, logging, and e-mailing. Typically, you set this up once and never touch it again, but you do have the flexibility to add or change how exceptions are handled after the project is deployed.

Remember these key points when setting up exception handling:

- ❏ For display to users, add a common page that hides the details of the exception; and give users a friendly message (as friendly as an error message can be).

- ❏ Add the `customErrors` section to the `web.config` file, setting the mode to RemoteOnly and the `defaultRedirect` to the custom error page.

- ❏ Add the appropriate references to the Microsoft Application Blocks.

- ❏ Configure the `web.config` file using the Enterprise Library Configuration tool.

- ❏ Add a Logging Application Block section to the `web.config` file and add an e-mail trace listener. Hook the All Events special source to use the e-mail trace listener.

- ❏ Add an Exception Handling Block section to the `web.config` file and add a new policy that catches the generic exception type, and add a logging handler to the exception type.

- ❏ Add a `Global.asax` file to the project and add the `ExceptionPolicy.Handle Exception (Server.GetLastError(), "Global Policy");` line to the `Application_Error` event.

- ❏ Customize the error message by editing the `Template` property of the TextFormatter node in the `web.config` file.

The previous four chapters have defined the architecture for the `PaidTimeOffSolution` example. Now its time to start using this architecture to build the functionality that Mary requested. You remember Mary, right? She's the user who is driving the requirements and who will be the ultimate judge of whether you get a raise this year. The next chapter builds the role-based security model that enables Mary or anyone with the correct permissions to create users and roles, and associate users with roles. The biggest difference between the role-based security in this solution and the default security model defined in the .NET Framework is the addition of an extra layer that enables users to associate capabilities to a role, and the capabilities are mapped to functionality in the system, not the role. The role is just a junction between users and capabilities. This will all be clear in the following chapters.

6

Role-Based Security

For some reason, security seems to be the last thing developers want to think about when developing a system. It's much more fun to create new pages, create databases, and play with the latest technology than it is to write boring old code where there isn't much bang for your buck. Wouldn't it be great if security were something you didn't have to think about and it were part of a framework that you could reuse and customize for your own applications? Well, you're in luck. This chapter provides just that. After reading this chapter, you'll have a framework in place that enables users to create roles and specify whether another user has read-only access, full access, partial access, or no access to a page.

Problem

Usually, when you review requirements with clients, they make a broad statement such as "we need security." This doesn't really help you much. Take Mary, for example. As I continued my discussions with her, she started to get a little more specific by saying a particular user should have access to a page but someone else shouldn't. Then, after showing her some prototypes, she asked if one person could view the page but not be able to change anything. Then she said, "Well, on this page I want to be able to click these two buttons, but someone else should only be able to click one button."

This chapter focuses on building a role-based security framework that can handle all types of scenarios, and one that enables you to control security down to the field level on each screen. After reading this chapter, you should never even have to ask the client about security anymore. Armed with this functionality, you can let clients keep changing their mind about how the pages work. Just don't let them know how easy it is to change them.

The other challenging issue with security is administration. How many applications have you built for which you become the security administrator because it takes some coding changes to create a user or grant access to a page? This isn't what developers are supposed to be spending time on. They should be coding (and occasionally let out to see the sunshine). Support is supposed to be handled by the help desk. The role-based security design for this solution remedies this problem by giving users the capability to manage security themselves by creating roles, creating users, and associating users with roles.

Design

Role-based security is not a new concept. In fact, the .NET Framework comes with built-in functionality to enable you to create roles, associate users with roles, and manage these tasks using the Web Site Administration Tool. The problem with this structure for the PaidTimeOff project is that you, as the developer, have to create the roles and associate them with specific pages in the application, not the user. Nor do you want to give users access to the Web Site Administration Tool to manage the security themselves.

In my opinion, the biggest challenge you face is deciding which roles go with which pages; and a role isn't really associated with a page, a capability is associated with a page, and that capability can be associated with one or more roles. The term "capability" refers to the smallest level of access a user can have in your system. For example, you may need to associate "run" capabilities for each report with different users. If you have 20 reports, then you would need 20 capabilities. You could set up an Accounting role that can only run accounting reports, but you could also set up an Administrator role that can run all reports.

A capability needs to be able to be defined as being read-only, editable, or potentially some other type of access, such as run or execute. This type of functionality isn't supported out of the box by the .NET Framework's security model. The pattern discussed in this chapter does address all of these issues, and clarifies the difference between a role and a capability and the access levels associated with each.

Role-Based Security Table Design

The tables shown in Figure 6-1 are the backbone of the role-based security model in the PaidTimeOff solution. Two of the tables you have seen already: ENTUserAccount and ENTMenuItem.

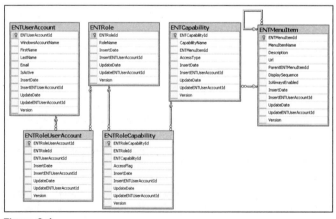

Figure 6-1

ENTRole Table

The `ENTRole` table stores the name of the role. For example, the user could create a "System Administrator" role or a "Paid Time Off Approver" role. Each record in this table can then be associated with multiple capabilities or multiple users.

ENTCapability Table

The `ENTCapability` table holds the name of a capability, the menu item the capability is associated with, and the access types that could be associated with this capability. The `AccessType` field maps to an enumeration with the following values:

❑ **ReadOnlyEdit (0):** Allows the user to choose no access, read-only access, or edit access for this capability.

❑ **ReadOnly (1):** Allows the user to choose no access or read-only access for this capability.

❑ **Edit (2):** Allows the user to choose no access or edit access for this capability.

For example, consider a web page that allows a user to submit a paid time off request. A record will be added to the `ENTMenuItem` table so the user can get to this page. Another record will be added to the `ENTCapability` table and point to the `ENTMenuItem` record. Users should either have no access to this page or have edit access to this page. Read-only access for this page does not make sense, so the `AccessType` for this capability record will be set to Edit, which indicates to the Role page to display options for "no access" or "edit access." Another page will be created that allows the user to manage states in the workflow engine. Again, a record will be added to the `ENTMenuItem` and `ENTCapability` tables. Users should have no access, read-only access, or edit access to this screen, so the `AccessType` will be set to ReadOnlyEdit. This will display three options on the role screen: none, read-only, or edit. The `ENTCapability` records are associated with `ENTMenuItem` records, so only pages to which users have read-only or edit access are displayed.

ENTRoleCapability Table

The `ENTRoleCapability` table is a junction table between the `ENTCapability` and `ENtRole` tables. This allows users to create roles themselves and associate the type of access for that capability for the role. The `AccessFlag` field specifies the type of access the user has for this capability. The `AccessFlag` maps to an enumeration in the application with the following values:

❑ None (0)

❑ ReadOnly (1)

❑ Edit (2)

For example, as mentioned earlier, if the user wanted to create a role that granted read-only access to the State Workflow page, then a record would be added to the `ENTRoleCapability` table that has an `AccessFlag` set to ReadOnly. Just to clarify, the `AccessType` field in the `ENTCapability` table signifies the options that should be displayed for this capability, and the `AccessFlag` field in the `ENTRole Capability` table signifies which option the user associated with this capability when it was associated with a role. Figure 6-2 shows a screenshot of what the capabilities section of the Role page will look like when we are finished implementing it.

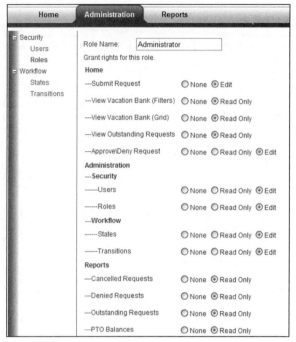

Figure 6-2

As you can see, the screen is divided up according to how the menu is structured, and radio buttons are used to display the AccessType for each capability. Note that two capabilities are associated with the "View Vacation Bank" page — one that allows users to see a grid displaying their own vacation bank, and one that allows users to see filters on the screen to enable them to view other employees' vacation banks. The View Vacation Bank page will be customized to handle specific screen-level security, but all other pages will use the default functionality.

ENTRoleUserAccount Table

The ENTRoleUserAccount table is a junction table that stores which users are associated with which roles. The bottom part of the Role page will have the section displayed in Figure 6-3. This allows the user to associate users with the role.

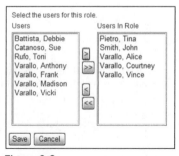

Figure 6-3

The users in the "Users In Role" list box are saved to the ENTRoleUserAccount table. The page uses two list boxes, which allow the user to move users in and out of the role. If you've ever implemented this type of functionality before, you probably know how much of a pain it is to move items from one box to another. The problem is that if you move the list items using JavaScript, they are not posted back to the server in the list box they were moved to dynamically. You end up having to use a hidden field to keep track of what each list box contains, and it becomes a hassle to manage. This page solves the problem by posting back using ASP.NET AJAX when items are moved back and forth — so when the Save button is clicked, the correct list items are posted back to the server.

The user can use the Role page to manage security, but the application must implement the access types throughout the application. If a user specifies None for a capability, then the menu item isn't even shown to the user. If the user has edit access to a page, then the screen is shown in normal mode, with all controls enabled and a Save button. For example, if the user has edit access to the User screen, it would look like Figure 6-4.

Figure 6-4

If the user has read-only access to a screen, then the controls should be disabled and the Save button will not appear. Figure 6-5 shows the read-only view of the same User screen.

Figure 6-5

Because all pages inherit from the same base page and all edit screens use the same master page, it is easy to implement this functionality. The next section shows you the plumbing behind the scenes that enables all this to work together.

Solution

The first step is to create the tables and stored procedures that the role-based security model needs, which are in a script file (available on the Wrox website) called Chapter6RoleBasedSecurity.sql. Run this script against the HRPaidTimeOff database. This script does not drop any objects, so if you have been following along in the previous chapters and creating the tables and stored procedures, you'll have to drop them manually. The script also adds some seed users in the system, which you'll need to change to match your domain and the user names on your network or local PC. The stored procedures that end with Insert, Update, Delete, SelectAll, and SelectById follow the same pattern defined in Chapter 2, so I won't review them here. Also included are a few nonstandard procedures, which are defined next.

The ENTRoleCapabilitySelectByENTRoleId stored procedure selects all the records from the ENTRole Capability junction table for a specific role:

```
CREATE PROCEDURE ENTRoleCapabilitySelectByENTRoleId
(
  @ENTRoleId int
)
AS
  SET NOCOUNT ON

  SELECT ENTRoleCapabilityId, ENTRoleId, ENTCapabilityId, AccessFlag, InsertDate,
         InsertENTUserAccountId,
         UpdateDate, UpdateENTUserAccountId, Version
    FROM ENTRoleCapability
   WHERE ENTRoleId = @ENTRoleId

  RETURN
```

The ENTRoleSelectByENTUserAccountId stored procedure selects all the roles associated with a user:

```
CREATE PROCEDURE ENTRoleSelectByENTUserAccountId
(
  @ENTUserAccountId int
)
AS
  SET NOCOUNT ON

    SELECT ENTRole.ENTRoleId, RoleName, ENTRole.InsertDate,
           ENTRole.InsertENTUserAccountId, ENTRole.UpdateDate,
           ENTRole.UpdateENTUserAccountId, ENTRole.Version
      FROM ENTRole
INNER JOIN ENTRoleUserAccount
        ON ENTRole.ENTRoleId = ENTRoleUserAccount.ENTRoleId
     WHERE ENTUserAccountId = @ENTUserAccountId

  RETURN
```

The `ENTRoleUserAccountSelectByENTRoleId` stored procedure selects all the users from the `ENTRoleUserAccount` table who are associated with a specific role. That's it as far as custom procedures are concerned:

```
CREATE PROCEDURE ENTRoleUserAccountSelectByENTRoleId
(
   @ENTRoleId int
)
AS
   SET NOCOUNT ON

   SELECT ENTRoleUserAccountId, ENTRoleId, ENTUserAccountId, InsertDate,
          InsertENTUserAccountId, UpdateDate,
          UpdateENTUserAccountId, Version
     FROM ENTRoleUserAccount
    WHERE ENTRoleId = @ENTRoleId

   RETURN
```

Entity Objects and Data Context

Once you have created the tables and stored procedures, you need to create the entity objects using the ORM Designer. Open the `HRPaidTimeOff.dbml` file in Visual Studio 2008 and remove any objects on the designer. Drag all six tables from the Server Explorer to the ORM Designer surface. Rearrange the tables so you are comfortable viewing them (see Figure 6-6).

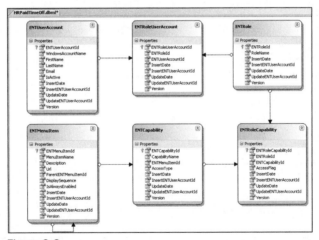

Figure 6-6

Now drag the `Insert`, `Update`, and `Delete` stored procedures to the Methods pane. Do not drag any of the `Select` procedures to the Methods pane because the designer will produce the wrong return object. Remember from Chapter 2 that if you want a stored procedure to return an instance of a table entity object, you need to drag and drop the stored procedure onto the table. Drag the `ENTCapabilitySelectAll` and `ENTCapabilitySelectById` stored procedures on top of the `ENTCapability` table. They will appear in the Methods pane, and if you look at their return type in the code-behind you'll see that they return the `ENTCapability` entity object:

```
[Function(Name="dbo.ENTCapabilitySelectAll")]
public ISingleResult<ENTCapability> ENTCapabilitySelectAll()
{
    IExecuteResult result = this.ExecuteMethodCall(this,
        ((MethodInfo)(MethodInfo.GetCurrentMethod())));
    return ((ISingleResult<ENTCapability>)(result.ReturnValue));
}
```

Finish dragging the other stored procedures to the appropriate table. The name of the stored procedure starts with the table name to which it is related. You now have all your entity objects and strongly typed methods on your `HRPaidTimeOff DataContext` object for the stored procedures.

Next, add code to the `CustomizedEntities.cs` file that changes the entity classes to implement the `IENTBaseEntity` interface:

```
namespace V2.PaidTimeOffDAL
{
    public partial class ENTUserAccount : IENTBaseEntity { }

    public partial class ENTMenuItem : IENTBaseEntity { }

    public partial class ENTRole : IENTBaseEntity { }

    public partial class ENTCapability : IENTBaseEntity { }

    public partial class ENTRoleCapability : IENTBaseEntity { }

    public partial class ENTRoleUserAccount : IENTBaseEntity { }
}
```

Data Classes

The next step is to create the data classes in the DAL. Each table should have a data class named *TABLEData* and they all should inherit from `ENTBaseData`. The `ENTCapabilityData` class is as follows:

```
public class ENTCapabilityData : ENTBaseData<ENTCapability>
{
    public override List<ENTCapability> Select()
    {
        using (HRPaidTimeOffDataContext db = new
            HRPaidTimeOffDataContext(DBHelper.GetHRPaidTimeOffConnectionString()))
        {
            return db.ENTCapabilitySelectAll().ToList();
        }
    }

    public override ENTCapability Select(int id)
```

```
        {
            using (HRPaidTimeOffDataContext db = new
                HRPaidTimeOffDataContext(DBHelper.GetHRPaidTimeOffConnectionString()))
            {
                return db.ENTCapabilitySelectById(id).SingleOrDefault();
            }
        }

        public override void Delete(HRPaidTimeOffDataContext db, int id)
        {
            throw new NotImplementedException();
        }
    }
```

ENTCapability is a static table that users will never be able to edit, so there is no need for insert, update, or delete functionality.

The ENTMenuItemData class is as follows:

```
public class ENTMenuItemData : ENTBaseData<ENTMenuItem>
{
    public override List<ENTMenuItem> Select()
    {
        using (HRPaidTimeOffDataContext db = new
            HRPaidTimeOffDataContext(DBHelper.GetHRPaidTimeOffConnectionString()))
        {
            return db.ENTMenuItemSelectAll().ToList();
        }
    }

    public override ENTMenuItem Select(int id)
    {
        throw new NotImplementedException();
    }

    public override void Delete(HRPaidTimeOffDataContext db, int id)
    {
        throw new NotImplementedException();
    }
}
```

This table is also never manipulated by a user and only needs to support select functionality.

The ENTRoleData class is a little more exciting, as it needs to allow insert, update, delete, and select functionality:

```
public class ENTRoleData : ENTBaseData<ENTRole>
{
    #region Overrides

    public override List<ENTRole> Select()
    {
        using (HRPaidTimeOffDataContext db = new
```

```
                    HRPaidTimeOffDataContext(DBHelper.GetHRPaidTimeOffConnectionString()))
        {
            return db.ENTRoleSelectAll().ToList();
        }
    }

    public override ENTRole Select(int id)
    {
        using (HRPaidTimeOffDataContext db = new
            HRPaidTimeOffDataContext(DBHelper.GetHRPaidTimeOffConnectionString()))
        {
            return db.ENTRoleSelectById(id).SingleOrDefault();
        }
    }

    public override void Delete(HRPaidTimeOffDataContext db, int id)
    {
        db.ENTRoleDelete(id);
    }

    #endregion Overrides

    #region Insert

    public int Insert(string connectionString, string roleName, int
        insertENTUserAccountId)
    {
        using (HRPaidTimeOffDataContext db = new
            HRPaidTimeOffDataContext(connectionString))
        {
            return Insert(db, roleName, insertENTUserAccountId);
        }
    }

    public int Insert(HRPaidTimeOffDataContext db, string roleName, int
        insertENTUserAccountId)
    {
        Nullable<int> entRoleId = 0;

        db.ENTRoleInsert(ref entRoleId, roleName, insertENTUserAccountId);

        return Convert.ToInt32(entRoleId);
    }

    #endregion Insert

    #region Update

    public bool Update(string connectionString, int entRoleId, string roleName, int
        updateENTUserAccountId, Binary version)
    {
        using (HRPaidTimeOffDataContext db = new
            HRPaidTimeOffDataContext(connectionString))
        {
```

```
            return Update(db, entRoleId, roleName, updateENTUserAccountId,
                version);
        }
    }

    public bool Update(HRPaidTimeOffDataContext db, int entRoleId, string roleName,
        int updateENTUserAccountId, Binary version)
    {
        int rowsAffected = db.ENTRoleUpdate(entRoleId, roleName,
            updateENTUserAccountId, version);

        return rowsAffected == 1;
    }

    #endregion Update

    #region Utility Methods

    public bool IsDuplicateRoleName(HRPaidTimeOffDataContext db, int entRoleId,
        string roleName)
    {
        return IsDuplicate(db, "ENTRole", "RoleName", "ENTRoleID", roleName,
            entRoleId);
    }

    public List<ENTRole> SelectByENTUserAccountId(int entUserAccountId)
    {
        using (HRPaidTimeOffDataContext db = new
            HRPaidTimeOffDataContext(DBHelper.GetHRPaidTimeOffConnectionString()))
        {
            return db.ENTRoleSelectByENTUserAccountId(entUserAccountId).ToList();
        }
    }

    #endregion Utility Methods
}
```

The `Select`, `Insert`, `Update`, and `Delete` methods follow the standard syntax that was defined in Chapter 2. Two utility methods that are not standard are worth mentioning. First is the `IsDuplicateRoleName` method, which is used to validate that a role name is unique. The second method is `SelectByENTUserAccountId`, which returns all the roles for a specific user.

The `ENTRoleCapabilityData` class also needs to support insert, update, and delete functionality and is implemented using the standard syntax defined above, so I won't show you the entire class. There is only one custom method in this class called `SelectByENTRoleId`, which returns the list of capability IDs associated with one role:

```
public class ENTRoleCapabilityData : ENTBaseData<ENTRoleCapability>
{
    public override List<ENTRoleCapability> Select()
    {
        using (HRPaidTimeOffDataContext db = new
            HRPaidTimeOffDataContext(DBHelper.GetHRPaidTimeOffConnectionString()))
```

```
        {
            return db.ENTRoleCapabilitySelectAll().ToList();
        }
    }

    public override ENTRoleCapability Select(int id)
    {
        using (HRPaidTimeOffDataContext db = new
            HRPaidTimeOffDataContext(DBHelper.GetHRPaidTimeOffConnectionString()))
        {
            return db.ENTRoleCapabilitySelectById(id).SingleOrDefault();
        }
    }

    public List<ENTRoleCapability> SelectByENTRoleId(int entRoleId)
    {
        using (HRPaidTimeOffDataContext db = new
            HRPaidTimeOffDataContext(DBHelper.GetHRPaidTimeOffConnectionString()))
        {
            return db.ENTRoleCapabilitySelectByENTRoleId(entRoleId).ToList();
        }
    }

    public override void Delete(HRPaidTimeOffDataContext db, int id)
    {
        db.ENTRoleCapabilityDelete(id);
    }

    public int Insert(string connectionString, int entRoleId, int entCapabilityId,
        byte accessFlag, int insertENTUserAccountId)
    {
        using (HRPaidTimeOffDataContext db = new
            HRPaidTimeOffDataContext(connectionString))
        {
            return Insert(db, entRoleId, entCapabilityId, accessFlag,
                insertENTUserAccountId);
        }
    }

    public int Insert(HRPaidTimeOffDataContext db, int entRoleId, int
        entCapabilityId, byte accessFlag, int insertENTUserAccountId)
    {
        Nullable<int> entRoleCapabilityId = 0;

        db.ENTRoleCapabilityInsert(ref entRoleCapabilityId, entRoleId,
            entCapabilityId, accessFlag, insertENTUserAccountId );

        return Convert.ToInt32(entRoleCapabilityId);
    }

    public bool Update(string connectionString, int entRoleCapabilityId, int
        entRoleId, int entCapabilityId, byte accessFlag, int
        updateENTUserAccountId, Binary version)
    {
```

```
        using (HRPaidTimeOffDataContext db = new
            HRPaidTimeOffDataContext(connectionString))
        {
            return Update(db, entRoleCapabilityId, entRoleId, entCapabilityId,
                accessFlag, updateENTUserAccountId, version);
        }
    }

    public bool Update(HRPaidTimeOffDataContext db, int entRoleCapabilityId, int
        entRoleId, int entCapabilityId, byte accessFlag, int
        updateENTUserAccountId, Binary version)
    {
        int rowsAffected = db.ENTRoleCapabilityUpdate(entRoleCapabilityId,
            entRoleId, entCapabilityId, accessFlag, updateENTUserAccountId,
            version);

        return rowsAffected == 1;
    }
}
```

The ENTRoleUserAccountData class is very similar to the ENTRoleCapabilityData class, as it needs insert, update, and delete functionality and only has one custom method called SelectByENTRoleId. This method returns a list of user IDs associated with a single role:

```
public class ENTRoleUserAccountData : ENTBaseData<ENTRoleUserAccount>
{
    public override List<ENTRoleUserAccount> Select()
    {
        using (HRPaidTimeOffDataContext db = new
            HRPaidTimeOffDataContext(DBHelper.GetHRPaidTimeOffConnectionString()))
        {
            return db.ENTRoleUserAccountSelectAll().ToList();
        }
    }

    public override ENTRoleUserAccount Select(int id)
    {
        using (HRPaidTimeOffDataContext db = new
            HRPaidTimeOffDataContext(DBHelper.GetHRPaidTimeOffConnectionString()))
        {
            return db.ENTRoleUserAccountSelectById(id).SingleOrDefault();
        }
    }

    public List<ENTRoleUserAccount> SelectByENTRoleId(int entRoleId)
    {
        using (HRPaidTimeOffDataContext db = new
            HRPaidTimeOffDataContext(DBHelper.GetHRPaidTimeOffConnectionString()))
        {
            return db.ENTRoleUserAccountSelectByENTRoleId(entRoleId).ToList();
        }
    }

    public override void Delete(HRPaidTimeOffDataContext db, int id)
```

```
        {
            db.ENTRoleUserAccountDelete(id);
        }

        public int Insert(string connectionString, int entRoleId, int entUserAccountId,
            int insertENTUserAccountId)
        {
            using (HRPaidTimeOffDataContext db = new
                HRPaidTimeOffDataContext(connectionString))
            {
                return Insert(db, entRoleId, entUserAccountId, insertENTUserAccountId);
            }
        }

        public int Insert(HRPaidTimeOffDataContext db, int entRoleId, int
            entUserAccountId, int insertENTUserAccountId)
        {
            Nullable<int> entRoleUserAccountId = 0;

            db.ENTRoleUserAccountInsert(ref entRoleUserAccountId, entRoleId,
                entUserAccountId, insertENTUserAccountId);

            return Convert.ToInt32(entRoleUserAccountId);
        }

        public bool Update(string connectionString, int entRoleUserAccountId, int
            entRoleId, int entUserAccountId, int updateENTUserAccountId, Binary
            version)
        {
            using (HRPaidTimeOffDataContext db = new
                HRPaidTimeOffDataContext(connectionString))
            {
                return Update(db, entRoleUserAccountId, entRoleId, entUserAccountId,
                    updateENTUserAccountId, version);
            }
        }

        public bool Update(HRPaidTimeOffDataContext db, int entRoleUserAccountId, int
            entRoleId, int entUserAccountId, int updateENTUserAccountId, Binary
            version)
        {
            int rowsAffected = db.ENTRoleUserAccountUpdate(entRoleUserAccountId,
                entRoleId, entUserAccountId, updateENTUserAccountId, version);

            return rowsAffected == 1;
        }
    }
}
```

The last data class is the ENTUserAccountData, which is unchanged from Chapter 2. Now that all the data classes are defined, you are ready to start building the business classes.

Business Classes

The business classes consist of the classes shown in Figure 6-7 and Figure 6-8.

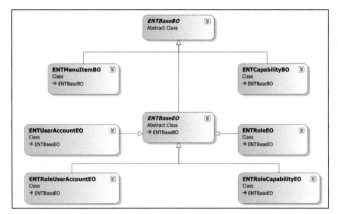

Figure 6-7

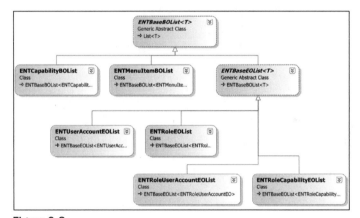

Figure 6-8

ENTCapabilityBO and ENTCapabilityBOList Classes

The ENTCapability and ENTCapabilityBOList classes are non-editable classes, so they inherit from the ENTBaseBO and ENTBaseBOList classes, respectively:

```
[Serializable()]
public class ENTCapabilityBO : ENTBaseBO
{
    public enum AccessTypeEnum
```

```
        {
            ReadOnlyEdit = 0,
            ReadOnly = 1,
            Edit = 2
        }

        public string CapabilityName { get; private set; }
        public Nullable<int> MenuItemId { get; private set; }
        public AccessTypeEnum AccessType { get; private set; }

        public override bool Load(int id)
        {
            ENTCapability capability = new ENTCapabilityData().Select(id);
            MapEntityToProperties(capability);
            return true;
        }

        protected override void MapEntityToCustomProperties(IENTBaseEntity entity)
        {
            ENTCapability capability = (ENTCapability)entity;

            ID = capability.ENTCapabilityId;
            CapabilityName = capability.CapabilityName;
            MenuItemId = capability.ENTMenuItemId;
            AccessType = (AccessTypeEnum)capability.AccessType;
        }

        protected override string GetDisplayText()
        {
            return CapabilityName;
        }
    }
}
```

The `AccessType` enumeration maps to the values in the `AccessType` field. This determines what types of access should be allowed for this capability. If you wanted to add more access levels, such as separating Delete from Edit, then you would add an item to the enumeration.

The `ENTCapabilityBOList` class inherits from the `ENTBaseBOList` object and implements the abstract methods using the same pattern defined in Chapter 3. There are only two custom methods for this class:

```
public ENTCapabilityBO GetByName(string capabilityName)
{
    return this.SingleOrDefault(c => c.CapabilityName == capabilityName);
}

public IEnumerable<ENTCapabilityBO> GetByMenuItemId(int entMenuItemId)
{
    return from c in this
           where c.MenuItemId == entMenuItemId
           orderby c.CapabilityName
           select c;
}
```

The `GetByName` method uses a lambda expression to find the object in this list matching the `capability Name` parameter. The `GetByMenuItemId` method uses a LINQ expression to return all the objects in this list that are associated with a single menu item, ordering them by the `CapabilityName` property.

ENTRoleCapabilityEO and ENTRoleCapabilityEOList Classes

These classes represent the junction table between the `ENTRole` and `ENTCapbility` tables. They both implement the same standard methods for classes that inherit from the `ENTBaseEO` and `ENTBaseEOList` classes defined in Chapter 3. The standard code is left out of this snippet intentionally; only the custom logic is displayed here, but the code available on the Wrox website has the full class definition:

```
[Serializable()]
public class ENTRoleCapabilityEO : ENTBaseEO
{
    public enum CapabiiltyAccessFlagEnum
    {
        None,
        ReadOnly,
        Edit
    }

    public ENTRoleCapabilityEO()
    {
        Capability = new ENTCapabilityBO();
    }

    public int ENTRoleId { get; set; }
    public CapabiiltyAccessFlagEnum AccessFlag { get; set; }
    public ENTCapabilityBO Capability { get; private set; }

    protected override void MapEntityToCustomProperties(IENTBaseEntity entity)
    {
        ENTRoleCapability roleCapability = (ENTRoleCapability)entity;

        ID = roleCapability.ENTRoleCapabilityId;
        ENTRoleId = roleCapability.ENTRoleId;
        AccessFlag = (CapabiiltyAccessFlagEnum)roleCapability.AccessFlag;
        Capability.Load(roleCapability.ENTCapabilityId);
    }
}
```

Notice that there is an enumeration that maps to the `AccessFlag` field. There is also a property defined as an `ENTCapabilityBO` object, which is loaded in the `MapEntityToCustomProperties` method. This represents the relationship between the `ENTCapability` record and the `ENTRoleCapability` record.

The `ENTRoleCapabilityEOList` class has a few custom methods:

```
[Serializable()]
public class ENTRoleCapabilityEOList : ENTBaseEOList<ENTRoleCapabilityEO>
{
    //Standard Overrides methods would go here.

    internal IEnumerable<ENTRoleCapabilityEO> GetByMenuItemId(int menuItemId)
```

```
    {
        return from rc in this
               where rc.Capability.MenuItemId == menuItemId
               select rc;
    }

    public ENTRoleCapabilityEO GetByCapabilityID(int capabilityId)
    {
        return this.SingleOrDefault(rc => rc.Capability.ID == capabilityId);
    }

    internal void LoadByENTRoleId(int entRoleId)
    {
        LoadFromList(new ENTRoleCapabilityData().SelectByENTRoleId(entRoleId));
    }
}
```

The Get methods use lambda expressions to find a specific object in the list. The LoadByENTRoleId method uses the custom select method in the DAL to populate the current instance with all capabilities for this role. Any method that starts with *Get* will search the current instance and return one or more objects from the list. Any method that starts with *Load* will retrieve data from the database and load the current instance.

ENTRoleUserAccountEO and ENTRoleUserAccountEOList Classes

These classes represent the junction table between the ENTRole and ENTUserAccount tables. The ENTRoleUserAccountEO class implements the ENTBaseEO class and has no special properties or methods, so I won't review the code here. The ENTRoleUserAccountEOList implements the ENTBaseEOList class and has the follow custom methods:

```
[Serializable()]
public class ENTRoleUserAccountEOList : ENTBaseEOList<ENTRoleUserAccountEO>
{
    //Standard Overrides methods would go here.

    public bool IsUserInRole(int userAccountId)
    {
        return (GetByUserAccountId(userAccountId) != null);
    }

    public ENTRoleUserAccountEO GetByUserAccountId(int userAccountId)
    {
        return this.SingleOrDefault(u => u.ENTUserAccountId == userAccountId);
    }

    internal void LoadByEntRoleId(int entRoleID)
    {
        LoadFromList(new ENTRoleUserAccountData().SelectByENTRoleId(entRoleID));
    }
}
```

The IsUserInRole method enables you to determine if a particular user is in this role. It calls the GetByUserAccountId method and returns true if null is not returned. The other methods follow the same pattern for searching and loading as defined by the previous classes.

ENTRoleEO Class

The ENTRoleEO class represents a role with its associated users and capabilities. This class inherits from the ENTBaseEO class because users can edit roles. The class declaration is as follows:

```
[Serializable()]
public class ENTRoleEO : ENTBaseEO
{
    ...
}
```

Roles consist of a unique name, a list of associated users, and a list of associated capabilities for the role:

```
public ENTRoleEO()
{
    RoleCapabilities = new ENTRoleCapabilityEOList();
    RoleUserAccounts = new ENTRoleUserAccountEOList();
}

public string RoleName { get; set; }
public ENTRoleCapabilityEOList RoleCapabilities { get; set; }
public ENTRoleUserAccountEOList RoleUserAccounts { get; set; }
```

The list objects must be instantiated in the constructor because the shorthand syntax is used for the property's declaration. The next step is to implement the abstract methods of the ENTBaseEO class. Load and MapEntityToCustomProperties use the exact same pattern defined in Chapter 3:

```
public override bool Load(int id)
{
    //Get a data reader from the database.
    ENTRole role = new ENTRoleData().Select(id);
    MapEntityToProperties(role);
    return true;
}

protected override void MapEntityToCustomProperties(IENTBaseEntity entity)
{
    ENTRole role = (ENTRole)entity;

    ID = role.ENTRoleId;
    RoleName = role.RoleName;
    RoleCapabilities.Load(ID);
    RoleUserAccounts.Load(ID);
}
```

The Save method must be able to save the record to the ENTRole table and all the records associated with this role in the ENTRoleUserAccount and ENTRoleCapability tables:

```
public override bool Save(HRPaidTimeOffDataContext db, ref ENTValidationErrors
    validationErrors, int userAccountId)
{
    if (DBAction == DBActionEnum.Save)
    {
```

```
        //Validate the object
        Validate(db, ref validationErrors);

        //Check if there were any validation errors
        if (validationErrors.Count == 0)
        {
            if (IsNewRecord())
            {
                //Add
                ID = new ENTRoleData().Insert(db, RoleName, userAccountId);

                //Since this was an add you need to update all the role ids for the
                //user and capability records
                foreach (ENTRoleCapabilityEO capability in RoleCapabilities)
                {
                    capability.ENTRoleId = ID;
                }

                foreach (ENTRoleUserAccountEO user in RoleUserAccounts)
                {
                    user.ENTRoleId = ID;
                }
            }
            else
            {
                //Update
                if (!new ENTRoleData().Update(db, ID, RoleName, userAccountId,
                    Version))
                {
                    UpdateFailed(ref validationErrors);
                    return false;
                }
            }

            //Now save the capabilities
            if (RoleCapabilities.Save(db, ref validationErrors, userAccountId))
            {
                //Now save the users
                if (RoleUserAccounts.Save(db, ref validationErrors, userAccountId))
                {
                    return true;
                }
                else
                {
                    return false;
                }
            }
            else
            {
                return false;
            }
        }
        else
        {
```

```
                    //Didn't pass validation.
                    return false;
            }
        }
        else
        {
            throw new Exception("DBAction not Save.");
        }
    }
```

Notice here that after a new record is added, the newly added ID for the role is associated with the capabilities and users associated with the role. After the role is added or updated, the capabilities and user accounts are saved in the same transaction. Remember that the ENTBaseEO class has a Save method that does not take a DataContext object. That method creates the DataContext and starts the transaction. All other calls to Save are enlisted in the same transaction because the overloaded Save method that takes a DataContext object as a parameter is called. The transaction is rolled back if any of the Save methods return false.

There are only two validation rules when saving a role. The name must be unique and it is required. The Validate method enforces these rules:

```
protected override void Validate(HRPaidTimeOffDataContext db, ref
    ENTValidationErrors validationErrors)
{
    if (RoleName.Trim().Length == 0)
    {
        validationErrors.Add("The name is required.");
    }

    //The role name must be unique.
    if (new ENTRoleData().IsDuplicateRoleName(db, ID, RoleName))
    {
        validationErrors.Add("The name must be unique.");
    }
}
```

Because users can delete roles, the DeleteForReal method must be implemented:

```
protected override void DeleteForReal(HRPaidTimeOffDataContext db)
{
    if (DBAction == DBActionEnum.Delete)
    {
        new ENTRoleData().Delete(db, ID);
    }
    else
    {
        throw new Exception("DBAction not delete.");
    }
}
```

The foreign key relationships between the ENTRole and ENTRoleUserAccount and the ENTRole and ENTRoleCapability tables are defined as *cascade delete relationships,* so deleting the ENTRole record deletes the child records. If the relationships did not cascade, then you could put the code to delete these records in the DeleteForReal method before deleting the ENTRole record.

The GetDisplayText method should return the role's name:

```
protected override string GetDisplayText()
{
    return RoleName;
}
```

ENTRoleEOList Class

The ENTRoleEOList class inherits from the ENTBaseEOList object and represents multiple records from the ENTRole table:

```
[Serializable()]
public class ENTRoleEOList : ENTBaseEOList<ENTRoleEO>
{
    public override void Load()
    {
        LoadFromList(new ENTRoleData().Select());
    }

    private void LoadFromList(List<ENTRole> roles)
    {
        if (roles.Count > 0)
        {
            foreach (ENTRole role in roles)
            {
                ENTRoleEO newRoleEO = new ENTRoleEO();
                newRoleEO.MapEntityToProperties(role);
                this.Add(newRoleEO);
            }
        }
    }

    internal ENTRoleEO GetByRoleId(int roleId)
    {
        return this.SingleOrDefault(r => r.ID == roleId);
    }

    internal void LoadByENTUserAccountId(int entUserAccountId)
    {
        LoadFromList(new ENTRoleData().SelectByENTUserAccountId(entUserAccountId));
    }
}
```

There are two nonstandard methods in this class: GetByRoleId and LoadByENTUserAccountId. GetByRoleId takes a role ID and uses a lambda expression to find the role in the list with the matching ID. If no object is found, then null will be returned because SingleOrDefault is being called. The LoadByENTUserAccountId method loads the current instance with all the roles a single user is associated with. Notice that this method retrieves the data from the DAL and uses the standard LoadFromList method to populate itself.

ENTMenuItemBO Class

The ENTMenuItemBO class was defined in Chapter 4 when the MenuTabs and MenuTree controls were created. Only one additional method, HasAccessToMenu, needs to be added to this class to support the role-based security:

```
public bool HasAccessToMenu(ENTUserAccountEO userAccount, ENTRoleEOList roles)
{
    if (IsAlwaysEnabled)
    {
        return true;
    }
    else
    {
        //Loop through all the roles this user is in.  The first time the user has
        //access to the menu item return true.  If you get through all the
        //roles then the user does not have access to this menu item.
        foreach (ENTRoleEO role in roles)
        {
            //Check if this user is in this role
            if (role.RoleUserAccounts.IsUserInRole(userAccount.ID))
            {
                //Try to find the capability with the menu item Id.
                IEnumerable<ENTRoleCapabilityEO> capabilities =
                    role.RoleCapabilities.GetByMenuItemId(ID);

                if ((capability != null) && (capability.AccessFlag !=
                    ENTRoleCapabilityEO.CapabiiltyAccessFlagEnum.None))
                {
                    //If the record is in the table and the user has access other
                    //then None then return true.
                    return true;
                }
            }
        }
    }

    //If it gets here then the user didn't have access to this menu item.  BUT they
    //may have access to one of its children, now check the children and if they
    //have access to any of them return true.
    if (ChildMenuItems.Count > 0)
    {
        foreach (ENTMenuItemBO child in ChildMenuItems)
        {
            if (child.HasAccessToMenu(userAccount, roles))
            {
                return true;
            }
        }
    }

    //If it never found a role with any capability then return false.
    return false;
}
```

This method determines whether a user has access to a specific menu item based on his or her roles. Because menu items can be nested, this method is recursive to check any child menu items. A recursive method is a method that calls itself.

ENTUserAccountEO Class

This class was also defined in earlier chapters and only one new method was added, `GetCapability Access`, which returns the least restrictive access a user has for a specific capability. Least restrictive means that if a user is in more than one role and one role has edit access and the other has read-only access, then the user has edit access for this capability:

```
public ENTRoleCapabilityEO.CapabiiltyAccessFlagEnum GetCapabilityAccess(int
    capabilityId, ENTRoleEOList rolesWithCapabilities)
{
    ENTRoleCapabilityEO.CapabiiltyAccessFlagEnum retVal =
        ENTRoleCapabilityEO.CapabiiltyAccessFlagEnum.None;

    //The roles in the user object do not include the capabilities.
    foreach (ENTRoleEO role in Roles)
    {
        ENTRoleEO roleWithCapabilities = rolesWithCapabilities.GetByRoleId(role.ID);

        foreach (ENTRoleCapabilityEO capability in
            roleWithCapabilities.RoleCapabilities)
        {
            if (capability.Capability.ID == capabilityId)
            {
                if (capability.AccessFlag ==
                    ENTRoleCapabilityEO.CapabiiltyAccessFlagEnum.Edit)
                {
                    return ENTRoleCapabilityEO.CapabiiltyAccessFlagEnum.Edit;
                }
                else if (capability.AccessFlag ==
                    ENTRoleCapabilityEO.CapabiiltyAccessFlagEnum.ReadOnly)
                {
                    //Since this is least restrictive temporarirly set the return
                    //value to read only.
                    retVal = ENTRoleCapabilityEO.CapabiiltyAccessFlagEnum.ReadOnly;
                }
            }
        }
    }

    return retVal;
}
```

ENTUserAccountEOList

Two methods need to be added to this class. The `LoadWithRoles` method loads the current instance with all users and all the roles each user is associated with:

```
public void LoadWithRoles()
{
```

```
    Load();

    foreach (ENTUserAccountEO user in this)
    {
        user.Roles.LoadByENTUserAccountId(user.ID);
    }
}
```

The `GetByWindowsAccountName` method searches the current instance for an `ENTUserAccountEO` object with the matching Windows account name:

```
public ENTUserAccountEO GetByWindowAccountName(string windowsAccountName)
{
    return this.SingleOrDefault(u => u.WindowsAccountName.ToUpper() ==
        windowsAccountName.ToUpper());
}
```

User Interface

Now that the DAL and BLL classes are defined, the user interface classes can be built. Numerous changes to the user interface are needed to accommodate the role-based security model. These include changes to the `MenuTabs` and `MenuTree` controls to determine whether the menu item should be displayed. The `BasePage` class will be updated to create a generic method to make a form read-only and to enable you to inject special code for nonstandard situations on a screen. The master pages need to be changed to show or hide the Save button or the Add button based on a user's security. The roles and users will be cached, so the `Globals` class must be changed to support this. Finally, the role grid screen and role edit screen must be built to enable users to create new roles, associate users with roles, and associate capabilities with roles.

Globals Class

Previously, the `Globals` class in the `PaidTimeOffUI` project had the list of menu items cached so the menu could be built without having to hit the database. This isn't the `Globals.asax` page, but rather the `Globals` class, that was added to the `App_Code` folder. Because users, roles, and capabilities do not change that often and are going to be used in a wide variety of locations, they are good candidates for caching. Add the following constants to the `Globals` class:

```
private const string CACHE_KEY_USERS = "Users";
private const string CACHE_KEY_ROLES = "Roles";
private const string CACHE_KEY_CAPABILITIES = "Capabilities";
```

These are the keys that will be used to retrieve the data from the cache. Next, add the methods to get the data from the cache and to load the data in the cache. These all use the same pattern that the menu items used in Chapter 4:

```
public static ENTUserAccountEOList GetUsers(Cache cache)
{
    //Check for the users
    if (cache[CACHE_KEY_USERS] == null)
    {
        LoadUsers(cache);
```

```
        }

        return (ENTUserAccountEOList)cache[CACHE_KEY_USERS];
    }

    public static ENTRoleEOList GetRoles(Cache cache)
    {
        //Check for the roles
        if (cache[CACHE_KEY_ROLES] == null)
        {
            LoadRoles(cache);
        }

        return (ENTRoleEOList)cache[CACHE_KEY_ROLES];
    }

    public static ENTCapabilityBOList GetCapabilities(Cache cache)
    {
        //Check for the roles
        if (cache[CACHE_KEY_CAPABILITIES] == null)
        {
            LoadCapabilities(cache);
        }

        return (ENTCapabilityBOList)cache[CACHE_KEY_CAPABILITIES];
    }

    public static void LoadUsers(Cache cache)
    {
        ENTUserAccountEOList users = new ENTUserAccountEOList();
        users.LoadWithRoles();

        cache.Remove(CACHE_KEY_USERS);
        cache[CACHE_KEY_USERS] = users;
    }

    public static void LoadRoles(Cache cache)
    {
        ENTRoleEOList roles = new ENTRoleEOList();
        roles.Load();

        cache.Remove(CACHE_KEY_ROLES);
        cache[CACHE_KEY_ROLES] = roles;
    }

    public static void LoadCapabilities(Cache cache)
    {
        ENTCapabilityBOList capabilities = new ENTCapabilityBOList();
        capabilities.Load();

        cache.Remove(CACHE_KEY_CAPABILITIES);
        cache[CACHE_KEY_CAPABILITIES] = capabilities;
    }
```

BasePage Class

The fact that we have a `BasePage` class is very useful in this situation because the majority of the changes can be made in this class, giving all pages the functionality by default. The first thing to add to this class is an abstract method that returns an array of strings designating the capability names associated with this page. Most of the time, a page has only one capability associated with it, but sometimes you need to separate a page's security into multiple sections, for which you need an array. Here is the method:

```
public abstract string[] CapabilityNames();
```

A typical implementation of this method in an inheriting class looks like this:

```
public override string[] CapabilityNames()
{
    return new string[] { "Users" };
}
```

Next, add two properties that determine whether the page is in read-only mode and whether security should be turned off for the page altogether:

```
public bool ReadOnly { get; set; }

public bool IgnoreCapabilityCheck { get; set; }
```

If a form is read-only, the input controls should be disabled, the Add and Save buttons should be hidden, and any links that perform actions such as delete should be hidden. Some pages that inherit from `BasePage` have no security associated with them, such as `ErrorPage.aspx` or `Administration.aspx` page. These pages should set the `IgnoreCapabilitiesCheck` to true in their `OnInit` method. This prevents the system from checking any security for the page at all. The default value for this property is false, so you have to explicitly turn this on.

Next, override the `OnInit` method of the `BasePage` class:

```
protected override void OnInit(EventArgs e)
{
    base.OnInit(e);

    CheckCapabilities();
}
```

This calls a new virtual method called `CheckCapabilities`:

```
public virtual void CheckCapabilities()
{
    if (IgnoreCapabilityCheck == false)
    {
        foreach (string capabilityName in CapabilityNames())
        {
            //Check if the user has the capability to view this screen
            ENTCapabilityBO capability =
```

```
                        Globals.GetCapabilities(this.Cache).GetByName(capabilityName);

            if (capability == null)
            {
                throw new Exception("Security is not enabled for this page. " +
                    this.ToString());
            }
            else
            {
                switch (CurrentUser.GetCapabilityAccess(capability.ID,
                    Globals.GetRoles(this.Cache)))
                {
                    case ENTRoleCapabilityEO.CapabiiltyAccessFlagEnum.None:
                        NoAccessToPage(capabilityName);
                        break;
                    case ENTRoleCapabilityEO.CapabiiltyAccessFlagEnum.ReadOnly:
                        MakeFormReadOnly(capabilityName, this.Controls);
                        break;
                    case ENTRoleCapabilityEO.CapabiiltyAccessFlagEnum.Edit:
                        //Do not make the form read only.
                        break;
                    default:
                        throw new Exception("Unknown access for this screen. " +
                            capability.CapabilityName);
                }
            }
            capability = null;
        }
    }
}
```

This method implements the standard rules for setting a form's state. The method loops around each capability returned in the `CapabilityNames` array and then validates that the string is a valid capability name. It then calls the `GetCapabilityAccess` method in the `ENTUserAccountEO` class to determine the type of access this user has for this capability. Remember that this method returns the least restrictive capability for the user. If the user does not have access to this page, then the `NoAccessToPage` virtual method is called. By default, this method throws an exception because users shouldn't even see any menu items for pages to which they do not have access:

```
protected void NoAccessToPage(string capabilityName)
{
    //The default implementation throws an error if the user came to a page and
    //they do not have access to the capability associated with that screen.
    //If a page has more than one capability you should override this method
    //because a user could  have access to one section but not another so you do
    //not want them to get an error
    throw new AccessViolationException("You do not have access to this screen.");
}
```

However, if a page has more than one capability associated with it, then you do not want to throw this error. You can override this method and handle this situation accordingly.

If the user has read-only access to the screen, then the `MakeFormReadOnly` method is called:

```
public virtual void MakeFormReadOnly(string capabilityName, ControlCollection
    controls)
{
    ReadOnly = true;
    MakeControlsReadOnly(controls);
    CustomReadOnlyLogic(capabilityName);
}
```

This method sets the `ReadOnly` property to true, disables the input controls on the screen, and then calls another virtual method called `CustomReadOnlyLogic`, which you could override if you needed to add special logic to a page that doesn't have standard controls. The `MakeControlReadOnly` method looks like this:

```
private void MakeControlsReadOnly(ControlCollection controls)
{
    foreach (Control c in controls)
    {
        if (c is TextBox)
        {
            ((TextBox)c).Enabled = false;
        }
        else if (c is RadioButton)
        {
            ((RadioButton)c).Enabled = false;
        }
        else if (c is DropDownList)
        {
            ((DropDownList)c).Enabled = false;
        }
        else if (c is CheckBox)
        {
            ((CheckBox)c).Enabled = false;
        }
        else if (c is RadioButtonList)
        {
            ((RadioButtonList)c).Enabled = false;
        }

        if (c.HasControls())
        {
            MakeControlsReadOnly(c.Controls);
        }
    }
}
```

This is another recursive method that loops through all the controls on the form and sets the `enabled` property to false for input controls. If the control has child controls, then the method is called again, passing in the child controls.

The `CustomReadOnlyLogic` method is virtual because most of the time you do not need custom logic. When you do, you can override this method. There is no logic in the virtual method in the `BasePage` class:

```
public virtual void CustomReadOnlyLogic(string capabilityName)
{
    //Override this method in a page that has custom logic for non standard
    //controls on the screen.
}
```

Later in this chapter, the `Role.aspx` page will provide an example of how to use this method.

The last step is to add a property to the `BasePage` class called `CurrentUser`. This will search the cached list of users in the `Globals` class and return the one that matches the Windows account name. The `this.User.Identity.Name` returns the Windows account name of the current user when anonymous access is turned off in IIS, and Integrated Windows Authentication is turned on:

```
public ENTUserAccountEO CurrentUser
{
  get
  {
    return
        Globals.GetUsers(this.Cache).GetByWindowAccountName(this.User.Identity.Name);
  }
}
```

MenuTabs Control

The `MenuTabs` control that was built in Chapter 4 needs to be changed to honor the new security model. Essentially, if a user has read-only or edit access to a menu item or any child of that menu item, then it needs to be shown. Two new properties must be added that enable the developer to specify the current user and the roles with the corresponding capabilities:

```
[Browsable(false)]
public ENTUserAccountEO UserAccount { get; set; }

[Browsable(false)]
public ENTRoleEOList Roles { get; set; }
```

The menu is built in the `RenderContents` method, so that is where the code must be changed to check whether a user has access to a specific menu. This can be accomplished by making a call to the business layer in the `ENTMenuItemBO` class:

```
//Loop around the top level items
foreach (ENTMenuItemBO mi in MenuItems)
{
    //Only show the tabs for the side menu item that the user has access to.
    if (mi.HasAccessToMenu(UserAccount, Roles))
    {
        //Check if this is the selected menu tab.
        if (mi.MenuItemName == topMenuItem.MenuItemName)
        {
```

```
            html += GetActiveTab(mi);
        }
        else
        {
            html += GetInactiveTab(mi);
        }
    }
}
```

The `UserAccount` and `Roles` properties must also be set in the `Page_Load` event of the `PaidTimeOff.master` page, which contains this control:

```
ENTUserAccountEO currentUser = ((BasePage)Page).CurrentUser;
MenuTabs1.Roles = Globals.GetRoles(this.Cache);
MenuTabs1.UserAccount = currentUser;
```

MenuTree Control

The `MenuTree` control also needs to determine if the menu items on the side menu should be shown or hidden based on a user's security. The same `UserAccount` and `Roles` properties that were added in the `MenuTabs` class should be added to this class, and the code in the `CreateChildMenu` method should be changed to check the user's capabilities for this menu item:

```
private void CreateChildMenu(TreeNodeCollection nodes, ENTMenuItemBOList menuItems)
{
    foreach (ENTMenuItemBO mi in menuItems)
    {
        //Check if the user has access to the menu or any children.
        if (mi.HasAccessToMenu(UserAccount, Roles))
        {
            //Create an instance of the menu
            TreeNode menuNode = new TreeNode(mi.MenuItemName, mi.ID.ToString(), "",
                    (string.IsNullOrEmpty(mi.Url) ? "" : RootPath + mi.Url), "");

            //Same code as before…
        }
    }
}
```

The `Page_Load` event in the `PaidTimeOff.master` page also needs to be changed to set the `UserAccount` and `Roles` properties the same way they are set for the `MenuTabs` control just described.

PaidTimeOffEditGrid.master

Now that the `BasePage` has been changed, you need to change the `PaidTimeOffEditGrid.master.cs` file to honor the `ReadOnly` property. Remember that this master page has the Add New button at the top of the screen. If the page is read-only, then this should be hidden:

```
protected override void OnPreRender(EventArgs e)
{
    base.OnPreRender(e);

    if (((BasePage)this.Page).ReadOnly)
```

```
    {
        //Hide the Add button
        btnAddNew.Visible = false;
    }
}
```

This code is executed in the `OnPreRender` event to hide this button after all the `PageInit` and `PageLoad` events have fired. There might be custom logic in these methods that change the `ReadOnly` property, so you want to ensure that this code fires last.

PaidTimeOffEditPage.master

Add similar functionality to the `PaidTimeOffEditPage.master` page to hide the Save button when the page is in read-only mode:

```
protected override void OnPreRender(EventArgs e)
{
    base.OnPreRender(e);

    if (((BasePage)this.Page).ReadOnly)
    {
        //Hide the save button
        btnSave.Visible = false;
    }
}
```

Role Grid Page

Now that all the plumbing is ready to support secured pages, you can create the screens that enable users to create roles, associate users with roles, and associate capabilities with roles. The `Roles.aspx` page displays the list of roles and enables users to add new roles, edit existing roles, or delete roles (see Figure 6-9).

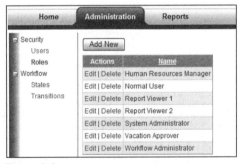

Figure 6-9

This page uses the `PaidTimeOffEditGrid.master` page and inherits from the `BasePage` class. It is trivial to set these types of pages up because most of the logic is in either the `BasePage` class, the master page, or the custom grid control. First, add the column constants and the `Page_Load` event:

```
private const int COL_INDEX_ACTION = 0;
private const int COL_INDEX_ROLE_NAME = 1;
```

```
protected void Page_Load(object sender, EventArgs e)
{
    Master.AddButton_Click += new
        PaidTimeOffEditGrid.ButtonClickedHandler(Master_AddButton_Click);

    if (!IsPostBack)
    {
        //Tell the control what class to create and what method to call to load the
        //class.
        cgvRoles.ListClassName = typeof(ENTRoleEOList).AssemblyQualifiedName;
        cgvRoles.LoadMethodName = "Load";

        //Action column-Contains the Edit and Delete links
        cgvRoles.AddBoundField("", "Actions", "");

        //Name
        cgvRoles.AddBoundField("DisplayText", "Name", "DisplayText");

        cgvRoles.DataBind();
    }
    else
    {
        string eventTarget = Page.Request.Form["__EVENTTARGET"].ToString();
        if (eventTarget.IndexOf("lbtnDelete") > -1)
        {
            //Rebind the grid so the delete event is captured.
            cgvRoles.DataBind();
        }
    }
}
```

The Page_Load binds the grid to an instance of the ENTRoleEOList object the first time the page is called. If this is a postback because a Delete link was clicked, then the grid is bound again because the link button was dynamically added to the grid. If the grid isn't rebound, the link button's click event is not hooked to the event handler on postback.

The next step is to dynamically add the Edit and Delete links in the cgvRoles_RowDataBound event. One difference here is that if the user has read-only access to the Roles capability, then the Edit link button text should be changed to View instead of Edit. The Delete link should be hidden if the user has only read-only access:

```
protected void cgvRoles_RowDataBound(object sender, GridViewRowEventArgs e)
{
    if (e.Row.RowType == DataControlRowType.DataRow)
    {
        //Add the edit link to the action column.
        HyperLink editLink = new HyperLink();
        if (ReadOnly)
        {
            editLink.Text = "View";
        }
        else
        {
            editLink.Text = "Edit";
        }
```

```
                editLink.NavigateUrl = "Role.aspx" + EncryptQueryString("id=" +
                    ((ENTRoleEO)e.Row.DataItem).ID.ToString());

                e.Row.Cells[COL_INDEX_ACTION].Controls.Add(editLink);

                //If the user has read only access then do not show this Delete link.
                if (ReadOnly == false)
                {
                    //Add a pipe between the Edit and Delete links
                    LiteralControl lc = new LiteralControl(" | ");
                    e.Row.Cells[COL_INDEX_ACTION].Controls.Add(lc);

                    //Add the Delete link
                    LinkButton lbtnDelete = new LinkButton();
                    lbtnDelete.ID = "lbtnDelete" +
                        ((ENTRoleEO)e.Row.DataItem).ID.ToString();
                    lbtnDelete.Text = "Delete";
                    lbtnDelete.CommandArgument = ((ENTRoleEO)e.Row.DataItem).ID.ToString();
                    lbtnDelete.OnClientClick = "return ConfirmDelete();";
                    lbtnDelete.Command += new CommandEventHandler(lbtnDelete_Command);
                    e.Row.Cells[COL_INDEX_ACTION].Controls.Add(lbtnDelete);
                }
            }
        }
```

Notice that when the Delete link is added, the id of the record is set to the `CommandArgument` property. This is passed in the `CommandEventArgs` parameter of the click event's event handler so the system knows which record to delete:

```
    void lbtnDelete_Command(object sender, CommandEventArgs e)
    {
        ENTValidationErrors validationErrors = new ENTValidationErrors();
        ENTRoleEO role = new ENTRoleEO();
        role.DBAction = ENTBaseEO.DBActionEnum.Delete;

        role.ID = Convert.ToInt32(e.CommandArgument);
        role.Delete(ref validationErrors, CurrentUser.ID);

        Master.ValidationErrors = validationErrors;

        cgvRoles.DataBind();
    }
```

The `lbtnDelete_Command` takes care of deleting the record using the business object and then rebinds the grid to remove the row.

The only other code in this file is the Add button's click event handler, which is the same as the pattern defined in Chapter 4 and the implementation of the two abstract methods in the `BasePage` class:

```
    void Master_AddButton_Click(object sender, EventArgs e)
    {
        Response.Redirect("Role.aspx" + EncryptQueryString("id=0"));
```

```
    }

    public override string MenuItemName()
    {
        return "Roles";
    }

    public override string[] CapabilityNames()
    {
        return new string[] { "Roles" };
    }
```

Role Edit Page

The Role.aspx page is used to add or edit roles and allow the user to associate users and capabilities with the role. The screen has three sections. The first is a textbox for the role's name. The second section includes all the capabilities defined for the system and a radio button list with a variable number of radio buttons based on the AccessType of the capability. This is dynamically created using the ENTCapability table. The third section has two list boxes: One displays all the users who are in the role; the other displays all users who are not. Four buttons between the list boxes enable the movement of one or all items from either box to the other.

Start by adding the Role.aspx page to the Administration folder and use the PaidTimeOffEditPage .master and inherit from the BaseEditPage, passing in ENTRoleEO for the generic. Follow the same steps defined in Chapter 4 to hook up the Save and Cancel button event handlers. The Cancel button's event handler should just call the GoToGridPage method.

The next step is to create the HTML for the page. Add a ScriptManager control to enable this page to support ASP.NET AJAX functionality. ASP.NET AJAX will be used to move users from list to list when the buttons are clicked:

```
<asp:ScriptManager ID="ScriptManager1" runat="server"></asp:ScriptManager>
<asp:UpdatePanel ID="UpdatePanel1" runat="server">
<ContentTemplate>
```

An HTML table is used to position the rest of the controls on the screen. The first row contains the role name controls. The third row contains an ASP.NET server-side table control. This table will be dynamically created with the capabilities, and the radio buttons associated with each capability:

```
<table>
    <tr>
        <td>Role Name:</td>
        <td><asp:TextBox ID="txtRoleName" runat="server"></asp:TextBox></td>
    </tr>
    <tr>
        <td colspan="2">Grant rights for this role.</td>
    </tr>
    <tr>
        <td colspan="2">
            <asp:Table id="tblCapabilities" runat="server"></asp:Table>
        </td>
    </tr>
```

The fourth row contains an embedded table that contains the two list boxes, and the four buttons that are used to pass users back and forth between the two:

```
        <tr>
            <td colspan="2">
                <table>
                    <tr>
                        <td colspan="3">
                            <asp:Label ID="lblUserHeader" runat="server"
                            Text="Select the users for this role."></asp:Label>
                        </td>
                    </tr>
                    <tr>
                        <td><asp:Label ID="lblUsers" runat="server"
                            Text="Users"></asp:Label></td>
                        <td> </td>
                        <td><asp:Label ID="Label2" runat="server" Text="Users In
                            Role"></asp:Label>
                        </td>
                    </tr>
                    <tr>
                        <td>
                            <asp:ListBox ID="lstUnselectedUsers" runat="server"
                            Rows="10" SelectionMode="Multiple"></asp:ListBox>
                        </td>
                        <td>
                            <asp:Button ID="btnMoveToSelected" runat="server" Text=">"
                            onclick="btnMoveToSelected_Click" /><br />
                            <asp:Button ID="btnMoveAllToSelected" runat="server"
                            Text=">>" onclick="btnMoveAllToSelected_Click" /><br />
                            <br />
                            <asp:Button ID="btnMoveToUnselected" runat="server"
                            Text="<" onclick="btnMoveToUnselected_Click" /><br />
                            <asp:Button ID="btnMoveAllToUnselected" runat="server"
                            Text="<<" onclick="btnMoveAllToUnselected_Click" /><br />
                        </td>
                        <td>
                            <asp:ListBox ID="lstSelectedUsers" runat="server" Rows="10"
                            SelectionMode="Multiple"></asp:ListBox>
                        </td>
                    </tr>
                </table>
            </td>
        </tr>
    </table>
    </ContentTemplate>
    </asp:UpdatePanel>
```

The next step is to create the code in the code-behind page that will dynamically build the capabilities table. This table should list all the capabilities according to how the menu is structured. If more than one capability is associated with a menu item, then the capability name should be listed in parentheses next to the menu item name. Because this grid is dynamically created, it should be generated in the `OnInit` method of the page so that it persists between postbacks:

```
protected override void OnInit(EventArgs e)
{
    //You need to build the table here so it retains state between postbacks.
    BuildCapabilityTable();
    base.OnInit(e);
}
```

The `BuildCapabilityTable` code is as follows:

```
private void BuildCapabilityTable()
{
    //Get the capabilities
    ENTCapabilityBOList capabilities = Globals.GetCapabilities(Page.Cache);

    //Get the menu items
    ENTMenuItemBOList menuItems = Globals.GetMenuItems(Page.Cache);

    AddCapabilitiesForMenuItems(menuItems, capabilities, "");
}
```

This just grabs the capabilities and menu items from the cache and calls another method called `AddCapabilitiesForMenuItems`, which is another recursive method that builds the nested tree for the menu items:

```
private void AddCapabilitiesForMenuItems(ENTMenuItemBOList menuItems,
    ENTCapabilityBOList capabilities, string indentation)
{
    //Loop around each menu item and create a row for each menu item and capability
    //associated with the menu item
    foreach (ENTMenuItemBO menuItem in menuItems)
    {
        //Get any capabilities with this menu item
        IEnumerable<ENTCapabilityBO> capabilitiesForMenuItem =
            capabilities.GetByMenuItemId(menuItem.ID);

        //If there are no capabilities associated with the menu then just display
        //the menu item name without the radio buttons.
        if (capabilitiesForMenuItem.Count() == 0)
        {
            //Just add the menu item to the row
            TableRow tr = new TableRow();
            TableCell tc = new TableCell();
            LiteralControl lc = new LiteralControl();
            lc.Text = indentation + menuItem.MenuItemName;
            tc.CssClass = "capabilityHeader";
            tc.Controls.Add(lc);
            tc.ColumnSpan = 3;
```

```
                tr.Cells.Add(tc);

                tblCapabilities.Rows.Add(tr);
        }
        else
        {
            //If there is only one capability associated with this menu item then
            //just display the menu item name and the radio buttons
            if (capabilitiesForMenuItem.Count() == 1)
            {
                AddCapabilityToTable(capabilitiesForMenuItem.ElementAt(0),
                    indentation + menuItem.MenuItemName);
            }
            else
            {
                //Add a row for each capability
                foreach (ENTCapabilityBO capability in capabilitiesForMenuItem)
                {
                    AddCapabilityToTable(capability, indentation +
                        menuItem.MenuItemName + " (" + capability.CapabilityName +
                        ")");
                }
            }
        }

        if (menuItem.ChildMenuItems.Count > 0)
        {
            AddCapabilitiesForMenuItems(menuItem.ChildMenuItems, capabilities,
                indentation + "---");
        }
    }
}
```

This method loops around each menu item in the list that is passed in and builds the nested tree. If any menu item has children, then it calls itself to display the child menu items. The cell that contains the radio buttons is created in the AddCapabilityToTable method:

```
private void AddCapabilityToTable(ENTCapabilityBO capability, string text)
{
    TableRow tr = new TableRow();

    //Name
    TableCell tc = new TableCell();
    LiteralControl lc = new LiteralControl();
    lc.Text = text;
    tc.Controls.Add(lc);
    tr.Cells.Add(tc);

    //access flag
    TableCell tc1 = new TableCell();

    RadioButtonList radioButtons = new RadioButtonList();
    radioButtons.ID = capability.ID.ToString();
```

```
            switch (capability.AccessType)
            {
                case ENTCapabilityBO.AccessTypeEnum.ReadOnlyEdit:
                    radioButtons.Items.Add(new ListItem("None",
                        ENTRoleCapabilityEO.CapabiiltyAccessFlagEnum.None.ToString()));

                    radioButtons.Items.Add(new ListItem("Read Only",
                        ENTRoleCapabilityEO.CapabiiltyAccessFlagEnum.ReadOnly.ToString()));

                    radioButtons.Items.Add(new ListItem("Edit",
                        ENTRoleCapabilityEO.CapabiiltyAccessFlagEnum.Edit.ToString()));

                    radioButtons.RepeatDirection = RepeatDirection.Horizontal;
                    radioButtons.RepeatLayout = RepeatLayout.Table;
                    break;

                case ENTCapabilityBO.AccessTypeEnum.ReadOnly:
                    radioButtons.Items.Add(new ListItem("None",
                        ENTRoleCapabilityEO.CapabiiltyAccessFlagEnum.None.ToString()));

                    radioButtons.Items.Add(new ListItem("Read Only",
                        ENTRoleCapabilityEO.CapabiiltyAccessFlagEnum.ReadOnly.ToString()));

                    radioButtons.RepeatDirection = RepeatDirection.Horizontal;
                    radioButtons.RepeatLayout = RepeatLayout.Table;
                    break;

                case ENTCapabilityBO.AccessTypeEnum.Edit:
                    radioButtons.Items.Add(new ListItem("None",
                        ENTRoleCapabilityEO.CapabiiltyAccessFlagEnum.None.ToString()));

                    radioButtons.Items.Add(new ListItem("Edit",
                        ENTRoleCapabilityEO.CapabiiltyAccessFlagEnum.Edit.ToString()));

                    radioButtons.RepeatDirection = RepeatDirection.Horizontal;
                    radioButtons.RepeatLayout = RepeatLayout.Table;
                    break;
            }

        tc1.Controls.Add(radioButtons);
        tr.Cells.Add(tc1);
        tblCapabilities.Rows.Add(tr);
    }
```

The number of radio buttons to display is based on the `AccessType` of the capability: `ReadOnlyEdit` shows all radio buttons, `ReadOnly` displays the None and Read-Only radio buttons, and `Edit` displays the None and Edit radio buttons.

These few methods build the grid but do not set the selected radio buttons. That is done later in the `LoadScreenFromObject` method. This method also sets the role name text box and puts users in the appropriate list box depending on whether they are in this role or not. It then persists the object in the `ViewState`:

```
protected override void LoadScreenFromObject(ENTRoleEO baseEO)
{
    ENTRoleEO role = (ENTRoleEO)baseEO;

    txtRoleName.Text = role.RoleName;

    //Select the capabilities
    for (int row = 0; row < tblCapabilities.Rows.Count; row++)
    {
        TableRow tr = tblCapabilities.Rows[row];

        if (tr.Cells.Count > 1)
        {
            //The 2nd cell has the radio list
            RadioButtonList radioButtons = (RadioButtonList)tr.Cells[1].Controls[0];

            //Check if the role has this capability
            ENTRoleCapabilityEO capability =
          role.RoleCapabilities.GetByCapabilityID(Convert.ToInt32(radioButtons.ID));

            if (capability != null)
            {
                //set the access
                radioButtons.SelectedValue = capability.AccessFlag.ToString();
            }
            else
            {
                //default to none.
                radioButtons.SelectedIndex = 0;
            }
            capability = null;
        }
    }

    //Select the users
    //Get all the users
    ENTUserAccountEOList users = Globals.GetUsers(Page.Cache);

    foreach (ENTUserAccountEO user in users)
    {
        if (role.RoleUserAccounts.IsUserInRole(user.ID))
        {
            lstSelectedUsers.Items.Add(new ListItem(user.DisplayText,
                user.ID.ToString()));
        }
        else
        {
            lstUnselectedUsers.Items.Add(new ListItem(user.DisplayText,
                user.ID.ToString()));
        }
    }

    ViewState[VIEW_STATE_KEY_ROLE] = role;
}
```

The next step is to implement the Save button's click event handler. The only difference between this method and the method described in Chapter 4 is that the users and roles should be reloaded in the cache on a successful save. Other than that, this code is boilerplate from the design pattern for the UI:

```
void Master_SaveButton_Click(object sender, EventArgs e)
{
        ENTValidationErrors validationErrors = new ENTValidationErrors();

        ENTRoleEO role = (ENTRoleEO)ViewState[VIEW_STATE_KEY_ROLE];
        LoadObjectFromScreen(role);

        if (!role.Save(ref validationErrors, CurrentUser.ID))
        {
            Master.ValidationErrors = validationErrors;
        }
        else
        {
            //Reload the globals
            Globals.LoadUsers(Page.Cache);
            Globals.LoadRoles(Page.Cache);
            GoToGridPage();
        }
}
```

This method calls `LoadObjectFromScreen`, which moves the values in the controls to the properties of the object. This method is a little tricky on this screen because three different tables are being maintained: `ENTRole`, `ENTRoleCapability`, and `ENTRoleUserAccount`. The only field on the `ENTRole` table is `RoleName`, so that is easy to set:

```
protected override void LoadObjectFromScreen(ENTRoleEO baseEO)
{
    baseEO.RoleName = txtRoleName.Text;
```

`ENTCapabilities` has a many-to-one relationship with the `ENTRole` table. This is implemented as a property of the `ENTRoleEO` object, which is of the `ENTRoleCapabilityEOList` type. The code loops through each row displayed in the `Capabilities` table on the screen, determines which radio button is selected, and then sets this value to the corresponding object in the `ENTRoleCapabilityEOList` object:

```
//Load the capabilities
for (int row = 0; row < tblCapabilities.Rows.Count; row++)
{
    TableRow tr = tblCapabilities.Rows[row];

    if (tr.Cells.Count > 1)
    {
        //The 2nd cell has the radio list
        RadioButtonList radioButtons = (RadioButtonList)tr.Cells[1].Controls[0];

        //The radio button's id contains the id of the capability.
        int capabilityId = Convert.ToInt32(radioButtons.ID);

        string value = radioButtons.SelectedValue;
```

```
                    ENTRoleCapabilityEO.CapabiiltyAccessFlagEnum accessFlag =
        (ENTRoleCapabilityEO.CapabiiltyAccessFlagEnum)Enum.Parse(typeof(ENTRoleCapabilityEO
        .CapabiiltyAccessFlagEnum), value);

                    //Try to find an existing record for this capability
                    ENTRoleCapabilityEO capability =
                        baseEO.RoleCapabilities.GetByCapabilityID(capabilityId);
                    if (capability == null)
                    {
                        //New record
                        ENTRoleCapabilityEO roleCapability = new ENTRoleCapabilityEO();
                        roleCapability.ENTRoleId = baseEO.ID;
                        roleCapability.Capability.ID = capabilityId;
                        roleCapability.AccessFlag = accessFlag;
                        baseEO.RoleCapabilities.Add(roleCapability);
                    }
                    else
                    {
                        //Update an existing record
                        capability.AccessFlag = accessFlag;
                    }
                }
            }
        }
```

The last step in this method is to load the users for this role. The tricky part here is that users could be added to the role or removed. The code first looks at all users in the list box who are in this role, adding any that weren't in the role before. Keeping the original object in the `ViewState` makes this simple to determine:

```
        //Load the selected users
        //Add any users that were not in the role before.
        foreach (ListItem li in lstSelectedUsers.Items)
        {
            //Check if they were already selected.
            if (baseEO.RoleUserAccounts.IsUserInRole(Convert.ToInt32(li.Value)) ==
                false)
            {
                //If they weren't then add them.
                baseEO.RoleUserAccounts.Add(new ENTRoleUserAccountEO { ENTUserAccountId
                    = Convert.ToInt32(li.Value), ENTRoleId = baseEO.ID });
            }
        }
```

The next step is to mark for deletion any users who were in the role before but have been removed:

```
        //Remove any users that used to be selected but now are not.
        foreach (ListItem li in lstUnselectedUsers.Items)
        {
            //Check if they were in the role before
            if (baseEO.RoleUserAccounts.IsUserInRole(Convert.ToInt32(li.Value)))
            {
                //Mark them for deletion.
                ENTRoleUserAccountEO user =
```

```
                baseEO.RoleUserAccounts.GetByUserAccountId(Convert.ToInt32(li.Value));

                user.DBAction = ENTBaseEO.DBActionEnum.Delete;
            }
        }
    }
```

Now, add the event handlers for the four buttons that will move users between the two list boxes:

```
    protected void btnMoveToSelected_Click(object sender, EventArgs e)
    {
        MoveItems(lstUnselectedUsers, lstSelectedUsers, false);
    }

    protected void btnMoveToUnselected_Click(object sender, EventArgs e)
    {
        MoveItems(lstSelectedUsers, lstUnselectedUsers, false);
    }

    protected void btnMoveAllToSelected_Click(object sender, EventArgs e)
    {
        MoveItems(lstUnselectedUsers, lstSelectedUsers, true);
    }

    protected void btnMoveAllToUnselected_Click(object sender, EventArgs e)
    {
        MoveItems(lstSelectedUsers, lstUnselectedUsers, true);
    }

    private void MoveItems(ListBox lstSource, ListBox lstDestination, bool moveAll)
    {
        for (int i = 0; i < lstSource.Items.Count; i++)
        {
            ListItem li = lstSource.Items[i];

            if ((moveAll == true) || (li.Selected == true))
            {
                //Add to destination
                li.Selected = false;
                lstDestination.Items.Add(li);
                lstSource.Items.RemoveAt(i);
                i--;
            }
        }
    }
```

Because this page has AJAX enabled, users won't even see the postback when they click the buttons.

The last step is to implement the security for this page. Implement the abstract method called CapabilityNames and pass back the capability that this page is associated with:

```
    public override string[] CapabilityNames()
    {
        return new string[] { "Roles" };
    }
```

The BasePage handles all the logic for making the textbox and radio controls read-only, but the list boxes that display the users in the role need to be explicitly hidden if a user has read-only rights to this screen. The arrow buttons that move users from one list box to the other should also be hidden. To do this, override the CustomReadOnlyLogic method:

```
public override void CustomReadOnlyLogic(string capabilityName)
{
    base.CustomReadOnlyLogic(capabilityName);

    //If this is read only then do not show the available choice for the users or
    //the buttons to swap between list boxes
    lstUnselectedUsers.Visible = false;
    btnMoveAllToSelected.Visible = false;
    btnMoveAllToUnselected.Visible = false;
    btnMoveToSelected.Visible = false;
    btnMoveToUnselected.Visible = false;
    lblUsers.Visible = false;
    lblUserHeader.Visible = false;
}
```

That's it. Now the screens are built that enable users to administer the application themselves, and the pattern for implementing security throughout the application has been defined. The first few pages that you build using this pattern will be the hardest to understand, but once you do it a few times, it becomes easy because it involves the exact same steps each time. Chapter 13 builds a code generator to generate most of this code for you, so you won't even have to write the repetitive code.

Summary

Recall from Chapter 1 that when Mary was explaining her requirements, she asked for some type of security. Although she could only vaguely describe what she wanted and didn't understand security terminology, by implementing the pattern designed in this chapter you have now successfully met Mary's requirements for role-based security.

The key points to remember when adding a new page and applying security to it are as follows:

❑ Add one or more records to the ENTMenuItem table. Usually, one record is added to the table for the two pages for data entry screens. The menu item navigates to the list page and from there the user can get to the data entry page.

❑ Add one or more records to the ENTCapability table. Usually, one record is used for both the list page and the data entry page, but in some situations more than one capability will be associated with a page. Remember to add the id of the menu item on the capability record.

❑ Set the correct AccessType on the ENTCapability record so it appears correctly on the Role screen. An enumeration maps to the AccessType field and can have three values: ReadOnlyEdit, ReadOnly, or Edit. You can add more if you want to customize the security for your own needs.

❑ When creating a page, you must override the CapabilityNames method and return an array of strings that map to the capabilities for this page. Most of the time this method returns only one capability name.

❑ If you have nonstandard input controls on a form or you need to implement special logic that isn't covered in the `BasePage.MakeFormReadOnly` method, then override the `CustomRead OnlyLogic` method and add your specific logic.

❑ If you have more then one capability associated with a page, then override the `NoAccessToPage` method to hide or disable the controls associated with that specific capability and prevent an exception from being thrown by the `BasePage` class.

❑ If your page does not have security associated with it, then set the `IgnoreCapabilityCheck` to true in the page's `OnInit` method.

❑ In any grid page that has Edit links, check the `ReadOnly` property of the page to determine whether the text of the link should be set to "Edit" or "View."

❑ In any grid page that has a Delete link, check the `ReadOnly` property of the page to determine whether the link should be shown.

The next chapter focuses on building the workflow engine that will be used to track the status of a paid time off request. The workflow in this application uses a state machine workflow that consists of states and transitions. The design is actually flexible enough that you could use it in any application that has an approval process, or even a more complex process such as a defect-tracking system. The design pattern enables you to make as many states and transitions as you like, so as you read the next chapter focus on the pattern rather than the specific implementation of the pattern. Remember that the goal of this book is to provide you with a framework that you can reuse in your own applications, and get that big raise the next time you have a performance review.

7

The Workflow Engine

How many applications have you written that have some type of workflow for which one user enters a request and a second user approves it? Or one user enters some data and a second person verifies it? In the real world these business processes are ubiquitous. Human resources might have a vacation request process, a travel request process, and even a weekend stay-over process. Many companies have new hire processes whereby new users must be set up on the network, entered into the payroll system, have their e-mail set up, have a phone ordered, and more. Software development shops have change request processes that require all requests to be approved before being worked on. The list goes on and on. If you take a moment to consider all the business applications you've built, you'll probably find that a good number of them include workflow.

In its most basic form, a *workflow* is any defined business process that entails an *issue* moving from one *state* to another; and it requires that the current *owner* of the issue *transition* the issue to an end point. A simple document approval workflow is represented in Figure 7-1.

Submitter

Initial Request

Waiting For Approval
Direct Manager

Approved

Closed
Submitter

Figure 7-1

Problem

In any given document workflow, there is always an initial submission that enters the waiting approval state. When it is waiting approval, the document must have an owner assigned to approve the document. The owner can then approve the document and the issue is transitioned to a closed state. Let's make things a little more complicated. For example, suppose the approver doesn't want to approve the document. It then has to be sent back to the submitter to be changed. The approver transitions the document back to the submitter, and the document is now in a resubmit state and the new owner is the original submitter. When a document is sent back to the submitter, the submitter can either resubmit the document for approval or cancel the request. If the issue is cancelled, the workflow ends. If it is sent back to the approver, then the state is changed again to waiting for approval and the owner is the approver. The document can go back and forth many times until it is approved. Once approved, the issue goes to a closed state and the owner is the submitter but the document is locked down. Of course, this procedure can get very ugly very fast, even with the simplest workflow containing only a few steps.

The goal of this chapter is to build a framework with a set of tables, classes, and controls that enable you to "hook" a workflow to an object in your system. This chapter uses the requirements defined by Mary for the paid time off approval process, but it is designed in such a way that you can extend it in your own applications and even set up multiple workflows in the same application for different types of objects.

Speaking from experience, the hardest part of using the workflow developed in this book is not the coding piece — it's getting users to accurately define all aspects of their business process. Typically, the client gives you the "happy path" when defining the requirements, and then a week after you've released the application they tell you about the exceptions. The workflow framework described here enables you to add features to the workflow without making any coding changes. It may sound daunting now, but keep reading; after walking through some concrete examples, everything will be clear by the end of the chapter.

Design

Let's go back to our conversation with Mary again to review her requirements and pick out those that are relevant to workflow.

Me: "So you want to automate the process of requesting vacation. I've used that template, so I know a little bit about the process, but I don't know what happens after my manager signs it. Can you tell me how the process is supposed to work?"

Mary: "When employees want to take a vacation or holiday, they are supposed to fill out the form, print it, sign it, and then hand it to their manager for approval and signature. The manager is then supposed to sign it and inter-office mail it to HR, where I check it against my Excel spreadsheet to ensure that the employee has enough days to cover the request. I then subtract the days in my spreadsheet. Also, people who want to take more than two weeks off at a time need to have their manager and a vice president sign off on the request. This really causes problems because the VPs are so busy they rarely send us the form."

Me: "Then you need a system that allows a user to request time off and then have workflow built into the system for the manager, vice president, and you to approve or deny the request. What the user enters will determine how many levels of approval are needed."

Mary: "Well, yes. I guess we would need to be able to deny the request too, but we usually just throw them out. It probably would be a good idea to keep them around so we could refer to them."

Based on this conversation and some common sense, the following statements can be made:

- There are seven states in the workflow: Waiting Direct Manger Approval, Waiting VP Approval, Waiting HR approval, Approved, Denied, Cancelled, and Resubmit.
- There are four groups of users: the Submitter, the Direct Manager, the VP, and the HR Administrator.
- When a request is in the Waiting Direct Manager Approval state, the direct manager owns the issue.
- When a request is in the Waiting VP Approval state, the VP owns the issue.
- When a request is in the Waiting HR Approval, Denied, or Cancelled state, the HR administrator owns the issue.
- When a request is in the Approved or Resubmit state, the submitter owns the issue.
- When a request is made it must go to the Waiting Direct Manager Approval state.
- When a request is in the Waiting Direct Manager Approval state, it can be denied, approved and sent to HR, approved and sent to the VP, or asked to be resubmitted.
- When a request is in the Waiting VP Approval state, it can be denied, approved, or asked to be resubmitted.
- When a request is in the Waiting HR Approval state, it can be denied, approved, or asked to be resubmitted.
- When a request is in the Approved state, the submitter can cancel it.
- When a request is in the Denied or Cancelled states, it cannot be transitioned to anyone else.
- When a request is in the Resubmit state, it can be cancelled or sent to the direct manager for approval again.

Graphically, this looks like what is shown in Figure 7-2.

Each picture represents a state, and each arrow emanating from a picture represents a transition. The user who should be assigned ownership in each state is in the picture's description. The workflow framework that is built in this chapter will enable you to create a workflow, create states in a workflow, create a group of users who are the available owners of an issue, and create transitions. A series of screens will be built that enable you or a trusted user to add any of these items after the launch of the application.

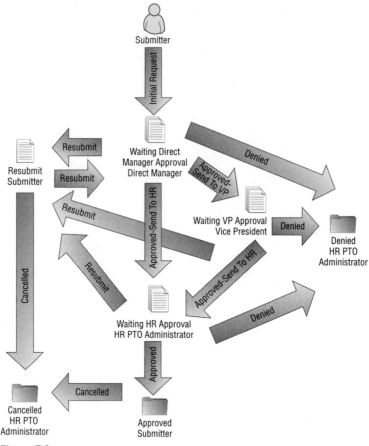

Figure 7-2

Workflow Table Design

Figure 7-3 consists of the tables that make up the data model for the workflow engine. The ENTWorkflow table is the main table. It consists of the name of the workflow and the fully qualified object name that this workflow should be associated with. Because the workflow engine is generic, it isn't specific to the actual types of issues being sent through the workflow. For this application, a new class called PTORequestEO will be created and hooked to the workflow.

The next table to describe is the ENTWFOwnerGroup table. This table is used to represent the list of users who can own an issue for any given state. For example, in the PTO Request application, the direct manager is the owner when the request is initially submitted and waiting direct manager approval. The direct manager will vary according to who made the request. The ENTWFOwnerGroup would contain a record with the name "Direct Manager," and the employees associated with this group will be added to the ENTWFOwnerGroupUserAccount table. Another group of users are the vice presidents, and the third group is the HR administrators. Each of these groups will have their own list of associated users.

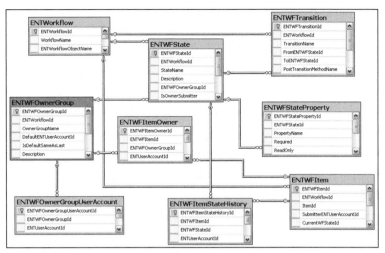

Figure 7-3

The `ENTWFState` table enables the user to define one or more states for this workflow. When defining a state, the user can optionally give it a description. There are also two more important fields. First is the `ENTWFOwnerGroupId`, which is required and tells the system which group owns the issue when it is in that state. For example, the Waiting Direct Manager Approval state would have this set to the Direct Managers group. The user who is assigned as the Direct Manager would be the owner whenever it goes to the Waiting Direct Manager Approval state. The second field is called `IsOwnerSubmitter`, which tells the system not to look at the `ENTWFOwnerGroupId`, but rather the person who submitted the request, and make them the owner. For example, when a request is sent back for resubmission, the state is changed to Resubmit but the owner should be the submitter.

The `ENTWFStateProperty` table is a child of the `ENTWFState` table, which stores all the property names for the object associated with this workflow. The user can enforce required and read-only business rules based on the state of the item. For example, when a request is submitted, the request date is required. When a request is in the Waiting Direct Manager Approval state, the request date should be read-only. If the request is sent back to the user for resubmission, then the request date should be editable again. This can be a very powerful feature in a complex workflow because you can enforce some business rules without having to change the system.

The `ENTWFTransition` table represents the allowed transitions from one state to another. For example, if a request is in the Waiting Direct Manager Approval state and the user wants to approve the request to send it to the HR administrator, then a transition would be created with the name "Approved–Send to HR Administrator," the `FromENTWFStateId` field would point to the Waiting Direct Manager Approval state, and the `ToENTWFStateId` field would point to the Waiting HR Administrator Approval state.

The last field in this table, `PostTransitionMethodName`, enables you to specify a method on the object associated with the workflow. This method will be executed dynamically after the transition is complete. An example of when you might use this is for an accounting workflow for approving costs. If a cost is approved, then you could subtract it from the budget, but only after it is approved.

The `ENTWFItem` table contains the associated ID of the record associated with the workflow. In our application, a new table called `PTORequest` will contain all the fields associated with a PTO request, and the ID of that record will be added to the `ENTWFItem` table to associate it with the workflow. The `SubmitterENTUserAccountId` field contains the ID for the user who submitted the original request. The `CurrentWFStateId` field stores the current state of the item in the workflow.

The `ENTWFItemOwner` table contains the specific users who can own the issue when it moves to a specific state. For example, if your direct manager is Bob, your VP is Jane, and the HR administrator is Mary, then this table would contain three records, each pointing to the `ENTWFOwnerGroup` and `ENTUserAccount` record.

The last table to describe is `ENTWFItemStateHistory`. This stores a history indicating every time an item was moved from state to state or the current owner of the item changed. Because all records also have the `Inserted Date` and `Inserted By` fields, you can determine how long an item has been sitting with any one person.

The `Chapter7WorkflowTables.sql` file contains the DDL statements to create these tables.

It's tough to visualize all this without going through the screens that these tables actually affect. Figure 7-4 shows a screen shot of the workflow control that will be built later in this chapter. It may be helpful to see how these tables are represented to users.

Figure 7-4

This control displays the item's current state and current owner. The owner is in parentheses. The Actions drop-down list contains all the transitions that are allowed when an issue is in the Waiting Direct Manager Approval state. The Users drop-down lists are dynamically created and display all groups that have been defined for this workflow and all users in the group. The last section displays a table with the state, the person who owned the request, the time they received the request, and who sent it to them. This grid will be very important to users when they are trying to determine who is associated with any bottleneck in the process. Just be prepared to print this out and bring it to the witch hunt meetings.

The next section describes each object in the workflow framework and builds the screens that enable users to create their own workflow. Once the workflow is built, the solution section in this chapter will build the PTO Request screen and associated objects, and show you how to hook this to the workflow.

Stored Procedures

A lot of stored procedures are used in the workflow framework but most of them are the standard Insert, Update, Delete, and Select. A few custom selects use different where clauses, but they are essentially the same. This section explains any of the custom procedures for the workflow that are worth mentioning.

The ENTWFOwnerGroup table has a field called IsDefaultSameAsLast that is used to default the owner to the same owner as the requestor's last request. This is useful for the Direct Manager Group because after users make their first request, subsequent requests will default to the same manager:

```
CREATE PROCEDURE ENTWFItemOwnerSelectLastUserByGroupId
(
    @ENTWFOwnerGroupId int,
    @ENTUserAccountId int
)
AS
    SET NOCOUNT ON

     SELECT TOP(1) ENTUserAccountId
        FROM ENTWFItem
  INNER JOIN ENTWFItemOwner
          ON ENTWFItem.ENTWFItemId = ENTWFItemOwner.ENTWFItemId
       WHERE ENTWFOwnerGroupId = @ENTWFOwnerGroupId
         AND ENTWFItem.InsertENTUserAccountId = @ENTUserAccountId
    ORDER BY ENTWFItem.InsertDate Desc

    RETURN
```

When defining owners, the name of the group must be unique across the workflow. The standard IsDuplicate method won't work because the requirement is to be unique across a workflow, not the entire table. To accomplish this, create the following custom stored procedure:

```
CREATE PROCEDURE ENTWFOwnerGroupSelectCountByNameWorkflowId
(
   @ENTWFOwnerGroupId int,
   @ENTWorkflowId int,
   @OwnerGroupName varchar(50)
)
AS
   SET NOCOUNT ON

   SELECT COUNT(1) AS CountOfNames
     FROM ENTWFOwnerGroup
    WHERE OwnerGroupName = @OwnerGroupName
      AND ENTWorkflowId = @ENTWorkflowId
      AND ENTWFOwnerGroupId <> @ENTWFOwnerGroupId

   RETURN
```

The following stored procedure is called when a user tries to delete a state. If a state is associated with an Owner Group, then it cannot be deleted. Recall that the ENTBaseEO business object class has a ValidateDelete method that can call this stored procedure to give users a friendly message if the state cannot be deleted:

```
CREATE PROCEDURE ENTWFStateSelectCountByENTWFOwnerGroupId
(
    @ENTWFOwnerGroupId int
)
AS
    SET NOCOUNT ON

    SELECT COUNT(1) AS CountOfStates
      FROM ENTWFState
     WHERE ENTWFOwnerGroupId = @ENTWFOwnerGroupId

    RETURN
```

This next stored procedure is interesting because it uses dynamic SQL to return the correct data. The goal of this procedure is to return the list of transitions that should be shown to the user based on the issue's current state. However, when an issue is being submitted for the first time, its state is not defined yet. You need to create a transition that has an ENTWFFromStateId of NULL. The stored procedure takes only one parameter, which could be NULL or an integer value. If the value passed in is NULL, then the where clause must use the IS NULL syntax. If it is not Null, then it must use the "=" syntax. However, because a dynamic SQL statement is being created, the Id must be converted to a string and appended to the rest of the SQL string. Here is an example:

```
CREATE PROCEDURE ENTWFTransitionSelectByFromStateId
(
    @FromENTWFStateId int
)
AS
    SET NOCOUNT ON

    DECLARE @SQL varchar(1000)

    SET @SQL = 'SELECT ENTWFTransitionId, ENTWFTransition.ENTWorkflowId,
        TransitionName, FromENTWFStateId, ToENTWFStateId, PostTransitionMethodName,
        ENTWFTransition.InsertDate, ENTWFTransition.InsertENTUserAccountId,
        ENTWFTransition.UpdateDate, ENTWFTransition.UpdateENTUserAccountId,
        ENTWFTransition.Version,
        ENTWFState.StateName AS FromStateName, ENTWFState1.StateName AS ToStateName
            FROM ENTWFTransition
      INNER JOIN ENTWFState AS ENTWFState1
            ON ENTWFState1.ENTWFStateId = ENTWFTransition.ToENTWFStateId
 LEFT OUTER JOIN ENTWFState
            ON ENTWFState.ENTWFStateId = ENTWFTransition.FromENTWFStateId '

    IF @FromENTWFStateId IS NULL
        SET @SQL = @SQL + 'WHERE FromENTWFStateId IS NULL'
    ELSE
        SET @SQL = @SQL + 'WHERE FromENTWFStateId = ' + CONVERT(varchar(15), @
                            FromENTWFStateId)
```

```
EXEC(@SQL)

RETURN
```

Notice that the `Select` clause returns the `FromStateName` and `ToStateName` columns by join-ing to the `ENTWFState` table. Because this stored procedure returns extra fields that are not in the `ENTWFTransition` table, the entity object must be customized to handle these fields. The other `Select` procedures for the `ENTWFTransition` table should also be customized to return these fields so the same entity object can be used for all `Select` stored procedures:

```
CREATE PROCEDURE ENTWFTransitionSelectAll
AS
    SET NOCOUNT ON

        SELECT ENTWFTransitionId, ENTWFTransition.ENTWorkflowId, TransitionName,
            FromENTWFStateId, ToENTWFStateId, PostTransitionMethodName,
            ENTWFTransition.InsertDate, ENTWFTransition.InsertENTUserAccountId,
            ENTWFTransition.UpdateDate, ENTWFTransition.UpdateENTUserAccountId,
            ENTWFTransition.Version,
            ENTWFState.StateName AS FromStateName,
            ENTWFState1.StateName AS ToStateName
          FROM ENTWFTransition
      INNER JOIN ENTWFState AS ENTWFState1
            ON ENTWFState1.ENTWFStateId = ENTWFTransition.ToENTWFStateId
LEFT OUTER JOIN ENTWFState
            ON ENTWFState.ENTWFStateId = ENTWFTransition.FromENTWFStateId

    RETURN
```

```
CREATE PROCEDURE ENTWFTransitionSelectById
(
    @ENTWFTransitionId int
)
AS
    SET NOCOUNT ON

        SELECT ENTWFTransitionId, ENTWFTransition.ENTWorkflowId, TransitionName,
            FromENTWFStateId, ToENTWFStateId, PostTransitionMethodName,
            ENTWFTransition.InsertDate, ENTWFTransition.InsertENTUserAccountId,
            ENTWFTransition.UpdateDate, ENTWFTransition.UpdateENTUserAccountId,
            ENTWFTransition.Version,
            ENTWFState.StateName AS FromStateName,
            ENTWFState1.StateName AS ToStateName
          FROM ENTWFTransition
      INNER JOIN ENTWFState AS ENTWFState1
            ON ENTWFState1.ENTWFStateId = ENTWFTransition.ToENTWFStateId
LEFT OUTER JOIN ENTWFState
            ON ENTWFState.ENTWFStateId = ENTWFTransition.FromENTWFStateId
         WHERE ENTWFTransitionId = @ENTWFTransitionId

    RETURN
```

There are a few other Select stored procedures that join to other tables and return extra fields, but they are not listed here for the sake of brevity. The Chapter7WorkflowStoredProcedures.sql file contains all the stored procedures, so you should run this file against your database before proceeding to create the entity objects.

Entity Objects and Data Context

Now that the workflow tables and stored procedures are created, you can create the entity objects in the DAL. Drag the ENTWorkflow, ENTWFState, ENTWFTransition, ENTWFOwnerGroup, ENTWFItemOwner, ENTWFStateProperty, ENTWFOwnerGroupUserAccount, ENTWFItemStateHistory, and ENTWFItem tables onto the ORM Designer (see Figure 7-5).

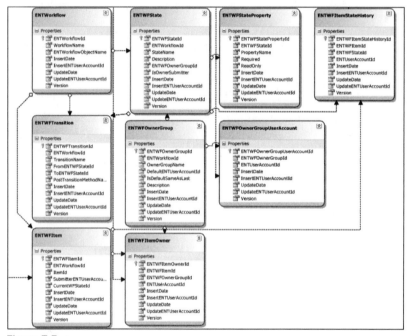

Figure 7-5

Next, drag all the Insert, Update, and Delete stored procedures that begin with ENTWF to the Methods pane. Multiple stored procedures can be highlighted at once by holding down the Ctrl key and clicking on the stored procedure name. You can then drag them to the Methods pane all at once. Do not drag any of the Select stored procedures yet because some of them have been customized, so the entity objects need to be customized first. Create the partial classes in the CustomizedEntities.cs file so the entity objects inherit from the IENTBaseEntity object:

```
public partial class ENTWorkflow : IENTBaseEntity { }

public partial class ENTWFOwnerGroup : IENTBaseEntity { }
```

```
    public partial class ENTWFState : IENTBaseEntity { }

    public partial class ENTWFStateProperty : IENTBaseEntity { }
```

Five classes need to be customized because the stored procedures return extra fields. They are
ENTWFTransition, ENTWFItem, ENTWFItemOwner, ENTWFItemStateHistory, and ENTWFOwner
GroupUserAccount. These classes should be created in the CustomizedEntities.cs file. To append
extra fields to an entity class, you need to create a member variable to store the field's value, create the
On*PropertyName*Changing and On*PropertyName*Changed partial methods, and create the property get
and set accessors. The property contains a Column attribute that contains the name of the member variable to store the data, the SQL Server type, whether it can be null, and whether this field should be used
for a concurrency check. Since the application isn't using LINQ to SQL's default functionality for concurrency, this can be set to Never.

Here is the code for the ENTWFTransition class, which contains the FromStateName and ToStateName
fields that are returned from the stored procedures. You need to add a using directive to the System
.Data.Linq.Mapping namespace at the top of the file.

```
    public partial class ENTWFTransition : IENTBaseEntity
    {
        private string _FromStateName;
        private string _ToStateName;

        partial void OnFromStateNameChanging(string value);
        partial void OnFromStateNameChanged();

        partial void OnToStateNameChanging(string value);
        partial void OnToStateNameChanged();

        [Column(Storage = "_FromStateName", DbType = "VarChar(50)", CanBeNull = true,
         UpdateCheck = UpdateCheck.Never)]
        public string FromStateName
        {
            get
            {
                return this._FromStateName;
            }
            set
            {
                if ((this._FromStateName != value))
                {
                    this.OnFromStateNameChanging(value);
                    this.SendPropertyChanging();
                    this._FromStateName = value;
                    this.SendPropertyChanged("FromStateName");
                    this.OnFromStateNameChanged();
                }
            }
        }

        [Column(Storage = "_ToStateName", DbType = "VarChar(50) NOT NULL", CanBeNull =
         false, UpdateCheck = UpdateCheck.Never)]
        public string ToStateName
```

```
        {
            get
            {
                return this._ToStateName;
            }
            set
            {
                if ((this._ToStateName != value))
                {
                    this.OnToStateNameChanging(value);
                    this.SendPropertyChanging();
                    this._ToStateName = value;
                    this.SendPropertyChanged("ToStateName");
                    this.OnToStateNameChanged();
                }
            }
        }
    }
}
```

The ENTWFItem class needs to be changed to store the submitter's user name. Since the field is a concatenation of the first name and the last name, the size must set to 102 to accommodate 50 characters for the first name, 50 characters for the last name, the comma, and the space:

```
public partial class ENTWFItem : IENTBaseEntity
{
    private string _SubmitterUserName;

    partial void OnSubmitterUserNameChanging(string value);
    partial void OnSubmitterUserNameChanged();

    [Column(Storage = "_SubmitterUserName", DbType = "VarChar(102)", UpdateCheck =
    UpdateCheck.Never)]
    public string SubmitterUserName
    {
        get
        {
            return this._SubmitterUserName;
        }
        set
        {
            if ((this._SubmitterUserName != value))
            {
                this.OnSubmitterUserNameChanging(value);
                this.SendPropertyChanging();
                this._SubmitterUserName = value;
                this.SendPropertyChanged("SubmitterUserName");
                this.OnSubmitterUserNameChanged();
            }
        }
    }
}
```

The `ENTWFItem` class needs to be changed to store the user's name who is designated as the owner of the issue for a specific state:

```
public partial class ENTWFItemOwner : IENTBaseEntity
{
    private string _UserName;

    partial void OnUserNameChanging(string value);
    partial void OnUserNameChanged();

    [Column(Storage = "_UserName", DbType = "VarChar(102)", UpdateCheck =
     UpdateCheck.Never)]
    public string UserName
    {
        get
        {
            return this._UserName;
        }
        set
        {
            if ((this._UserName != value))
            {
                this.OnUserNameChanging(value);
                this.SendPropertyChanging();
                this._UserName = value;
                this.SendPropertyChanged("UserName");
                this.OnUserNameChanged();
            }
        }
    }
}
```

The `ENTWFItemStateHistory` needs to be changed to return the state name, the owner, and the person who transitioned the item. The person who transitioned the item can be determined by looking at the `InsertedBy` field:

```
public partial class ENTWFItemStateHistory : IENTBaseEntity
{
    private string _StateName;
    private string _OwnerName;
    private string _InsertedBy;

    partial void OnStateNameChanging(string value);
    partial void OnStateNameChanged();

    partial void OnOwnerNameChanging(string value);
    partial void OnOwnerNameChanged();

    partial void OnInsertedByChanging(string value);
    partial void OnInsertedByChanged();
```

```
[Column(Storage = "_StateName", DbType = "VarChar(50)", UpdateCheck =
UpdateCheck.Never)]
public string StateName
{
    get
    {
        return this._StateName;
    }
    set
    {
        if ((this._StateName != value))
        {
            this.OnStateNameChanging(value);
            this.SendPropertyChanging();
            this._StateName = value;
            this.SendPropertyChanged("StateName");
            this.OnStateNameChanged();
        }
    }
}

[Column(Storage = "_OwnerName", DbType = "VarChar(102) NOT NULL", CanBeNull =
false, UpdateCheck = UpdateCheck.Never)]
public string OwnerName
{
    get
    {
        return this._OwnerName;
    }
    set
    {
        if ((this._OwnerName != value))
        {
            this.OnOwnerNameChanging(value);
            this.SendPropertyChanging();
            this._OwnerName = value;
            this.SendPropertyChanged("OwnerName");
            this.OnOwnerNameChanged();
        }
    }
}

[Column(Storage = "_InsertedBy", DbType = "VarChar(102) NOT NULL", CanBeNull =
false, UpdateCheck = UpdateCheck.Never)]
public string InsertedBy
{
    get
    {
        return this._InsertedBy;
    }
    set
    {
        if ((this.InsertedBy != value))
        {
```

```
                  this.OnInsertedByChanging(value);
                  this.SendPropertyChanging();
                  this._InsertedBy = value;
                  this.SendPropertyChanged("InsertedBy");
                  this.OnInsertedByChanged();
               }
           }
       }
   }
```

The `ENTWFOwnerGroupUserAccount` class also needs to be changed to return the user's name:

```
public partial class ENTWFOwnerGroupUserAccount : IENTBaseEntity
{
    private string _UserName;

    partial void OnUserNameChanging(string value);
    partial void OnUserNameChanged();

    [Column(Storage = "_UserName", DbType = "VarChar(102)", UpdateCheck =
     UpdateCheck.Never)]
    public string UserName
    {
        get
        {
            return this._UserName;
        }
        set
        {
            if ((this._UserName != value))
            {
                this.OnUserNameChanging(value);
                this.SendPropertyChanging();
                this._UserName = value;
                this.SendPropertyChanged("UserName");
                this.OnUserNameChanged();
            }
        }
    }
}
```

Now you can drag the `Select` stored procedures, except the `ENTWFTransitionSelectByFromStateId`, onto their respective tables. This will create the methods in the `DataContext` that return the table's entity object. The `ENTWFTransitionSelectByFromStateId` uses dynamic SQL, so you would get an error if you tried to drop it on the `ENTWFTransition` table in the ORM Designer. You want the method to return the table's entity object, but you can't count on the ORM Designer to do it for you. Drag the stored procedure to the Methods pane and then open the `HRPaidTimeOff.designer.cs` file. Search for the `ENTWFTransitionSelectByFromStateId` method:

```
[Function(Name="dbo.ENTWFTransitionSelectByFromStateId")]
public int ENTWFTransitionSelectByFromStateId([Parameter(Name="FromENTWFStateId",
    DbType="Int")] System.Nullable<int> fromENTWFStateId)
{
```

```
    IExecuteResult result = this.ExecuteMethodCall(this,
        ((MethodInfo)(MethodInfo.GetCurrentMethod())), fromENTWFStateId);
    return ((int)(result.ReturnValue));
}
```

By default, the return value is an `int`, which is incorrect. You could modify the method to return the entity object, but then every time a change was made to the ORM Designer, you would have to remember to change it again. To solve this problem you can create a partial class for the `HRPaidTimeOff` `DataContext` and add this method.

Delete the method from the ORM Designer. Right-click on the `V2.PaidTimeOffDAL` project, add a new class named `HRPaidTimeOffDataContext.cs`, and click the Add button. Add three `using` statements to the class:

```
using System.Data.Linq.Mapping;
using System.Data.Linq;
using System.Reflection;
```

Change the declaration of the class so that it is public, partial, and inherits from the `System.Data`.`Linq.DataContext` class:

```
public partial class HRPaidTimeOffDataContext : System.Data.Linq.DataContext
```

Now add the method signature for the stored procedure. The method should have an attribute that tells LINQ to SQL the name of the stored procedure to call:

```
[Function(Name = "dbo.ENTWFTransitionSelectByFromStateId")]
public ISingleResult<ENTWFTransition> ENTWFTransitionSelectByFromStateId(
    [Parameter(Name = "FromENTWFStateId", DbType = "Int")] System.Nullable<int>
    fromENTWFStateId)
```

The body of the method should execute the stored procedure and return the result:

```
IExecuteResult result = this.ExecuteMethodCall(this, ((MethodInfo)
    (MethodInfo.GetCurrentMethod())), fromENTWFStateId);

return ((ISingleResult<ENTWFTransition>)(result.ReturnValue));
```

Now you don't have to worry about this method being overwritten when the ORM Designer is changed because this class is outside the `designer.cs` file.

The next step is to add the data classes to the DAL for each table. Add the files to the `Framework` folder in the DAL project. Each data class follows the same pattern defined in Chapter 2, so they all have `Insert`, `Update`, `Delete`, and `Select` methods. In Chapter 13, a code generator is created that will automatically generate this code for you. For now, you're probably better off just using the code included with the book and including the files in your own project. Some of the classes have methods for duplicate checks and custom selects, but there is nothing special worth noting about them so they are omitted in this section.

Business Classes

The business classes contain the validation rules and business logic for creating a workflow. Again, most of this code is generic and was defined in Chapter 3. All the objects inherit from the ENTBaseEO or ENTBaseEOList class and implement the abstract methods defined in the base class. As stated earlier, a code generator will be built in Chapter 13 that creates all of this code for you automatically. This section defines each business class and reviews only the methods or properties that deviate from the norm.

ENTWorkflowEO and ENTWorkfflowEOList

The ENTWorkflowEO and ENTWorkflowEOList classes do not have any extra methods or properties. The only custom code needed for the ENTWorkflowEO object is in the Validate and ValidateDelete methods. The workflow name and object name are required and must be unique. The system should also prevent a user from deleting a workflow if a record exists in the ENTWFItem table associated with that workflow:

```
protected override void Validate(HRPaidTimeOffDataContext db, ref
    ENTValidationErrors validationErrors)
{
    if (WorkflowName.Trim() == "")
    {
        validationErrors.Add("The workflow name is required.");
    }
    else
    {
        //The name must be unique.
        if (new ENTWorkflowData().IsDuplicateWorkflowName(db, ID, WorkflowName))
        {
            validationErrors.Add("The name must be unique.");
        }
    }

    //The object name is required
    if (ENTWorkflowObjectName.Trim() == "")
    {
        validationErrors.Add("The class name is required.");
    }
    else
    {
        //The object name must be unique
        if (new ENTWorkflowData().IsDuplicateObjectName(db, ID,
            ENTWorkflowObjectName))
        {
            validationErrors.Add("This class already has a workflow associated with
                            it.");
        }
    }
}
protected override void ValidateDelete(HRPaidTimeOffDataContext db, ref
    ENTValidationErrors validationErrors)
{
```

```
    //Nothing to validate.
    if (new ENTWorkflowData().IsWorkflowAssociatedWithItem(db, ID))
    {
        validationErrors.Add("The workflow can not be deleted because there are
                              items associated with this workflow.");
    }
}
```

ENTWFStateEO and ENTWFStatePropertyEO

The ENTWFStateEO class has all the fields from the ENTWFState table as properties, plus an extra property that represents the one-to-many relationship between the ENTWFState and ENTWFStateProperty tables:

```
public ENTWFStatePropertyEOList ENTWFStateProperties { get; private set; }
```

The constructor should be changed so that this object is instantiated when the object is created, preventing users from getting a null reference exception:

```
public ENTWFStateEO()
{
    ENTWFStateProperties = new ENTWFStatePropertyEOList();
}
```

MapEntityToCustomProperties must be modified so that when a state object is being loaded, the associated child objects are loaded:

```
protected override void MapEntityToCustomProperties(IENTBaseEntity entity)
{
    ENTWFState eNTWFState = (ENTWFState)entity;

    ID = eNTWFState.ENTWFStateId;
    ENTWorkflowId = eNTWFState.ENTWorkflowId;
    StateName = eNTWFState.StateName;
    Description = eNTWFState.Description;
    IsOwnerSubmitter = eNTWFState.IsOwnerSubmitter;
    ENTWFOwnerGroupId = eNTWFState.ENTWFOwnerGroupId;
    ENTWFStateProperties.Load(ID)
}
```

When saving a record, all the state property records must be saved in the same transaction, so the Save method must be modified to reflect this:

```
public override bool Save(HRPaidTimeOffDataContext db, ref ENTValidationErrors
    validationErrors, int userAccountId)
{
    if (DBAction == DBActionEnum.Save)
    {
        //Validate the object
        Validate(db, ref validationErrors);

        //Check if there were any validation errors
        if (validationErrors.Count == 0)
```

```
            {
                if (IsNewRecord())
                {
                    //Add
                    ID = new ENTWFStateData().Insert(db, ENTWorkflowId, StateName,
                        Description, ENTWFOwnerGroupId, IsOwnerSubmitter,
                        userAccountId);

                    //Update the ID on all the ENTWFStateProperty objects
                    foreach (ENTWFStatePropertyEO stateProperty in
                        ENTWFStateProperties)
                    {
                        stateProperty.ENTWFStateId = ID;
                    }
                }
                else
                {
                    //Update
                    if (!new ENTWFStateData().Update(db, ID, ENTWorkflowId, StateName,
                        Description, ENTWFOwnerGroupId, IsOwnerSubmitter,
                        userAccountId, Version))
                    {
                        UpdateFailed(ref validationErrors);
                        return false;
                    }
                }

                //Delete all the existing ENTWFStateProperty records
                ENTWFStateProperties.Delete(db, ID);

                //Add the records that were chosen on the screen.
                if (ENTWFStateProperties.Save(db, ref validationErrors, userAccountId))
                {
                    return true;
                }
                else
                {
                    return false;
                }
            }
            else
            {
                //Didn't pass validation.
                return false;
            }
        }
        else
        {
            throw new Exception("DBAction not Save.");
        }
    }
}
```

Notice that for this one-to-many relationship, the child records are deleted each time and re-added each time the state is saved.

The `Validate` methods must also be modified to reflect required and unique fields, but they follow the same pattern as all the other `Validate` methods so they are not covered here.

The `ENTWFStateEOList` object has one extra method that overloads the `Load` method and takes a workflow `Id` as a parameter. This enables you to load the list with states for only one workflow:

```
public void Load(int entWorkflowId)
{
    LoadFromList(new ENTWFStateData().SelectByENTWorkflowId(entWorkflowId));
}
```

The `ENTWFStatePropertyEO` class has no special logic but the `ENTWFStatePropertyEOList` has four custom methods. The first two are overloads of the `Load` method again:

```
internal void Load(int entWFStateId)
{
    using (HRPaidTimeOffDataContext db = new
        HRPaidTimeOffDataContext(DBHelper.GetHRPaidTimeOffConnectionString()))
    {
        Load(db, entWFStateId);
    }
}

internal void Load(HRPaidTimeOffDataContext db, int entWFStateId)
{
    LoadFromList(new ENTWFStatePropertyData().SelectByENTWFStateId(db,
        entWFStateId));
}
```

Both of these methods enable you to load the list with records for a specific state — the only difference is one takes a `DataContext` object and the other doesn't.

A `Delete` method must be added to the class because the `Save` method of `ENTWFState` deletes all the records associated with the state. This calls a method in the DAL that calls the stored procedure to delete all the records for the state:

```
internal void Delete(HRPaidTimeOffDataContext db, int entWFStateId)
{
    new ENTWFStatePropertyData().DeleteByENTWFStateId(db, entWFStateId);
}
```

The last custom method searches the current instance to find an object by its property name. It uses a lambda expression to find the object:

```
public ENTWFStatePropertyEO GetByPropertyName(string propertyName)
{
    return this.SingleOrDefault<ENTWFStatePropertyEO>(sp => sp.PropertyName ==
        propertyName);
}
```

Remember that the pattern for methods that populate the list start with the word `Load`, and methods that search the list for elements start with `Get`.

ENTWFTransitionEO

ENTWFTransitionEO has two extra properties that do not map to fields in the ENTWFTransition table:
FromStateName and ToStateName. These need to be declared as properties, and they are loaded in the
MapEntityToCustomProperties method:

```
public string FromStateName { get; private set; }
public string ToStateName { get; private set; }

protected override void MapEntityToCustomProperties(IENTBaseEntity entity)
{
    ENTWFTransition eNTWFTransition = (ENTWFTransition)entity;

    ID = eNTWFTransition.ENTWFTransitionId;
    ENTWorkflowId = eNTWFTransition.ENTWorkflowId;
    TransitionName = eNTWFTransition.TransitionName;
    FromENTWFStateId = eNTWFTransition.FromENTWFStateId;
    FromStateName = eNTWFTransition.FromStateName;
    ToENTWFStateId = eNTWFTransition.ToENTWFStateId;
    ToStateName = eNTWFTransition.ToStateName;
    PostTransitionMethodName = eNTWFTransition.PostTransitionMethodName;
}
```

The ENTWFTransitionEOList class has two custom methods. The first loads the current instance with
all the transitions by the FromStateId. This is used when viewing a request and you need to know
which transitions should be shown to the user based on the request's current state. The Load method
calls the DAL, which calls the stored procedure that uses the dynamic SQL statement:

```
public void Load(int fromStateId)
{
    LoadFromList(new ENTWFTransitionData().SelectByFromStateId(fromStateId));
}
```

The second custom method gets a transition from the current instance by using a lambda expression:

```
internal ENTWFTransitionEO Get(int entWFTransitionId)
{
    return this.Single(t => t.ID == entWFTransitionId);
}
```

ENTWFOwnerGroupEO and ENTWFOwnerGroupUserAccountEO

ENTWFOwnerGroup has one extra property that reflects the one-to-many relationship between
an ENTWFOwnerGroup and ENTWFOwnerGroupUserAccount tables. This is represented by the
ENTWFOwnerGroupUserAccountEOList object:

```
public ENTWFOwnerGroupUserAccountEOList UserAccounts { get; private set; }

public ENTWFOwnerGroupEO()
{
    UserAccounts = new ENTWFOwnerGroupUserAccountEOList();
}
```

The `MapEntityToCustomProperties` method must be changed to load the `UserAccounts` property, following the exact same pattern as all the other objects:

```
protected override void MapEntityToCustomProperties(IENTBaseEntity entity)
{
    ENTWFOwnerGroup eNTWFOwnerGroup = (ENTWFOwnerGroup)entity;

    ID = eNTWFOwnerGroup.ENTWFOwnerGroupId;
    ENTWorkflowId = eNTWFOwnerGroup.ENTWorkflowId;
    OwnerGroupName = eNTWFOwnerGroup.OwnerGroupName;
    DefaultENTUserAccountId = eNTWFOwnerGroup.DefaultENTUserAccountId;
    IsDefaultSameAsLast = eNTWFOwnerGroup.IsDefaultSameAsLast;
    Description = eNTWFOwnerGroup.Description;
    UserAccounts.Load(ID);
}
```

The `Save` method also needs to be changed so that the `ENTWFOwnerGroupUserAccount` records are added or updated in the same transaction as the `ETNWFOwnerGroup` record:

```
if (IsNewRecord())
{
    //Add
    ID = new ENTWFOwnerGroupData().Insert(db, ENTWorkflowId, OwnerGroupName,
        DefaultENTUserAccountId, IsDefaultSameAsLast, Description, userAccountId);

    foreach (ENTWFOwnerGroupUserAccountEO user in UserAccounts)
    {
        user.ENTWFOwnerGroupId = ID;
    }
}
else
{
    //Update
    if (!new ENTWFOwnerGroupData().Update(db, ID, ENTWorkflowId, OwnerGroupName,
        DefaultENTUserAccountId, IsDefaultSameAsLast, Description, userAccountId,
        Version))
    {
        UpdateFailed(ref validationErrors);
        return false;
    }
}

//Now save the users
if (UserAccounts.Save(db, ref validationErrors, userAccountId))
{
    return true;
}
else
{
    return false;
}
```

The `ENTWFOwnerGroupEOList` object has two custom methods. The first loads the current instance with all the owner groups associated with a workflow:

```
public void Load(int entWorkflowId)
{
    LoadFromList(new ENTWFOwnerGroupData().SelectByENTWorkflowId(entWorkflowId));
}
```

The second gets an `ENTWFOwnerGroup` object from the current instance based on the `Id`:

```
public ENTWFOwnerGroupEO GetByENTWFOwnerGroupId(int entWFOwnerGroupId)
{
    return this.Single(og => og.ID == entWFOwnerGroupId);
}
```

`ENTWFOwnerGroupUserAccountEO` has one extra property that reflects the user name associated with the `ENTUserAccountId` on the record. The property must be added and the `MapEntityToCustom Propeties` method must be customized to reflect this:

```
public string UserName { get; set; }

protected override void MapEntityToCustomProperties(IENTBaseEntity entity)
{
    ENTWFOwnerGroupUserAccount eNTWFOwnerGroupUserAccount =
        (ENTWFOwnerGroupUserAccount)entity;

    ID = eNTWFOwnerGroupUserAccount.ENTWFOwnerGroupUserAccountId;
    ENTWFOwnerGroupId = eNTWFOwnerGroupUserAccount.ENTWFOwnerGroupId;
    ENTUserAccountId = eNTWFOwnerGroupUserAccount.ENTUserAccountId;
    UserName = eNTWFOwnerGroupUserAccount.UserName;
}
```

The `ENTWFOwnerGroupUserAccountEOList` object has three custom methods. The first takes a user account `Id` and determines whether the user is in the group. This calls the second method, which uses a lambda expression to search the current instance for the object:

```
public bool IsUserInGroup(int entUserAccountId)
{
    return (GetByUserAccountId(entUserAccountId) != null);
}

public ENTWFOwnerGroupUserAccountEO GetByUserAccountId(int userAccountId)
{
    return this.SingleOrDefault(u => u.ENTUserAccountId == userAccountId);
}
```

The third method loads the current instance with all records for a specific owner group:

```
public void Load(int entWFOwnerGroupId)
{
    LoadFromList(new
    ENTWFOwnerGroupUserAccountData().SelectByENTWFOwnerGroupId(entWFOwnerGroupId));
}
```

ENTWFItemEO, ENTWFItemOwnerEO, and ENTWFItemStateHistoryEO

The `ENTWFItemEO` class has one custom property that reflects the submitter's user name. The property must be added and the `MapEntityToCustomProperties` must be changed to reflect this:

```
public string SubmitterUserName { get; private set; }

protected override void MapEntityToCustomProperties(IENTBaseEntity entity)
{
    ENTWFItem eNTWFItem = (ENTWFItem)entity;

    ID = eNTWFItem.ENTWFItemId;
    ENTWorkflowId = eNTWFItem.ENTWorkflowId;
    ItemId = eNTWFItem.ItemId;
    SubmitterENTUserAccountId = eNTWFItem.SubmitterENTUserAccountId;
    SubmitterUserName = eNTWFItem.SubmitterUserName;
    CurrentWFStateId = eNTWFItem.CurrentWFStateId;
}
```

The same is true for the `ENTWFItemOwnerEO` class:

```
public string UserName { get; private set; }

protected override void MapEntityToCustomProperties(IENTBaseEntity entity)
{
    ENTWFItemOwner eNTWFItemOwner = (ENTWFItemOwner)entity;

    ID = eNTWFItemOwner.ENTWFItemOwnerId;
    ENTWFItemId = eNTWFItemOwner.ENTWFItemId;
    ENTWFOwnerGroupId = eNTWFItemOwner.ENTWFOwnerGroupId;
    ENTUserAccountId = eNTWFItemOwner.ENTUserAccountId;
    UserName = eNTWFItemOwner.UserName;
}
```

The `ENTWFItemOwnerEOList` class has two custom methods that are very similar to the others — one loads the current instance by an `ENTWFItemId` and the other gets an object from the current instance based on the owner group `Id`:

```
public void Load(int entWFItemId)
{
    //Get the entity object from the DAL.
    LoadFromList(new ENTWFItemOwnerData().SelectByENTWFItemId(entWFItemId));
}

public ENTWFItemOwnerEO GetByENTWFOwnerGroupId(int ownerGroupId)
{
    return this.Single(o => o.ENTWFOwnerGroupId == ownerGroupId);
}
```

The `ENTWFItemStateHistoryEO` has three custom properties that reflect the name of the state, the owner's name, and the name of the person who inserted the record in this table. The properties need to be defined as strings, and the `MapEntityToCustomProperties` method must be changed to set these properties:

```
public string StateName { get; private set; }
public string OwnerName { get; private set; }
public string InsertedBy { get; private set; }

protected override void MapEntityToCustomProperties(IENTBaseEntity entity)
{
    ENTWFItemStateHistory eNTWFItemStateHistory = (ENTWFItemStateHistory)entity;

    ID = eNTWFItemStateHistory.ENTWFItemStateHistoryId;
    ENTWFItemId = eNTWFItemStateHistory.ENTWFItemId;
    ENTWFStateId = eNTWFItemStateHistory.ENTWFStateId;
    ENTUserAccountId = eNTWFItemStateHistory.ENTUserAccountId;

    StateName = eNTWFItemStateHistory.StateName;
    OwnerName = eNTWFItemStateHistory.OwnerName;
    InsertedBy = eNTWFItemStateHistory.InsertedBy;
}
```

ENTBaseWorkflowEO

The `ENTBaseWorkflowEO` class is the base class for any object that needs to have workflow capabilities. Remember that when a workflow is defined, an object name is associated with the workflow. This object must inherit from the `ENTBaseWorkflowEO` object, which has all the functionality for moving an item through a workflow.

Add a new class to the `Framework` folder in the BLL project and call it `ENTBaseWorkflowEO`. Change the class declaration to make it serializable, public, and inherit from the `ENTBaseEO` class:

```
[Serializable]
public abstract class ENTBaseWorkflowEO : ENTBaseEO
{
    ...
}
```

Add the following properties:

```
public ENTWorkflowEO Workflow { get; private set; }

public ENTWFItemEO WFItem { get; private set; }

public ENTWFOwnerGroupEOList WFOwnerGroups { get; private set; }

public ENTWFItemOwnerEOList WFOwners { get; private set; }

public ENTWFItemStateHistoryEOList WFStateHistory { get; private set; }

public ENTWFTransitionEOList WFTransitions { get; private set; }

public int ENTWFTransitionId { get; set; }
public ENTBaseEO OriginalItem{ get; set; }
```

As you can see, all the other objects that were just created are properties of this object, plus two additional properties. The first is `ENTWFTransitionId`. This property is set by a consumer of the object that wants to transition an item. The second property, `OriginalItem`, is an `ENTBaseEO` object. This is used when determining whether a field is read-only.

The `ValidateWorkflow` method looks at the original item's properties and the current item's properties to determine whether there is a difference. If they are different and the property is marked as read-only, then the record won't be saved to the database and a message is returned to the user.

Add another property now that reflects the item's current state. This cannot use the shortcut property syntax because there is some custom logic in the get accessor, so you have to add the member variable also:

```
private ENTWFStateEO _currentState = new ENTWFStateEO();

public ENTWFStateEO CurrentState
{
    get
    {
        if (WFItem.CurrentWFStateId != _currentState.ID)
        {
            _currentState = new ENTWFStateEO();
            _currentState.Load(WFItem.CurrentWFStateId);
            return _currentState;
        }
        else
        {
            return _currentState;
        }
    }
}
```

Add two more read-only properties that return the current owner's ID and the current owner's name:

```
public int CurrentOwnerENTUserAccountId
{
    get
    {
        //Determine the current owner by the current state
        if (WFItem.CurrentWFStateId != 0)
        {
            if (CurrentState.IsOwnerSubmitter)
            {
                return WFItem.SubmitterENTUserAccountId;
            }
            else
            {
                return Convert.ToInt32(WFOwners.GetByENTWFOwnerGroupId(
Convert.ToInt32(CurrentState.ENTWFOwnerGroupId)).ENTUserAccountId);
            }
        }
        else
        {
```

```
                        return 0;
                    }
                }
            }


    public string CurrentOwnerUserName
    {
        get
        {
            //Determine the current owner by the current state
            if (WFItem.CurrentWFStateId != 0)
            {
                if (CurrentState.IsOwnerSubmitter)
                {
                    return WFItem.SubmitterUserName;
                }
                else
                {
                    return WFOwners.GetByENTWFOwnerGroupId(
Convert.ToInt32(CurrentState.ENTWFOwnerGroupId)).UserName;
                }
            }
            else
            {
                return "";
            }
        }
    }
```

Next, add the constructor. This needs to instantiate all the properties:

```
public ENTBaseWorkflowEO() : base()
{
    Workflow = new ENTWorkflowEO();
    WFItem = new ENTWFItemEO();
    WFOwnerGroups = new ENTWFOwnerGroupEOList();
    WFOwners = new ENTWFItemOwnerEOList();
    WFStateHistory = new ENTWFItemStateHistoryEOList();
    WFTransitions = new ENTWFTransitionEOList();
}
```

The next step is to add the methods for this class. Because this class inherits from the ENTBaseEO object, there are already abstract methods for the Save, Validate, Load, and Init methods. This object needs to take care of similar methods for the workflow objects, so four new methods will be added that take care of this. The first is the SaveWorkflow method:

```
public bool SaveWorkflow(HRPaidTimeOffDataContext db, ref ENTValidationErrors
    validationErrors, ENTBaseEO item, int userAccountId)
{
    WFItem.ItemId = item.ID;

    ValidateWorkflow(db, ref validationErrors, item);
```

```
        if (validationErrors.Count == 0)
        {
            //Set the ID for all the child owner objects
            foreach (ENTWFItemOwnerEO entWFItemOwner in WFOwners)
            {
                entWFItemOwner.ENTWFItemId = item.ID;
            }

            foreach (ENTWFItemStateHistoryEO entWFItemStateHistory in WFStateHistory)
            {
                entWFItemStateHistory.ENTWFItemId = item.ID;
            }

            if (WFItem.Save(db, ref validationErrors, userAccountId))
            {
                foreach (ENTWFItemOwnerEO wfItemOwner in WFOwners)
                {
                    wfItemOwner.ENTWFItemId = WFItem.ID;

                    if (wfItemOwner.Save(db, ref validationErrors, userAccountId) ==
                        false)
                    {
                        return false;
                    }
                }

                foreach (ENTWFItemStateHistoryEO wfItemStateHistory in WFStateHistory)
                {
                    wfItemStateHistory.ENTWFItemId = WFItem.ID;

                    if (wfItemStateHistory.Save(db, ref validationErrors,
                        userAccountId) == false)
                    {
                        return false;
                    }
                }

                //Call any methods the transition requires
                if (ENTWFTransitionId != 0)
                {
                    ENTWFTransitionEO entWFTransition =
                        WFTransitions.Get(ENTWFTransitionId);

                    if (entWFTransition.PostTransitionMethodName != null)
                    {
                        //Create an instance of the object
                      Type objectType = Type.GetType(Workflow.ENTWorkflowObjectName);

                        objectType.InvokeMember(entWFTransition.PostTransitionMethodName,
                            BindingFlags.InvokeMethod, null, item, new object[] { db });
                    }
                }

            return true;
```

```
        }
        else
        {
            //Failed item save.
            return false;
        }
    }
    else
    {
        //Failed Validation
        return false;
    }
}
```

The `SaveWorkflow` method should be called by the parent object's `Save` method. The first thing this method does is validate the workflow by calling the `ValidateWorkflow` method, which you'll add next. If the workflow doesn't pass validation, then the `SaveWorkflow` method returns false and passes back the list of validation errors. The calling procedure should roll back the transaction. If the workflow passes validation, then all the child objects for the item have their `ID` set to the item's `ID`. Because the method that called this was the parent object's `Save` method, you don't know whether the user added or updated the record so this is just a safeguard.

The next step saves the `WFItem` record. If that succeeds, then the foreign key needs to be added to all of the `ENTWFItemOwner` and `ENTWFItemStateHistory` records. These are also saved by calling their `Save` method.

The next section is where it gets interesting. The method checks whether the `ENTWFTransitionId` is not equal to zero. Not equal to zero means that the user transitioned the item. Recall that the `ENTWFTransition` table has a field for the `PostTransitionMethodName`. The system is supposed to execute this method after successful completion of the transition. The `Save` method first checks whether the user is transitioning the item, and then whether there is a `PostTransitionMethodName` set for the transition. If there is, then it uses reflection to execute the method and passes in the `Data Context` object. The `DataContext` object must be passed in so that everything is wrapped in the same transaction.

Now add the `ValidateWorkflow` method. This method ensures that there is a current state for the item, and confirms that any read-only properties for the current state are not blank and that any read-only properties didn't change from their original state:

```
private void ValidateWorkflow(HRPaidTimeOffDataContext db, ref ENTValidationErrors
    validationErrors, ENTBaseEO item)
{
    //The current owner is required.
    if (CurrentOwnerENTUserAccountId == 0)
    {
        validationErrors.Add("Please select the " +
            WFOwnerGroups.GetByENTWFOwnerGroupId(
            Convert.ToInt32(CurrentState.ENTWFOwnerGroupId)).OwnerGroupName + ".");
    }

    if (OriginalItem == null)
```

```
        {
            throw new Exception("The original item was not sent to the workflow save
                            method.");
        }
    else
    {
        //Check required fields.
        ENTWFStatePropertyEOList entWFStateProperties = new
            ENTWFStatePropertyEOList();

        entWFStateProperties.Load(db, WFItem.CurrentWFStateId);

        Type objectType = Type.GetType(Workflow.ENTWorkflowObjectName);

        foreach (ENTWFStatePropertyEO entWFStateProperty in entWFStateProperties)
        {
            if (entWFStateProperty.Required)
            {
                PropertyInfo property =
                    objectType.GetProperty(entWFStateProperty.PropertyName);

                //Create an error message string in case of an error.
                string errorMessage = "The " + entWFStateProperty.PropertyName +
                                    " is required.";

                if (property.PropertyType.IsEnum)
                {
                    Array a = Enum.GetValues(property.PropertyType);

                    int value = Convert.ToInt32(property.GetValue(item, null));
                    bool isValid = false;

                    //Check that the value is one of the enumerated values.
                    foreach (int i in a)
                    {
                        if (i == value)
                        {
                            isValid = true;
                            break;
                        }
                    }

                    if (isValid == false)
                    {
                        validationErrors.Add(errorMessage);
                    }
                }
                else
                {
                    switch (property.PropertyType.Name)
                    {
                        case "Int32":
                            if (Convert.ToInt32(property.GetValue(item, null)) == 0)
                            {
```

```
                                validationErrors.Add(errorMessage);
                        }
                            break;
                    case "String":
                        if ((property.GetValue(item, null) == null) ||
                            (property.GetValue(item, null).ToString() ==
                             string.Empty))
                    {
                        validationErrors.Add(errorMessage);
                    }
                        break;
                    case "DateTime":
                        if ((property.GetValue(item, null) == null) ||
                            (Convert.ToDateTime(property.GetValue(item, null))
                             == DateTime.MinValue))
                        {
                            validationErrors.Add(errorMessage);
                        }
                        break;
                    case "Nullable`1":
                        if (property.GetValue(item, null) == null)
                        {
                            validationErrors.Add(errorMessage);
                        }
                        break;
                    default:
                        throw new Exception("Property type unknown.");
                }
            }
        }

        //Check if this field is read only. Only check read only fields if the
        //record was already submitted.
        if (((ENTBaseWorkflowEO)OriginalItem).CurrentState.ID != 0)
        {
            if (entWFStateProperty.ReadOnly)
            {
                PropertyInfo property =
                    objectType.GetProperty(entWFStateProperty.PropertyName);

                if (property.GetValue(item, null).ToString() !=
                    property.GetValue(OriginalItem, null).ToString())
                {
                    validationErrors.Add("The " +
                        entWFStateProperty.PropertyName +
                        " can not be changed.");
                }
            }
        }
    }
}
```

The next method to add is `LoadWorkflow`. This method loads the `WFItem` object, any owner groups associated with this workflow, the users who are designated for each owner group, the state history for this item, the list of transitions that are valid for this item based on its current state, and the current state of the object:

```
public void LoadWorkflow(string className, int itemId)
{
    //Get the workflow object by class name
    if (Workflow.LoadByObjectName(className))
    {
        //Load the WFItem using the itemId, this is the not the same as the primary
        //key for the WFItem.
        WFItem.LoadByItemId(Workflow.ID, itemId);

        //Get all owner groups for this workflow
        WFOwnerGroups.Load(Workflow.ID);

        //Get the owners for this item
        WFOwners.Load(WFItem.ID);

        //Add any owner groups that aren't in the list
        foreach (ENTWFOwnerGroupEO wfOwnerGroup in WFOwnerGroups)
        {
            ENTWFItemOwnerEO wfItemOwner = WFOwners.SingleOrDefault(o =>
                o.ENTWFOwnerGroupId == wfOwnerGroup.ID);

            if (wfItemOwner == null)
            {
                //Add this with a blank user
                WFOwners.Add(new ENTWFItemOwnerEO {
                    ENTWFItemId = itemId,
                    ENTWFOwnerGroupId = wfOwnerGroup.ID
                    });
            }
        }

        //Get all the state histories
        WFStateHistory.Load(WFItem.ID);

        //Load the transitions based on the current state.
        WFTransitions.Load(WFItem.CurrentWFStateId);

        //Load the current state.
        _currentState = new ENTWFStateEO();
        _currentState.Load(WFItem.CurrentWFStateId);
    }
    else
    {
        throw new Exception("Workflow not set correctly. Please associate this
                        item with a workflow.");
    }
}
```

The last method to add is the `InitWorkflow` method. This method will default the owner for each owner group. If the owner group was defined to default the owner to the same owner for this user's last request, then the logic figures out who that was and sets them as the default. If the owner group has a specific user designated as the owner, then they are set as the owner. The last part of the method loads the transitions that are valid for a new item:

```csharp
public void InitWorkflow(string className)
{
    //Get the workflow object by class name
    if (Workflow.LoadByObjectName(className))
    {
        //Get all unique owners for this workflow
        WFOwnerGroups.Load(Workflow.ID);

        //Add an owner group to the work flow owners
        foreach (ENTWFOwnerGroupEO entWFOwnerGroup in WFOwnerGroups)
        {
            Nullable<int> entUserAccountId = null;

            if (entWFOwnerGroup.IsDefaultSameAsLast)
            {
                //Get this user's last request and set it as the default.
                ENTWFItemOwnerSelectLastUserByGroupIdResult lastUser = new
                    ENTWFItemOwnerData().SelectLastUserByGroupId(entWFOwnerGroup.ID,
                    WFItem.SubmitterENTUserAccountId);

                if ((lastUser != null) && (lastUser.ENTUserAccountId != null))
                {
                    entUserAccountId = lastUser.ENTUserAccountId;
                }
            }
            else
            {
                //set the owner to the default one selected for this group.
                entUserAccountId = entWFOwnerGroup.DefaultENTUserAccountId;
            }

            //Add this item owner with the default user.
            WFOwners.Add(new ENTWFItemOwnerEO {
                ENTUserAccountId = entUserAccountId,
                ENTWFOwnerGroupId = entWFOwnerGroup.ID });
        }

        //Load the transitions based on the current state.
        WFTransitions.Load(WFItem.CurrentWFStateId);
    }
    else
    {
        throw new Exception("Workflow not set correctly. Please associate this item
                            with a workflow.");
    }
}
```

This is probably a little hard to follow until you see the screens in action in the solution, but this gives you an introduction to how the classes work.

The User Interface

One of the goals of this chapter is to give certain users the capability to change the workflow after the application has been released to production. This should be restricted to a few users of the application and should fall under the Administration section in the menu. The role-based security model that was built in Chapter 6 enables you to set up a role that has access to these menu items and then add the appropriate users to that role. The following menu item records should be added for the workflow administration screens:

MenuItemName	Url	ParentENT MenuItemId	Display Sequence	IsAlways Enabled
Workflow		Administration (ID)	4	False
Workflows	Administration\ Workflows.aspx	Workflow (ID)	1	False
Owners	Administration\ WorlflowOwners.aspx	Workflow (ID)	2	False
States	Administration\ WorkflowStates.aspx	Workflow (ID)	3	False
Transitions	Administration\ WorkflowTransitions.aspx	Workflow (ID)	4	False

The following capability records should also be added:

CapabilityName	ENTMenuItemId	AccessType
Workflows	Workflows Menu Item ID	0
Owners	Workflows Menu Item ID	0
States	Workflows Menu Item ID	0
Transitions	Workflows Menu Item ID	0

Workflows

The Workflows menu item navigates to the list of workflows defined for this application and allows the user to add, edit, or delete a workflow. Add a new Web form to the Administration folder and name it Workflows.aspx (see Figure 7-6).

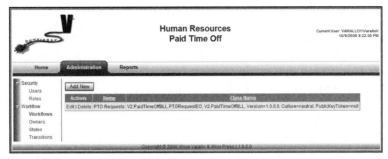

Figure 7-6

This should use the `PaidTimeOffEditGrid` master page. View the markup and add the tag to point to the master page:

```
<%@ MasterType virtualPath="~/PaidTimeOffEditGrid.master"%>
```

Add a custom `GridView` control to the page and name it `cgvWorkflows`.

Switch to the code-behind page and add a `using` directive that references the `V2.PaidTimeOffBLL` `.Framework` namespace. Change the class declaration so the page inherits from the `BasePage` class. Implement the abstract members by right-clicking on BasePage and selecting Implement Abstract Class. This will add the `MenuItemName` and `CapabilityNames` methods. In the `MenuItemName` method, return "Workflows." In the `CapabilityNames` method, return a string array with "Workflows" as the only element. The grid will have three columns only, so add the column index constants to the class:

```
private const int COL_INDEX_ACTION = 0;
private const int COL_INDEX_WORKFLOW_NAME = 1;
private const int COL_INDEX_OBJECT_NAME = 2;
```

Next, add the code to the `Page_Load` that hooks the Add button click event to the button and loads the grid:

```
protected void Page_Load(object sender, EventArgs e)
{
    Master.AddButton_Click += new
        PaidTimeOffEditGrid.ButtonClickedHandler(Master_AddButton_Click);

    if (!IsPostBack)
    {
        //Tell the control what class to create and what method to call to load the
        //class.
        cgvWorkflows.ListClassName = typeof(ENTWorkflowEOList).AssemblyQualifiedName;
        cgvWorkflows.LoadMethodName = "Load";

        //Action column-Contains the Edit link
        cgvWorkflows.AddBoundField("", "Actions", "");

        //Name
        cgvWorkflows.AddBoundField("DisplayText", "Name", "DisplayText");
```

```
        cgvWorkflows.AddBoundField("ENTWorkflowObjectName", "Class Name",
                            "ENTWorkflowObjectName");

    cgvWorkflows.DataBind();
  }
  else
  {
    string eventTarget = Page.Request.Form["__EVENTTARGET"].ToString();
    if (eventTarget.IndexOf("lbtnDelete") > -1)
    {
        //Rebind the grid so the delete event is captured.
        cgvWorkflows.DataBind();
    }
  }
}
```

Add the Add button's click event handler:

```
void Master_AddButton_Click(object sender, EventArgs e)
{
    Response.Redirect("Workflow.aspx" + EncryptQueryString("id=0"));
}
```

In order to add the Edit and Delete links, you need to create the OnRowBound event handler. You can automatically generate this handler by going back to the design view of the page, clicking on the cgvWorkflow grid, clicking on the properties window, and clicking the lightning bolt at the top. Now double-click on the RowDataBound line (see Figure 7-7).

Figure 7-7

Add the following code to the `RowDataBound` event handler:

```
if (e.Row.RowType == DataControlRowType.DataRow)
{
    //Add the edit link to the action column.
    HyperLink editLink = new HyperLink();
    if (ReadOnly)
    {
        editLink.Text = "View";
    }
    else
    {
        editLink.Text = "Edit";
    }
    editLink.NavigateUrl = "Workflow.aspx" + EncryptQueryString("id=" +
        ((ENTWorkflowEO)e.Row.DataItem).ID.ToString());

    e.Row.Cells[COL_INDEX_ACTION].Controls.Add(editLink);

    //If the user has read only access then do not show this Delete link.
    if (ReadOnly == false)
    {
        //Add a pipe between the Edit and Delete links
        LiteralControl lc = new LiteralControl(" | ");
        e.Row.Cells[COL_INDEX_ACTION].Controls.Add(lc);

        //Add the Delete link
        LinkButton lbtnDelete = new LinkButton();
        lbtnDelete.ID = "lbtnDelete" +((ENTWorkflowEO)e.Row.DataItem).ID.ToString();
        lbtnDelete.Text = "Delete";
        lbtnDelete.CommandArgument = ((ENTWorkflowEO)e.Row.DataItem).ID.ToString();
        lbtnDelete.OnClientClick = "return ConfirmDelete();";
        lbtnDelete.Command += new CommandEventHandler(lbtnDelete_Command);
        e.Row.Cells[COL_INDEX_ACTION].Controls.Add(lbtnDelete);
    }
}
```

The last piece of code to add is the Delete link's click event handler:

```
void lbtnDelete_Command(object sender, CommandEventArgs e)
{
    ENTValidationErrors validationErrors = new ENTValidationErrors();
    ENTWorkflowEO workflow = new ENTWorkflowEO();
    workflow.DBAction = ENTBaseEO.DBActionEnum.Delete;
    workflow.ID = Convert.ToInt32(e.CommandArgument);
    workflow.Delete(ref validationErrors, CurrentUser.ID);

    Master.ValidationErrors = validationErrors;

    cgvWorkflows.DataBind();
}
```

All of this code is very similar to the code described in Chapter 4 so I won't repeat it again for the other pages in this chapter. The same pattern exists for all of the grid pages, so you can copy the pages from the sample code for the rest of the pages.

Now that you have the grid page, you can create the edit page. This simple page has two fields: the name of the workflow and the list of classes that inherit from the ENTBaseWorkflowEO class (see Figure 7-8).

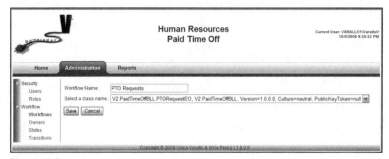

Figure 7-8

Add another page to the Administration folder and call it Workflow.aspx. This page uses the PaidTime OffEditPage master page. View the markup for this page and add a tag to point to the master page:

```
<%@ MasterType virtualPath="~/PaidTimeOffEditPage.master"%>
```

Add the following tags for the rest of the screen:

```
<table>
    <tr>
        <td>Workflow Name:</td>
        <td><asp:TextBox ID="txtWorkflowName" runat="server"></asp:TextBox></td>
    </tr>
    <tr>
        <td>Select a class name.:</td>
        <td><asp:DropDownList runat="server" ID="ddlObjectName">
            </asp:DropDownList></td>
    </tr>
</table>
```

Now open the code-behind page and add a using directive to the System.Reflection namespace. Change the class declaration to inherit from BaseEditPage and pass in the ENTWorkflowEO object for the generic class. Right-click on BaseEditPage and select Implement Abstract Class. Next, hook up the save and cancel event handlers in the Page_Load event:

```
Master.SaveButton_Click += new
    PaidTimeOffEditPage.ButtonClickedHandler(Master_SaveButton_Click);

Master.CancelButton_Click += new
    PaidTimeOffEditPage.ButtonClickedHandler(Master_CancelButton_Click);
```

Create the Cancel button's event hander:

```
void Master_CancelButton_Click(object sender, EventArgs e)
{
    GoToGridPage();
}
```

Then create the Save button's event handler:

```
void Master_SaveButton_Click(object sender, EventArgs e)
{
    ENTValidationErrors validationErrors = new ENTValidationErrors();

    ENTWorkflowEO workflow = (ENTWorkflowEO)ViewState[VIEW_STATE_KEY_WORKFLOW];
    LoadObjectFromScreen(workflow);

    if (!workflow.Save(ref validationErrors, CurrentUser.ID))
    {
        Master.ValidationErrors = validationErrors;
    }
    else
    {
        GoToGridPage();
    }
}
```

The only thing left to do is implement the abstract methods. Change the `MenuItemName` method to return "Workflow" and change the `CapabilityNames` method to return a string array with "Workflows" as the only element. Change the `GoToGridPage` so that it redirects the user to the `Workflows.aspx` page. Add the code to the `LoadObjectFromScreen` method so that the object's properties are set to the values on the screen:

```
protected override void LoadObjectFromScreen(ENTWorkflowEO baseEO)
{
    ENTWorkflowEO workflow = (ENTWorkflowEO)baseEO;

    workflow.WorkflowName = txtWorkflowName.Text;
    workflow.ENTWorkflowObjectName = ddlObjectName.Text;
}
```

The `LoadScreenFromObject` loads the control's values from the object's properties and persists the object in the page's `ViewState`. Create a constant at the top of the module that stores the key for the `ViewState` item:

```
private const string VIEW_STATE_KEY_WORKFLOW = "Workflow";

protected override void LoadScreenFromObject(ENTWorkflowEO baseEO)
{
    ENTWorkflowEO workflow = (ENTWorkflowEO)baseEO;

    txtWorkflowName.Text = workflow.WorkflowName;
    if (workflow.ENTWorkflowObjectName != null)
    {
        ddlObjectName.Items.FindByText(workflow.ENTWorkflowObjectName).Selected = true;
    }

    ViewState[VIEW_STATE_KEY_WORKFLOW] = workflow;
}
```

The last method to implement is the `LoadControls` method, which loads the drop-down list with all classes that inherit from the `ENTBaseWorkflowEO` object:

```
protected override void LoadControls()
{
    //Load the drop down list with the objects in this BLL.
    Assembly assembly = Assembly.Load("V2.PaidTimeOffBLL");

    Type[] types = assembly.GetTypes();

    foreach (Type t in types)
    {
        if ((t.IsClass) && (t.BaseType == typeof(ENTBaseWorkflowEO)))
        {
            ddlObjectName.Items.Add(t.AssemblyQualifiedName);
        }
    }
}
```

Again, this is very similar to the pattern described in Chapter 4, so I won't review all the code for the other screens unless something deviates from the norm.

Owners

The owners are the groups of people who can own an issue when it is in a specific state. Add a new page to the `Administration` folder and name it `WorkflowOwners.aspx`. It should inherit from the `PaidTimeOffEditGrid` master page. Follow the same steps defined earlier for creating the grid page. The screen should look like Figure 7-9.

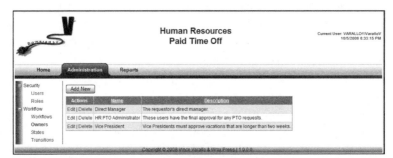

Figure 7-9

Now add the `WorkflowOwner.aspx` page, which inherits from the `PaidTimeOffEditPage` master page. Follow the same steps just described for creating an edit page. The goal of this page is to enable users to create owner groups and associate users with the group. The page should look like Figure 7-10.

There are only two tricky parts to this screen — the first is how the default owner drop-down list and the checkbox interact, and the second is the list of users to associate with the group.

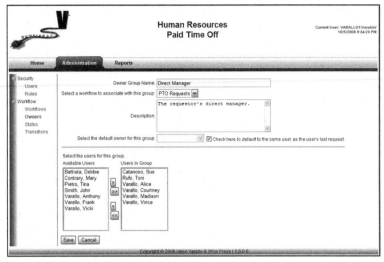

Figure 7-10

The screen should prevent a user from selecting a user from the drop-down list and having the box checked. The features are mutually exclusive. The first step is to set the `AutoPostback` property to true on the checkbox. Then double-click on the checkbox to create the `CheckedChange` event handler. Add the following code to the event handler:

```
protected void chkSameAsLast_CheckedChanged(object sender, EventArgs e)
{
    SetScreenStateForCheckbox(chkSameAsLast.Checked);
}

private void SetScreenStateForCheckbox(bool isChecked)
{
    if (!ReadOnly)
    {
        if (isChecked)
        {
            ddlDefaultOwner.SelectedIndex = 0;
            ddlDefaultOwner.Enabled = false;
        }
        else
        {
            ddlDefaultOwner.Enabled = true;
        }
    }
}
```

Change the `LoadScreenFromObject` method to call the `SetScreenStateForCheckbox` method when the screen is loaded:

```
chkSameAsLast.Checked = wfOwnerGroup.IsDefaultSameAsLast;
SetScreenStateForCheckbox(chkSameAsLast.Checked);
```

If the checkbox is checked, then the drop-down list becomes disabled and the selected index is set to 0, which is the blank list item. If the checkbox is not checked, then the checkbox is enabled. This can get ugly for the user if the screen keeps posting back each time the box is checked, so this page is a good candidate for AJAX functionality. To enable the AJAX functionality, you need to add a `ScriptManager` control to the page and then add an `UpdatePanel` control after the `ScriptManager`. The HTML table that contains all the controls should then go in the `ContentTemplate` tags in the `UpdatePanel`. Here is the code snippet:

```
<asp:ScriptManager ID="ScriptManager1" runat="server"></asp:ScriptManager>

<asp:UpdatePanel ID="UpdatePanel1" runat="server">
   <ContentTemplate>
      <table>
         <tr>
            ...
         </tr>
      </table>
   </ContentTemplate>
</asp:UpdatePanel>
```

That's all you need to do to AJAXify the page. The second tricky part of this page is allowing the user to associate users with this group. This is similar to the `Role.aspx` page where you associate users with a role. The only difference is that the source objects are different. The two list boxes are populated in the `LoadScreenFromObject` method:

```
//Get all the users
ENTUserAccountEOList users = Globals.GetUsers(Page.Cache);

foreach (ENTUserAccountEO user in users)
{
 if (wfOwnerGroup.UserAccounts.IsUserInGroup(user.ID))
 {
  lstSelectedUsers.Items.Add(new ListItem(user.DisplayText, user.ID.ToString()));
 }
 else
 {
  lstUnselectedUsers.Items.Add(new ListItem(user.DisplayText, user.ID.ToString()));
 }
}
```

The four arrow buttons that move users between the lists also need to maintain the users in the default drop-down list because only a user in the group should be able to be selected as the default:

```
protected void btnMoveToSelected_Click(object sender, EventArgs e)
{
    AddToDefaultDropDown(false);
    MoveItems(lstUnselectedUsers, lstSelectedUsers, false);
}

protected void btnMoveAllToSelected_Click(object sender, EventArgs e)
{
    AddToDefaultDropDown(true);
    MoveItems(lstUnselectedUsers, lstSelectedUsers, true);
```

```
    }

    protected void btnMoveAllToUnselected_Click(object sender, EventArgs e)
    {
        RemoveFromDropDown(true);
        MoveItems(lstSelectedUsers, lstUnselectedUsers, true);
    }

    protected void btnMoveToUnselected_Click(object sender, EventArgs e)
    {
        RemoveFromDropDown(false);
        MoveItems(lstSelectedUsers, lstUnselectedUsers, false);
    }

    private void AddToDefaultDropDown(bool all)
    {
        foreach (ListItem li in lstUnselectedUsers.Items)
        {
            if ((li.Selected) || (all))
            {
                ddlDefaultOwner.Items.Add(li);
            }
        }
    }

    private void RemoveFromDropDown(bool all)
    {
        foreach (ListItem li in lstSelectedUsers.Items)
        {
            if ((li.Selected) || (all))
            {
                ddlDefaultOwner.Items.Remove(ddlDefaultOwner.Items.FindByValue(li.Value));
            }
        }
    }

    private void MoveItems(ListBox lstSource, ListBox lstDestination, bool moveAll)
    {
        for (int i = 0; i < lstSource.Items.Count; i++)
        {
            ListItem li = lstSource.Items[i];

            if ((moveAll == true) || (li.Selected == true))
            {
                //Add to destination
                li.Selected = false;
                lstDestination.Items.Add(li);
                lstSource.Items.RemoveAt(i);
                i--;
            }
        }
    }
}
```

Because this page already has the AJAX controls, the user will not see the web page posting back for all of these buttons.

States

The states screens allow the user to add, update, or delete new states and set which properties are required or read-only. The two pages are WorkflowStates.aspx and WorkflowState.aspx. The WorkflowStates.aspx page is the grid page and contains no custom code. The WorkflowState.aspx page is the edit page and looks like Figure 7-11.

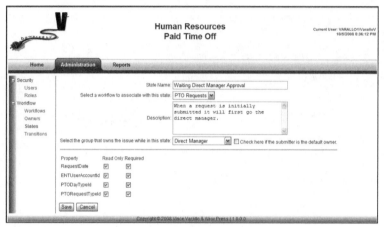

Figure 7-11

For this page, it is worth walking through each method. The workflow drop-down list allows the user to associate this state with a workflow. The owner drop-down list only displays owners associated with the selected workflow. The bottom of the screen uses reflection to list all the properties for the object that are associated with the workflow. When the user changes the workflow drop-down list, the owners and property list dynamically change, so the AJAX controls are used on this page also.

View the HTML markup and add the standard tag for the master page. Then add the following code in the Content control:

```
<asp:ScriptManager ID="ScriptManager1" runat="server"></asp:ScriptManager>
<asp:UpdatePanel ID="UpdatePanel1" runat="server">
<ContentTemplate>
  <table>
    <tr>
      <td style="text-align: right">State Name:</td>
      <td><asp:TextBox ID="txtStateName" runat="server" Width="300px">
          </asp:TextBox>
      </td>
    </tr>
    <tr>
      <td style="text-align: right">Select a workflow to associate with this
          state:</td>
      <td><asp:DropDownList runat="server" ID="ddlWorkflow" AutoPostBack="True"
          onselectedindexchanged="ddlWorkflow_SelectedIndexChanged">
          </asp:DropDownList>
      </td>
```

```
        </tr>
        <tr>
          <td style="text-align: right">Description:</td>
          <td><asp:TextBox ID="txtDescription" runat="server" Rows="5"
              TextMode="MultiLine" Width="300px"></asp:TextBox>
          </td>
        </tr>
        <tr>
          <td style="text-align: right">Select the group that owns the issue while in
              this state:</td>
          <td><asp:DropDownList runat="server" ID="ddlWFOwnerGroup" >
              </asp:DropDownList>
            <asp:CheckBox ID="chkIsSubmitter" runat="server" AutoPostBack="True"
                oncheckedchanged="chkIsSubmitter_CheckedChanged"
                Text="Check here if the submitter is the default owner." />
          </td>
        </tr>
        <tr>
          <td colspan="2"><hr /></td>
        </tr>
        <tr>
          <td colspan="2"><asp:Table runat="server" ID="tblProperties"></asp:Table>
          </td>
        </tr>
      </table>
    </ContentTemplate>
  </asp:UpdatePanel>
```

The important thing to note here is that the section that lists the object's properties is a table, called tblPropeties, without any rows. The code-behind will populate this table dynamically.

Now open the code-behind page and change the class so it inherits from the BaseEditPage class and pass in the ENTWFStateEO object as the generic parameter. Automatically implement the abstract member of the base class the same way as before. Add the standard code to the MenuItemName, GoToGridPage, and CapabilityNames methods.

Add the following code to the Page_load event:

```
protected void Page_Load(object sender, EventArgs e)
{
    Master.SaveButton_Click += new
        PaidTimeOffEditPage.ButtonClickedHandler(Master_SaveButton_Click);
    Master.CancelButton_Click += new
        PaidTimeOffEditPage.ButtonClickedHandler(Master_CancelButton_Click);

    if (ddlWorkflow.SelectedValue != "")
    {
        ENTWFStateEO entWFState = (ENTWFStateEO)ViewState[VIEW_STATE_KEY_STATE];
        LoadPropertiesTable(Convert.ToInt32(ddlWorkflow.SelectedValue),
                            entWFState);
    }
}
```

This hooks the event handler for the Add and Cancel buttons and calls a method that will build the properties HTML table. This isn't checking the `IsPostback` property of the page because this table is dynamically built, and if it weren't rebuilt in the `Page_Load` it would not retain its state between postbacks. The `LoadPropertiesTable` method is as follows:

```
private void LoadPropertiesTable(int entWorkflowId, ENTWFStateEO entWFStateEO)
{
```

The method first ensures that the workflow is selected and exists. If it exists, then the table's header row is created with a column for the property's name, a Read-only checkbox, and a Required checkbox:

```
if (entWorkflowId != 0)
{
    ENTWorkflowEO workflow = new ENTWorkflowEO();
    if (workflow.Load(entWorkflowId))
    {
        tblProperties.Rows.Clear();

        //Add header
        TableRow trHeader = new TableRow();
        TableCell tc1 = new TableCell();
        tc1.Text = "Property";
        trHeader.Cells.Add(tc1);

        TableCell tc2 = new TableCell();
        tc2.Text = "Read Only";
        trHeader.Cells.Add(tc2);

        TableCell tc3 = new TableCell();
        tc3.Text = "Required";
        trHeader.Cells.Add(tc3);

        tblProperties.Rows.Add(trHeader);
```

After the header row is added, the workflow's associated object's properties are retrieved using reflection. Only properties that are declared at the instance level and are public should be retrieved. You don't want to list all the properties in the class's base object:

```
//Get all the public instance properties for the object.
PropertyInfo[]properties =
    Type.GetType(workflow.ENTWorkflowObjectName).GetProperties(
    BindingFlags.Instance | BindingFlags.DeclaredOnly |
    BindingFlags.Public);
```

The properties are returned in a `PropertyInfo` array and then enumerated to show a row in the HTML table if the property has a public set accessor. If the property doesn't have a public set method, then the user cannot change it and so it should not be listed:

```
//Populate the table with all the fields.
foreach (PropertyInfo prop in properties)
{
    //Only show properties the have a public set property.
    MethodInfo[] methodInfo = prop.GetAccessors();
```

```
//Get the set method
IEnumerable<MethodInfo> set =
  from m in methodInfo
  where m.Name.StartsWith("set")
  select m;

if (set.Count() > 0)
{
  if (set.Single<MethodInfo>().IsPublic)
  {
```

Try to find this property in the state's list of saved properties. If the state is being added for the first time, then the list will be empty; but if the state already exists, then the value that has already been saved for this property should be reflected in the Read-only and Required checkboxes:

```
ENTWFStatePropertyEO entWFStateProperty = new
    ENTWFStatePropertyEO();

if (entWFStateEO.ENTWorkflowId ==
    Convert.ToInt32(ddlWorkflow.SelectedValue))
{
  //Try to find this property in the ENTWFStateObject
  entWFStateProperty =
    entWFStateEO.ENTWFStateProperties.GetByPropertyName(prop.Name);

  if (entWFStateProperty == null)
  {
    entWFStateProperty = new ENTWFStatePropertyEO();
  }
}

TableRow tr = new TableRow();

//Name of property
TableCell tcName = new TableCell();
tcName.Text = prop.Name;
tr.Cells.Add(tcName);

//Read Only checkbox
TableCell tcReadOnly = new TableCell();
CheckBox chkReadOnly = new CheckBox();
chkReadOnly.Enabled = !ReadOnly;
chkReadOnly.Checked = entWFStateProperty.ReadOnly;
tcReadOnly.Controls.Add(chkReadOnly);
tr.Cells.Add(tcReadOnly);

//Required checkbox
TableCell tcRequired = new TableCell();
CheckBox chkRequired = new CheckBox();
chkRequired.Enabled = !ReadOnly;
chkRequired.Checked = entWFStateProperty.Required;
tcRequired.Controls.Add(chkRequired);
tr.Cells.Add(tcRequired);

tblProperties.Rows.Add(tr);
```

```
                }
              }
            }
          }
        else
        {
          throw new Exception("The workflow can not be found in the database.");
        }
      }
    }
}
```

The next method to implement is the LoadControls method. This method loads the workflow drop-down list and inserts a blank in the owner group drop-down list:

```
protected override void LoadControls()
{
    //workflows
    ENTWorkflowEOList workflows = new ENTWorkflowEOList();
    workflows.Load();

    ddlWorkflow.DataSource = workflows;
    ddlWorkflow.DataTextField = "DisplayText";
    ddlWorkflow.DataValueField = "ID";
    ddlWorkflow.DataBind();

    ddlWorkflow.Items.Insert(0, new ListItem("", "0"));

    ddlWFOwnerGroup.Items.Insert(0, new ListItem("", "0"));
}
```

Next, implement the LoadScreenFromObject method. This method sets the text of the textbox controls and the checked property of the IsSubmitter checkbox. If a workflow is chosen, then the property table is rebuilt. The owner drop-down list is populated with the owner groups associated with this workflow:

```
protected override void LoadScreenFromObject(ENTWFStateEO baseEO)
{
    ENTWFStateEO state = (ENTWFStateEO)baseEO;

    txtStateName.Text = state.StateName;
    txtDescription.Text = state.Description;
    chkIsSubmitter.Checked = state.IsOwnerSubmitter;

    //Check if a workflow is selected.
    if (state.ENTWorkflowId != 0)
    {
        ddlWorkflow.Items.FindByValue(state.ENTWorkflowId.ToString()).Selected = true;

        //Load the properties table for this workflow.
        LoadPropertiesTable(state.ENTWorkflowId, baseEO);

        //Load the owner groups associated with this workflow.
        LoadOwnerGroupList(state.ENTWorkflowId);
```

```
        //Check if there is a owner group selected.
        if (state.ENTWFOwnerGroupId != null)
        {
         ddlWFOwnerGroup.Items.FindByValue(state.ENTWFOwnerGroupId.ToString()).Selected
            = true;
        }
    }

    SetControlStateByCheckbox();
    ViewState[VIEW_STATE_KEY_STATE] = baseEO;
}
```

This method calls two methods that have not been identified yet. The first is the `LoadOwnerGroupList` method. This method loads all the owner groups for a specific workflow:

```
private void LoadOwnerGroupList(int workflowId)
{
    ENTWFOwnerGroupEOList wfOwnerGroups = new ENTWFOwnerGroupEOList();
    wfOwnerGroups.Load(workflowId);

    ddlWFOwnerGroup.DataSource = wfOwnerGroups;
    ddlWFOwnerGroup.DataTextField = "DisplayText";
    ddlWFOwnerGroup.DataValueField = "ID";
    ddlWFOwnerGroup.DataBind();

    ddlWFOwnerGroup.Items.Insert(0, new ListItem("", "0"));
}
```

The second sets the owner drop-down list's `enabled` property based on the value of the checkbox. This is similar to the owner page where if the `IsSubmitted` checkbox is checked, then the drop-down list should be disabled. The two options are mutually exclusive:

```
private void SetControlStateByCheckbox()
{
    if (chkIsSubmitter.Checked)
    {
        ddlWFOwnerGroup.SelectedIndex = 0;
        ddlWFOwnerGroup.Enabled = false;
    }
    else
    {
        ddlWFOwnerGroup.Enabled = true;
    }
}
```

Now change the `chkIsSubmitter` checkbox so that `AutoPostBack` is true and create the `chkIsSub-mitter_CheckedChanged` event handler to call the `SetControlStateByCheckbox` method:

```
protected void chkIsSubmitter_CheckedChanged(object sender, EventArgs e)
{
    SetControlStateByCheckbox();
}
```

Next, because the property table and the owner drop-down list are tied to the workflow, you need to set the `AutoPostBack` property of the `ddlWorkflow` drop-down list to true and add the `ddlWorkFlow _SelectedIndexChanged` event handler to repopulate the table and owner drop-down:

```
protected void ddlWorkflow_SelectedIndexChanged(object sender, EventArgs e)
{
    LoadOwnerGroupList(Convert.ToInt32(ddlWorkflow.SelectedValue));

    ENTWFStateEO entWFState = (ENTWFStateEO)ViewState[VIEW_STATE_KEY_STATE];
    LoadPropertiesTable(Convert.ToInt32(ddlWorkflow.SelectedValue), entWFState);
}
```

Now implement the `LoadObjectFromScreen` method. The only tricky part here is getting the value of the checkboxes that were dynamically added to the page. The table has three columns; the second contains the Read-only checkbox and the third contains the Required checkbox. You can get to these controls by looking at the cell's `Controls` property. The checkbox should be the only control in the cell, so you can reference it by the zero index. Because the `Save` method of the `ENTWFState` object always deletes all the `ENTWFStateProperty` records, you can always add the values to the `ENTWFStateProperties` list:

```
protected override void LoadObjectFromScreen(ENTWFStateEO baseEO)
{
    baseEO.StateName = txtStateName.Text;
    baseEO.ENTWorkflowId = Convert.ToInt32(ddlWorkflow.SelectedValue);
    baseEO.Description = txtDescription.Text;
    baseEO.ENTWFOwnerGroupId = Convert.ToInt32(ddlWFOwnerGroup.SelectedValue);
    baseEO.IsOwnerSubmitter = chkIsSubmitter.Checked;

    baseEO.ENTWFStateProperties.Clear();

    //Load the properties
    if (tblProperties.Rows.Count > 1)
    {
        //skip the header
        for (int row = 1; row < tblProperties.Rows.Count; row++)
        {
            TableRow tr = tblProperties.Rows[row];

            bool readOnly = ((CheckBox)tr.Cells[1].Controls[0]).Checked;

            bool required = ((CheckBox)tr.Cells[2].Controls[0]).Checked;

            string propertyName = tr.Cells[0].Text;

            baseEO.ENTWFStateProperties.Add(new ENTWFStatePropertyEO
            {
                ENTWFStateId = baseEO.ID,
                PropertyName = propertyName,
                ReadOnly = readOnly,
                Required = required
            });
        }
    }
}
```

The last two methods to implement are the button click event handlers. These use the standard code but I list them here for clarity:

```
void Master_CancelButton_Click(object sender, EventArgs e)
{
    GoToGridPage();
}

void Master_SaveButton_Click(object sender, EventArgs e)
{
    ENTValidationErrors validationErrors = new ENTValidationErrors();

    ENTWFStateEO state = (ENTWFStateEO)ViewState[VIEW_STATE_KEY_STATE];
    LoadObjectFromScreen(state);

    if (!state.Save(ref validationErrors, CurrentUser.ID))
    {
        Master.ValidationErrors = validationErrors;
    }
    else
    {
        GoToGridPage();
    }
}
```

Transitions

The transitions screens enable users to set up transitions between two states and associate a method to be called after the transition is saved. Two pages need to be added to the `Administration` folder: the `WorkflowTransitions.aspx` page and the `WorkflowTransition.aspx` page. The first page has no special methods so you can use the same method just described to create this screen. The screen looks like the one shown in Figure 7-12.

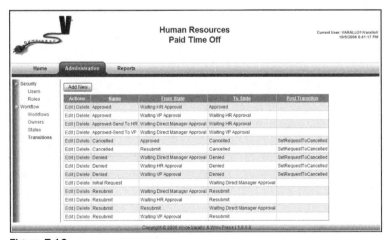

Figure 7-12

The second page is the edit page, shown in Figure 7-13.

Figure 7-13

The only tricky part to this screen is the loading of the post transition method drop-down list. This list should be populated with methods of the object associated with the workflow. Only methods that are public instance methods and have a single parameter that takes a `DataContext` object should be listed. Remember that the `ENTBaseWorkflowEO` object calls this method dynamically and passes in the `DataContext` object:

```
private void LoadMethodDropDownList(int entWorkflowId)
{
  ENTWorkflowEO workflow = new ENTWorkflowEO();
  if (workflow.Load(entWorkflowId))
  {
    //Create an instance of the type.
    MethodInfo[] methods = Type.GetType(workflow.ENTWorkflowObjectName).GetMethods(
      BindingFlags.Instance | BindingFlags.DeclaredOnly | BindingFlags.Public );

    //Load the methods for this workflow that return a boolean value into the
    //conditions drop down list.
    foreach (MethodInfo mi in methods)
    {
      //Only methods that take a parameter of a data context can be used.
      ParameterInfo[] parameters = mi.GetParameters();
      if (parameters.Length == 1)
      {
        if (parameters[0].ParameterType ==
            typeof(V2.PaidTimeOffDAL.HRPaidTimeOffDataContext))
        {
          ddlPostTransitionMethodName.Items.Add(mi.Name);
        }
      }
    }

    ddlPostTransitionMethodName.Items.Insert(0, "");
  }
  else
  {
```

```
        throw new Exception("The workflow can not be found in the database.");
    }
}
```

The rest of the code for this page is fairly standard so refer to the sample code if you would like to review it.

Now all the administrative screens are built so you can build your own workflows. The only problem now is that you don't have an object to hook it to. The next section will show you how to accomplish this by hooking the workflow to the Paid Time Off request workflow.

Solution

Let's turn our focus back to Mary and her requirements for requesting paid time off. After returning for another conversation with Mary, this is what I was able to drag out of her:

❑   The system must capture who is making the request.

❑   The system must capture the day being requested off.

❑   The system must enable the user to choose either a full day or a half day.

❑   The system must enable the user to choose among three types of days off: vacation, personal, or unpaid leave.

❑   The system must enable the HR administrator to enter each employee vacation bank for vacation and personal days.

❑   The system must ensure that people cannot request a day off that is a company holiday.

❑   The system must allow the user to copy each user's vacation bank from year to year.

❑   The system must allow a user to carry over five unused vacation days each year.

PTO Table Design

OK, this isn't so bad. Figure 7-14 shows the data model that will support these requirements.

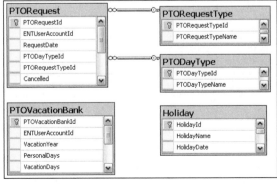

Figure 7-14

The `PTORequest` table is the main table that contains all the user's requests. The `ENTUserAccountId` field reflects the user making the request. The `RequestDate` field stores the date the user is requesting off. The `PTODayTypeId` field is a foreign key to the `PTODayType` table that denotes either a full day off, or just the a.m. or p.m. The `PTORequestTypeId` field is a foreign key to the `PTORequestTypeId` table that denotes either vacation time, personal time, or unpaid time. The `Cancelled` field is set to true if this request is cancelled or denied.

The `PTOVacationBank` table holds each employee's vacation and personal days for each year. The `Holiday` table contains all the company holidays. No big shakes so far.

The `Chapter7PTOTables.sql` file contains the script to create these tables.

Now that the tables are defined, the store procedures need to be created. The `PTORequestType` and `PTODayType` tables are not editable by the user, so all they need are the `SelectAll` and `SelectById` stored procedures. The `Holiday` table is editable by the user, so it needs the five standard procedures for `Insert`, `Update`, `Delete`, `SelectAll`, and `SelectById`. The `PTORequest` table has the five standard procedures, four custom select procedures, and a custom update procedure. The first custom select procedure selects all records for a specific user:

```
CREATE PROCEDURE PTORequestSelectByENTUserAccountId
(
    @ENTUserAccountId int
)
AS
    SET NOCOUNT ON

    SELECT PTORequestId, ENTUserAccountId, RequestDate, PTODayTypeId,
            PTORequestTypeId, InsertDate, InsertENTUserAccountId, UpdateDate,
            UpdateENTUserAccountId, Version
      FROM PTORequest
     WHERE ENTUserAccountId = @ENTUserAccountId

    RETURN
```

The second custom select procedure returns the total number of days by request type for a user and year. The fields that are returned do not map to the `PTORequest` table, but rather a resultset, with six fields that reflect each count that is returned. This one is pretty slick:

```
CREATE PROCEDURE PTORequestSelectByENTUserAccountIdYear
(
@PTORequestId int,
    @ENTUserAccountId int,
    @VacationYear smallint
)
AS
    SET NOCOUNT ON

    SELECT (SELECT COUNT(1)
              FROM PTORequest
             WHERE ENTUserAccountId = @ENTUserAccountId
               AND PTORequest.PTORequestId <> @PTORequestId
```

```
                  AND YEAR(RequestDate) = @VacationYear
                  AND PTORequestTypeId = 1
                  AND PTODayTypeId = 1
                  AND Cancelled = 0) AS CountOfFullVacation,
    (SELECT COUNT(1) * 0.5
       FROM PTORequest
      WHERE ENTUserAccountId = @ENTUserAccountId
        AND PTORequest.PTORequestId <> @PTORequestId
        AND YEAR(RequestDate) = @VacationYear
        AND PTORequestTypeId = 1
        AND PTODayTypeId <> 1
        AND Cancelled = 0) AS CountOfHalfVacation,
    (SELECT COUNT(1)
       FROM PTORequest
      WHERE ENTUserAccountId = @ENTUserAccountId
        AND PTORequest.PTORequestId <> @PTORequestId
        AND YEAR(RequestDate) = @VacationYear
        AND PTORequestTypeId = 2
        AND PTODayTypeId = 1
        AND Cancelled = 0) AS CountOfFullPersonal,
    (SELECT COUNT(1) * 0.5
       FROM PTORequest
      WHERE ENTUserAccountId = @ENTUserAccountId
        AND PTORequest.PTORequestId <> @PTORequestId
        AND YEAR(RequestDate) = @VacationYear
        AND PTORequestTypeId = 2
        AND PTODayTypeId <> 1
        AND Cancelled = 0) AS CountOfHalfPersonal,
    (SELECT COUNT(1)
       FROM PTORequest
      WHERE ENTUserAccountId = @ENTUserAccountId
        AND PTORequest.PTORequestId <> @PTORequestId
        AND YEAR(RequestDate) = @VacationYear
        AND PTORequestTypeId = 3
        AND PTODayTypeId = 1
        AND Cancelled = 0) AS CountOfFullUnpaid,
    (SELECT COUNT(1) * 0.5
       FROM PTORequest
      WHERE ENTUserAccountId = @ENTUserAccountId
        AND PTORequest.PTORequestId <> @PTORequestId
        AND YEAR(RequestDate) = @VacationYear
        AND PTORequestTypeId = 3
        AND PTODayTypeId <> 1
        AND Cancelled = 0) AS CountOfHalfUnPaid

RETURN
```

The third custom select procedure selects all the requests for a given user but excludes the one that has the ID passed in as a parameter. This is used when users are editing an existing request so that they cannot choose a date that was already requested:

```
CREATE PROCEDURE PTORequestSelectPreviousByENTUserAccountId
(
@PTORequestId int,
```

```
        @ENTUserAccountId int
)
AS
    SET NOCOUNT ON

    SELECT PTORequestId, ENTUserAccountId, RequestDate, PTODayTypeId,
           PTORequestTypeId, InsertDate, InsertENTUserAccountId, UpdateDate,
           UpdateENTUserAccountId, Version
      FROM PTORequest
     WHERE ENTUserAccountId = @ENTUserAccountId
       AND PTORequest.PTORequestId <> @PTORequestId
       AND Cancelled = 0

    RETURN
```

The fourth custom select procedure selects all the requests that a specific user currently owns:

```
CREATE PROCEDURE PTORequestSelectByCurrentOwner
(
    @ENTUserAccountId int,
    @ENTWorkflowObjectName varchar(255)
)
AS
    SET NOCOUNT ON

    SELECT PTORequestId, ENTUserAccountId, RequestDate, PTODayTypeId,
           PTORequestTypeId, InsertDate, InsertENTUserAccountId, UpdateDate,
           UpdateENTUserAccountId, Version
      FROM PTORequest
INNER JOIN (SELECT ItemId, ENTWFItemOwner.ENTUserAccountId AS OwnerId
              FROM ENTWFItem
        INNER JOIN ENTWorkflow
                ON ENTWFItem.ENTWorkflowId = ENTWorkflow.ENTWorkflowId
        INNER JOIN ENTWFState
                ON ENTWFItem.CurrentWFStateId = ENTWFState.ENTWFStateId
        INNER JOIN ENTWFItemOwner
                ON ENTWFItem.ENTWFItemId = ENTWFItemOwner.ENTWFItemId
             WHERE ENTWorkflowObjectName = @ENTWorkflowObjectName
               AND ENTWFState.ENTWFOwnerGroupId = ENTWFItemOwner.ENTWFOwnerGroupId)
                AS Item
        ON PTORequest.PTORequestId = Item.ItemId
     WHERE Item.OwnerId = @ENTUserAccountId
       AND Cancelled = 0

    RETURN
```

This joins the PTORequest table to the workflow tables using a nested Select statement. When creating queries with this syntax, the nested Select statement should be aliased; and any fields that are used in the join, where clause, or select clause of the main query must be selected in the nested Select clause.

The custom update procedure sets the `Cancelled` field to true for a specific request:

```
CREATE PROCEDURE PTORequestUpdateCancelled
(
    @PTORequestId  int,
    @Cancelled bit
)
AS
    SET NOCOUNT ON

    UPDATE PTORequest
       SET
            Cancelled = @Cancelled
     WHERE PTORequestId = @PTORequestId
```

The `PTOVacationBank` table has all five standard procedures plus two custom select procedures and two other custom procedures. The first custom select procedure selects an individual employee's vacation bank. Notice that this procedure returns the user's name by joining to the `ENTUserAccount` table, so the entity object needs to be customized to reflect this:

```
CREATE PROCEDURE PTOVacationBankSelectByUserAccountIdYear
(
    @ENTUserAccountid int,
    @VacationYear smallint
)
AS
    SET NOCOUNT ON

    SELECT PTOVacationBankId, PTOVacationBank.ENTUserAccountId, VacationYear,
           PersonalDays, VacationDays, PTOVacationBank.InsertDate,
           PTOVacationBank.InsertENTUserAccountId, PTOVacationBank.UpdateDate,
           PTOVacationBank.UpdateENTUserAccountId, PTOVacationBank.Version,
           LastName + ', ' + FirstName AS UserName
      FROM PTOVacationBank
INNER JOIN ENTUserAccount
        ON PTOVacationBank.ENTUserAccountId = ENTUserAccount.ENTUserAccountId
     WHERE PTOVacationBank.ENTUserAccountid = @ENTUserAccountId
       AND VacationYear = @VacationYear

    RETURN
```

The second custom select procedure retrieves a resultset of distinct years that exist in the table:

```
CREATE PROCEDURE PTOVacationBankSelectDistinctYears
AS
    SET NOCOUNT ON

    SELECT DISTINCT VacationYear
      FROM PTOVacationBank

    RETURN
```

The next custom procedure will copy all the records for a given year to another year for each employee who does not have records in the PTOVacationBank table for the year being copied to:

```
CREATE PROCEDURE PTOVacationBankCopyYear
(
  @FromYear smallint,
  @ToYear smallint,
  @InsertENTUserAccountId int
)
AS
  SET NOCOUNT ON

  INSERT INTO PTOVacationBank(ENTUserAccountId, VacationYear, PersonalDays,
          VacationDays, InsertDate, InsertENTUserAccountId, UpdateDate,
          UpdateENTUserAccountID)
  SELECT ENTUserAccountId, @ToYear, PersonalDays, VacationDays, GetDate(),
       @InsertENTUserAccountId, GetDate(), @InsertENTUserAccountId
    FROM PTOVacationBank
   WHERE VacationYear = @FromYear
     AND ENTUserAccountID NOT IN (SELECT ENTUserAccountID
                                    FROM PTOVacationBank
                                   WHERE VacationYear = @ToYear)

  RETURN
```

The last custom procedure checks if a user already has a vacation bank for a given year:

```
CREATE PROCEDURE PTOVacationBankIsDuplicate
(
    @PTOVacationBankId int,
    @ENTUserAccountId int,
    @VacationYear smallint
)
AS
    SET NOCOUNT ON

    SELECT Count(1) AS CountOfDuplicates
      FROM PTOVacationBank
     WHERE PTOVacationBankId <> @PTOVacationBankId
       AND ENTUserAccountId = @ENTUserAccountId
       AND VacationYear = @VacationYear

    RETURN
```

All the stored procedures can be found in the Chapter7PTOStoredProcedures.sql file.

Entity Objects and DataContext Objects

Open the ORM Designer and drag the five tables onto the design surface as shown in Figure 7-15.

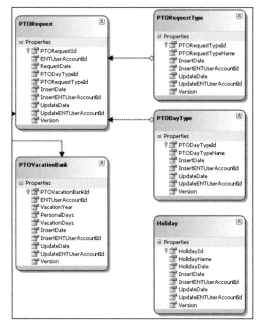

Figure 7-15

Drag all the Insert, Update, and Delete stored procedures to the Methods pane and then drag the select procedures for the PTORequestType, PTODayType, Holiday, and PTORequest tables on top of each respective table so the return type is the table's entity object. Because the PTOVacationBank select procedures return extra fields, you must customize the entity object before creating the stored procedure methods in the DataContext. Add the following class to the CustomizedEntities.cs file:

```
public partial class PTOVacationBank : IENTBaseEntity
{
    private string _UserName;

    partial void OnUserNameChanging(string value);
    partial void OnUserNameChanged();

    [Column(Storage = "_UserName", DbType = "VarChar(102)", UpdateCheck =
    UpdateCheck.Never)]
    public string UserName
    {
        get
        {
            return this._UserName;
        }
        set
        {
            if ((this._UserName != value))
```

```
            {
                this.OnUserNameChanging(value);
                this.SendPropertyChanging();
                this._UserName = value;
                this.SendPropertyChanged("UserName");
                this.OnUserNameChanged();
            }
        }
    }
}
```

Now you can drag the select procedures onto the table in the ORM Designer and the correct return type will be returned by the method.

The other custom select stored procedures that do not return resultsets that map to a table should be added to the Methods pane by dragging them directly to it. Each one will have a custom class created that is named the same as the stored procedure, with the word *Result* appended to it. These stored procedures are PTORequestSelectByENTUserAccountIdYear, PTOVacationBankIsDuplicate, and PTOVacationBankSelectDistinctYears.

The next step is to create the partial classes in the CustomizedEntities.cs file:

```
public partial class PTORequest : IENTBaseEntity { }

public partial class Holiday : IENTBaseEntity { }

public partial class PTODayType : IENTBaseEntity { }

public partial class PTORequestType : IENTBaseEntity { }
```

Now you can add the data classes for each table. The only difference between these classes and those that you have created before is that they are not in the Framework folder because these are specific to this application. The code available on the Wrox website has these classes, so you may want to just copy them to your project if you are following along.

Business Classes

Each of these tables has a business class associated with it. PTODayType and PTORequestType cannot be edited, so those classes inherit from the ENTBaseBO and ENTBaseBOList objects. The only customization to these classes is an enumeration. The PTODayTypeBO has an enumeration called PTODayType Enum that represents the three values this table can contain. These must match the ID of each record in the table:

```
public enum PTODayTypeEnum
{
    Full = 1,
    AM = 2,
    PM = 3
}
```

The `PTORequestTypeBO` class has an enumeration called `PTORequestTypeEnum` that represents the three values this table can contain. These must match the ID of each record in the table:

```
public enum PTORequestTypeEnum
{
    Vacation = 1,
    Personal = 2,
    Unpaid = 3
}
```

The `Holiday` table is editable, so the business classes inherit from the `ENTBaseEO` and `ENTBaseEOList` classes. Everything in these classes is boilerplate from the standard design except for two custom methods that should be added to the `HolidayEOList` class:

```
public bool IsHoliday(DateTime date)
{
    return (GetHoliday(date) != null);
}

public HolidayEO GetHoliday(DateTime date)
{
    return this.SingleOrDefault(h => h.HolidayDate == date);
}
```

The `IsHoliday` method searches the current list and returns true if the date passed in is a holiday. The `GetHoliday` method uses a lambda expression to search the current instance for a holiday with the date passed in.

The `PTOVacationBank` table is editable, so its business classes also inherit from the `ENTBaseEO` and `ENTBaseEOList` classes. Again, the standard methods should be implemented same as described earlier, and three custom methods need to be added to the `PTOVacationBankEO` class. The first returns an array list of distinct years that have records in the table:

```
public static ArrayList GetDistinctYears()
{
    ArrayList years = new ArrayList();

    List<PTOVacationBankSelectDistinctYearsResult> ptoYears = new
        PTOVacationBankData().SelectDistinctYears();

    foreach (PTOVacationBankSelectDistinctYearsResult ptoYear in ptoYears)
    {
        years.Add(ptoYear.VacationYear);
    }

    return years;
}
```

The second method enables the user to copy one year to another. This just calls the method in the DAL that calls the stored procedure that does this:

```
public static void CopyYear(short fromYear, short toYear, int userAccountId)
{
    new PTOVacationBankData().CopyYear(fromYear, toYear, userAccountId);
}
```

The last method overloads the `Load` method so that a specific employee's vacation bank can be loaded into the current instance:

```
public bool Load(int userAccountId, short year)
{
    PTOVacationBank pTOVacationBank = new
        PTOVacationBankData().SelectByUserAccountIdYear(userAccountId, year);

    MapEntityToProperties(pTOVacationBank);
    return pTOVacationBank != null;
}
```

The last business classes to create are for the `PTORequest` table. These classes will be hooked to the workflow to enable the request to pass from person to person. Add a new class to the `PaidTimeOffBLL` project and name it `PTORequestEO`. Change the class declaration so it is serializable and inherits from the `ENTBaseWorkflowEO` class:

```
[Serializable()]
public class PTORequestEO : ENTBaseWorkflowEO
```

Because the `ENTBaseWorkflowEO` object inherits from the `ENTBaseEO` object, you must implement the same abstract methods that you did for the other objects. A few extra lines of code need to be added to some of the methods to get the workflow to work. In the `MapEntityToCustomProperties` method, you need to call the `LoadWorkflow` method in the base class:

```
protected override void MapEntityToCustomProperties(IENTBaseEntity entity)
{
    PTORequest pTORequest = (PTORequest)entity;

    ID = pTORequest.PTORequestId;
    ENTUserAccountId = pTORequest.ENTUserAccountId;
    RequestDate = pTORequest.RequestDate;
    PTODayTypeId = (PTODayTypeBO.PTODayTypeEnum)pTORequest.PTODayTypeId;
    PTORequestTypeId =
    (PTORequestTypeBO.PTORequestTypeEnum)pTORequest.PTORequestTypeId;
    base.LoadWorkflow(this.GetType().AssemblyQualifiedName, ID);
}
```

The `Save` method must be customized to call the `SaveWorkflow` method in the base class:

```
public override bool Save(HRPaidTimeOffDataContext db, ref ENTValidationErrors
validationErrors, int userAccountId)
{
```

```
if (DBAction == DBActionEnum.Save)
{
    //Validate the object
    Validate(db, ref validationErrors);

    //Check if there were any validation errors
    if (validationErrors.Count == 0)
    {
        bool isNewRecord = IsNewRecord();
        if (isNewRecord)
        {
            //Add
            ID = new PTORequestData().Insert(db, ENTUserAccountId, RequestDate,
                Convert.ToInt32(PTODayTypeId), Convert.ToInt32(PTORequestTypeId),
                userAccountId);
        }
        else
        {
            //Update
            if (!new PTORequestData().Update(db, ID, ENTUserAccountId,
                  RequestDate, Convert.ToInt32(PTODayTypeId),
                  Convert.ToInt32(PTORequestTypeId), userAccountId, Version))
            {
                UpdateFailed(ref validationErrors);
                if (isNewRecord)
                    ID = 0;
                return false;
            }
        }

        if (base.SaveWorkflow(db, ref validationErrors, this, userAccountId))
        {
            return true;
        }
        else
        {
            if (isNewRecord)
                ID = 0;
            return false;
        }
    }
    else
    {
        //Didn't pass validation.
        ID = 0;
        return false;
    }
}
else
{
    throw new Exception("DBAction not Save.");
}
}
```

All the other abstract methods should be implemented the same way as before, and the code is included with the sample application. There is one method worth mentioning, however. The `GetDisplayText` method looks like this:

```
protected override string GetDisplayText()
{
    return RequestDate.ToStandardDateFormat();
}
```

The `RequestDate`'s type is `DateTime`. If you look at all the methods on the `DateTime` object, you won't find one called `ToStandardDateFormat`, so how does this work? It's made possible with another new feature in .NET 3.5 called *extension methods*, which enable you to extend an existing class by adding methods to it. The sample application adds two methods to the `DateTime` class that aren't there by default. To do this, add a new class to `PaidTimeOffBLL` called `ExtensionMethods`. The code for this class is as follows:

```
public static class ExtensionMethods
{
  public static bool IsWeekend(this DateTime d)
  {
      if ((d.DayOfWeek == DayOfWeek.Saturday) || (d.DayOfWeek == DayOfWeek.Sunday))
      {
        return true;
      }
      else
      {
        return false;
      }
  }

  public static string ToStandardDateFormat(this DateTime d)
  {
      return d.ToString("MM/dd/yyyy");
  }
}
```

The rules for creating an extension method are straightforward: They must be declared as static and the first parameter must include the *this* keyword followed by the class you want to extend. You can add more parameters to the declaration if you need to pass other parameters to the function. The first extension method is called `IsWeekend`, which returns true if the date is a Saturday or Sunday. The second extension method is called `ToStandardDateFormat`, which returns the date in the format MM/dd/yyyy. If this application needed to be international and the dates had to be displayed in dd/MM/yyyy format, you would only need to change this one method.

The `PTORequestEO` class has two custom methods. The first updates the current record to cancelled:

```
public void SetRequestToCancelled(HRPaidTimeOffDataContext db)
{
    new PTORequestData().UpdateCancelled(db, ID, true);
}
```

This has the signature that is needed by a `WFTransition` method. This is called whenever a request is cancelled or denied by the workflow.

The second custom method returns the employee's list of used days based on a specific year:

```
public static void GetUsed(ref double usedPersonalDays, ref double
    usedVacationDays, ref double unpaid, int ptoRequestId, int userAccountId,
    short year)
{
  PTORequestSelectByENTUserAccountIdYearResult result = new
      PTORequestData().SelectByENTUserAccountIdYear(ptoRequestId,
      userAccountId, year);

  if (result != null)
  {
    usedVacationDays = Convert.ToDouble(result.CountOfFullVacation +
                       result.CountOfHalfVacation);

    usedPersonalDays = Convert.ToDouble(result.CountOfFullPersonal +
                       result.CountOfHalfPersonal);

    unpaid = Convert.ToDouble(result.CountOfFullUnpaid +
             result.CountOfHalfUnPaid);
  }
  else
  {
    usedPersonalDays = 0;
    usedVacationDays = 0;
    unpaid = 0;
  }
}
```

The `PTORequestEOList` class has three custom methods. The first loads the current instance with all previous vacation days, excluding the current request:

```
public void LoadPreviousByENTUserAccountId(int ptoRequestId, int entUserAccountId)
{
  LoadFromList(new PTORequestData().SelectPreviousByENTUserAccountId(ptoRequestId,
          entUserAccountId));
}
```

The second method loads the current instance with all the requests for a specific employee:

```
public void LoadByENTUserAccountId(int entUserAccountId)
{
  LoadFromList(new PTORequestData().SelectByENTUserAccountId(entUserAccountId));
}
```

The third method returns a list of `PTORequestEO` objects from the current instance based on a request date. For example, a user could enter two separate requests for half days on the same day, so this must return a list rather than a single instance:

```
public List<PTORequestEO> GetByRequestDate(DateTime requestDate)
{
    var ret =
        from r in this
        where r.RequestDate == requestDate
```

```
            select r;

    return ret.ToList();
}
```

User Interface

Now that the `PTORequestEO` object is created, you can use the workflow screens to build the PTO Request workflow that Mary defined. Build the PTO Request workflow following these steps:

1. Launch the application and click the Administration tab. Assuming you created a role with the capability to edit all the workflow screens and added yourself to the role, you should see all four workflow menu items: Workflows, Owners, States, and Transitions.

2. Click the Workflows menu item to bring up the list of workflows.

3. Click the Add New button. The `Workflow.aspx` screen should appear. Enter **PTO Request** for the name and select V2.PaidTimeOffBLL.PTORequestEO, V2.PaidTimeOffBLL, Version=1.0.0.0, Culture=neutral, and PublicKeyToken=null from the drop-down list. This should be the only item in the list, as it is the only object that inherits from the `ENTBaseWorkflowEO` class.

4. Click the Save button.

5. To create the owners who are associated with this workflow, click on the Owners menu item, which brings up the list of owners.

6. Click the Add New button. The `WorkflowOwner.aspx` page should appear. Enter **Direct Manager** for the name, select the PTO Request item from the workflow list, enter a Description, and then check the "Check here to default to the same user as the user's last request" checkbox.

7. Add some of the users in the Available Users list to this group and click the Save button. Repeat the same steps to create the Vice President and HR PTO Administrator groups. When creating the HR PTO Administrator group, choose a specific user to default to, rather than check the box. Usually, only one person in HR manages the requests.

8. To add the states for this workflow, click on the States menu item and then click the Add New button. Enter **Waiting Direct Manager Approval** for the name. Select the PTO Request workflow from the workflow list. Enter a description and then select the Direct Manager owner from the "Select the group that owns this issue while in this state" drop-down list.

9. Check all eight checkboxes for Read-Only and Required properties. The screen should show four properties: `ENTUserAccountId`, `RequestDate`, `PTODayTypeId`, and `PTORequestTypeId`. All of these must be filled in for the request to be submitted to the Direct Manager, and the Direct Manager should not be allowed to change them. Click the Save button.

10. Create another state called **Waiting VP Approval** and set the Vice President as the owner. Check off all eight boxes again. Then create states called "Waiting HR Approval," "Denied," and "Cancelled," and set the HR PTO Administrator as the owner. Check off all eight boxes for each state.

11. Create a state called **Approved** and check the box called "Check here if the submitter is the default owner." All the checkboxes for the properties should be checked. The last state to create is the **Resubmit** state. This should also have the "Check here if the submitter is the default owner" option checked. Mark the `RequestDate`, `ENTUserAccountId`, `PTODayTypeId`, and `PTORequest TypeId` as Required. Only the `ENTUserAccountId` should be checked as Read-Only because when a request is in this state the user can change the `RequestDate`, `PTODayTypeId`, and the `PTORequestTypeId` fields and resubmit the request to the manager.

The next step is to create the transitions. All of the arrows defined in Figure 7-16 should be created as a transition. When defining transitions, at least one must have a From state that is blank. This is the transition that will be listed when the user first makes a request. Set up the transitions as shown in Figure 7-16.

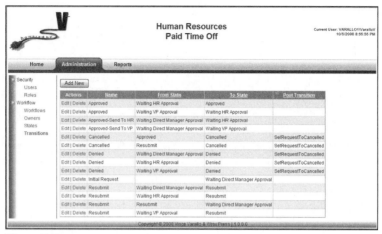

Figure 7-16

As you can see, even the simplest workflows have a lot of variations, and coding all this logic for each application you create could take quite a bit of time. It is hoped that these four workflow screens will save you time for your future applications.

Holidays

At this point, you're getting closer to being able to use the workflow engine, but a few screens still need to be created to enable users to enter a PTO request. The first is the holiday screen. This screen should only be used by an administrator in HR to set up the company. Add the following record to the ENTMenuItem table.

MenuItem Name	Url	ParentENT MenuItemId	Display Sequence	IsAlways Enabled
Holidays	Administration/Holidays.aspx	Administration (ID)	1	False

The following capability record should also be added.

CapabilityName	ENTMenuItemId	AccessType
Holidays	Holidays Menu Item ID	0

Now add a new Web Form called Holidays.aspx to the Administration folder and use the PaidTimeOffEditGrid master page. This page should be hooked to the HolidayEOList class using the same logic as the other grid pages.

The next step is to add the `Holiday.aspx` page to the `Administration` folder. This is the edit page, so it should use the `PaidTimeOffEditPage` master page. The screen should look like Figure 7-17.

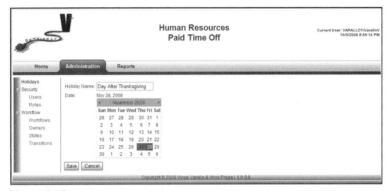

Figure 7-17

This page uses the built-in ASP.NET calendar control that comes with Visual Studio. It displays previously entered holidays in red and displays the date the user is selecting for the new holiday in green. This is accomplished by adding code to the `DayRender` and `SelectionChanged` events for the calendar control:

```
protected void calHolidayDate_DayRender(object sender, DayRenderEventArgs e)
{
    HolidayEO holiday = holidays.GetHoliday(e.Day.Date);

    HolidayEO currentHoliday = (HolidayEO)ViewState[VIEW_STATE_KEY_HOLIDAY];

    if ((holiday != null) && (holiday.ID != currentHoliday.ID))
    {
        e.Cell.Text = "H";
        e.Cell.BackColor = Color.Red;
        e.Cell.ToolTip = holiday.HolidayName;
    }
}

protected void calHolidayDate_SelectionChanged(object sender, EventArgs e)
{
    SetSelectedDateLabel();
}

private void SetSelectedDateLabel()
{
    lblSelectedDate.Text = calHolidayDate.SelectedDate.ToString("MMM dd, yyyy");
}
```

The `holidays` object is a cached list of previously entered holidays. All the other code in this screen is implemented like the other pages.

Vacation Bank

The next screens to create are the screens that manage a user's vacation bank. These screens should also be managed by the HR administrator, so they should be placed under the Administration menu. Add the following records to the ENTMenuItem and ENTCapability tables.

MenuItem Name	Url	ParentENT MenuItemId	Display Sequence	IsAlways Enabled
Vacation Banks	Administration/ VacationBanks.aspx	Administration (ID)	3	False

CapabilityName	ENTMenuItemId	AccessType
Vacation Banks	Vacation Banks Menu Item ID	0

Add the VacationBanks.aspx page to the Administration folder. It follows the same pattern as all the other grid pages with one exception: A button needs to be added to enable users to copy from one year to the next (see Figure 7-18).

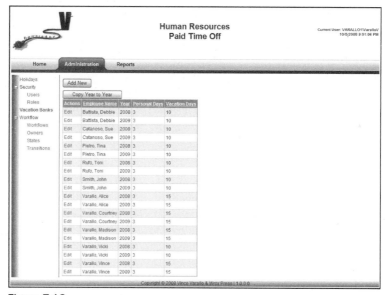

Figure 7-18

The copy button's click event should redirect users to a new page called CopyVacationBank.aspx. This is a simple page with two drop-down lists that enable users to copy from one year to the next (see Figure 7-19).

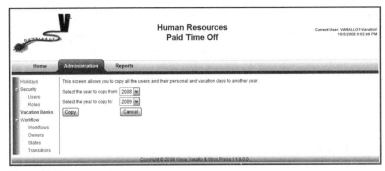

Figure 7-19

The Cancel button redirects the user back to the `VacationBanks.aspx` page. The Copy button's click event code is as follows:

```
protected void btnCopy_Click(object sender, EventArgs e)
{
    ENTValidationErrors validationErrors = new ENTValidationErrors();

    if (ddlFrom.Text == ddlTo.Text)
    {
        validationErrors.Add("The from and to years can not be the same.");
        ValidationErrorMessages1.ValidationErrors = validationErrors;
    }
    else
    {
        PTOVacationBankEO.CopyYear(Convert.ToInt16(ddlFrom.Text),
            Convert.ToInt16(ddlTo.Text), CurrentUser.ID);
        Response.Redirect("VacationBanks.aspx");
    }
}
```

The actual copying occurs in the `PTOVacactionBankCopyYear` stored procedure.

The next page to add is the `VacationBank.aspx` edit page. This page enables users to enter a specific employee's vacation bank. The Add New button and Edit link on the `VacationBanks.aspx` page redirect the user to the following page (see Figure 7-20).

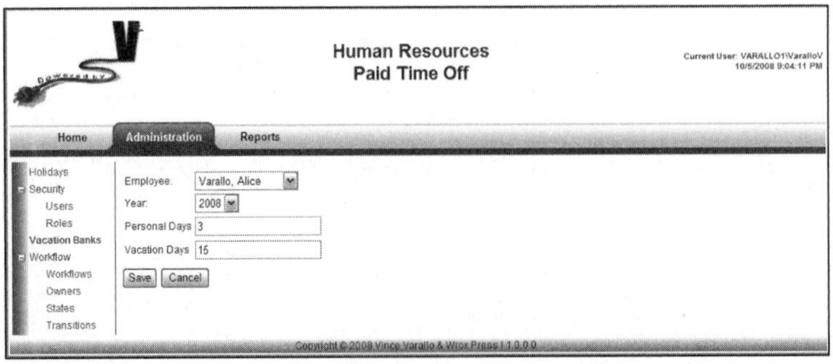

Figure 7-20

There nothing special about this screen so you can copy the file from the sample project to see the code-behind for this page.

Submit Request

OK, it's finally time to create the page, shown in Figure 7-21, that has all the magic in it to enable a user to submit a request and to enable other users to move it along in the process.

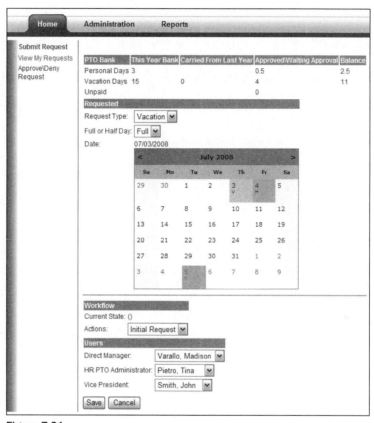

Figure 7-21

Because this page is supposed to be accessible to general users, its menu item will be placed under the Home tab. Add the following records to the ENTMenuItem and ENTCapability tables.

MenuItem Name	Url	ParentENT MenuItemId	Display Sequence	IsAlways Enabled
Submit Request	PTORequest.aspx	Home (ID)	1	False

CapabilityName	ENTMenuItemId	AccessType
Submit Request	Submit Request Menu Item ID	2

There is no need for read-only access to this page because it will be used to submit requests, so set the `AccessType` field to 2, which denotes None\Edit.

Add a new page to the root directory of the project and name it `PTORequest.aspx`. This page should use the `PaidTimeOffEditPage` master page and inherit from the `BaseEditPage` class. The screen needs to be explained in two parts. Everything from the calendar control on up is the first part. Everything below the calendar control is the second part, which is really a server-side control specific to the workflow functionality. The HTML for the top part of the screen is as follows:

```
<table>
  <tr class="gridViewHeader">
    <td>PTO Bank</td>
    <td>This Year Bank</td>
    <td>Carried From Last Year</td>
    <td>Approved\Waiting Approval</td>
    <td>Balance</td>
  </tr>
  <tr>
    <td>Personal Days</td>
    <td><asp:Label runat="server" ID="lblPersonalDaysBank"></asp:Label></td>
    <td></td>
    <td><asp:Label runat="server" ID="lblPersonalDaysUsed"></asp:Label></td>
    <td><asp:Label runat="server" ID="lblPersonalBalance"></asp:Label></td>
  </tr>
  <tr>
    <td>Vacation Days</td>
    <td><asp:Label runat="server" ID="lblVacationDaysBank"></asp:Label></td>
    <td><asp:Label runat="server" ID="lblVacationCarry"></asp:Label></td>
    <td><asp:Label runat="server" ID="lblVacationDaysUsed"></asp:Label></td>
    <td><asp:Label runat="server" ID="lblVacationBalance"></asp:Label></td>
  </tr>
  <tr>
    <td>Unpaid</td>
    <td></td>
    <td></td>
    <td><asp:Label runat="server" ID="lblUnpaidUsed"></asp:Label></td>
    <td></td>
  </tr>
</table>
<table>
  <tr class="gridViewHeader">
    <td colspan="2">Requested</td>
  </tr>
  <tr>
    <td runat="server">Request Type:</td>
    <td runat="server"><asp:DropDownList runat="server" ID="ddlPTORequestType"
      AutoPostBack="True"></asp:DropDownList></td>
  </tr>
  <tr>
    <td runat="server">Full or Half Day:</td>
    <td runat="server"><asp:DropDownList runat="server" ID="ddlPTODayType"
      AutoPostBack="True"></asp:DropDownList></td>
  </tr>
```

```
<tr>
    <td runat="server" valign="top">Date:</td>
    <td><asp:Label runat="server" ID="lblRequestDate"></asp:Label>
        <asp:Calendar ID="calFullDay" runat="server"
            ondayrender="calFullDay_DayRender"
            BackColor="White" BorderColor="#999999" CellPadding="4"
            DayNameFormat="Shortest" Font-Names="Verdana" Font-Size="8pt"
            ForeColor="Black"
            Height="250px" Width="300px"
            onselectionchanged="calFullDay_SelectionChanged"
            onvisiblemonthchanged="calFullDay_VisibleMonthChanged" >
            <SelectedDayStyle Font-Bold="False" ForeColor="Black" />
            <SelectorStyle BackColor="#CCCCCC" />
            <WeekendDayStyle BackColor="#FFFFCC" />
            <TodayDayStyle ForeColor="Black" />
            <OtherMonthDayStyle ForeColor="#808080" />
            <DayStyle HorizontalAlign="Left" VerticalAlign="Top" />
            <NextPrevStyle VerticalAlign="Bottom" />
            <DayHeaderStyle BackColor="#CCCCCC" Font-Bold="True" Font-Size="7pt" />
            <TitleStyle BackColor="#999999" BorderColor="Black" Font-Bold="True" />
        </asp:Calendar>
    </td>
</tr>
</table>
```

The PTO bank at the top of the screen enables users to see the number of days allowed for the year selected in the calendar control. It also shows how many days were carried over from the previous year, how many have been used for this year, and how many remain. All of the logic to calculate this was already defined in the business and data classes; the screen is just displaying the results.

The second part of the screen enables users to select the request type, the day type, and the day being requested off. This calendar control displays all holidays and previously entered PTO requests in blue. The current requested day is displayed in green.

The second part of the screen uses a new server-side control built specifically for the workflow. Before placing the control on this page, you need to create it:

1. Add a new ASP.NET Web Server control to the V2.FrameworkControls project and name the file WorkflowController.cs.

2. Remove the default Text property and code for the RenderContents method. Because this control is a composite control, it will override the CreateChildControls method to build the controls dynamically. Also, in order for this control to retain its state between postbacks, it must implement the INamingContainer interface. This is a strange interface because there are no methods to actually implement. The documentation about this interface states that it is used to guarantee that all child controls of the control have a unique ID. It doesn't say anything about how it is needed to keep the child control's state between postbacks, but that is what it does:

```
public class WorkflowController : WebControl, INamingContainer
{
    ...
}
```

3.   Now add the member variables for the control. The member variables are the child controls that will be created by this control:

```
private Label lblCurrentState = new Label();
private Label lblActions = new Label();
private DropDownList ddlTransitions = new DropDownList();
private HtmlTable tblWFUserGroups = new HtmlTable();
private CustomGridView cgvWFStateHistory = new CustomGridView();
```

The lblCurrentState Label displays the request's current state and owner. The lblActions Label just displays the "Action" label next to the ddlTransitions drop-down list. The ddlTransitions drop-down list displays all the available transitions based on the request's current state. The tblWFUserGroups control is a dynamically built HTML table that contains a row for each owner group associated with this workflow. cgvWFStateHistory is a custom GridView control that displays the history of the states and owners.

The next step is to add the properties. There are three:

```
public string WorkflowObjectName { get; set; }
public ENTBaseEO BaseEOObject { get; set; }
public ENTWorkflowEO Workflow { get; private set; }
```

The WorkflowObjectName and BaseEOObject properties must be set by the page that contains this control. The next method to implement is the CreateChildControls method, which instantiates the controls and adds them to the Controls collection for the server control:

```
protected override void  CreateChildControls()
{
    base.CreateChildControls();

    HtmlTable tblWorkflow = new HtmlTable();

    //Row 1
    HtmlTableRow tr1 = new HtmlTableRow();
    tr1.Attributes.Add("class", "gridViewHeader");

    HtmlTableCell tcR1C1 = new HtmlTableCell();
    tcR1C1.ColSpan = 2;
    tcR1C1.InnerText = "Workflow";
    tr1.Cells.Add(tcR1C1);
    tblWorkflow.Rows.Add(tr1);

    //Row 2
    HtmlTableRow tr2 = new HtmlTableRow();
    HtmlTableCell tcR2C1 = new HtmlTableCell();
    tcR2C1.InnerText = "Current State:";
    tr2.Cells.Add(tcR2C1);

    HtmlTableCell tcR2C2 = new HtmlTableCell();

    lblCurrentState.ID = "lblCurrentState";
    tcR2C2.Controls.Add(lblCurrentState);
    tr2.Cells.Add(tcR2C2);
```

```
      tblWorkflow.Rows.Add(tr2);

      //Row 3
      HtmlTableRow tr3 = new HtmlTableRow();
      HtmlTableCell tcR3C1 = new HtmlTableCell();

      lblActions.ID = "lblActions";
      lblActions.Text = "Actions:";
      tcR3C1.Controls.Add(lblActions);
      tr3.Cells.Add(tcR3C1);

      HtmlTableCell tcR3C2 = new HtmlTableCell();

      ddlTransitions.ID = "ddlTransitions";
      tcR3C2.Controls.Add(ddlTransitions);
      tr3.Cells.Add(tcR3C2);
      tblWorkflow.Rows.Add(tr3);

      Controls.Add(tblWorkflow);

      //Add the owners
      CreateWFGroupOwnersTable();

      //Add custom grid view control
      cgvWFStateHistory.ID = "cgvWFStateHistory";
      Controls.Add(cgvWFStateHistory);
}
```

The first row contains a single cell with the workflow header. The second row contains two cells. The first cell contains the text "Current State:" and the second cell contains the current state label that was defined as a member-level variable. The third row contains two cells. The first cell contains the text "Actions:" and the second cell contains the ddlTransitions drop-down list. The table is then added to the Controls collection by calling the Add method. Next, the owner rows are added in the CreateWFGroupOwnersTable method:

```
private void CreateWFGroupOwnersTable()
{
    HtmlTableRow tr1 = new HtmlTableRow();
    HtmlTableCell tc1 = new HtmlTableCell();
    tc1.Attributes.Add("class", "gridViewHeader");
    tc1.ColSpan = 2;
    tc1.InnerText = "Users";
    tr1.Cells.Add(tc1);
    tblWFUserGroups.Rows.Add(tr1);

    //Get the workflow associated with this object.
    Workflow = new ENTWorkflowEO();
    Workflow.LoadByObjectName(WorkflowObjectName);

    //Get the groups associated with this workflow
    ENTWFOwnerGroupEOList entWFOwnerGroups = new ENTWFOwnerGroupEOList();
    entWFOwnerGroups.Load(Workflow.ID);

    //Create the table for all the owner groups
```

```
            foreach (ENTWFOwnerGroupEO wfOwnerGroup in entWFOwnerGroups)
            {
                HtmlTableRow tr = new HtmlTableRow();

                HtmlTableCell tcName = new HtmlTableCell();
                tcName.InnerText = wfOwnerGroup.OwnerGroupName + ":";
                tcName.Attributes.Add("ENTWFOwnerGroupId", wfOwnerGroup.ID.ToString());
                tr.Cells.Add(tcName);

                HtmlTableCell tcUsers = new HtmlTableCell();
                DropDownList ddlUsers = new DropDownList();
                ddlUsers.DataSource = wfOwnerGroup.UserAccounts;
                ddlUsers.DataTextField = "UserName";
                ddlUsers.DataValueField = "ENTUserAccountId";
                ddlUsers.DataBind();
                ddlUsers.Items.Insert(0, new ListItem("", "0"));

                tcUsers.Controls.Add(ddlUsers);
                tr.Cells.Add(tcUsers);

                tblWFUserGroups.Rows.Add(tr);
            }

        Controls.Add(tblWFUserGroups);
    }
```

This method creates a row for each owner group associated with the workflow and adds a drop-down list with the appropriate users.

The `CreateChildControls` method only adds the controls to the custom server control; it doesn't set the values of these controls. A custom method must be added to the control to set these values, which will be called by the Page's `LoadScreenFromObject` method. This new method is called `LoadControlFromObject` but you probably guessed that already:

```
public void LoadControlFromObject(ENTBaseWorkflowEO baseWorkflowEO, int
    currentUserId)
{
```

Calling `this.EnsureChildControls` guarantees that these controls are already created when this method is called:

```
    this.EnsureChildControls();
```

Loop around each row in the table with the owner drop-own lists and select the correct item from the list:

```
    //Select the user for the group
    for (int row = 1; row < tblWFUserGroups.Rows.Count; row++)
    {
      HtmlTableRow tr = tblWFUserGroups.Rows[row];

      //The owner group id is an attribute in the first cell
      int entWFOwnerGroupId =
```

```
        Convert.ToInt32(tr.Cells[0].Attributes["ENTWFOwnerGroupId"]);

    DropDownList ddlUsers = (DropDownList)tr.Cells[1].Controls[0];

    //Select the correct record.
    ENTWFItemOwnerEO itemOwner =
      baseWorkflowEO.WFOwners.GetByENTWFOwnerGroupId(entWFOwnerGroupId);

    if (itemOwner.ENTUserAccountId == null)
    {
      ddlUsers.SelectedIndex = 0;
    }
    else
    {
      ddlUsers.Items.FindByValue( itemOwner.ENTUserAccountId.ToString()).Selected =
        true;
    }
}
```

Now set the current state label by using the `baseWorkflowEO` object's current state property:

```
//Set the current state label.
lblCurrentState.Text = baseWorkflowEO.CurrentState.StateName + " (" +
  baseWorkflowEO.CurrentOwnerUserName + ")";
```

Check whether the item has any transitions associated with it. Some states have no transitions because of the business rules of the application. For example, Cancelled has no transitions because the user shouldn't be able to change the request if it was cancelled.

```
    if (baseWorkflowEO.WFTransitions.Count == 0)
    {
      //Hide Transitions
      lblActions.Visible = false;
      ddlTransitions.Visible = false;
    }
    else
    {
      //Load the transition drop down
      ddlTransitions.DataSource = baseWorkflowEO.WFTransitions;
      ddlTransitions.DataTextField = "DisplayText";
      ddlTransitions.DataValueField = "ID";
      ddlTransitions.DataBind();
    }

    //If this is a new item then there must be a transition picked.
    if (baseWorkflowEO.ID != 0)
    {
      ddlTransitions.Items.Insert(0, new ListItem("", "0"));

      //If this is an existing item and the current user is not the current owner
      //then do not let them transition the item.
      if (currentUserId != baseWorkflowEO.CurrentOwnerENTUserAccountId)
      {
        lblActions.Visible = false;
```

```
      ddlTransitions.Visible = false;
   }
 }
```

Finally, load the custom GridView with all the state history objects associated with this item:

```
//Load the state history grid
cgvWFStateHistory.ListClassName =
  typeof(ENTWFItemStateHistoryEOList).AssemblyQualifiedName;

cgvWFStateHistory.LoadMethodName = "Load";
cgvWFStateHistory.LoadMethodParameters.Add(baseWorkflowEO.WFItem.ID);
cgvWFStateHistory.SortExpressionLast = "InsertDate";

//Name
cgvWFStateHistory.AddBoundField("StateName", "State", "");
cgvWFStateHistory.AddBoundField("OwnerName", "Owner", "");
cgvWFStateHistory.AddBoundField("InsertDate", "Date", "");
cgvWFStateHistory.AddBoundField("InsertedBy", "Moved By", "");

cgvWFStateHistory.DataBind();
}
```

The last method to add to the control is LoadObjectFromControl, which is similar to the LoadObjectFromScreen method. This method sets the object's properties based on the values selected in the control:

```
public void LoadObjectFromControl(ENTBaseWorkflowEO baseWorkflowEO)
{
  this.EnsureChildControls();

  baseWorkflowEO.WFItem.ItemId = baseWorkflowEO.ID;
  baseWorkflowEO.WFItem.ENTWorkflowId = baseWorkflowEO.Workflow.ID;
```

Loop around each row in the owners table to get the users who have been selected:

```
//Get the users that have been selected to be owners for this workflow.
for (int row = 1; row < tblWFUserGroups.Rows.Count; row++)
{
  HtmlTableRow tr = tblWFUserGroups.Rows[row];

  //Get selected user id
  int entUserAccountId =
    Convert.ToInt32(((DropDownList)tr.Cells[1].Controls[0]).SelectedValue);

  //Try to find the owner group
  int entWFOwnerGroupId =
    Convert.ToInt32(tr.Cells[0].Attributes["ENTWFOwnerGroupId"]);

  ENTWFItemOwnerEO itemOwner =
    baseWorkflowEO.WFOwners.GetByENTWFOwnerGroupId(entWFOwnerGroupId);

  if (itemOwner == null)
```

```
      {
        //This must be added to the object
        baseWorkflowEO.WFOwners.Add(new ENTWFItemOwnerEO
        {
          ENTUserAccountId = entUserAccountId,
          ENTWFItemId = baseWorkflowEO.ID,
          ENTWFOwnerGroupId = entWFOwnerGroupId
        });
      }
      else
      {
        //Set the id of the selected user
        itemOwner.ENTUserAccountId = entUserAccountId;
      }
    }
```

If the user is transitioning the item, then you need to get the state they are transitioning to and add to the state history. If the user isn't transitioning the item but changing the current owner, then a record should be added to the state history with the new owner:

```
//Check if the user is transitioning this item
baseWorkflowEO.ENTWFTransitionId = Convert.ToInt32(ddlTransitions.SelectedValue);
if (baseWorkflowEO.ENTWFTransitionId != 0)
{
  //Change the current state.
  ENTWFTransitionEO transition = new ENTWFTransitionEO();
  transition.Load(baseWorkflowEO.ENTWFTransitionId);

  baseWorkflowEO.WFItem.CurrentWFStateId = transition.ToENTWFStateId;

  //Add to state history
  baseWorkflowEO.WFStateHistory.Add(new ENTWFItemStateHistoryEO
  {
      ENTWFStateId = baseWorkflowEO.WFItem.CurrentWFStateId,
      ENTUserAccountId = baseWorkflowEO.CurrentOwnerENTUserAccountId
  });
}
else
{
  //Check if the user change the owner by chaning, this should be shown in the
  //state history also.
  if (baseWorkflowEO.CurrentOwnerENTUserAccountId !=
    ((ENTBaseWorkflowEO)baseWorkflowEO.OriginalItem).CurrentOwnerENTUserAccountId)
  {
    //Add to state history
    baseWorkflowEO.WFStateHistory.Add(new ENTWFItemStateHistoryEO
    {
      ENTWFStateId = baseWorkflowEO.WFItem.CurrentWFStateId,
      ENTUserAccountId = baseWorkflowEO.CurrentOwnerENTUserAccountId
    });
  }
}
```

This control is the real workhorse for the workflow's functionality, and because it is in a server control you can easily add it to multiple pages in this project or other projects.

Now add the control to the HTML in the PTORequest.aspx page:

```
<cc1:WorkflowController runat="server" ID="wfcPTORequest">
  </cc1:WorkflowController>
```

Open the code-behind page for the PTORequest.aspx page and change the class so it inherits from the BaseEditPage and pass in the PTORequestEO object as the generic parameter. Implement all the abstract methods as you have done before.

Now some extra functionality in this page needs some explaining. The calendar control needs to know which days are holidays or weekends, and which days have already been requested off, so users can't enter a duplicate request. In addition, if a request is for a half day, a user needs to be able to click on the day to request the second half of the day off. Therefore, you need to handle this in the calendar's DayRender event, but you don't want to have to grab all the holidays and prior days off each time this event fires, so create two member variables that will be loaded in the Page_Load event and then used in the subsequent events:

```
private HolidayEOList _holidays = new HolidayEOList();
private PTORequestEOList _priorDaysOff = new PTORequestEOList();

protected void Page_Load(object sender, EventArgs e)
{
  Master.SaveButton_Click += new
    PaidTimeOffEditPage.ButtonClickedHandler(Master_SaveButton_Click);
  Master.CancelButton_Click += new
    PaidTimeOffEditPage.ButtonClickedHandler(Master_CancelButton_Click);

  _holidays.Load();

  //Load the list of days this user has already requested. This is used in the
  //calendar's day render event to disable those days.
  int entUserAccountId;
  int ptoRequestId;

  PTORequestEO ptoRequest = (PTORequestEO)ViewState[VIEW_STATE_KEY_PTOREQUEST];

  if (ptoRequest == null)
  {
    //Check if the id was passed from the query string
    ptoRequestId = GetId();

    if (ptoRequestId == 0)
    {
      //This will be 0 if a new record is being added the first time in this page
      entUserAccountId = CurrentUser.ID;
    }
    else
    {
      ptoRequest = new PTORequestEO();
      ptoRequest.Load(ptoRequestId);
```

```
          entUserAccountId = ptoRequest.ENTUserAccountId;
      }
   }
   else
   {
      entUserAccountId = ptoRequest.ENTUserAccountId;
      ptoRequestId = ptoRequest.ID;
   }

   _priorDaysOff.LoadPreviousByENTUserAccountId(ptoRequestId, entUserAccountId);
}
```

The DayRender event uses these cached objects to determine each day's cell:

```
protected void calFullDay_DayRender(object sender, DayRenderEventArgs e)
{
   if (calFullDay.SelectedDate == e.Day.Date)
   {
      SetPTORequestCellText(e, e.Day.Date,
        (PTORequestTypeBO.PTORequestTypeEnum)Convert.ToInt32(
        ddlPTORequestType.SelectedValue),
        (PTODayTypeBO.PTODayTypeEnum)Convert.ToInt32(ddlPTODayType.SelectedValue),
        Color.LightGreen);

      //check if there is another request for this day. This could happen if the
      //user requested two half days on the same day.
      List<PTORequestEO> ptoRequests = _priorDaysOff.GetByRequestDate(e.Day.Date);
      if (ptoRequests.Count != 0)
      {
         foreach (PTORequestEO ptoRequest in ptoRequests)
         {
            SetPTORequestCellText(e, e.Day.Date, ptoRequest.PTORequestTypeId,
              ptoRequest.PTODayTypeId, Color.LightGreen);
         }
      }
   }
   else
   {
      if (e.Day.Date.IsWeekend())
      {
         e.Day.IsSelectable = false;
      }
      else
      {
         HolidayEO holiday = _holidays.GetHoliday(e.Day.Date);
         if (holiday != null)
         {
            SetHolidayCell(e, holiday);
         }
         else
         {
          List<PTORequestEO> ptoRequests = _priorDaysOff.GetByRequestDate(e.Day.Date);

          if (ptoRequests.Count != 0)
```

```
          {
            foreach (PTORequestEO ptoRequest in ptoRequests)
            {
              SetPriorPTOCell(e, ptoRequest);
            }

            if (ptoRequests.Count > 1)
            {
              e.Day.IsSelectable = false;
            }
          }
        }
      }
    }
  }
}
```

This method calls a couple of helper methods to set the cell's properties. `SetPTORequestCellText` will add a letter indicating the type of day off requested: vacation, personal, or unpaid. If it is a half day, it will append a.m. or p.m. to the text:

```csharp
private void SetPTORequestCellText(DayRenderEventArgs e, DateTime requestDate,
    PTORequestTypeBO.PTORequestTypeEnum requestType,
    PTODayTypeBO.PTODayTypeEnum dayType, Color color)
{
  string text;

  switch (requestType)
  {
    case PTORequestTypeBO.PTORequestTypeEnum.Vacation:
      text = "V";
      break;
    case PTORequestTypeBO.PTORequestTypeEnum.Personal:
      text = "P";
      break;
    case PTORequestTypeBO.PTORequestTypeEnum.Unpaid:
      text = "U";
      break;
    default:
      throw new Exception("Unknown request type.");
  }

  switch (dayType)
  {
    case PTODayTypeBO.PTODayTypeEnum.AM:
      text += "-AM";
      e.Day.IsSelectable = true;
      break;
    case PTODayTypeBO.PTODayTypeEnum.PM:
      text += "-PM";
      e.Day.IsSelectable = true;
      break;
    case PTODayTypeBO.PTODayTypeEnum.Full:
```

```
      e.Day.IsSelectable = false;
      break;
   default:
      throw new Exception("Unknown day type.");
}

Label lbl = new Label();
lbl.Text = text;
lbl.Font.Size = 6;

e.Cell.Controls.Add(new LiteralControl("<br />"));
e.Cell.Controls.Add(lbl);

e.Cell.BackColor = color;
}
```

The `SetHolidayCell` adds an "H" to the cell's text to signify that this is a holiday, and sets its tooltip to the name of the holiday:

```
private void SetHolidayCell(DayRenderEventArgs e, HolidayEO holiday)
{
   e.Day.IsSelectable = false;
   e.Cell.Controls.Add(new LiteralControl("<br />"));

   Label lbl = new Label();
   lbl.Text = "H";
   lbl.Font.Size = 6;
   e.Cell.Controls.Add(lbl);

   e.Cell.ToolTip = holiday.HolidayName;
   e.Cell.BackColor = Color.LightSkyBlue;
}
```

The `SetPriorPTOCell` method calls the `SetPTORequestCell` method and passes in a different background color:

```
private void SetPriorPTOCell(DayRenderEventArgs e, PTORequestEO ptoRequest)
{
   SetPTORequestCellText(e, ptoRequest.RequestDate,
      ptoRequest.PTORequestTypeId, ptoRequest.PTODayTypeId, Color.LightSkyBlue);
}
```

You need to take a few extra steps because this page has the workflow control on it. First, override the `OnInit` method of the page and set the workflow control's `WorkflowObjectName` property:

```
protected override void OnInit(EventArgs e)
{
   base.OnInit(e);

   wfcPTORequest.WorkflowObjectName = typeof(PTORequestEO).AssemblyQualifiedName;
}
```

Next, change the `LoadObjectFromScreen` method to call the control's `LoadObjectFromControl` method.

```
protected override void LoadObjectFromScreen(PTORequestEO baseEO)
{
    baseEO.PTORequestTypeId = (PTORequestTypeBO.PTORequestTypeEnum)Convert.ToInt32(
        ddlPTORequestType.SelectedValue);
    baseEO.PTODayTypeId = (PTODayTypeBO.PTODayTypeEnum)Convert.ToInt32(
        ddlPTODayType.SelectedValue);
    baseEO.RequestDate = calFullDay.SelectedDate;

    wfcPTORequest.LoadObjectFromControl(baseEO);
}
```

The `LoadScreenFromObject` method must also be changed to load the control:

```
protected override void LoadScreenFromObject(PTORequestEO baseEO)
{
    ddlPTORequestType.Items.FindByValue(Convert.ToInt32(
        baseEO.PTORequestTypeId).ToString()).Selected = true;

    ddlPTODayType.Items.FindByValue(Convert.ToInt32(
        baseEO.PTODayTypeId).ToString()).Selected = true;

    calFullDay.SelectedDate = baseEO.RequestDate;

    lblRequestDate.Text = calFullDay.SelectedDate.ToStandardDateFormat();
    calFullDay.VisibleDate = calFullDay.SelectedDate;

    wfcPTORequest.LoadControlFromObject(baseEO, CurrentUser.ID);

    SetBalances(Convert.ToInt16(baseEO.RequestDate.Year), baseEO.ENTUserAccountId,
        baseEO.ID);

    ViewState[VIEW_STATE_KEY_PTOREQUEST] = baseEO;
}
```

This method also calls another custom method to load the vacation bank at the top of the screen. You can view the sample code available on the Wrox website for this, but all it does is set the labels at the top of the screen.

The `LoadNew` method that exists in the `BaseEditPage` must also be overridden so that it calls the workflow's `InitWorkflow` method. By default, the `LoadNew` method calls only the `BaseEO` object's `Init` method, but the workflow's `InitWorkflow` method requires some parameters that aren't passed to the `Init` method:

```
protected override void LoadNew()
{
    PTORequestEO ptoRequest = new PTORequestEO();
    CreateNew(ref ptoRequest);
    LoadScreenFromObject(ptoRequest);
}
```

```
private void CreateNew(ref PTORequestEO ptoRequest)
{
  //PTO specific
  ptoRequest = new PTORequestEO();
  ptoRequest.Init();
  ptoRequest.RequestDate = GetBusinessDay(DateTime.Today);
  ptoRequest.ENTUserAccountId = CurrentUser.ID;

  //Workflow specific
  ptoRequest.WFItem.SubmitterENTUserAccountId = CurrentUser.ID;
  ptoRequest.InitWorkflow(typeof(PTORequestEO).AssemblyQualifiedName);
}
```

The last change that is required is in the SaveButton event handler. In order for the workflow to compare original values and new values when a property is marked as read-only, the original PTORequest object must be loaded and passed to the workflow:

```
void Master_SaveButton_Click(object sender, EventArgs e)
{
  ENTValidationErrors validationErrors = new ENTValidationErrors();
  PTORequestEO ptoRequest = (PTORequestEO)ViewState[VIEW_STATE_KEY_
PTOREQUEST];

  //Get the original state of the object.
  PTORequestEO originalPTORequest = new PTORequestEO();
  originalPTORequest.Load(ptoRequest.ID);
  ptoRequest.OriginalItem = (ENTBaseEO)originalPTORequest;

  LoadObjectFromScreen(ptoRequest);

  if (!ptoRequest.Save(ref validationErrors, CurrentUser.ID))
  {
    //Reload the object. If any validation errors occurred after a property
was
    //changed then the object would retain that changed property. You want to
    //revert back to what it was originally.
    if ((ptoRequest == null) || (ptoRequest.ID == 0))
    {
      CreateNew(ref ptoRequest);
    }
    else
    {
      ptoRequest = originalPTORequest;;
    }

    ViewState[VIEW_STATE_KEY_PTOREQUEST] = ptoRequest;
    Master.ValidationErrors = validationErrors;
  }
  else
  {
    GoToGridPage();
  }
}
```

View My Requests

Now that users can submit requests, they need to be able to view their requests and check their status. Add a new menu item called View My Requests, which will point to a new page called PTORequests. aspx (see Figure 7-22).

Figure 7-22

Add the following records to the ENTMenuItem and ENTCapability tables.

MenuItem Name	Url	ParentENT MenuItemId	Display Sequence	IsAlways Enabled
View My Requests	PTORequests.aspx	Home (ID)	2	False

CapabilityName	ENTMenuItemId	AccessType
View My Requests	View My Requests Menu Item ID	2

Add a new page called PTORequests.aspx to the root directory of the project and use the PaidTimeOff EditGrid master page to change the class so it inherits from BasePage. This page has some nonstandard features. First, notice in Figure 7-22 that the button doesn't say "Add New." The text of the button in the master page is changed in the Page_Load event to make it more meaningful for this page. Second, the PTORequestEOList object's method to load a request for the current user takes a parameter, so you must add the parameter to the custom GridView's method parameters array list by calling the LoadMethodParameters method:

```
protected void Page_Load(object sender, EventArgs e)
{
   Master.AddButton_Click += new
      PaidTimeOffEditGrid.ButtonClickedHandler(Master_AddButton_Click);

   if (!IsPostBack)
   {
      Button addButton = Master.btnAddNewRef();
      addButton.Text = "Make Another Request";
```

```
            //Tell the control what class to create and what method to call to load the
            //class.
            cgvPTORequests.ListClassName = typeof(PTORequestEOList).AssemblyQualifiedName;
            cgvPTORequests.LoadMethodName = "LoadByENTUserAccountId";
            cgvPTORequests.LoadMethodParameters.Add(CurrentUser.ID);

            //Action column-Contains the Edit link
            cgvPTORequests.AddBoundField("", "Actions", "");

            cgvPTORequests.AddBoundField("RequestDateString", "Request Date",
              "RequestDate");
            cgvPTORequests.AddBoundField("RequestTypeString", "Type", "RequestTypeString");
            cgvPTORequests.AddBoundField("", "Status", "");
            cgvPTORequests.AddBoundField("", "Current Owner", "");
            cgvPTORequests.AddBoundField("", "Date Submitted", "");

            //Default the sort to the request date
            cgvPTORequests.SortExpressionLast = "RequestDate";

            cgvPTORequests.DataBind();
        }
    }
```

Another difference with this page is that the current state name and current owner properties are not on the PTORequestEO object. The RowDataBound event must be customized to look to the workflow properties to set these columns correctly. Also, the date submitted must be formatted using the ToStandardDateFormat method:

```
    protected void cgvPTORequests_RowDataBound(object sender, GridViewRowEventArgs e)
    {
      if (e.Row.RowType == DataControlRowType.DataRow)
      {
        //Add the edit link to the action column.
        HyperLink editLink = new HyperLink();
        if (ReadOnly)
        {
          editLink.Text = "View";
        }
        else
        {
          editLink.Text = "Edit";
        }
        editLink.NavigateUrl = "PTORequest.aspx" + EncryptQueryString("id=" +
          ((PTORequestEO)e.Row.DataItem).ID.ToString());

        e.Row.Cells[COL_INDEX_ACTION].Controls.Add(editLink);

        //Get the state and show that as the status
        e.Row.Cells[COL_INDEX_STATUS].Text =
          ((PTORequestEO)e.Row.DataItem).CurrentState.StateName;

        e.Row.Cells[COL_INDEX_CURRENT_OWNER].Text =
          ((PTORequestEO)e.Row.DataItem).CurrentOwnerUserName;
```

```
        e.Row.Cells[COL_INDEX_DATE_SUBMITTED].Text =
          ((PTORequestEO)e.Row.DataItem).InsertDate.ToStandardDateFormat();
    }
}
```

Approve/Deny Requests

The last page to create is the page that approvers will use to list all the requests in their queue waiting to be approved. This page is very similar to the View My Requests page except that the Add New button should be hidden and the page should only list requests for which the current user is the owner (see Figure 7-23).

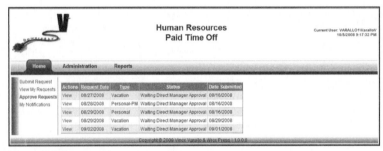

Figure 7-23

Add the following records to the ENTMenuItem and ENTCapability tables.

MenuItem Name	Url	ParentENT MenuItemId	Display Sequence	IsAlways Enabled
Approve Requests	PTORequestApprove.aspx	Home (ID)	3	False

CapabilityName	ENTMenuItemId	AccessType
Approve Requests	Approve Requests Menu Item ID	0

Add a new page called PTORequestApprove.aspx and set the master page to the PaidTimeOffEditGrid master page. Most of the code is the same as the PTORequests.aspx page so I won't review it all. The method to load only requests for which the current owner is the current user is called LoadByCurrent OwnerId, so change the page load to reflect this:

```
cgvPTORequests.LoadMethodName = "LoadByCurrentOwnerId";
cgvPTORequests.LoadMethodParameters.Add(CurrentUser.ID);
```

If users click the View link, they will be redirected to the PTORequest.aspx page. Here they can select an action from the Transitions drop-down list and move the request along in the process.

However, by default, they are sent back to the View My Requests page. Instead, they should be sent back to this page. To fix this, add another parameter to the query string in the `RowDataBound` event when it adds the Edit link:

```
editLink.NavigateUrl = "PTORequest.aspx" + EncryptQueryString("id=" +
    ((PTORequestEO)e.Row.DataItem).ID.ToString() + "&Approving=true");
```

Now the `PTORequest.aspx` page must be changed to honor this setting. Open the `PTORequest`'s code-behind page and make the following changes to the `GoToGridPage` method:

```
protected override void GoToGridPage()
{
  bool approving = false;
  NameValueCollection queryString =
    DecryptQueryString(Request.QueryString.ToString());

  if (queryString != null)
  {
    //Check if the user came from the approval screen.
    string approvingQueryString = queryString["Approving"];

    if (approvingQueryString != null)
    {
      approving = true;
    }
  }

  if (approving)
  {
    Response.Redirect("PTORequestApprove.aspx");
  }
  else
  {
    Response.Redirect("PTORequests.aspx");
  }
}
```

Summary

If you made it through this chapter and understand every concept, then congratulations — you are way ahead of the game! However, most readers might need to review the chapter a few times or take a thorough look at the sample application to really understand what is going on. Even if you don't use the workflow features described in this chapter, some concepts are generic enough to use in your application. This chapter created extension methods, which are new to .NET 3.5; created a pattern to dynamically create read-only and required properties at runtime; used lambda expressions to search through lists; and created some complex queries in the stored procedures. It is hoped that these little nuggets were enough to make the chapter worth reading; and if you get the entire concept behind the workflow, then even better.

The key points to remember when creating a workflow are as follows:

❑ You need a good understanding of the business process from the client. As shown in this simple example, the number of states and transitions can explode. A clear understanding of the client's requirements for their business process will always be the hardest step in the process. It usually helps to create a workflow diagram and walk through the entire process with the client.

❑ All workflows must have groups of users who can own an issue. This needs to be defined in the requirements.

❑ All workflows must have states that have an owner group associated with them, and you can optionally assign a default owner. The default owner can be either a user in the owner list or the submitter.

❑ Workflows use transitions to move items from state to state. The transitions are represented by arrows in a standard workflow diagram.

❑ Transitions enable you to execute code dynamically after the transition is complete.

❑ Workflows are associated with a business object that must inherit from the `ENTBaseWorkflowEO` object.

❑ The business object must call the `LoadWorkflow` method in the `MapEntityToCustom Properties` method.

❑ The business object must call the `SaveWorkflow` method in the `Save` method.

❑ The page that manages the business object must use the `WorkflowController` custom server control to enable users to move the request through the workflow.

❑ The page's `OnInit` method must be overridden to set the `WorkflowController`'s `WorkflowObjectName` property to the name of the business object.

❑ The `Save` button's click event must create a copy of the original request to enable the workflow to check for read-only fields.

❑ The page's `LoadNew` method must be overridden to call the workflow's `InitWorkflow` method.

❑ The page's `LoadObjectFromScreen` method must call the `WorkflowController`'s `LoadObjectFromControl` method.

❑ The page's `LoadScreenFromObject` method must call the `WorkflowController`'s `LoadControlFromObject` method.

While you were reading this chapter I went back and showed Mary the application and she was quite happy with how it has turned out so far. Her first question was "How do I know I have something waiting for me to approve?" Well, right now she has to open the application and look at the list in the Approve Requests screen. Her next statement was "I need the system to notify me when something is in my queue or when somebody cancels a request." That brings us to the next chapter, which designs the notification pattern for this application. It will enable Mary to set up her own notification system and send e-mails to anybody who registers for a notification.

8

Notifications

Another key piece of functionality that enterprise applications usually require is the capability to send notifications when specific events occur in the system. The notification is usually an e-mail message that is sent to a user. Some applications define notifications as *alerts,* which is essentially the same thing. The system is proactively communicating with users to let them know that certain events occurred or certain actions need to be followed up on. For applications that have workflow, notifications are key pieces of functionality that people tend to rely on to let them know they are supposed to do something. It is helpful if the e-mail message has a link back to the application and the specific screen that enables the user to take action. Once users get used to receiving these e-mails they become dependent on them, which is a great selling feature for your application. Mary didn't consider this functionality in our first conversation, but from experience I knew she would eventually ask for it so I brought it up. Luckily, the framework being built in this book has this capability, so it is easy to add this functionality without extending the deadline of the project too much.

Problem

For the Paid Time Off application, users should be notified whenever they become the "owner" of an issue, whenever a request they submitted changes state, or when a request goes to a specific state such as cancelled or denied. The last thing you want to do is give users an excuse about why they didn't follow up on a request. You can help Mary stay on top of the game by having the system nudge each user by sending them an e-mail letting them know they are supposed to do something.

This chapter creates a pattern for sending e-mails, registering for notifications, and even allowing users to customize the message that is sent for a specific notification. This chapter also uses a Windows service to work in the background to poll for unsent e-mails and fire them off behind the scenes without coupling this functionality with the actual website. Windows services can be quite handy in conjunction with a web application because not all situations should be handled using the web interface. There are plenty of situations in which a background process can be utilized to automate certain tasks such as sending e-mails.

The main goals of this chapter are as follows:

❑ Understand how to create a Windows service and use a `Timer` object to automate tasks.

❑ Define a pattern for sending e-mails that is not coupled with the design of the website.

❑ Create functionality that enables users to register for predefined notifications in the system.

❑ Enable users to customize the text of the e-mails that are sent by the notifications and dynamically change the content based on the paid time off request.

Design

It is relatively easy to create an e-mail message and send it to a recipient using the .NET Framework. The following few lines of code will accomplish that:

```
//Add the following using directive to the beginning of the file
//using System.Net.Mail;

SmtpClient client = new SmtpClient("127.00.00.1");

MailMessage mail = new MailMessage(new MailAddress("from@PoweredByV2.com"),
                                   new MailAddress("to@hotmail.com"));
mail.Subject = "test";
mail.Body = "test";
client.Send(mail);
```

SmtpClient Class

The `SmtpClient` class represents the object that handles sending a message. When you create the `SmtpClient` object, you set the SMTP server's address so the system knows where to relay the message. You can also pass in a port number to the constructor if needed or set the `Port` property after the object is created. The following table provides a short description of all the properties for the `SmtpClient` class.

Property	Description
ClientCertificates	Specifies which certificates should be used to establish the Secure Sockets Layer (SSL) connection
Credentials	Gets or sets the credentials used to authenticate the sender
DeliveryMethod	Specifies how outgoing e-mail messages will be handled
EnableSsl	Specifies whether the SmtpClient uses Secure Sockets Layer (SSL) to encrypt the connection
Host	Gets or sets the name or IP address of the host used for SMTP transactions
PickupDirectoryLocation	Gets or sets the folder where applications save e-mail messages to be processed by the local SMTP server

Property	Description
Port	Gets or sets the port used for SMTP transactions
ServicePoint	Gets the network connection used to transmit the e-mail message
Timeout	Gets or sets a value that specifies the amount of time after which a synchronous Send call times out
UseDefaultCredentials	Gets or sets a Boolean value that controls whether the DefaultCredentials are sent with requests

You can leave most of these properties untouched when using the SmtpClient class except for Host. The SmtpClient class also has numerous methods, but the most important are listed here.

Method	Description
Send	Overloaded. Sends an e-mail message to an SMTP server for delivery. These methods block while the message is being transmitted.
SendAsync	Overloaded. Sends an e-mail message. These methods do not block the calling thread.
SendAsyncCancel	Cancels an asynchronous operation to send an e-mail message.

The Send method connects to the server and sends the e-mail message. Processing is not returned back to the calling procedure until the method is complete. The SendAsync method sends the message to the server asynchronously. You can capture when the command is complete by catching the SendCompleted event from the SmtpClient object.

The complete list of methods can be found at http://msdn.microsoft.com/en-us/library/system .net.mail.smtpclient_members.aspx.

The next class to examine is the MailMessage class. This class is used to represent the message that you want to send. The complete list of methods and properties for this class can be found at http://msdn .microsoft.com/en-us/library/system.net.mail.mailmessage_members.aspx. The following table describes its properties.

Property	Description
AlternateViews	Gets the attachment collection used to store alternative forms of the message body
Attachments	Gets the attachment collection used to store data attached to this e-mail message
Bcc	Gets the address collection that contains the blind carbon copy (BCC) recipients for this e-mail message
Body	Gets or sets the message body

Property	Description
BodyEncoding	Gets or sets the encoding used to encode the message body
CC	Gets the address collection that contains the carbon copy (CC) recipients for this e-mail message
DeliveryNotificationOptions	Gets or sets the delivery notifications for this e-mail message
From	Gets or sets the From address for this e-mail message
Headers	Gets the e-mail headers that are transmitted with this e-mail message
IsBodyHtml	Gets or sets a value indicating whether the e-mail message body is in HTML
Priority	Gets or sets the priority of this e-mail message
ReplyTo	Gets or sets the ReplyTo address for the message
Sender	Gets or sets the sender's address for the e-mail message
Subject	Gets or sets the subject line for the e-mail message
SubjectEncoding	Gets or sets the encoding used for the subject content for the e-mail message
To	Gets the address collection that contains the recipients of the e-mail message

These properties are fairly straightforward. The important thing to note here is that the `Bcc`, `CC`, `From`, and `To` properties are collections of `MailAddress` objects. If you want to add an address to any of these properties, then you call the `Add` method of the collection.

You can find the complete list of methods and properties for the `MailAddress` class at `http://msdn .microsoft.com/en-us/library/system.net.mail.mailaddress_members.aspx`. Here is a list of its properties.

Property	Description
Address	Gets the e-mail address specified when this instance was created
DisplayName	Gets the display name composed from the display name and address information specified when this instance was created
Host	Gets the host portion of the address specified when this instance was created
User	Gets the user information from the address specified when this instance was created

The preceding sample code calls the `MailMessage` overloaded constructor, which takes two `MailAddress` objects for the `From` and `To` addresses. It then sets the `subject` and `body` properties and sends the message by calling the `Send` method. No big shakes going on here. As long as you have a valid SMTP server, the code will work.

There is also a special section that you can add to your application's configuration file to set the properties of the `SmtpClient` object dynamically. The section must be nested in the `configuration` section in the application's configuration file. For an ASP.NET application, the configuration file is the `web.config` file. For a Windows Forms or Windows server application, the `app.config` file is the configuration file:

```
<system.net>
    <mailSettings>
        <smtp deliveryMethod="Network">
            <network host="yourserverip"
            userName="username"
            password="pwd"
            port="80" />
        </smtp>
    </mailSettings>
</system.net>
```

This enables you to change the server without having to recompile the application. You simply need to set the `host` attribute to your SMTP server. The other settings depend on how your server is set up. If you added this to your configuration file, ran the sample code, and put a breakpoint after the `SmtpClient` object was created, you would notice that all of the properties are set according to the configuration file. This is quite convenient, as e-mail servers or passwords can change at any time.

Designing the Database Tables

You could add this code everywhere that you want to send an e-mail in your application, but the problem you could run into is that the application may crash if the notification fails. For example, if a user enters a request and the e-mail server is down for some reason, you don't want the system to fail and never send the e-mail. The system should enable the user to create the request and be able to send the e-mail once the server is back up. You essentially need to decouple the notification functionality from the actual functionality. The design for this section will create a table to hold all of the notifications that are to be sent and then create a separate Windows service that runs in the background to process the requests. That way, if the server is down, the requests will pile up in the table. Once the server is back up, the Windows service will send all the e-mails that are waiting in the queue. The application that is handling the data entry piece simply needs to add records to the e-mail queue, which reduces the risk of a failure. Sure, the application could fail if there were a bug while adding to the e-mail table, but that is less likely to occur than a server being down.

The other feature that users usually need when sending e-mails is a template for the subject and body sections of the e-mail that contains tokens that can be replaced by real values at runtime. For example, if an e-mail needs to include the ID of the request, it must be generated dynamically when the e-mail message is created. This can be done by using the `StringBuilder` class and the `Replace` method. It is also helpful to add a link in the body of the e-mail that will take the user to the page containing the request. Because the message will contain a hyperlink, the message must be sent in HTML format.

This section will also build the tables, classes, and screens needed to create the e-mail templates and the code to handle the token-based replacement of content. The first step is to create the table that will be used to handle the queue of e-mails. Add a table to the `HRPaidTimeOff` database called `ENTEmail`. Again, because this functionality is not specific to any one application, the table name starts with `ENT` because it is part of the Enterprise Framework being built in this book (see Figure 8-1).

ENTEmail			
Column Name	Data Type		Allow Nulls
🔑 ENTEmailId	int		☐
ToEmailAddress	varchar(MAX)		☐
CCEmailAddress	varchar(MAX)		☑
BCCEmailAddress	varchar(MAX)		☑
FromEmailAddress	varchar(255)		☐
Subject	varchar(MAX)		☐
Body	varchar(MAX)		☐
EmailStatusFlag	tinyint		☐
InsertDate	datetime		☐
InsertENTUserAccountId	int		☐
UpdateDate	datetime		☐
UpdateENTUserAccou...	int		☐
Version	timestamp		☐
			☐

Figure 8-1

The `To`, `CC`, and `BCC` e-mail address fields are varchar max fields and expect a semicolon delimited string of addresses. The `FromEmailAddress` field can only be one address so it is limited to 255 characters. The `Subject` and `Body` fields contain the subject of the text and the message of the e-mail, respectively. Any token replacements should be handled before getting into this table. The `EmailStatusFlag` field is either a zero or a one. Zero means not sent and one means sent.

Add the standard five stored procedures that insert, update, delete, and select all records, and select a record by ID. There is only one custom select stored procedure that selects all the records that have not been sent. You can view the `Chapter8NotificationStoredProcedures.sql` file to see the code for these procedures. Next, add the table to the `DataContext` using the ORM Designer. Add the stored procedures to the Methods pane, create the partial class in the `CustomizedEntities` file, and create the `ENTEmailData` class. This takes care of all of the data access needed for this table.

Now create the `ENTEmailEO` and `ENTEmailEOList` classes as you have done before. An enumeration should be added to the `ENTEmailEO` class for the `EmailStatusFlag` field:

```
public enum EmailStatusFlagEnum
{
    NotSent = 0,
    Sent = 1
}
```

Also add a custom method to the `ENTEmailEOList` class that loads the current instance with all of the unsent e-mail. The method name should be called `LoadUnsent`. The complete classes can be copied from the sample project available on the Wrox website.

The next step is to create the Windows Service project:

1. Open the `PaidTimeOffSolution` file in Visual Studio. Right-click on the solution and choose Add New Project.

2. Choose the Window Service project type and name the project **V2.EmailService**. Make sure the location is pointing to the solution folder.

3. Click the Add button. This will create a new Windows Service project with a class called `Service1`, and the designer for the `Service1` class will be displayed in Visual Studio.

4. Click the link that says "Click here to switch to code view." This will display the class that was created for you:

```
public partial class Service1 : ServiceBase
{
    public Service1()
    {
        InitializeComponent();
    }

    protected override void OnStart(string[] args)
    {
    }

    protected override void OnStop()
    {
    }
}
```

The OnStart method is fired when the service is started, and the OnStop method is fired when the service is stopped. The e-mail service should run every so often and look for unsent records in the ENTEmail table and send them. To accomplish this polling mechanism, an instance of the Timer class will be used. This is a class that is defined in the System.Timers namespace. This class enables you to specify the polling interval and will fire an Elapsed event at your specified interval. Add a reference to the V2.PaidTimeOffBLL project and the System.Configuration namespace. Add the following using directives to the top of the Service1 class:

```
using System.Timers;
using System.Configuration;
using V2.PaidTimeOffBLL.Framework;
using System.Net.Mail;
```

Now add a member variable for the Timer object:

```
private Timer _emailTimer;
```

When the service starts, it should instantiate the Timer object and set its interval, which is stored in the application's configuration file so that it can be changed without recompiling. Right-click on the V2.EmailService project and select Add New Item. Select the Application Configuration File template and click the Add button. Replace the configuration section in the file with the following text:

```
<configuration>
  <appSettings >
    <add key="TimerInterval" value="60000"/>
  </appSettings>
</configuration>
```

The TimerInterval is in milliseconds so a value of 60000 will run every minute. Create a constant in the Service1 class that has the key for this setting:

```
private const string APP_CONFIG_TIMER_INTERVAL = "TimerInterval";
```

Next, add the following code to the `OnStart` method to read the setting and enable the timer:

```
//Instantiate a timer.
_emailTimer = new Timer();

//Check if the timer interval has been set.
string timerInterval = ConfigurationManager.AppSettings[APP_CONFIG_TIMER_INTERVAL];

if (timerInterval != "")
{
    _emailTimer.Interval = Convert.ToDouble(timerInterval);
}
else
{
    //Default to 60 seconds
    _emailTimer.Interval = 60000;
}

//Hook the Elapsed event to the event handler
_emailTimer.Elapsed += new ElapsedEventHandler(_emailTimer_Elapsed);

//Start the timer.
_emailTimer.Enabled = true;
```

The `ElapsedEventHandler` method must be created to handle the `Elapsed` event. This method will be called whenever the timer fires and it should handle sending any e-mails and switching their status to "Sent" in the table. The method is as follows:

```
void _emailTimer_Elapsed(object sender, ElapsedEventArgs e)
{
  try
  {
    //Check if there are any emails that need to be sent
    ENTEmailEOList emails = new ENTEmailEOList();
    emails.LoadUnsent();

    if (emails.Count != 0)
    {
      ENTValidationErrors validationErrors = new ENTValidationErrors();

      //if there are then send one at a time
      SmtpClient client = new SmtpClient();

      foreach (ENTEmailEO email in emails)
      {
        MailMessage message = new MailMessage();

        message.From = new MailAddress(email.FromEmailAddress);
        AddAddresses(email.ToEmailAddress, message.To);
        AddAddresses(email.CCEmailAddress, message.CC);
        AddAddresses(email.BCCEmailAddress, message.Bcc);

        message.Subject = email.Subject;
        message.Body = email.Body;
```

```
            message.IsBodyHtml = true;

            client.Send(message);

            //Update record after the email is sent
            email.EmailStatusFlag = ENTEmailEO.EmailStatusFlagEnum.Sent;
            if (!email.Save(ref validationErrors, _entUserAccountId))
            {
                foreach (ENTValidationError ve in validationErrors)
                {
                    EventLog ev = new EventLog();
                    ev.Source = "EmailService";
                    ev.WriteEntry(ve.ErrorMessage, EventLogEntryType.Error);
                }
            }
        }
    }
}
catch (Exception exception)
{
    EventLog ev = new EventLog();
    ev.Source = "EmailService";
    ev.WriteEntry(exception.Message, EventLogEntryType.Error);
}
}
```

This method calls a custom method called `AddAddress` that will take the semicolon delimited string in the `To`, `CC`, or `Bcc` address fields, split it up, and add each address to the `MailAddressCollection`:

```
private void AddAddresses(string emailAddresses, MailAddressCollection
    mailAddressCollection)
{
    if (emailAddresses != null)
    {
        string[] addresses = emailAddresses.Split(new char[] { ';' });

        foreach (string address in addresses)
        {
            mailAddressCollection.Add(address);
        }
    }
}
```

The `Elapsed` event handler also changes the status of an e-mail to Sent after the e-mail message is sent. In order to update the `ENTEmail` record, you need to pass in a valid `ENTUserAccountId` because the `Update` method updates the `UpdatedENTUserAccountId` field. This ID is also stored in the `App.config` file and loaded when the service starts. If the setting is missing from the `App.config` file, the service should log a message to the event log and stop.

Add the setting to the `App.config` file. The value should be set to a valid user ID in your database:

```
<add key="ENTUserAccountId" value="1"/>
```

Add a constant for the key to the Service1 class:

```
private const string APP_CONFIG_ENT_USER_ACCOUNT_ID = "ENTUserAccountId";
```

Now add a member variable in the Service1 class that can store this value:

```
private int _entUserAccountId;
```

Add the code to the OnStart event to read this value and fail if it does not exist. This should be added before the timer is instantiated:

```
//Get the user account id that should be used to update the record.
string entUserAccountId =
    ConfigurationManager.AppSettings[APP_CONFIG_ENT_USER_ACCOUNT_ID];

if ((entUserAccountId == "") || (int.TryParse(entUserAccountId, out
    _entUserAccountId) == false))
{
    //Log an event to the event log
    EventLog ev = new EventLog();
    ev.Source = "V2EmailService";
    ev.WriteEntry("The ENTUserAccountId must be configured in the application
                  configuration file before starting this service. This value should
                  be set to the valid ENTUserAccountId in the ENTUserAccount table
                  which will be used to update the email record after it has been
                  sent.", EventLogEntryType.Error);
    //Stop the service
    this.Stop();
}
```

The reason why this must be logged to the event log is because that is how a service communicates with the user. There is no interface for the service, so the event log is an easy place to store messages that you need to communicate back to the user.

The next step is to add code to the OnStop event to stop the timer:

```
protected override void OnStop()
{
    _emailTimer.Enabled = false;
}
```

The last step is to add the setting for the connection string and e-mail server to the App.config file. This should be after the appSetting section in the file:

```
<connectionStrings>
    <add name="HRPaidTimeOffConnString"
        connectionString="Data Source=VARALLO1;Initial Catalog=HRPaidTimeOff;User
                          ID=V2Application;Password=pwd"
        providerName=""/>
</connectionStrings>

<system.net>
    <mailSettings>
```

```
            <smtp deliveryMethod="Network">
                <network host="smtpserver"
                userName="admin@PoweredByV2.com"
                password="password"
                port="80" />
            </smtp>
        </mailSettings>
    </system.net>
```

Now that you have the class fully defined, you need to test it. If you set the V2.EmailService project as the startup project for the solution and run the project, you will get the message shown in Figure 8-2.

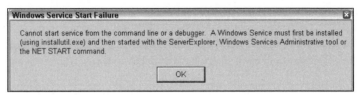

Figure 8-2

Unfortunately, you cannot run a Windows service using the run command in Visual Studio. You have to install the compiled .exe as a service in order to run it. This can make debugging quite challenging but there is a trick you can use to step through the code even though you are running the executable. First, install the service as requested using the following steps. The installutil.exe file, installed by the .NET Framework, is a command-line tool to install and uninstall services.

From the Start button, open the Visual Studio Command Prompt and navigate All Programs ➪ Microsoft Visual Studio 2008 ➪ Visual Studio Tools ➪ Visual Studio Command Prompt. Build the V2.EmailService project in Visual Studio and then change the directory in the command prompt to the folder where the .exe file was built. Enter the following command after the directory is changed: **Installutil.exe V2.EmailService.exe**. Click enter. A bunch of mumbo jumbo will appear in the command window. Essentially, it is telling you that the install failed. That's because you have to add an installer file to the Windows service project in order for it to be successfully installed. An installer file is a special file that tells the system which account to run the service as, what its name is, how it should start up, and so on.

To add an installer, right-click on the Service1.cs file and select View Designer. Right-click anywhere on the gray designer surface and select Add Installer. This creates a file called ProjectInstaller.cs and opens the designer for this file. Notice that two objects are already in the file design surface: the serviceInstaller1 and the serviceProcessInstaller1, as shown in Figure 8-3. Click the service Installer1 icon to view its properties. The Description property is what users will see in the Services window in the Administrative Tools on the computer where the service is installed.

Set the Description to "This service sends e-mails based on the ENTEmail table." The DisplayName property is the friendly name that users will see in the Services window. Set this to V2 Email Service. The other property to be aware of is the StartType. This should be set to Automatic, which tells Windows to automatically start this service when the computer starts. You can change this to Manual or Disable for a specific business need, but for our project leave this at Automatic.

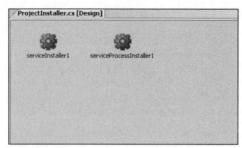

ProjectInstaller.cs [Design]

serviceInstaller1   serviceProcessInstaller1

Figure 8-3

Click the `serviceProcessInstaller1` icon to view its properties. The `Account` is the important property to set for this object. The options for Account are as follows:

Type	Description
LocalService	An account that acts as a nonprivileged user on the local computer, and presents anonymous credentials to any remote server.
NetworkService	An account that provides extensive local privileges, and presents the computer's credentials to any remote server.
LocalSystem	An account, used by the service control manager, that has extensive privileges on the local computer and acts as the computer on the network.
User	An account defined by a specific user on the network. Specifying User for the `ServiceProcessInstaller.Account` member causes the system to prompt for a valid user name and password when the service is installed, unless you set values for both the `Username` and `Password` properties of your `ServiceProcessInstaller` instance.

Services should run with the least privileges, so leave this at LocalService. Now you can rebuild the `V2.EmailService` project with the installer information. You may get an error indicating that the executable is locked. If you do, simply close Visual Studio and open it again. Once the executable is created, you can run the `installutil` command again. This time it should run successfully. If it does, you should see the `V2 Email Service` in the Services window (see Figure 8-4).

Right-click on the V2 Email Service in the Services window and start the process. You can now test that the service is running correctly by adding a record to the `ENTEmail` table. Be sure to set the To and From e-mail addresses, and the status should be zero. After you add the record, the e-mail should be sent within the next minute. If all goes well, then you have nothing to worry about; but usually it takes a few tries to get this right. The fact that you have to run compiled code to test the application and you can't step through the code to see what is actually going on is a challenge. However, there is a trick to stepping through the code. Right-click on the service in the Services window and stop the service. Go back into Visual Studio and add the following line to the `OnStart` event:

```
#if DEBUG
    Debugger.Launch();
#endif
```

This is a conditional compile statement. It specifies that if this has been compiled for debugging, then launch the debugger. This will cause the Visual Studio Just-In-Time Debugger window to be shown (see Figure 8-5).

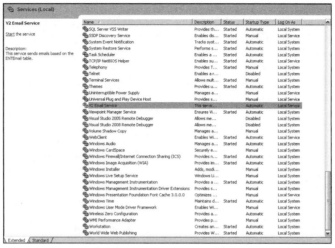

Figure 8-4

Figure 8-5

Recompile the V2 Email Service project and then start the service again. You should get the Visual Studio Just-In-Time Debugger window right away. Select "New instance of Visual Studio 2008" and click the Yes button. You'll now be able to step through the code in the OnStart event. Just remember when you release this to production that you recompile the Release version and deploy that executable so users do not get this message.

Solution

The e-mail Windows service takes care of sending e-mails and decouples the process of sending the e-mail from the application. The application should still work if an e-mail fails to send because the e-mail server is down. This section builds the notification functionality that is used for the workflow framework built in the previous chapter. This is done by adding records to the e-mail table when specific events happen during the approval process. For the Paid Time Off application, three types of notifications will be set up. First, the system should notify users when they become the owner of an issue. For example, when a request is submitted and sent to the direct manager, the direct manger should get an e-mail with a link to the item that was just submitted. The system should also notify users anytime an item they submitted changes state. That way, the original submitter will be notified after his or her manager, VP, or HR administrator approves the request.

The system should also allow users to specify that they want to be notified when a request goes to a specific state. For example, if I am the submitter's direct manager and have already approved their request and the submitter then cancels the request, I want to be notified. When a request is cancelled, it does not go back to the direct manager, so there needs to be some way for the direct manager to be notified.

Users should also be allowed to "subscribe" to any of the three notifications. That way, if users only want to be notified when they become the owner of an issue, they can turn the other two notifications off.

The last set of requirements for this section concern the text of the e-mail. The system needs to enable administrators to customize the message that should be sent for each e-mail. In addition, the system should enable users to set up dynamic text so that item ID, current owner, current state, and the submitted date can appear in the message. Finally, the system should enable users to add a link back to the item in the e-mail.

Defining Tables for Notification Services

Let's take care of defining the tables for the notifications first. Figure 8-6 shows a diagram of the three notification tables.

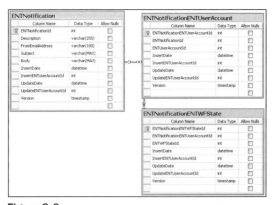

Figure 8-6

You can use the `Chapter8NotificationTables.sql` file to create these tables. This file will also create three default records in the `ENTNotification` table that represent the three notifications being created in this chapter. If you needed to customize the application and add more "types" of notifications, you would add them to this table. The `Description` field contains a user-friendly description of the notification that will be displayed to the user. The `FromEmailAddress` contains a valid e-mail address for the sender of the e-mail. This would typically be an administrator account, as all e-mails will be sent from here. If the user should reply to the e-mail, it goes to this account, so choose this wisely — you don't want to put your e-mail address in there. The `Subject` and `Body` fields contain the text of the subject and the body of the e-mail, respectively. Think of these fields as templated text containing tokens that the system will replace with dynamic data. The body text will be formatted as HTML, so you can also add HTML tags to create links, formatted data, images, or line breaks. The body text for the "I became the owner of an issue" notification looks like this:

```
Please review the following item.<br>
<br>
Item Id: <WFITEMID><br>
State: <WFSTATE><br>
Owner: <WFOWNER><br>
Submit Date: <WFSUBMITDATE><br>
<br>
<LINK>
```

The `<br>` will be displayed in the e-mail as HTML, so this forces a line break. The other text in brackets are tokens that will be replaced by dynamic data when the e-mail is created. In this example, there are five token fields. `<WFITEMID>` will be replaced with the request's ID. `<WFSTATE>` will be replaced with the current state of the request. `<WFOWNER>` will be replaced by the user name of the current owner. `<WFSUBMITDATE>` will be replaced with the date the request was submitted. `<LINK>` will be replaced by a link that says "Click here to view this item" and will provide a hyperlink to the page that contains the request.

The `ENTNotificationENTUserAccount` table contains the users who have registered to receive a specific notification. This is a junction table between the `ENTNotification` table and the `ENTUserAccount` table. The `ENTNotificationENTWFState` table is specific to the third notification mentioned earlier, which enables a user to subscribe to a notification when an item enters a specific state.

The five standard stored procedures are used for these tables, as well as a few custom select and delete procedures. The stored procedures are in the `Chapter8NotificationStoredProcedure.sql` file. There is nothing special about these procedures so they are not reviewed here, but you can look at them in the file. After you add the tables and the stored procedures to the `HRPaidTimeOff` database, you should use the ORM Designer to create the entity objects and `DataContext` methods for these tables and stored procedures. Then add the `ENTNotificationData`, `ENTNotificationENTUserAccountData`, `ENTNotificationENTWFStateData` classes to the DAL; and add the partial class for each class in the `CustomizedEntities` file.

Business Objects for E-mail Notifications

The next step is to create the business classes. Each table has a corresponding `EO` and `EOList`. The majority of this code follows the same pattern that has been defined before for loading, saving, and deleting the records. The `ENTNotificationEO` does have one special method called `ReplaceTokens` that handles replacing the tokens that exist in the `Subject` and `Body` fields. To accomplish this, a new class called `Token` should be added to the BLL project. This is a simple class that just contains the text for the token and the value that should replace the token:

```
public class Token
{
    public string TokenString { get; set; }
    public string Value { get; set; }
}
```

The code for the `ReplaceTokens` method takes a list of `Token` objects and loops through each one to find and replace the token in the supplied string:

```
public static string ReplaceTokens(List<Token> tokens, string template)
{
    StringBuilder sb = new StringBuilder(template);

    foreach (Token token in tokens)
    {
        sb.Replace(token.TokenString, token.Value);
    }

    return sb.ToString();
}
```

The `ENTNotificationENTUserAccountEO` class has a bit of custom code that is worth mentioning. First, a member variable must be added that represents the list of states that can be associated with the notification. For most notifications this will be null, but for the third notification this list will contain the list of states the user can choose to register for:

```
private ENTNotificationENTWFStateEOList _notificationStates;
```

Next, a custom property should be added to the class that enables the user to optionally load this object when calling the `Load` method:

```
public bool LoadStates { get; set; }
```

The `MapEntityToCustomProperties` method must then be customized to respect this property:

```
protected override void MapEntityToCustomProperties(IENTBaseEntity entity)
{
  ENTNotificationENTUserAccount eNTNotificationENTUserAccount =
    (ENTNotificationENTUserAccount)entity;

  ID = eNTNotificationENTUserAccount.ENTNotificationENTUserAccountId;
  ENTNotificationId = eNTNotificationENTUserAccount.ENTNotificationId;
  ENTUserAccountId = eNTNotificationENTUserAccount.ENTUserAccountId;

  if (LoadStates)
  {
    _notificationStates.Load(ID);
  }
}
```

By default, this should be set to true, so the constructor should be changed to set this value to true. It should also instantiate the _notificationStates object so the user doesn't get an "invalid use of null" exception:

```
public ENTNotificationENTUserAccountEO()
{
    LoadStates = true;
    _notificationStates = new ENTNotificationENTWFStateEOList();
}
```

The Save method also needs to be customized because when saving a notification, the child records must be saved in the same transaction. This will follow the same pattern defined earlier in the book whereby the child records are deleted and then re-added on each save:

```
public override bool Save(HRPaidTimeOffDataContext db, ref ENTValidationErrors
    validationErrors, int userAccountId)
{
  if (DBAction == DBActionEnum.Save)
  {
    //Validate the object
    Validate(db, ref validationErrors);

    //Check if there were any validation errors
    if (validationErrors.Count == 0)
    {
      if (IsNewRecord())
      {
        //Add
        ID = new ENTNotificationENTUserAccountData().Insert(db, ENTNotificationId,
                ENTUserAccountId, userAccountId);

        foreach (ENTNotificationENTWFStateEO notificationState in
                _notificationStates)
        {
          notificationState.ENTNotificationENTUserAccountId = ID;
        }
      }
      else
      {
        //Update
        if (!new ENTNotificationENTUserAccountData().Update(db, ID,
                ENTNotificationId, ENTUserAccountId, userAccountId, Version))
        {
          UpdateFailed(ref validationErrors);
          return false;
        }
      }

      //Delete all the states associated with this user
      _notificationStates.Delete(db, ID);

      //Add the states that were selected.
      return _notificationStates.Save(db, ref validationErrors, userAccountId);
    }
```

```
    else
    {
      //Didn't pass validation.
      return false;
    }
  }
  else
  {
    throw new Exception("DBAction not Save.");
  }
}
```

There are a few other methods that load lists and get objects from lists, and they can be found in the sample code. They use the same pattern already defined.

The next step is to create the screen that will enable an administrator to define the template with the "from" e-mail address, the subject, and the body for the three notifications. You must first add the ENTMenuItem and ENTCapability records to the database. The menu item should be located under the Administration tab and when the user clicks on it, the system should display the list of notifications that have been defined.

MenuItem Name	Url	ParentENT MenuItemId	Display Sequence	IsAlways Enabled
Notification Templates	Administration\ NotificationTemplates.aspx	Administration (ID)	3	False

CapabilityName	ENTMenuItemId	AccessType
Notification Templates	Notification Templates Menu Item ID	0

Notifications cannot be created by the user because you, as the developer, have to create the code to catch the notification, so there is no need for the Add button on this screen. In addition, the user should not be able to delete the notifications either. The screen should look like Figure 8-7.

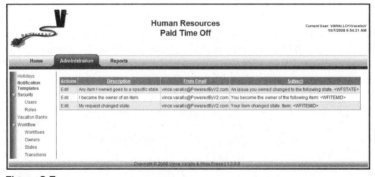

Figure 8-7

To accomplish this, add a new page to the `Administration` folder and call it `Notification Templates.aspx`. This page should use the `PaidTimeOffEditGrid` master page and implement the `BasePage` class. Add the custom `GridView` control to the page and the directive to identify the master page, as you've done before. The code-behind for this page is much simpler because there is no need for adding and deleting:

```
private const int COL_INDEX_ACTION = 0;
private const int COL_INDEX_WORKFLOW_NAME = 1;
private const int COL_INDEX_OBJECT_NAME = 2;

protected void Page_Load(object sender, EventArgs e)
{
  Master.btnAddNewRef().Visible = false;

  if (!IsPostBack)
  {
    //Tell the control what class to create and what method to call to load the
    //class.
    cgvNotificationTemplates.ListClassName =
        typeof(ENTNotificationEOList).AssemblyQualifiedName;
    cgvNotificationTemplates.LoadMethodName = "Load";

    //Action column-Contains the Edit link
    cgvNotificationTemplates.AddBoundField("", "Actions", "");

    //Name
    cgvNotificationTemplates.AddBoundField("Description", "Description",
                                  "Description");
    cgvNotificationTemplates.AddBoundField("FromEmailAddress", "From Email",
                                  "FromEmailAddress");
    cgvNotificationTemplates.AddBoundField("Subject", "Subject", "Subject");

    cgvNotificationTemplates.DataBind();
  }
}

protected void cgvNotificationTemplates_RowDataBound(object sender,
    GridViewRowEventArgs e)
{
  if (e.Row.RowType == DataControlRowType.DataRow)
  {
    //Add the edit link to the action column.
    HyperLink editLink = new HyperLink();
    if (ReadOnly)
    {
      editLink.Text = "View";
    }
    else
    {
      editLink.Text = "Edit";
    }
    editLink.NavigateUrl = "NotificationTemplate.aspx" + EncryptQueryString("id=" +
        ((ENTNotificationEO)e.Row.DataItem).ID.ToString());
```

```
        e.Row.Cells[COL_INDEX_ACTION].Controls.Add(editLink);
    }
}

public override string MenuItemName()
{
    return "Notification Templates";
}

public override string[] CapabilityNames()
{
    return new string[] { "Notification Templates" };
}
```

When users click the Edit link, it should take them to the page to update this record, as shown in Figure 8-8.

Figure 8-8

This screen displays the description of the notification and enables the user to change the other three fields. Because this is where the user can add the tokens to the text of the e-mail, the list of available tokens and their meaning are displayed on the right side of the screen.

Create this page by adding another page to the Administration folder called Notification Template.aspx and make it use the PaidTimeOffEditPage master page. This page should inherit from the BaseEditPage class. The HTML is straightforward so I won't list it here. The code-behind is also quite simple and follows the same pattern defined previously:

```
private const string VIEW_STATE_KEY_NOTIFICATION = "Notification";

protected void Page_Load(object sender, EventArgs e)
```

```
{
  Master.SaveButton_Click += new
    PaidTimeOffEditPage.ButtonClickedHandler(Master_SaveButton_Click);
  Master.CancelButton_Click += new
    PaidTimeOffEditPage.ButtonClickedHandler(Master_CancelButton_Click);
}

void Master_CancelButton_Click(object sender, EventArgs e)
{
  GoToGridPage();
}

void Master_SaveButton_Click(object sender, EventArgs e)
{
  ENTValidationErrors validationErrors = new ENTValidationErrors();
  ENTNotificationEO notification =
    (ENTNotificationEO)ViewState[VIEW_STATE_KEY_NOTIFICATION];

  LoadObjectFromScreen(notification);

  if (!notification.Save(ref validationErrors, 1))
  {
    Master.ValidationErrors = validationErrors;
  }
  else
  {
    GoToGridPage();
  }
}

protected override void LoadObjectFromScreen(ENTNotificationEO baseEO)
{
  baseEO.FromEmailAddress = txtFromEmailAddress.Text;
  baseEO.Subject = txtSubject.Text;
  baseEO.Body = txtBody.Text;
}

protected override void LoadScreenFromObject(ENTNotificationEO baseEO)
{
  lblDescription.Text = baseEO.Description;
  txtFromEmailAddress.Text = baseEO.FromEmailAddress;
  txtSubject.Text = baseEO.Subject;
  txtBody.Text = baseEO.Body;

  ViewState[VIEW_STATE_KEY_NOTIFICATION] = baseEO;
}

protected override void GoToGridPage()
{
  Response.Redirect("NotificationTemplates.aspx");
}

public override string MenuItemName()
{
```

```
      return "Notification Templates";
   }

   public override string[] CapabilityNames()
   {
      return new string[] { "Notification Templates" };
   }
```

Now users can manage the text of the e-mail themselves without any assistance from the developer and it will even have dynamically generated text with a link to the issue.

Creating the Notification Registration Screen

The next step is to create the screen that enables users to register for a notification. This screen will be different from the rest because it won't have a grid screen and an edit screen. It doesn't make any sense to make users view a list of the three notifications and then navigate to another screen just to turn the notification on. Instead, users are only presented with one screen containing checkboxes, which users can check off depending on which notifications they want to be registered for. Because this functionality should be available to general users, its menu item will be placed under the Home tab; its name is My Notifications. Clicking the My Notifications link takes users to the screen shown in Figure 8-9.

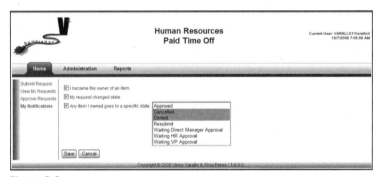

Figure 8-9

This window manages two tables at the same time: `ENTNotificationENTUserAccount` and `ENTNotificationENTWFState`.

There is a problem with the business objects as they are defined currently. The `ENTNotification ENTUserAccountEO` class only saves one record at a time but this screen needs to save all three records at once, plus the related state records. To solve this problem, create a custom edit object called `MyNotifications` in the BLL that inherits from the `ENTBaseEO` class and contains a list of `ENTNotificationENTUserAccount` objects:

```
[Serializable]
public class MyNotificationsEO : ENTBaseEO
{
   private ENTNotificationENTUserAccountEOList _userNotifications;

   public MyNotificationsEO()
```

```
    {
      _userNotifications = new ENTNotificationENTUserAccountEOList();
    }

    public ENTNotificationENTUserAccountEOList UserNotifications
    {
      get { return _userNotifications; }
    }
```

The `Save` method simply calls the `Save` method on the list object, which saves all the records in one transaction:

```
    public override bool Save(HRPaidTimeOffDataContext db, ref ENTValidationErrors
      validationErrors, int userAccountId)
    {
      if (DBAction == DBActionEnum.Save)
      {
        //Validate the object
        Validate(db, ref validationErrors);

        //Check if there were any validation errors
        if (validationErrors.Count == 0)
        {
          return _userNotifications.Save(db, ref validationErrors, userAccountId);
        }
        else
        {
          //Didn't pass validation.
          return false;
        }
      }
      else
      {
        throw new Exception("DBAction not Save.");
      }
    }
```

The default `Load` method for this object does not work because the screen does not display any records based on the ID of the record. It must display the list of notifications that the current logged on user has registered for:

```
    public override bool Load(int id)
    {
      throw new NotImplementedException();
    }

    public void LoadByENTUserAccountId(int entUserAccountId)
    {
      _userNotifications.Load(entUserAccountId);
    }
}
```

Now you can add a new page to the root directory and name it MyNotifications.aspx. This page should use the PaidTimeOffEditPage master page and inherit from the BaseEditPage class and pass in the MyNotificationsEO object as the generic parameter. Since this entire screen is built dynamically from the data in the database, you only need to add the HTML table to the markup that will contain the three notifications rows:

```
<table runat="server" id="tblNotifications"></table>
```

Everything else is handled in the code-behind page. Each row in the table will contain a checkbox for any notification defined in the ENTNotification table, and it will be checked if there is a record in the ENTNotificationENTUserAccount table for the current user. To create the table, you must override the OnInit method because you want the table to remain between postbacks. This method will also add a list box of all the states for the third notification, which is dependent upon state:

```
protected override void OnInit(EventArgs e)
{
    base.OnInit(e);

    //Build the notification list.
    ENTNotificationEOList notifications = new ENTNotificationEOList();
    notifications.Load();

    foreach (ENTNotificationEO notification in notifications)
    {
        HtmlTableRow tr = new HtmlTableRow();

        //the first cell contains a checkbox
        HtmlTableCell tc1 = new HtmlTableCell();
        tc1.Attributes.Add("NotificationId", notification.ID.ToString());

        CheckBox chkNotify = new CheckBox();
        chkNotify.Text = notification.Description;
        chkNotify.ID = "chk" + notification.ID.ToString();
        tc1.Controls.Add(chkNotify);
        tc1.VAlign = "top";
        tr.Cells.Add(tc1);

        //if this is the state notification then add a listbox to the second cell.
        if ((ENTNotificationEO.NotificationType)notification.ID ==
            ENTNotificationEO.NotificationType.IssueIOwnedGoesToState)
        {
            HtmlTableCell tc2 = new HtmlTableCell();

            ListBox lstStates = new ListBox();
            lstStates.SelectionMode = ListSelectionMode.Multiple;

            //get the states
            ENTWFStateEOList states = new ENTWFStateEOList();
            states.Load();
            List<ENTWFStateEO> sortedStates = states.SortByPropertyName("StateName",
                true);

            if (states.Count > 0)
```

```
    {
      lstStates.DataSource = sortedStates;
      lstStates.DataTextField = "DisplayText";
      lstStates.DataValueField = "ID";
      lstStates.DataBind();

      lstStates.Rows = states.Count;
    }
    tc2.Controls.Add(lstStates);

    tr.Cells.Add(tc2);
  }
  else
  {
    tc1.ColSpan = 2;
  }
  tblNotifications.Rows.Add(tr);
 }
}
```

This method will just build the table with the available options. The `LoadScreenFromObject` method will then check the boxes and highlight items in the State list box based on the user's notifications:

```
protected override void LoadScreenFromObject(MyNotificationsEO baseEO)
{
  foreach (HtmlTableRow tr in tblNotifications.Rows)
  {
    //Cell one has the checkbox and the id for the notification.
    ENTNotificationEO.NotificationType notificationType =
      (ENTNotificationEO.NotificationType)
        int.Parse(tr.Cells[0].Attributes["NotificationId"].ToString());

    //Try to find this in notifications the user already registered for.
    ENTNotificationENTUserAccountEO myNotification =
      baseEO.UserNotifications.Get(notificationType);

    if (myNotification != null)
    {
      //Check the box
      ((CheckBox)tr.Cells[0].Controls[0]).Checked = true;

      if (notificationType ==
          ENTNotificationEO.NotificationType.IssueIOwnedGoesToState)
      {
        ListBox lstStates = (ListBox)tr.Cells[1].Controls[0];

        //Highlight each state in the list box.
        foreach (ENTNotificationENTWFStateEO state in
                 myNotification.NotificationStates)
        {
          //Find this item in the list box.
          foreach (ListItem li in lstStates.Items)
          {
            if (li.Value == state.ENTWFStateId.ToString())
```

```
        {
            //Set it to selected.
            li.Selected = true;
            break;
        }
      }
    }
  }
}

ViewState[VIEW_STATE_KEY_MYNOTIFICATIONS] = baseEO;
}
```

The only other tricky part to this screen is loading the object from the screen. This is done in the LoadObjectFromScreen method, which will loop through each row in the HTML table and set the correct properties on the MyNotificationEO object:

```
protected override void LoadObjectFromScreen(MyNotificationsEO baseEO)
{
  foreach (HtmlTableRow tr in tblNotifications.Rows)
  {
    //Cell one has the checkbox and the id for the notification.
    ENTNotificationEO.NotificationType notificationType =
      (ENTNotificationEO.NotificationType)
        ((int.Parse(tr.Cells[0].Attributes["NotificationId"].ToString())));

    bool isChecked = ((CheckBox)tr.Cells[0].Controls[0]).Checked;

    //Try to find this in notifications the user already registered for.
    ENTNotificationENTUserAccountEO myNotification =
        baseEO.UserNotifications.Get(notificationType);

    //If it wasn't in the list already then add it if the checkbox is checked.
    if (myNotification == null)
    {
      if (isChecked)
      {
        myNotification = new ENTNotificationENTUserAccountEO();
        myNotification.ENTNotificationId = (int)notificationType;
        myNotification.ENTUserAccountId = CurrentUser.ID;

        baseEO.UserNotifications.Add(myNotification);
      }
    }
    else
    {
      //if the user previously registered for this notification and now they
      //unchecked the box then mark this record for deletion.
      if (isChecked == false)
      {
        myNotification.DBAction = ENTBaseEO.DBActionEnum.Delete;
      }
```

```
    }

        //If this is the state notification then add the states that were selected.
        if ((isChecked) && (notificationType ==
           ENTNotificationEO.NotificationType.IssueIOwnedGoesToState))
        {
          myNotification.NotificationStates.Clear();
          ListBox lstState = (ListBox)tr.Cells[1].Controls[0];

          foreach (ListItem li in lstState.Items)
          {
            if (li.Selected == true)
            {
              myNotification.NotificationStates.Add(new ENTNotificationENTWFStateEO
                {
                  ENTNotificationENTUserAccountId = myNotification.ID,
                  ENTWFStateId = int.Parse(li.Value)
                });
            }
          }
        }
      }
    }
  }
}
```

That's the only custom code for this screen. Everything else uses the same pattern defined earlier for the other events and overridden methods.

The next step is to add the code to the ENTBaseWorkflowEO class, which will add records to the ENTEmail table if a user is registered for any of the three notifications. This is accomplished by changing the existing SaveWorkflow method because you want all of these records to be saved in the same transaction as the other records. The following code shows the complete SaveWorkflow method (changed code is highlighted):

```
public bool SaveWorkflow(HRPaidTimeOffDataContext db, ref ENTValidationErrors
    validationErrors, ENTBaseEO item, int userAccountId)
{
WFItem.ItemId = item.ID;

ValidateWorkflow(db, ref validationErrors, item);

if (validationErrors.Count == 0)
{
  //Set the ID for all the child owner objects
  foreach (ENTWFItemOwnerEO entWFItemOwner in WFOwners)
  {
    entWFItemOwner.ENTWFItemId = item.ID;
  }

  foreach (ENTWFItemStateHistoryEO entWFItemStateHistory in WFStateHistory)
  {
    entWFItemStateHistory.ENTWFItemId = item.ID;
  }

  if (WFItem.Save(db, ref validationErrors, userAccountId))
```

```
{
  foreach (ENTWFItemOwnerEO wfItemOwner in WFOwners)
  {
    wfItemOwner.ENTWFItemId = WFItem.ID;

    if (wfItemOwner.Save(db, ref validationErrors, userAccountId) == false)
    {
      return false;
    }
  }

  foreach (ENTWFItemStateHistoryEO wfItemStateHistory in WFStateHistory)
  {
    if (wfItemStateHistory.IsNewRecord())
    {
      //A state history is only added if an item changes state or a different
      //person becomes the owner.  Send notification if user became owner,
      //Check if the new owner is registered to recieve a notification when they
      //become the owner of an item.
      ENTNotificationEO myNotification = new ENTNotificationEO();
      if (myNotification.Load(db,
          ENTNotificationEO.NotificationType.IBecameOwnerOfIssue,
          wfItemStateHistory.ENTUserAccountId))
      {
        //Get the new owner's email address
        ENTUserAccountEO newOwner = new ENTUserAccountEO();
        newOwner.Load(db, wfItemStateHistory.ENTUserAccountId);

        ENTEmailEO email = new ENTEmailEO
          {
            FromEmailAddress = myNotification.FromEmailAddress,
            Subject = ReplaceTokens(myNotification.Subject, item),
            Body = ReplaceTokens(myNotification.Body, item),
            EmailStatusFlag = ENTEmailEO.EmailStatusFlagEnum.NotSent,
            ToEmailAddress = newOwner.Email
          };

        email.Save(db, ref validationErrors, userAccountId);
      }
    }

    wfItemStateHistory.ENTWFItemId = WFItem.ID;

    if (wfItemStateHistory.Save(db, ref validationErrors, userAccountId) ==
        false)
    {
      return false;
    }
  }

  //Call any methods the transition requires
  if (ENTWFTransitionId != 0)
  {
    ENTWFTransitionEO entWFTransition = WFTransitions.Get(ENTWFTransitionId);
```

```
if (entWFTransition.PostTransitionMethodName != null)
{
  //Create an instance of the object
  Type objectType = Type.GetType(Workflow.ENTWorkflowObjectName);

  //Call the method to load the object
  objectType.InvokeMember(entWFTransition.PostTransitionMethodName,
    BindingFlags.InvokeMethod, null, item, new object[] { db });
}

//Send notifications if user requests to be notified when their issue changes
//state, Chapter 8.
ENTNotificationEO issueChangedStateNotification = new ENTNotificationEO();
if (issueChangedStateNotification.Load(db,
    ENTNotificationEO.NotificationType.MyRequestChangedState,
    WFItem.SubmitterENTUserAccountId))
{
  //Get the submitters email address.
  ENTUserAccountEO submitter = new ENTUserAccountEO();
  submitter.Load(db, WFItem.SubmitterENTUserAccountId);

  ENTEmailEO email = new ENTEmailEO
    {
      FromEmailAddress = issueChangedStateNotification.FromEmailAddress,
      Subject = ReplaceTokens(issueChangedStateNotification.Subject, item),
      Body = ReplaceTokens(issueChangedStateNotification.Body, item),
      EmailStatusFlag = ENTEmailEO.EmailStatusFlagEnum.NotSent,
      ToEmailAddress = submitter.Email
    };

  email.Save(db, ref validationErrors, userAccountId);
}

//Check if anyone registered for this notification for the current state.
ENTNotificationENTUserAccountEOList goesToStateNotification = new
    ENTNotificationENTUserAccountEOList();

goesToStateNotification.Load(db, WFItem.CurrentWFStateId,
    ENTNotificationEO.NotificationType.IssueIOwnedGoesToState);

if (goesToStateNotification.Count > 0)
{
  //Get the notification details to send the email.
  ENTNotificationEO notification = new ENTNotificationEO();
  notification.Load(db,
    (int)ENTNotificationEO.NotificationType.IssueIOwnedGoesToState);

  //Send notifications if user requests to be notified if they owned an issue
  //an it reaches a specific state.
  foreach(ENTWFItemOwnerEO owner in WFOwners)
  {
    ENTNotificationENTUserAccountEO notifyForState =
    goesToStateNotification.GetByENTUserAccountId(
    (int)owner.ENTUserAccountId);
```

```
                    if (notifyForState != null)
                    {
                        //Get the owner's email address.
                        ENTUserAccountEO ownerUserAccount = new ENTUserAccountEO();
                        ownerUserAccount.Load(db, (int)owner.ENTUserAccountId);

                        ENTEmailEO email = new ENTEmailEO
                          {
                            FromEmailAddress = notification.FromEmailAddress,
                            Subject = ReplaceTokens(notification.Subject, item),
                            Body = ReplaceTokens(notification.Body, item),
                            EmailStatusFlag = ENTEmailEO.EmailStatusFlagEnum.NotSent,
                            ToEmailAddress = ownerUserAccount.Email
                          };

                        email.Save(db, ref validationErrors, userAccountId);
                    }
                }
            }
        }

        return true;
    }
    else
    {
        //Failed item save.
        return false;
    }
}
else
{
    //Failed Validation
    return false;
}
}
}
```

This method relies on one new method called `ReplaceTokens` that contains the logic for setting the token values. It replaces the text in the e-mail subject or body based on the template set up by the user:

```
private string ReplaceTokens(string text, ENTBaseEO baseEO)
{
  List<Token> tokens = new List<Token>();

  //state
  tokens.Add(new Token{TokenString="<WFSTATE>", Value=CurrentState.StateName});

  //owner
  tokens.Add(new Token{TokenString = "<WFOWNER>", Value = CurrentOwnerUserName});

  //itemid
  tokens.Add(new Token{TokenString = "<WFITEMID>", Value = baseEO.ID.ToString() });
```

```
    //submit date
    tokens.Add(new Token{TokenString = "<WFSUBMITDATE>", Value = (WFItem.InsertDate
            == DateTime.MinValue ? DateTime.Now.ToStandardDateFormat() :
                                    WFItem.InsertDate.ToStandardDateFormat()) });

    //link, get the page from the workflow.
    tokens.Add(new Token { TokenString = "<LINK>", Value = "<a href='" +
        NotificationPage + StringHelpers.EncryptQueryString("id=" +
        WFItem.ItemId.ToString()) + "'>Click here to view the item.</a>" });

    return ENTNotificationEO.ReplaceTokens(tokens, text);
}
```

Notice that if the <LINK> token is in the string it is replaced by a hyperlink using the NotificationPage property of this object. This is also a new property that must be added to the BaseWorkflowEO class. The value for this property should be set in the WorkflowController class created in Chapter 7. This is the control that must be on the page that the user uses to move the request through the workflow. The LoadObjectFromControl method in the WorkflowController class should set this property:

```
baseWorkflowEO.NotificationPage = this.Context.Request.Url.AbsoluteUri;
```

This is handled in the control because you might have more than one workflow defined in your project for different types of requests. Each type of request should have its own edit page with this control on it. The control will know the name of the page it is in using its Context object. The link created in the e-mail should bring users to the appropriate page based on the request.

That's all that is needed to get the notifications to work in the workflow. You could create other custom notification for events such as when a user logs on, when a user runs a report, when a password is changed, and so on. It's as simple as adding a record to the ENTNotification table and adding the code to the appropriate event when a notification should be fired. The sample in this chapter was quite simple but it exposed you to a pattern that you can customize to meet your own needs.

Summary

Now Mary has a little bit more functionality in her Paid Time Off application and she's quite happy with the progress. She can monitor everything that is going on in the application and she doesn't have to worry about chasing people down to approve requests because they will automatically get an e-mail when an issue moves to them for approval. She can also control the text of the e-mail message and her users can decide whether they want to receive notifications or not.

Not only does Mary have more functionality, it is hoped that you gained some insight into notification patterns, and Windows services also. It may seem strange to find a chapter about Windows services in an ASP.NET book, but there are plenty of situations in which they come in handy in a web application. They're especially helpful in situations where a long-running process needs to be kicked off on a regular basis. A service could be built to run the process, and an e-mail can be sent when the job completes. Again, the possibilities are endless, but you can use the timer pattern described in this chapter in your own applications.

Of course, after showing Mary the latest and greatest version of the application, she is asking for more stuff. She is preparing for an audit of her department and she needs to be able to print a report that lists all the roles and users defined in the system. She also needs to be able to report on the status of any requests, so all this hard work building e-mail notifications netted us about two minutes of praise and now it's back to the drawing board.

The next chapter will show you how to create reports using the Crystal Reports for .NET objects that is included free with Visual Studio 2008. These reports not only add polish to your application, they can also make or break an application. Once you see the pattern for creating reports, you'll be able to add new reports in a matter of minutes, not days.

9

Reporting

For some reason, reporting always seems to be an afterthought when it comes to developing an application. Everybody is concerned about the design of the data entry screens and what data should be collected, but far too often applications are built and quickly become a data graveyard. The data goes in but it never comes out. Problems always seem to arise near the end of the development cycle when users start thinking about reports, and then they realize that they aren't collecting the right information or they don't have enough information for a report to make sense. In these situations, you are forced to tell the user that either you can't create the report or you have to make wholesale changes to the application in order to accomplish what they want. That's not a position you ever want to be in.

Another issue with reporting is that many applications don't even include reporting, and an entirely different tool and application is used for reports. There are plenty of tools that just handle reporting, such as Business Objects Web Intelligence, Crystal Reports, Hyperion, SQL Server Reporting Services — the list goes on and on. Producing reports takes an entirely different skill set than the typical programmer possesses.

Problem

Mary has asked for a couple of reports so far. She needs a report that will display the roles that have been defined in the application. She needs a report that displays any requests that are in the system, including their status. Unfortunately, she has no money in her budget for third-party tools for printing, so what are you going to do? Fortunately, Visual Studio comes with a free version of Crystal Reports for .NET that may be the answer you are looking for.

Visual Studio has shipped with Crystal Reports for .NET since its inception, and it is a perfectly viable option for creating reports directly in an ASP.NET application. It looks much more professional when the user can print directly from the application, rather than telling them to go to some other site.

This chapter will build some reports for the Paid Time Off application that enables users to print directly from the application, export to PDF, and still conform to the three-layered architecture.

Design

You have plenty of options when it comes to reporting and all of them are perfectly feasible as long as they accomplish the business need and do not hinder performance. One of the requests for the Paid Time Off application is for a report that displays the list of users and the capabilities associated with a role. This is a great report for an auditor.

Here are the requirements for the Role report:

❑   The company name must be at the top of each page of the report.

❑   The report must list each capability associated with a role and state the type of access (either Read Only or Edit). Access types of None should be hidden.

❑   The report must list each user associated with the role.

❑   The report must print each role on a separate page.

❑   Each page of the report must display the date and time the report was printed.

❑   Each page of the report must display the current page number and the total number of pages.

Figure 9-1 shows a screen shot of the report.

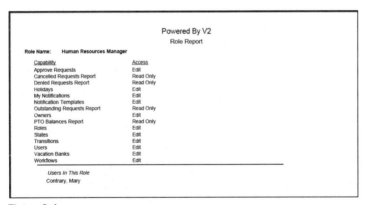

Figure 9-1

To create this report using Crystal Reports, follow these steps:

1.   Add a new folder to the `PaidTimeOffUI` project and call it "Reports."

2.   Right-click on this folder and select Add New Item.

3.   Choose Crystal Reports from the dialog, name the file `Roles.rpt`, and then click the Add button. This adds the file to the project and then brings up the Crystal Reports Gallery dialog, shown in Figure 9-2.

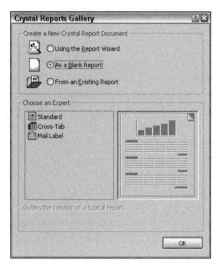

Figure 9-2

Choose the radio button for As a Blank Report and click OK. The Crystal Reports designer will appear, shown in Figure 9-3.

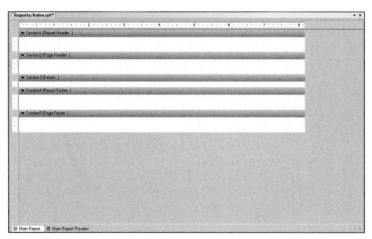

Figure 9-3

By default there are five sections in the report, but you can add more for grouping purposes or even split a group into multiple sections:

❑   Section one is the report header, which appears only on the first page of the report.

❑   The second section is the page header. This section appears at the top of each page in the report. This is usually where the company name and report name are placed.

❑   The third section is the details section. This is the section where the data is placed on a report. Think of the details section as the rows in a GridView control. When you bind data to the report, the rows in your data source are displayed here.

❑   The fourth section is the report footer. This is displayed only on the last page and is great for grand totals.

❑   The last section is the page footer, which appears on each page. This is a great place to put page numbers or the date when the report was printed.

Note in Figure 9-1 that the company name and the name of the report are at the top of the page. This should be displayed on each page, so it should be placed in the page header section. Since there is nothing to display in the report header, this section is hidden. To hide the report header, right-click on the gray bar that says "Section1 (Report Header)" and then select "Suppress (No Drill Down)." This will make the section appear with gray lines through it. To add the company name to the page header, right-click anywhere in the white space in the page header section. Select Insert ➪ Text Object from the pop-up menu. This will ghost a text box where your mouse is located. Hover the mouse pointer over the left side of the page header and left-click. This will drop a text box on the report and the cursor will be in the text box waiting for input. Enter your company name in the text box and then expand the width of the text box so it is the entire width of the report. You can expand the width by clicking on the border and dragging the window handles to the right.

Next, format the text box. Right-click on the text box and select Format Object from the pop-up menu. This brings up the Format Editor. You have several options when it comes to formatting a text box, as shown in Figure 9-4.

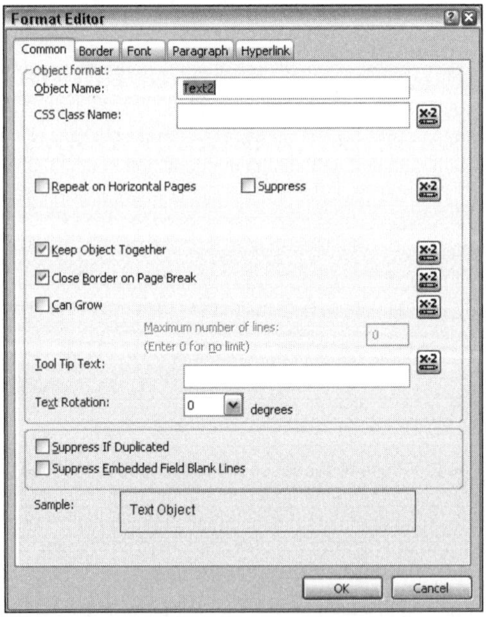

Figure 9-4

An important setting to note on the Common tab is the Can Grow setting. This enables the text box to grow vertically if the length of the data happens to be longer than width of the box. This is helpful when printing large text fields such as notes. For the company header, all you want to do is center the text and make it size 14. To do so, click the Paragraph tab and change the Alignment drop-down in the Horizontal Alignment section to Centered. Now click the Font tab and change the size to 14. Click the OK button and the text box should reflect your changes.

Because the font size is changed to 14, you may have to make the height of the text box larger to accommodate the change. Repeat the same steps to add a second text box that contains the name of the report. For this demo, the report name is "Roles Report." Make the font for this text box 12, as this is a subheader. If you need to make the page header section taller, you can hover the mouse pointer over the top border of Section 3 until it becomes a line with an arrow on the top and bottom. Left-click and drag the mouse pointer down to expand the section. The report should now look like Figure 9-5.

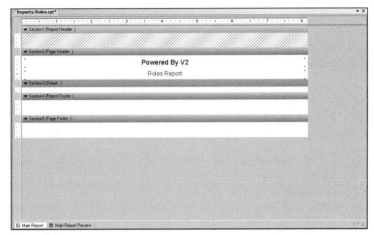

Figure 9-5

Now add the page footer. For this sample, the page footer should contain the page number, in the format of "Page N of M," and the date and time the report was printed. This should be shown on each page, so it should be placed in the page footer section. The report footer section can be suppressed by following the same instructions as above:

1. Add the page numbers by right-clicking in the page footer section and selecting Insert ⇨ Special Field ⇨ Page N of M.

2. Drag the text box onto the report and make it the width of the report so it can be centered. To center the text, right-click on the field and select Format Object. The Horizontal Alignment combo is on the Common tab, instead of the Paragraph tab for "Special Fields."

3. Add the date and time the report was printed. You could use two special fields called `Print Date` and `Print Time` for this, but it should be displayed as one field. To do this, you create a *formula field*. Formula fields are very powerful in Crystal Reports because they enable you to write script code that you can use to do almost anything in a report. You can use `if` logic, `for` loops, financial calculations, string manipulation, and much more. To create a formula field, right-click on the Formula Fields node in the Field Explorer window. The Field Explorer window is only valid for Crystal Reports and should be located on either side of the Visual Studio designer (see Figure 9-6).

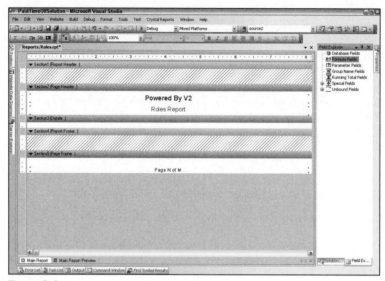

Figure 9-6

When you right-click on the Formula Fields node, select New. This will display a dialog for the formula name. Enter **PrintDateTime** for the name and click the Use Editor button. This opens the Formula Editor dialog, shown in Figure 9-7.

Figure 9-7

The tree on the left lists any formula fields in the report, as well as any conditional formatting formulas added to the report. The three panes to the right of the tree control display any fields in the data source for the report; all the built-in functions Crystal Reports offers; and the operators that can be used in the formulas. Expand the Functions tree and then expand the Date and Time node. Notice that there are numerous other functions for dates than just the ones that were offered in the Special Fields. The one we are interested in is the `CurrentDateTime` function. Double-click on the CurrentDateTime node and it will be added to the bottom pane. This is where the formula text is actually coded. Keywords appear in blue and the syntax is similar to VB. Click the Save and Close toolbar item to save your changes.

Now you can drag the `PrintDateTime` formula field from the Field Explorer window to the report footer just above the page number text box. Change the width and center the field as you've done before. The report should now look like Figure 9-8.

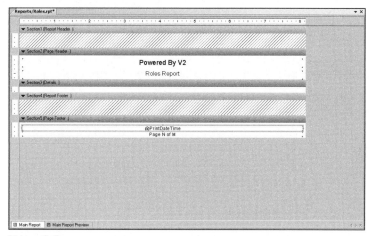

Figure 9-8

The easy part is over. Now the data has to be added to the report.

Directly Connecting to the Database

The first attempt at this report uses the Crystal Reports Database Expert tool to retrieve the data needed for the report:

1. Right-click on the details section and select Database ⇨ Database Expert from the pop-up menu. This brings up the Database Expert window. Expand the plus sign next to the Create New Connection folder.

2. Click on the plus sign next to the OLE DB (ADO) folder. This will bring up the OLE DB (ADO) dialog, which essentially creates a connection to a database (see Figure 9-9).

3. Choose Microsoft OLE DB Provider for SQL Server from the list of providers and click the Next button.

4. The next screen asks for the server, user ID, password, and database that you want to connect to. Enter the appropriate information to connect to the `HRPaidTimeOff` database, click Next, and then click Finish on the last screen. This brings you back to the Database Expert window. You should see a connection to the `HRPaidTimeOff` database in the OLE DB (ADO) folder.

Figure 9-9

5. Click the plus sign next to the database name to display the schemas. Expand the dbo schema and then expand the tables (see Figure 9-10).

Use this screen to choose which tables you want to report on and to define the relationships between the tables. Highlight the ENTCapability, ENTRole, and ENTRoleCapability tables and click the arrow button to move the tables to the right pane.

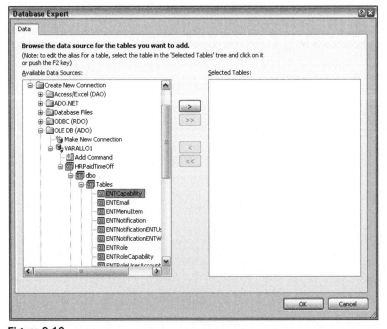

Figure 9-10

6. Click the OK button. This brings up the Links window, where you can define the relationships between the tables (see Figure 9-11).

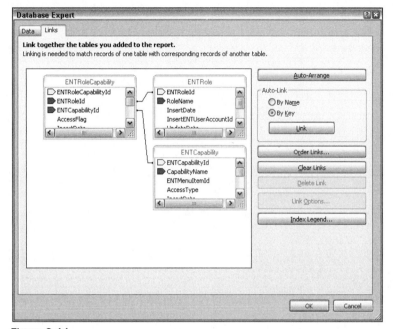

Figure 9-11

The ENTRole table is the parent table and each row in this table may or may not have capabilities associated with it. In order for the data to be shown correctly, you need to create a right outer join between the ENTRole and ENTRoleCapability tables. To do this, right-click on the line between these two tables and choose Link Options. This opens the Link Options window, shown in Figure 9-12. Select the Right Outer Join option and click the OK button.

Figure 9-12

You need to also change the link between the ENTRoleCapability and ENTCapability tables to be a Left Outer Join using the same steps just described. When you're done, click the OK button twice to return to the report.

Note in the Field Explorer window that the Database Fields node now has the three tables listed below it. Expand the ENTCapability node and then drag the CapabilityName field onto the details section in the report. You can preview the data by clicking the Main Report Preview button at the bottom of the report designer (see Figure 9-13).

Figure 9-13

The Main Report and Main Report Preview buttons enable you to toggle back and forth between the design view and the print preview. The preview of the report looks like Figure 9-14.

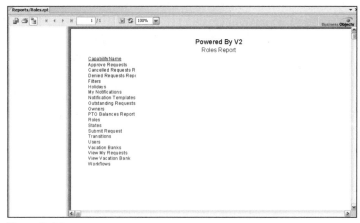

Figure 9-14

If everything is set up correctly, you should see a single list of capabilities, although this is not what you want. You really want to see each role's list of capabilities. To do this, you need to insert a group in the details section. Switch back to design view by clicking on the Main Report button at the bottom of the report designer. Right-click anywhere in the white space in the details section and select Insert ⇨ Group from the pop-up menu. The Insert Group dialog should appear (see Figure 9-15). Select the RoleName field under the ENTRole table and click the OK button.

This adds two sections to the report, one for the group header and one for the group footer. Crystal Reports automatically adds the group name field in bold in the group header section. For this report, add a text box to the left of the group name field and set the text to "Role Name:." You'll have to move the group name box slightly to the right to fit the text box. Change the font of the text box to bold to match the group name field. Now if you preview the report, you should see the list of capabilities under each role defined in your database.

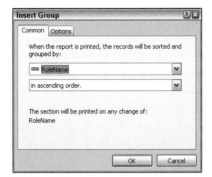

Figure 9-15

The next issue to resolve is the requirement that each role should be displayed on a separate page. To do this, right-click on the gray bar for the GroupFooterSection1 section. Select Section Expert from the pop-up menu. This displays the Section Expert dialog, shown in Figure 9-16.

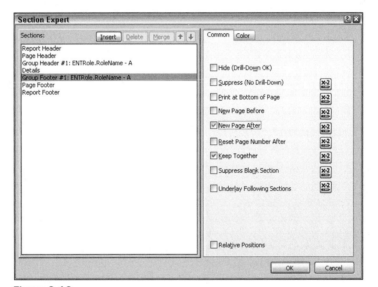

Figure 9-16

Check the New Page After option, click the OK button, and preview the report again. This time each role should start on a new page.

The next step is to add a formula field that translates the `AccessFlag` field in the `ENTRoleCapability` table to None, Read Only, or Edit. Remember that this field contains zero, one, or two: zero means none, one means read only, and two means edit access. Right-click on the Formula Fields in the Field Explorer and select New. Name the field **AccessFlagText** and click the Use Editor button. Enter the following code in the Formula Editor, shown in Figure 9-17:

```
if {ENTRoleCapability.AccessFlag} = 0 then
    'None'
else
    if {ENTRoleCapability.AccessFlag} = 1 then
        'Read Only'
    else
        if {ENTRoleCapability.AccessFlag} = 2 then
            'Edit'
        else
            'Unknown'
```

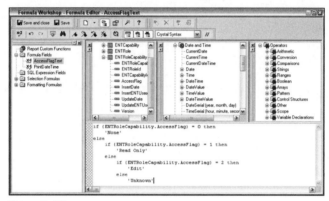

Figure 9-17

This code will return a string with the correct text for the access flag. Click the Save and Close button. Drag the `AccessFlagText` field from the Field Explorer to the right of the capability name field in the details section. Notice that each time you add a field to the details section, a column header is also added to the page header section. This can look confusing when a group is added to the report, so I like to drag the column headers to the group header section below the group name. To do this, you need to make the group header section taller and then simply drag the fields from the page header. Change the text to **Capability** and **Access** in each of the text boxes. Preview the report again and it should look like Figure 9-18.

Notice that the capabilities are not listed in alphabetical order. To fix this, right-click on any white space in the report and select Report ⇨ Record Sort Expert from the pop-up menu. The Record Sort Export dialog should appear. Click on the `CapabilityName` field in the list of Available Fields and move it to the Sort Fields list (see Figure 9-19).

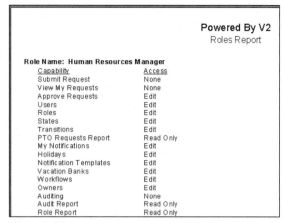

Figure 9-18

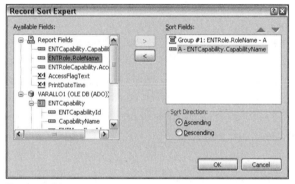

Figure 9-19

Click the OK button and preview the report again. The capability names are now sorted correctly.

The next step is to hide any detail lines where the access type is None:

1. Go back to design view for the report, right-click on the gray bar for the details section, and select Section Expert from the pop-up menu. The Section Expert dialog should appear and the details section item should be selected in the Sections list.

2. Check the box next to Suppress (No Drill-Down) and then click on the button to the right of the checkbox. This opens the Formula Editor again, where you can create a formula that returns true or false to conditionally format the section.

3. Expand the tables under the database server name and then expand the ENTRoleCapability table to view its fields.

4. Double-click on the `AccessFlag` field to add it to the editor pane. Change the formula to the one shown in Figure 9-20.

Figure 9-20

This will return true when the access flag is zero and suppress the current line. Click the Save and Close button and then click the OK button on the Section Expert dialog. Preview the report again; the detail line that had "None" before should be hidden.

The next step is a little tricky. The requirements state that the report should also display all the users associated with the role. The problem is that the detail lines are already repeating on the `CapabilityName` field. Users cannot be added to the details section because the report would display too many rows because of the join between the two tables. This is where a *subreport* comes in handy. A subreport enables you to embed a report inside another report and link the two reports on a shared field. For this report, users will be listed in the group footer section so that they only appear once per group after the list of capabilities has been displayed:

1. Right-click in the group footer section and select Insert ➪ Subreport from the pop-up menu.

2. Drop the subreport in the group footer section. This will display the Insert Subreport dialog, shown in Figure 9-21.

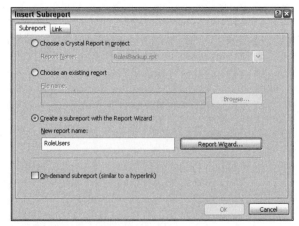

Figure 9-21

3. Select the "Create a subreport with the Report Wizard" option.

4. Enter **RoleUsers** for the report name and then click the Report Wizard button. The first screen of the wizard enables you to select different tables for the subreport.

5. Select the ENTRole, ENTRoleUserAccount, and ENTUserAccount tables from the HRPaidTimeOff database and move them to the Selected Tables list by clicking the arrow button. Click the Next button to define the links between the tables. The link between the ENTRoleUserAccount and ENTRole tables should be a right outer join, and the link between the ENTRoleUserAccount and ENTUserAccount tables should be a left outer join. Change these links by right-clicking on the link between the tables and choosing the correct options in the dialog.

6. Click the Next button in the wizard. The next screen asks which fields you want to display on the report. Because the report should first display the user's last name and then the first name separated by a comma, you can skip this step. You'll create a formula to display the name this way.

7. Click the Next button to display the Report Styles screen.

8. Choose Standard from the list and click the Finish button.

9. Click the OK button on the Insert Subreport dialog. You should now see a box in the group footer section called RoleUsers.

Now you have to define the field that will be used to link the main report to the subreport. Right-click on the RoleUsers subreport box and select Change Subreport Links from the pop-up menu. Select RoleName from the list of Available Fields and move it to the Field(s) to link to list. Click the OK button.

To view the subreport in design mode, right-click on the subreport box and select Edit Subreport from the pop-up menu. This will display the embedded subreport. Notice at the bottom of the screen that a third button appeared for the subreport. You can now use these buttons to toggle between the three views (see Figure 9-22).

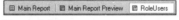

Figure 9-22

Now add a new formula to the subreport for the user's first and last name. Right-click on the Formula Fields node in the Field Explorer and select New. Enter **UserName** for the name of the formula and click the Use Editor button. Enter the following for the formula:

```
{ENTUserAccount.LastName} + ', ' + {ENTUserAccount.FirstName}
```

Strings in Crystal Reports are surrounded by single quotes, and the plus sign is used for concatenation. Click the Save and Close button and then add the new field to the details section in the subreport. Remove the UserName text object that was added to the report header section and remove the Print Date box from that section. Insert a new text object in the report header and set the text to **Users In Role**. Right-click on the ReportFooterSection2 section's gray bar and suppress this section also. The subreport should look like the one shown in Figure 9-23.

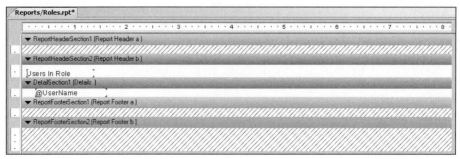

Figure 9-23

The last step for the subreport is to sort the report by the UserName formula field. Do this by again using the Report Sort Expert:

1. Click back to the Main Report view and right-click on the subreport. By default, the subreport appears in a black box. This report should show only the top border and nothing else.

2. Select Format Object from the pop-up menu.

3. Click the Border tab and change the right, left, and bottom borders to None.

4. Click the OK button and preview the report.

The report is now designed as per the requirements.

Report Viewer

Now that you have a report, you need to enable users to view it. Crystal Reports comes with a handy control that enables you to do just that, and it has paging, export, search, and drill-down capabilities. This section covers adding this control to a page to enable users to view the Role report.

Right-click on the Reports folder and add a new Web Form called ReportViewer.aspx. This should not use any master page because reports always appear in a separate window without any menu. Change the view of the form to design view and add a CrystalReportsViewer control to the form. This control is located in the Reporting group in the toolbox (see Figure 9-24).

When you add the viewer, the Crystal Report Viewer Tasks window will appear on the design surface, as shown in Figure 9-25.

Uncheck the box next to Enable Database Logon Prompting. If this were checked, the control would allow users to enter the database user name and password. This should never be shown to users. Instead, the code-behind will handle all the database parameters.

Figure 9-24

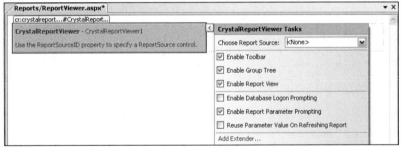

Figure 9-25

Double-click on the web Form to open the code-behind page. Add the following `using` directives to the top of the class:

```
using CrystalDecisions.CrystalReports.Engine;
using CrystalDecisions.Shared;
```

These two namespaces contain the classes that expose the object model that manipulates the Crystal Reports objects. You can do almost anything with this object model, and a single chapter in one book cannot cover it all. For this example, you only need to open the report file, set the database parameters, and then hook it to the viewer. Add the following lines of code to the `Page_Load` event to open the report file:

```
ReportDocument report = new ReportDocument();
report.Load(Server.MapPath("Roles.rpt"));
```

ReportDocument is the class that represents the report file just created. The Load method takes a report file path and loads the definition of the file. You can use the ReportDocument object to change groups, sort, set selection formulas, and many other tasks.

Because this report is connecting directly to the database, you need to set the location for each table in the report to your database. The ReportDocument object has a property called Database that has a collection property of Tables. To set their location, use a ConnectionInfo object, which is in the Crystal Descisions namespace. You also have to set the location for each table in the subreport. To do this, create a helper function that takes a Tables collection and sets the location:

```
private void SetTableLocation(Tables tables)
{
    ConnectionInfo connectionInfo = new ConnectionInfo();

    connectionInfo.ServerName = "VARALLO1";
    connectionInfo.DatabaseName = "HRPaidTimeOff";
    connectionInfo.UserID = "V2Application";
    connectionInfo.Password = "wrox";

    foreach (CrystalDecisions.CrystalReports.Engine.Table table in tables)
    {
        TableLogOnInfo tableLogOnInfo = table.LogOnInfo;
        tableLogOnInfo.ConnectionInfo = connectionInfo;
        table.ApplyLogOnInfo(tableLogOnInfo);
    }
}
```

Replace the ServerName, DatabaseName, UserID, and Password with your settings. The Page_Load event can call this method to set the location for the tables in the main report and the subreport:

```
ReportDocument report = new ReportDocument();
report.Load(Server.MapPath("Roles.rpt"));
```

```
//Set the location for the main report.
SetTableLocation(report.Database.Tables);
```

```
//Set the location for any of the subreports.
foreach (ReportDocument rd in report.Subreports)
{
    SetTableLocation(rd.Database.Tables);
}
```

The last step is to set the report source for the control:

```
CrystalReportViewer1.ReportSource = report;
```

If you set the startup page to this page and run the report, you should see the page shown in Figure 9-26.

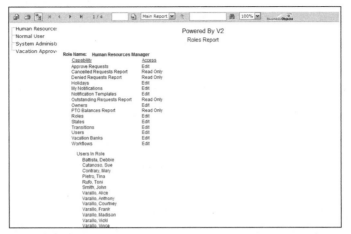

Figure 9-26

You can use the toolbar on the viewer to export the report, scroll through each page, search, change the zoom, and toggle the drill-down tree so it is hidden. This is nice, but there is one major problem with this control: Every time you page through the report, the page posts back to the server and runs the entire logic all over again. This is not ideal behavior. I've never used this control in a production-level application. Instead of displaying the report in the viewer you can display it in PDF format, which doesn't post back to the server as the user is paging through the report. Let's change this page to display the report in PDF, rather than use the viewer.

Delete the `CrystalReportViewer` control from the page and remove the code in the `Page_Load` event that sets the report source for the control. Add the following lines of code after the table locations have been set:

```
report.ExportToHttpResponse(ExportFormatType.PortableDocFormat, Response, false, "");
```

The `ExportToHttpResponse` method of the `report` object will pump the output from the report to the specified format. You can also export to Excel, Word, Text, and many other formats.

Run the project again and the report should be displayed in Acrobat Reader if it is installed. This is a free viewer, so installing it on a user's desktop shouldn't be a problem. You could easily change the output format by changing the `ExportFormatType` to Word, Excel, or even text files.

At this point you are probably thinking that I must be crazy, because I just created a report that completely violates everything about the three-layered architecture that has been built in each of the previous chapters. Well, you're right, but I wanted to show you how you can easily incorporate a report into an application. The next section uses the three-layered architecture to create this same report. The only problem with the three-layered approach is that you cannot preview the report with real data because the data source isn't connected to the database at design time, so you have to actually run the report to preview it. Of course, you can always connect to the database directly as just described. Pick your poison!

Three-Layered Architecture

In keeping with the pattern defined in this book so far, the data for any report should be retrieved via a stored procedure; a method should be added to the `DataContext` to call the stored procedure; a data class should call the method on the `DataContext`; a business class should call the data class; and the UI should call the business class to retrieve the data and display it to the user.

Start by adding two stored procedures to retrieve the data for the roles, capabilities, and users:

```
CREATE PROCEDURE ReportRoleCapability
AS
  SET NOCOUNT ON

    SELECT ENTRole.RoleName, ENTRoleCapability.AccessFlag,
           ENTCapability.CapabilityName
      FROM ENTCapability
INNER JOIN ENTRoleCapability
        ON ENTCapability.ENTCapabilityId = ENTRoleCapability.ENTCapabilityId
INNER JOIN ENTRole
        ON ENTRoleCapability.ENTRoleId = ENTRole.ENTRoleId

  RETURN
```

```
CREATE PROCEDURE ReportRoleUserAccount
AS
  SET NOCOUNT ON

         SELECT RoleName, FirstName, LastName
           FROM ENTUserAccount
RIGHT OUTER JOIN ENTRoleUserAccount
             ON ENTUserAccount.ENTUserAccountId =
                ENTRoleUserAccount.ENTUserAccountId
RIGHT OUTER JOIN ENTRole
             ON ENTRoleUserAccount.ENTRoleId = ENTRole.ENTRoleId

  RETURN
```

The first stored procedure will be used for the main report; the second will be used by the subreport.

Next, add the two stored procedures as methods to the `DataContext`. Open the `HRPaidTimeOff.dbml` file in the ORM Designer and drag the two stored procedures to the Methods pane. This will create the methods in the `DataContext` and create two classes that represent a custom entity object returned from the method. The two classes are called `ReportRoleCapabilityResult` and `ReportRoleUser AccountResult`.

Add a folder under the `Framework` folder in the DAL project that will contain all the data classes used for reporting off of framework tables. Reporting classes do not insert, update, or delete, so they do not inherit from the `ENTBaseData` class. Since there is no object to inherit from and all these classes simply retrieve data, they will be created as static classes and the methods will be static. Add a class to the

Reports folder and name it ReportENTRoleData. This class should be made public and static and should contain the two methods to call the two stored procedures:

```
public static class ReportENTRoleData
{
    public static List<ReportRoleCapabilityResult> SelectCapabilities()
    {
        using (HRPaidTimeOffDataContext db = new
            HRPaidTimeOffDataContext(DBHelper.GetHRPaidTimeOffConnectionString()))
        {
            return db.ReportRoleCapability().ToList();
        }
    }

    public static List<ReportRoleUserAccountResult> SelectUserAccounts()
    {
        using (HRPaidTimeOffDataContext db = new
            HRPaidTimeOffDataContext(DBHelper.GetHRPaidTimeOffConnectionString()))
        {
            return db.ReportRoleUserAccount().ToList();
        }
    }
}
```

The data layer is complete, so the next step is to create the business class.

Again, create a folder under the Framework folder in the BLL project and call it Reports. Add a class to the Reports folder and name it ReportENTRole. The report classes will be different from the other business class because it only acts as a pass-through between the UI and the DAL. The data retrieved from the DAL will not be traversed through and added to a list of business objects. Instead, the raw data retrieved from the DAL is passed back to the UI. There is one change, though: The data is returned from the DAL as a list of entity objects. The entity objects are defined in the DAL and if the UI calls a method in the BLL that returns an object defined in the DAL, then it would need a reference to the DAL, which isn't allowed. To get around this, the business layer passes back the data as an array of type object. The object array can then be bound to the Crystal Reports. Here is the code for the business class:

```
public static class ReportENTRole
{
    public static object[] SelectCapabilities()
    {
        return ReportENTRoleData.SelectCapabilities().ToArray();
    }

    public static object[] SelectUserAccounts()
    {
        return ReportENTRoleData.SelectUserAccounts().ToArray();
    }
}
```

Notice that this class is static, as no object state is needed.

Now that the business object is defined you can create the UI. This gets a little tricky when defining the report because you cannot connect to the database when designing the report. Instead, when you create a report in a three-layered environment, you need to create a schema file that represents the fields returned from the database. This schema file acts as a placeholder for where the real fields will be located in the data source for the report. You'll never actually use the schema file for anything but design-time support for the report. However, you can create a typed dataset, load it with data, and bind that to a report — but that would bypass the DAL so that option isn't shown here.

Add another folder under the Reports folder in the UI project and call the folder **Schemas**. Right-click on the Schemas folder and select Add New Item from the pop-up menu. Choose Dataset for the type of file, name the file ReportRoleCapability.xsd, and click the Add button. You'll get a message saying that you should add this type of file to the App_Code folder but you should ignore this message and click No. This will add the file to the project and open the schema file in the designer. Drag a TableAdapter from the toolbox to the design surface. This will bring up the TableAdapter Configuration Wizard. The first screen asks which connection string to use. Select the connection string in the web.config file for the HRPaidTimeOff database and click Next. The next screen asks you to choose the Command Type (see Figure 9-27).

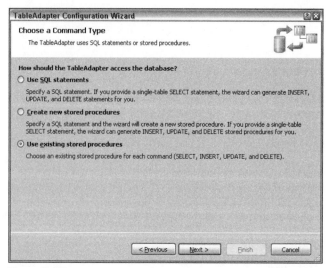

Figure 9-27

Choose the option "Use existing stored procedures" and click Next. The next screen enables you to choose which stored procedure should be used for the Select method of the DataSet (see Figure 9-28).

Select the ReportRoleCapability stored procedure from the list and click Next. The next screen, shown in Figure 9-29, asks you to name the methods for the Table Adapter that will fill this DataSet. Since this DataSet is only being used as a placeholder (to enable the report to know what the schema looks like), you do not need this method.

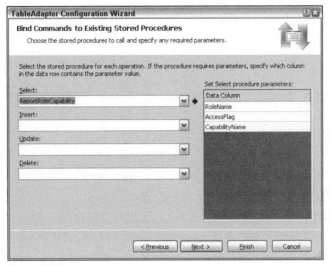

Figure 9-28

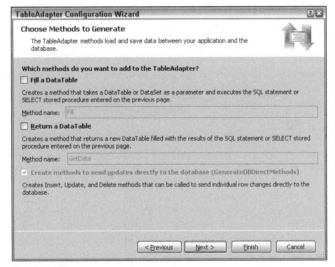

Figure 9-29

Uncheck the Fill a DataTable and Return a DataTable options and click the Next button. You'll get a message saying that only the DataTable will be created, which is exactly what you want, so click OK. The Wizard Result screen will appear. Click Finish to create the DataSet for the stored procedure. Repeat the same steps to create a new DataSet for the ReportRoleUserAccount stored procedure.

Now you can create the Crystal Reports. Right-click on the `Reports` folder and add a new Crystal Reports file called `Roles3Layer.rpt`. The Crystal Reports Gallery dialog will appear. Select Using the Report Wizard and click OK. The next screen prompts you for the location of the data. Click the plus sign next to Create New Connection, and then click the plus sign next to ADO.NET.

You may be prompted at this point to choose the location of the schema file; if not, double-click on the Make New Connection node (see Figure 9-30).

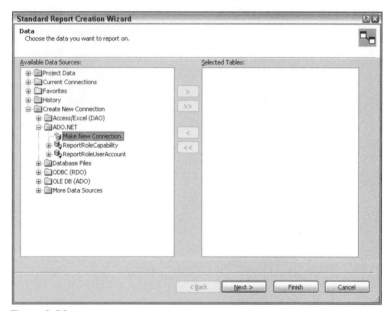

Figure 9-30

The Connection window should appear. All you need to do is select the `ReportRoleCapability.xsd` file you just created and then click Finish (see Figure 9-31).

This will add the ReportRoleCapability node under the ADO.NET node. Select the ReportRoleCapability node and click the button to move the object to the Selected Tables list. Click Next. This enables you to select the available fields for the report. Select the `CapabilityName` field and click the arrow button to move it to the Fields to Display list. Click Next. The next screen enables you to select the grouping fields. Select the `RoleName` field and click the arrow button to move the field to the Group By list. Click Next. The next screen enables you to add summaries but this report doesn't have any so just click Next.

Although you can filter report records from the next screen, just click Next without adding any filters. The next screen enables you to select a style for the report. Select Standard and click Finish. This will display the report in design view. You can treat this report the same way as defined earlier when the report was "connected" to the database.

Repeat the preceding steps to add the headers, the footers, and the `AccessFlagText` formula field. Once that is done, you can add the subreport to the GroupFooterSection1 section just as you did before. The only difference this time is that when you create the subreport, you need to add a connection to the `RoleUserAccount.xsd` file. Other than that, everything is done the exact same way.

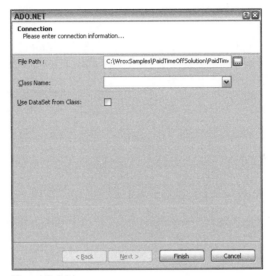

Figure 9-31

Now that the report is created, you need to create the viewer page to display the report. Add a new page to the `Reports` folder in the UI project called `ReportView3Layer.aspx`. This should not use a master page. Now add the following `using` directives:

```
using CrystalDecisions.CrystalReports.Engine;
using CrystalDecisions.Shared;
using V2.PaidTimeOffBLL.Framework.Reports;
```

In the `Page_Load` event, add the following:

```
ReportDocument report = new ReportDocument();
report.Load(Server.MapPath("Roles3Layer.rpt"));
```

```
//Get the data
report.SetDataSource(ReportENTRole.SelectCapabilities());
```

```
report.Subreports[0].SetDataSource(ReportENTRole.SelectUserAccounts());
```

```
report.ExportToHttpResponse(ExportFormatType.WordForWindows, Response, false, "");
```

The only difference between this page and the other viewer page is that the data for the report is associated with the report by calling the `SetDataSource` method. This method can take a `DataSet`, a `DataTable`, an object that implements `IDataReader`, or an object that implements `IEnumerable`. Since our business layer returns an array of objects, this method works. Set this page as the startup page for the project and run the solution. You should get the exact same report that was displayed when the report was connected to the database. A lot of steps were included in this section, so if it didn't work you can view the sample code for this chapter and copy the code from there.

Solution

Now that a pattern is defined for generating reports, let's create a report in the Paid Time Off solution that enables users to print a listing of their requests. The My Requests report, shown in Figure 9-32, will display a list of all requests for the current user.

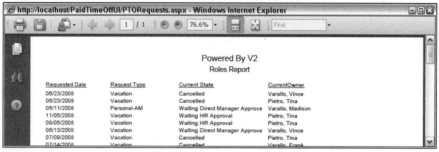

Figure 9-32

This is similar to the View My Requests page created in Chapter 7, and in fact that is the page from which users should be able to print this report. Start by creating the stored procedure that will retrieve this data. You might assume that the query already exists because a page already displays this data but the object that populates the grid is not denormalized, so a new stored procedure needs to be created that denormalizes the data in order for it to be used as a data source for the report. The stored procedure must accept a user account ID, and must know which workflow to join to because the query has to display the current state and current owner of the request. Remember that an application can have more than one workflow and the object name is unique across workflows, so you can use that to determine which records in the ENTWFItem table belong to this workflow:

```
CREATE PROCEDURE ReportMyPTORequests
(
    @ENTWorkflowObjectName varchar(255),
    @ENTUserAccountId int
)
AS
    SET NOCOUNT ON

    SELECT ENTUserAccount.LastName, ENTUserAccount.FirstName,
           PTORequest.RequestDate, PTODayType.PTODayTypeName,
           PTORequestType.PTORequestTypeName,
           ENTWFState.StateName AS CurrentState,
           CurrentOwner.LastName AS CurrentOwnerLastName,
           CurrentOwner.FirstName AS CurrentOwnerFirstName
      FROM ENTWorkflow
INNER JOIN ENTWFItem ON ENTWorkflow.ENTWorkflowId = ENTWFItem.ENTWorkflowId
INNER JOIN PTORequest
INNER JOIN PTODayType ON PTORequest.PTODayTypeId = PTODayType.PTODayTypeId
INNER JOIN PTORequestType ON PTORequest.PTORequestTypeId =
           PTORequestType.PTORequestTypeId
        ON ENTWFItem.ItemId = PTORequest.PTORequestId
INNER JOIN ENTUserAccount ON PTORequest.ENTUserAccountId =
           ENTUserAccount.ENTUserAccountId
```

```
        INNER JOIN ENTWFState ON ENTWFItem.CurrentWFStateId = ENTWFState.ENTWFStateId
        INNER JOIN ENTWFItemOwner ON ENTWFState.ENTWFOwnerGroupId =
                ENTWFItemOwner.ENTWFOwnerGroupId
            AND ENTWFItem.ENTWFItemId = ENTWFItemOwner.ENTWFItemId
        INNER JOIN ENTUserAccount AS CurrentOwner ON ENTWFItemOwner.ENTUserAccountId =
                CurrentOwner.ENTUserAccountId
            WHERE PTORequest.ENTUserAccountId = @ENTUserAccountId
            AND ENTWorkflowObjectName = @ENTWorkflowObjectName

        RETURN
```

Notice that the `CurrentState` and `CurrentOwner` fields are pulled from the `ENTWFState` and `ENTUserAccount` tables but aliased in the `Select` clause to clearly indicate what is being returned from the query. The field names in the `Select` clause should match the schema, and this will be built for the report. After the stored procedure is created, add the method to the `DataContext` by dragging it to the Methods pane in the ORM Designer.

Next, add the DAL class that will call this stored procedure. This report is specific to the Paid Time Off application, so it should not be a part of the framework reports. Create a new folder directly under the `PaidTimeOffDAL` project called `Reports` that will contain all the data classes for reports that are not part of the framework. Add a new class to the `Reports` folder and name it `ReportMyPTORequestsData`. Change the class declaration so it is public and static and add the following method:

```
public static class ReportMyPTORequestsData
{
  public static List<ReportMyPTORequestsResult> Select(string
      entWorkflowObjectName, int entUserAccountId)
  {
    using (HRPaidTimeOffDataContext db = new
           HRPaidTimeOffDataContext(DBHelper.GetHRPaidTimeOffConnectionString()))
    {
      return db.ReportMyPTORequests(entWorkflowObjectName,
                              entUserAccountId).ToList();
    }
  }
}
```

The `ReportMyPTORequestsResult` class was created automatically when you used the ORM Designer to create the method on the `DataContext`.

Now create the business class that will call this method and pass the data back to the UI. Create a new folder in the `PaidTimeOffBLL` project and name it `Reports`. Add a new class to this folder and name it `ReportMyPTORequests`. It should be declared as public and static, and the following method should be added:

```
public static class ReportMyPTORequests
{
 public static object[] Select(int entUserAccountId)
 {
   return ReportMyPTORequestsData.Select(typeof(PTORequestEO).AssemblyQualifiedName,
                            entUserAccountId).ToArray();
 }
}
```

The `PTORequestEO` object is the base object for this workflow, so its fully qualified assembly name should be passed as the `entWorkflowObjectName` parameter.

Next, create the schema for the report. Add a new `DataSet` file to the `Reports/Schemas` folder in the `PaidTimeOffUI` project. Name the file `ReportMyPTORequest.xsd`. Drag a `TableAdapter` object from the toolbar onto the designer and go through the wizard to use the `ReportMyPTORequests` stored procedure as the `Select` method for the `DataSet` as defined above. Remember to uncheck the boxes to generate the `Fill` and `GetData` methods when running through the wizard. This `DataSet` will only be used as a placeholder for the report to know what fields are in the data source. The `DataSet` should look like the one shown in Figure 9-33.

Figure 9-33

The next step is to add the report file:

1. Add a new Crystal Reports file to the `Reports` folder and name the file `MyPTORequests.rpt`. When the Crystal Reports Gallery wizard appears, choose the As a Blank Report option and click the OK button.

2. Right-click on any white space in the report and select Database ⇨ Database Expert from the pop-up menu.

3. Expand the Create New Connection node and then expand the ADO.NET node. This will bring up a dialog that enables you to select the schema file you just created.

4. Enter the file path to the `ReportMyPTORequest.xsd` file and leave all the other fields blank.

5. Click the Finish button. The `ReportMyPTORequest` object will appear in the Available Data Sources list.

6. Click the arrow button to move the object to the list of Selected Tables and then click the OK button.

The fields in the `DataSet` now appear in the Field Explorer window and you can start dragging fields to the appropriate section in the report. Figure 9-34 shows how the report should look in design mode.

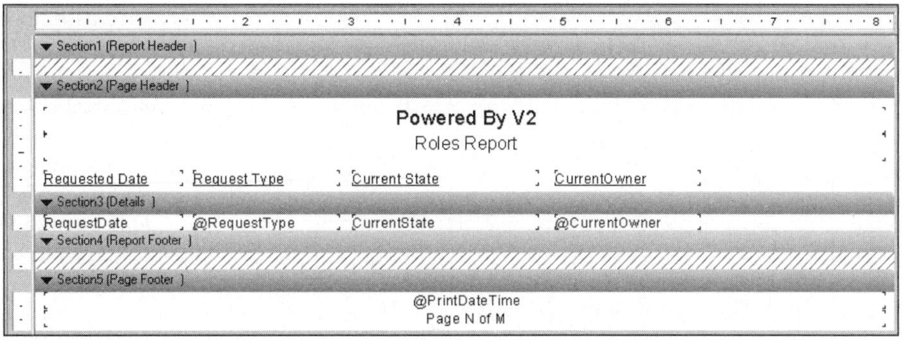

Figure 9-34

Notice the two formula fields in the details section. You can always tell which fields are formula fields because they begin with the @ sign. You have to add these two formulas before dragging them onto the report. To create the two formula fields, right-click on the Formula Fields node in the Field Explorer and select New. Enter the name of the formula and click the Use Editor button. The @RequestType formula is as follows:

```
if {ReportMyPTORequests.PTODayTypeName} = 'Full' then
    {ReportMyPTORequests.PTORequestTypeName}
else
    {ReportMyPTORequests.PTORequestTypeName} + '-' +
        {ReportMyPTORequests.PTODayTypeName}
```

This formula will indicate whether the request is for a full day or a half day, and whether it is a personal or vacation request. The @CurrentOwner formula is as follows.

```
{ReportMyPTORequests.CurrentOwnerLastName} + ', ' +
{ReportMyPTORequests.CurrentOwnerFirstName}
```

This formula displays the current owner's last name and first name separated by a comma. The rest of the fields can be added as defined in the Design section of this chapter.

Now that you have the report, the business classes, the data classes, and the stored procedure, you need to add a place for the user to print the report. The View My Request page is the best place to add this report since users will already be looking at a grid of their requests. This page uses the `PaidTimeOffEditGrid` master page, and in fact all pages that inherit from this page will most likely need print functionality. Therefore, the Print button can be added to the edit grid master page and hidden by default so that each individual page can either show or hide the Print button.

Open the `PaidTimeOffEditGrid` master page and add a new button named `btnPrint` to the right of the Add New button. Set its `Visibility` property to false. Set the `OnClick` attribute to `btnPrint_Click` and create the event handler. The HTML should look like this:

```
<table>
  <tr>
    <td>
      <asp:Button ID="btnAddNew" runat="server" Text="Add New"
                  click="btnAddNew_Click" />
    </td>
    <td>
      <asp:Button ID="btnPrint" runat="server" Text="Print" Visible="false"
                  OnClick="btnPrint_Click" />
    </td>
  </tr>
</table>
```

Open the code-behind for this page and add an event declaration to the class. This event will be used by any page that uses this master page and needs to catch the Print button's click event:

```
public event ButtonClickedHandler PrintButton_Click;
```

Now add the event handler code:

```
protected void btnPrint_Click(object sender, EventArgs e)
{
    if (PrintButton_Click != null)
    {
        PrintButton_Click(sender, e);
    }
}
```

The last step is to add a property that enables the child pages to reference the Print button and set its `Visibility` property:

```
public Button btnPrintRef()
{
    return btnPrint;
}
```

Now the master page displays the Print button but you need to add code to the `PTORequests.aspx` page to handle the special logic for the My Requests report. Open the code-behind page for the `PTORequests.aspx` page. Add the following `using` directives for the Crystal Reports objects and the new `Report` class you just created in the business layer:

```
using CrystalDecisions.CrystalReports.Engine;
using CrystalDecisions.Shared;
using V2.PaidTimeOffBLL.Reports;
```

Next, hook the Print button's click event in the master page to an event handler in this page. Add the following code to the `Page_Load` event:

```
Master.PrintButton_Click += new
    PaidTimeOffEditGrid.ButtonClickedHandler(Master_PrintButton_Click);
```

This works like the Add button's click event. As you type this text in Visual Studio, it will prompt you to automatically generate the event hander declaration. Indicate yes so the code is built for you. There is one more change to the `Page_Load` event: Make the Print button visible. Remember that by default it is hidden because all the other pages do not have print functionality yet:

```
Master.btnPrintRef().Visible = true;
```

Now add the code to the Print button's event handler:

```
void Master_PrintButton_Click(object sender, EventArgs e)
    {
        ReportDocument report = new ReportDocument();
        report.Load(Server.MapPath("Reports/MyPTORequests.rpt"));

        //Get the data
        report.SetDataSource(ReportMyPTORequests.Select(CurrentUser.ID));

        report.ExportToHttpResponse(ExportFormatType.PortableDocFormat, Response,
            false, "");
    }
```

This is very simple. All you need to do is create an instance of the Crystal Reports object, set its `DataSource` to the data returned by the business class, and then export the report in PDF format to the response object.

If you run the project, navigate to the View My Requests page, and click the Print button, the report should appear in the browser as a PDF. However, this isn't exactly what you want. The report should actually appear in a new window, and the current page should remain in the browser. This can be accomplished with a little bit of JavaScript magic. The Print button should call the `window.open` method but the logic to print the report is in the Print button's event handler in server-side code. You could create a new page that contains this logic in its page load event to load the report, but then you would have to create a new page for every report you want to print. You also wouldn't be able to pass data to the page easily. You would have to use the query string to pass in the parameters of the report.

There is a much cleaner solution. This solution opens a new window and passes in a "Please Wait" page as the source. The postback still occurs and the event handler in the page fires, but the target is changed so that the output of the click event is actually rendered in the new window. To accomplish this, create JavaScript in the `BasePage` class, as any page that needs to be printed can create the script, and add it to a button's `onclick` attribute. Here is the code that generates the JavaScript:

```
public string GetPrintButtonScript(Button btn)
{
    StringBuilder printButtonScript = new StringBuilder();
```

```
        //Get the postback script.
        string postback = this.Page.ClientScript.GetPostBackEventReference(btn, "");

        //Change target to a new window.  Name the window the current date and time so
        //multiple windows can be opened.
        printButtonScript.Append("var today = new Date();");
        printButtonScript.Append("var newWindowName = today.getFullYear().toString() +
           today.getMonth().toString() + today.getDate().toString() +
           today.getHours().toString() + today.getHours().toString() +
           today.getMinutes().toString() + today.getSeconds().toString() +
           today.getMilliseconds().toString();");

        printButtonScript.Append("document.forms[0].target = newWindowName;");

        //Show the please wait screen.
        printButtonScript.Append("window.open('Reports/PleaseWait.html', newWindowName,
                           'scrollbars=yes,status=no,resizable=yes');");

        //Add the postback script.
        printButtonScript.Append(postback + ";");

        //Reset target back to itself so other controls will post back to this form.
        printButtonScript.Append("document.forms[0].target='_self';");

        printButtonScript.Append("return false;" + Environment.NewLine);

        return printButtonScript.ToString();
    }
```

This method enables you to pass in any button to generate the script, and returns the string that should be added to the button's `onclick` attribute. To add a script to the button's attribute, add the following code in the `Page_Load` event:

```
    Master.btnPrintRef().Attributes.Add("onclick",
        GetPrintButtonScript(Master.btnPrintRef()));
```

Let's review the entire script to see what is going on here. The first line receives a string that the JavaScript can call to mimic the postback that the Print button's click event would normally do. Remember that the postback events are actually just JavaScript functions that the ASP.NET framework adds to the page when it is rendered.

The next step begins to build a string that is essentially a bunch of JavaScript commands that you want to run when the button is clicked. The next line creates a date variable and then creates a string that consists of the current date, to the millisecond. This string is used as the new window's name. The date is used because if the user clicks the button more than once, it should open in a new window, not the same window as before. The window's name is stored in the `newWindowName` variable and passed into the `window.open` method.

The next line is where the magic happens. The target of the current form is changed to the new window. This allows the postback event to fire but the response is actually sent back to the new window. The next line opens the new `PleaseWait.html` page, which is just a plain HTML page. This will appear as the report is being generated and then it is replaced by the PDF document when the report is sent back as the response. The next line appends the postback call to the script so that after the window is opened, the page actually posts back to the server and the Print button's click event fires. The next line sets the target back to itself. This is very important because if you have any other controls on the form that post back to the server, they would post to the new window. Setting the target back to _self avoids that problem.

Add a new HTML page named PleaseWait.html to the project and add some text to let users know that processing is occurring. If you added the GetPrintButtonScript method to the BasePage class and added the line in the Page_Load event to call this script, you should have the desired result. Run the project again and click the Print button. This time the report should appear in a separate window. If you click the Print button again it should appear in another new window. If you click the Make New Request button, it should redirect to the new page in the same window (see Figure 9-35).

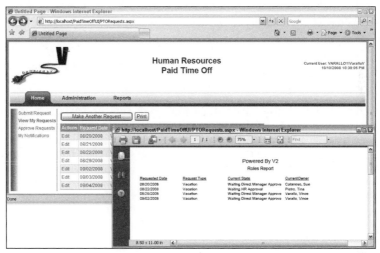

Figure 9-35

Summary

This chapter described a pattern for creating reports within an enterprise-level application. The Crystal Reports for .NET objects are a great add-on to Visual Studio that enable you to easily generate reports in any application, and the Crystal Reports designer enables you to customize nearly every aspect of the report. The Crystal object model enables you to manipulate the report at runtime. You can change groups, sorting, selection formulas, formula fields, and almost any aspect of the report. It is definitely a top-notch tool when it comes to reporting.

The steps to create a Crystal Reports are as follows:

❑   Create a stored procedure with a denormalized view of the data.

❑   Add the stored procedure to the methods of the DataContext object.

❑   Create a data class in the DAL to call the DataContext's method.

❑ Create a business class in the BLL to call the Data class. This class should return the data as an object array.

❑ Create a DataSet in the UI layer that will be used as the placeholder for the fields in the report. The dataset will never be used at runtime — it is merely a schema that the report designer needs to enable you to design the report.

❑ Add a Crystal Reports file to the project and use the schema as the database source.

❑ Add a button or use a button on a master page to display the report. The button's onclick attribute should call the GetPrintButtonScript method in the BasePage class to show the report in a new window correctly.

❑ Add code to the Print button's OnClick event to create the report object, load the report file, set its data source, and send the report back as a PDF to the Response object.

When I showed Mary the My Request report and the Role report she was quite happy; but like most clients, she wanted more. Her immediate reaction was to ask for a whole slew of new reports. She now wants a report that displays a list of outstanding requests, a report that shows the requests by current owner, and a report of approved requests. After talking it over with her for a few moments, I figured out that she wants the same report each time, but that the criteria for each report are different.

This leads into the next chapter, which creates a server-side control that enables a user to dynamically create a where clause that can be applied to a report or even a List object. The QueryBuilder control is specifically designed to address Mary's new need: the same report with different criteria. The control is smart enough to handle ANDs and ORs and even predecessors. It can save you a lot of time when it comes to reports and lists of data, and it gives users a lot of flexibility when using your application.

10

The Query Builder Control

When dealing with data, some common features eventually make their way into most systems. Data often needs to be presented in a table-like fashion on the screen, displayed in a report, or exported to a file in a standard format such as .csv or Excel. When displaying data in a table, users often have to page through data to find specific records. When displaying data in a report, users can use Find or Search functionality in the report viewer to find exactly what they are looking for. In many cases, users are directed to export the data from the system to Excel and then muck around with the rows and columns to filter the data they are looking for. I tend to think of HTML tables, reports, and exports as different interfaces wrapped on top of the exact same business objects that retrieve the data. All of these processes need to pull data from the database and display it to the user in different forms. The business layer doesn't really care what format the data is in. It just needs to serve it back in a way that the user interface can understand, and users often need the capability to present the data in the same fashion, but filter it differently.

Problem

In the Paid Time Off application, Mary liked the My PTO Requests report built in the previous chapter, but then asked for the same data to be displayed in an Outstanding Requests report, a Current Owner report, and an Approved Requests report. The Outstanding Requests report can be considered the same report but with requests that have a status not equal to Approved, Denied, or Cancelled. The Current Owner report displays the same columns but the report is filtered on the current owner of the request. The Approved Requests report displays the same columns but has a filter such that the status of the requests is equal to Approved. Wouldn't it be great if you had a control that you could place on a page that enabled users to build a filter to be applied to the data before it is displayed in an HTML table, report, or export so you wouldn't have to spend time writing the same code over and over again? Well, that is exactly what this chapter is going to build.

This chapter will build a server-side control that enables users to dynamically build a filter for any data, and use AND\OR logic and even predecessor logic. The control will also incorporate ASP.NET AJAX to dynamically populate drop-down lists and list boxes as the user is defining the query. You'll also learn how to create your own custom attributes that can decorate a class to describe the metadata about the class. This is how field names can be displayed as "friendly" names to the user.

Design

Figure 10-1 shows a screen shot of the query builder control that we are going to create.

Figure 10-1

The first control is a drop-down list of all the fields the user can query by. The second drop-down list contains a list of comparison operators such as Equals, Not Equals, Is In List, Is Not In List, Greater Than, Greater Than or Equal To, Less Than, Less Than Or Equal To, Is Blank, and Is Not Blank. The comparison operators are converted into syntax that the database understands. For example, Not Equals converts to <> and Is Blank converts to `Is NULL`. The third drop-down list contains the list of data that is in the Select a Field drop-down list. If the comparison operator is "Is In List" or "Is Not In List," then this is displayed as a list box. You populate the data in this list by making an ASP.NET AJAX call back to the server after the user has selected the field and comparison.

This gets a little tricky because when the screen posts back, it can take some time to fill the list. Therefore, a "Please Wait" modal dialog is displayed while the processing is occurring on the server. The modal dialog is an extender control that can be found in the ASP.NET AJAX Control Toolkit, which can be downloaded free at `www.codeplex.com/AjaxControlToolkit/Release/ProjectReleases.aspx?Release Id=16488`. The buttons after the drop-down lists are used to add the filter to the Filters To Apply list box. Users can add an `AND` or an `OR` clause, remove a line, or add or remove parentheses. The dynamic `AND` and `OR` functionality makes this control very powerful. The Filters To Apply list box simply displays the filters that will be applied to the data returned to the user interface. Again, the UI can be a report, an HTML table, or an export file, and the control can be placed on any page and applied to any business object that supports querying.

ENTBaseQueryData

So far, most of the queries that retrieve data from the database have been in stored procedures. This takes advantage of pre-compilation and optimizes the execution path. When it comes to building a custom `whereClause`, the advantages of stored procedures become less valuable. You essentially have to convert the SQL statement in the stored procedure to a varchar variable and then append the where clause. You then call EXEC or sp_executesql and pass in the SQL statement to execute the query. One problem is that you lose the pre-compiled functionality of stored procedures.

Another consideration that you must take into account is the functionality of the query builder control that fills the drop-down list with data. The main query that returns the data has a Select clause containing all the fields that are passed back to the report or HTML table. When querying for a specific field, only that field needs to be returned from the database. The SQL statement's From clause should be the same, so the application needs to be able to pull out specific pieces of the base SQL statement and execute them in pieces. For these reasons, the SQL statement will not be in a stored procedure but instead built dynamically in the data access layer.

In order to create common functionality for all Data classes that need to support dynamic querying, a base class needs to be created. Add a new class to the Framework folder in the V2.PaidTimeOffDAL project and name the class ENTBaseQueryData. Add the following code to the class:

```
public abstract class ENTBaseQueryData<T>
{
    protected abstract string SelectClause();

    protected abstract string FromClause();

    public List<LookupData> GetLookup(string lookupFieldName, string valueField)
    {
        using (HRPaidTimeOffDataContext db = new
            HRPaidTimeOffDataContext(DBHelper.GetHRPaidTimeOffConnectionString()))
        {
            return db.ExecuteQuery<LookupData>("SELECT DISTINCT " + lookupFieldName
                    + " AS Text, " + valueField + " AS Value " +
                    FromClause(), new Object[] { }).ToList();
        }
    }

    public List<T> Run(string whereClause)
    {
        using (HRPaidTimeOffDataContext db = new
            HRPaidTimeOffDataContext(DBHelper.GetHRPaidTimeOffConnectionString()))
        {
            return db.ExecuteQuery<T>(SelectClause() + FromClause() + whereClause,
                    new Object[] { }).ToList();
        }
    }
}
```

This is an abstract class that has two abstract methods. The first abstract method is called SelectClause. An object that inherits from this class should implement this method and simply return the Select clause that should be used in the SQL statement. The same is true for the FromClause method except this method should only return the From clause of the SQL statement.

The next method, called GetLookup, is used to retrieve all the data for a specific field. This method enables you to pass in two field names: one for the field that will be displayed to the user and one that will be used to capture the value for the displayed data. For example, you would want to display the text for the request's current status but when you query the database you want to query by the ID because it will be faster. This method passes back a generic list of a new class called `LookupData`. This class is defined later in this chapter. Notice that the `GetLookup` method uses the `From` clause that will be defined in the implementing class.

The next method, `Run`, is used to concatenate the `Select`, `From`, and `Where` clauses together and execute them against the database. This method returns a generic `List` object. The generic object should be an entity object in the data layer that is passed back to the business layer.

Now that the base class is defined, let's go back to the `ReportMyPTORequestsData` class used in the previous chapter to create the My PTO Requests report:

```
public static class ReportMyPTORequestsData
{
  public static List<ReportMyPTORequestsResult> Select(string
    entWorkflowObjectName, int entUserAccountId)
  {
    using (HRPaidTimeOffDataContext db = new
           HRPaidTimeOffDataContext(DBHelper.GetHRPaidTimeOffConnectionString()))
    {
      return db.ReportMyPTORequests(entWorkflowObjectName,
             entUserAccountId).ToList();
    }
  }
}
```

This class calls a stored procedure and returns the result in a generic `List` object. The SQL in the stored procedure is listed here:

```
    SELECT  ENTUserAccount.LastName, ENTUserAccount.FirstName,
            PTORequest.RequestDate, PTODayType.PTODayTypeName,
            PTORequestType.PTORequestTypeName, ENTWFState.StateName AS CurrentState,
            CurrentOwner.LastName AS CurrentOwnerLastName, CurrentOwner.FirstName AS
            CurrentOwnerFirstName
      FROM  ENTWorkflow
INNER JOIN  ENTWFItem ON ENTWorkflow.ENTWorkflowId = ENTWFItem.ENTWorkflowId
INNER JOIN  PTORequest
INNER JOIN  PTODayType ON PTORequest.PTODayTypeId = PTODayType.PTODayTypeId
INNER JOIN  PTORequestType ON PTORequest.PTORequestTypeId =
            PTORequestType.PTORequestTypeId
        ON  ENTWFItem.ItemId = PTORequest.PTORequestId
INNER JOIN  ENTUserAccount ON PTORequest.ENTUserAccountId =
            ENTUserAccount.ENTUserAccountId
INNER JOIN  ENTWFState ON ENTWFItem.CurrentWFStateId = ENTWFState.ENTWFStateId
INNER JOIN  ENTWFItemOwner ON ENTWFState.ENTWFOwnerGroupId =
            ENTWFItemOwner.ENTWFOwnerGroupId
       AND  ENTWFItem.ENTWFItemId = ENTWFItemOwner.ENTWFItemId
INNER JOIN  ENTUserAccount AS CurrentOwner ON ENTWFItemOwner.ENTUserAccountId =
            CurrentOwner.ENTUserAccountId
     WHERE  PTORequest.ENTUserAccountId = @ENTUserAccountId
       AND  ENTWorkflowObjectName = @ENTWorkflowObjectName
```

This will be the basis for the SQL in the new data class that supports dynamic queries. Add a new class to the `Reports` folder in the `V2.PaidTimeOffDAL` project and name the class `ReportPTORequests QueryData`. Change the class declaration so it is public and inherits from the `ENTBaseQueryData` class. Implement the `SelectClause` and `FromClause` abstract methods by chopping the stored procedure's SQL statement as follows:

```
public class ReportPTORequestsQueryData :
    ENTBaseQueryData<ReportMyPTORequestsResult>
{
  protected override string SelectClause()
  {
    return "SELECT ENTUserAccount.LastName, ENTUserAccount.FirstName, " +
           " PTORequest.RequestDate, PTODayType.PTODayTypeName, "  +
           " PTORequestType.PTORequestTypeName, ENTWFState.StateName AS " +
           " CurrentState, CurrentOwner.LastName AS CurrentOwnerLastName, " +
           " CurrentOwner.FirstName AS CurrentOwnerFirstName ";
  }

  protected override string FromClause()
  {
    return "FROM ENTWorkflow " +
    "INNER JOIN ENTWFItem ON ENTWorkflow.ENTWorkflowId = ENTWFItem.ENTWorkflowId " +
    "INNER JOIN PTORequest " +
    "INNER JOIN PTODayType ON PTORequest.PTODayTypeId = PTODayType.PTODayTypeId " +
    "INNER JOIN PTORequestType ON PTORequest.PTORequestTypeId = " +
             " PTORequestType.PTORequestTypeId " +
            "ON ENTWFItem.ItemId = PTORequest.PTORequestId " +
    "INNER JOIN ENTUserAccount ON PTORequest.ENTUserAccountId = " +
             " ENTUserAccount.ENTUserAccountId " +
    "INNER JOIN ENTWFState ON ENTWFItem.CurrentWFStateId =ENTWFState.ENTWFStateId" +
    "INNER JOIN ENTWFItemOwner ON ENTWFState.ENTWFOwnerGroupId = " +
             " ENTWFItemOwner.ENTWFOwnerGroupId " +
           "AND ENTWFItem.ENTWFItemId = ENTWFItemOwner.ENTWFItemId " +
    "INNER JOIN ENTUserAccount AS CurrentOwner ON ENTWFItemOwner.ENTUserAccountId="+
             " CurrentOwner.ENTUserAccountId ";
  }
}
```

The next part gets interesting. The user interface needs to know which fields are available for this query, a friendly name for each field, and the type of data in the field. The data layer should be the only layer that knows anything about database fields, so the data class will be responsible for serving this information back to the business layer. To accomplish this, a custom attribute class will be used.

Attributes are special classes that enable you to decorate a class, property, method, enum, and so on with information about the class. When you look at an entity class created by the ORM Designer, you will notice that it is filled with attributes above each class, property, and method. The attributes are the text in the square brackets "[ ]".

The first custom attribute that will be created is called `QueryFieldAttribute`. This attribute is used to decorate the data class with the fields that should be exposed to the user. Since this `QueryFieldAttribute` class isn't really a data class and isn't really a business class, it will be placed in a new project in the solution that will essentially be used like a type library. The new project will then be referenced by the data layer, the business layer, and the user interface.

361

Add a new class library project to the `PaidTimeOffSolution` solution and name the project `V2.Common`. Remove the `Class1.cs` file that was created in the project and add a new class file called `QueryFieldAttribute`. This class should inherit from the `Attribute` class in the .NET Framework. Here is the code for the entire class:

```csharp
[AttributeUsage(AttributeTargets.Class, AllowMultiple = true)]
[Serializable]
public class QueryFieldAttribute : Attribute
{
  public enum QueryFieldTypeEnum
  {
    NotSet,
    String,
    Date,
    Number,
    Boolean,
    Lookup
  }

  public QueryFieldAttribute(string fieldName, string friendlyFieldName,
                             QueryFieldTypeEnum fieldType)
  {
    FieldName = fieldName;
    FriendlyFieldName = friendlyFieldName;
    FieldType = fieldType;
  }

  public string FieldName { get; set; }
  public string FriendlyFieldName { get; set; }
  public QueryFieldTypeEnum FieldType { get; set; }
  public string LookupFieldName { get; set; }
}
```

When you create an attribute class, the standard naming convention includes "Attribute" at the end of the class name. When using the class, you only need to refer to the first part of the class name, excluding the word "Attribute." The `QueryFieldAttribute` class has two attributes itself. The first is called `Attribute Usage`. You use this attribute to define how this attribute class can be used. The `AttributeTargets` enumeration enables you to define whether this should be used for a class, a property, an enum, and so on. You can even specify "All," which enables you to use the attribute for anything in a class. You can also optionally specify that this attribute can occur multiple times for the same element it describes. In our case, there will be a `QueryFieldAttribute` for each field that can be queried, so `AllowMultiple` is set to true. The default value is false. This class is also defined as serializable because the control built later in this chapter stores the query fields in the `ViewState` of the page.

The `QueryFieldTypeEnum` enumeration is a custom enumeration that defines the type of the field. Again, the custom control needs to know this to format the data correctly. The next part of the code snippet shows the constructor. Any fields that you consider required should be a parameter in the constructor. For this example, `fieldName`, `friendlyFieldName`, and `fieldType` are required. After these three properties are defined, a fourth optional property is declared, `LookupFieldName`. This property enables you to select the text to be displayed to the user while using the `FieldName` to store the value. This is useful for lookup tables that contain a primary key to a record in a lookup table. That's all that is needed for this class.

If you refer back to the stored procedure for the My PTO Requests report, you'll notice that the Where clause has two fields: ENTUserAccountID and ENTWorkflowObjectName. The ENTWorkflowObject Name is required by this query and users should not be able to choose this. Therefore, a second custom attribute class will be created that defines any required fields and values in the custom query. Add a new class to the V2.Common project and name the class RequiredQueryFieldAttribute:

```
[AttributeUsage(AttributeTargets.Class, AllowMultiple = true)]
[Serializable]
public class RequiredQueryFieldAttribute : Attribute
{
  public RequiredQueryFieldAttribute(string clause)
  {
    Clause = clause;
  }

  public string Clause{ get; set;}
}
```

All you need when defining this attribute is the hard-coded clause that must be part of your query. It may be easier to understand once you see an example. Go back to the V2.PaidTimeOffDAL project and add a reference to the V2.Common project. Open the ReportPTORequestsQueryData class that you just created and add a using directive to reference V2.Common. Add the following custom attributes above the class declaration:

```
[QueryField("CurrentOwner.LastName + ', ' + CurrentOwner.FirstName",
          "Current Owner", QueryFieldAttribute.QueryFieldTypeEnum.String)]
[QueryField("ENTWFState.StateName", "Current State",
          QueryFieldAttribute.QueryFieldTypeEnum.String)]
[QueryField("PTODayType.PTODayTypeName", "Day Type",
          QueryFieldAttribute.QueryFieldTypeEnum.String)]
[QueryField("convert(varchar, PTORequest.RequestDate, 101)", "Request Date",
          QueryFieldAttribute.QueryFieldTypeEnum.Date)]
[QueryField("PTORequestType.PTORequestTypeName", "Request Type",
          QueryFieldAttribute.QueryFieldTypeEnum.String)]
[QueryField("ENTUserAccount.LastName + ', ' + ENTUserAccount.FirstName",
          "Requestor", QueryFieldAttribute.QueryFieldTypeEnum.String)]
[RequiredQueryField("ENTWorkflowObjectName = 'V2.PaidTimeOffBLL.PTORequestEO,
      V2.PaidTimeOffBLL, Version=1.0.0.0, Culture=neutral, PublicKeyToken=null'")]
public class ReportPTORequestsQueryData:ENTBaseQueryData<ReportMyPTORequestsResult>
```

As you can see when referencing the QueryFieldAttribute class, you only need to specify QueryField in the actual attribute tag. The first parameter in the constructor is the field name. The first query field concatenates the current owner's last name and first name and displays this using the "friendly" name Current Owner. This data class enables users to query by six different fields: current owner, current state, day type, request date, request type, and requestor. The field name can be a SQL expression such as a concatenation or in the case of a request date, a custom format. There is one required field, ENTWorkflowObjectName, which has its value set to the name of the PTORequestEO class's fully qualified name.

ENTBaseQueryBO

Now that the data layer has been defined, the business layer can be built. A new base class called `ENTBaseQueryBO` will be created for all classes that need to support querying. Add this new class to the `V2.PaidTimeOffBLL` project. The code is as follows:

```
public class ENTBaseQueryBO<T, R>
        where T : ENTBaseQueryData<R>, new()
{
  public object[] GetCustomAttributes()
  {
    return typeof(T).GetCustomAttributes(false);
  }

  public List<LookupData> GetLookup(string lookupFieldName, string valueField)
  {
    T reportData = new T();
    return reportData.GetLookup(lookupFieldName, valueField);
  }

  public virtual object[] Select(string whereClause)
  {
    T reportData = new T();
    return (object[])(object)reportData.Run(whereClause).ToArray();
  }
}
```

This class has two generics. The first generic, `T`, must be a class that inherits from the `ENTBaseQueryData` class. Essentially, this has to be a class in the data layer that supports querying. The second generic is the type of object that the data class returns. In the preceding example, the `ReportPTORequestQueryData` class returns a list of `ReportMyPTORequestsResult` objects. Remember that the `ReportMyPTORequests Result` object was created in Chapter 9 using the ORM Designer for the `ReportMyPTORequest` stored procedure.

The first method in the `ENTBaseQueryBO` object uses reflection to return an array of custom attributes for the data class. This is how you access the `QueryField` attributes. The next method, `GetLookup`, simply passes the field and value field to the data layer's `GetLookup` method. This always returns a list of `LookupData` objects. The last method is the `Select`, which calls the `Run` method in the data class and passes in the `where` clause. This is the method that will execute the query and return the results to the UI.

Now is a good time to add the `LookupData` class. Because this class is used across layers, like a type library, it should be added to the `V2.Common` project:

```
public class LookupData
{
    public object Text { get; set; }
    public object Value { get; set; }
}
```

This class is very simple and is used to populate drop-down lists and list boxes with the text and the value.

Now that the base class is defined, you need to create the business class that calls the ReportPTORequests QueryData class. Add a new class to the V2.PaidTimeOffBLL project and name it ReportPTORequests. This class should inherit from the ENTBaseQueryBO class:

```
public class ReportPTORequests : ENTBaseQueryBO<ReportPTORequestsQueryData,
                                                ReportMyPTORequestsResult>
{

}
```

Pass in the ReportPTORequestsQueryData class for the first generic class and the ReportMyPTORequests Result class for the second generic class. That's all that is needed for this class. All of the logic is handled in the base class. If you needed to add any special logic you could override the default implementations in the base, but for this example the default is fine.

Query Builder Custom Control

The next step is to create the custom server-side control that enables users to dynamically build the where clause for the query. The reason it is a control is because you can drop this control on any form that needs querying capabilities, such as a report, an HTML table, or an export screen. The control is a composite control that will look like what was shown in Figure 10-1.

Add three references to the V2.FrameworkControls project to AjaxControlToolkit, V2.Common, and System.Web.Extensions. Now add a new server control to the V2.FrameworkControls project and name it QueryBuilder. Remove the code for the default Text property and the RenderContents method. Because this control will be a composite control, it will be built in the CreateChildControls method, rather than the RenderContents method.

Refer to Figure 10-1 again to see how the control is rendered at runtime so you can follow along when building this control. Unless you have a good idea of what the final control looks like, it is hard to conceptualize. The first step is to add member variables for each control:

```
private DropDownList _ddlFields;
private DropDownList _ddlComparison;
private DropDownList _ddlValues;
private ListBox _lstValues;
private ListBox _lstWhereClause;

private Button _btnAdd;
private Button _btnAddAnd;
private Button _btnAddOr;
private Button _btnRemoveLine;
private Button _btnLeftParen;
private Button _btnRightParen;
private Button _btnRemoveLeftParen;
private Button _btnRemoveRightParen;

private UpdatePanel _updatePanel;
private Panel _pleaseWaitPanel;
HiddenField _hidDummyField;
private ModalPopupExtender _mde;
```

_ddlFields is a drop-down list that contains the query fields defined in the data class. _ddlComparison contains the comparison operators. The _ddlValues and _lstValues represent a drop-down list or a list box of the values in the database for the selected field. If the comparison operator is "In List" or "Is Not In List," then the list box is shown so the user can select multiple values. The other comparison operators use the drop-down list because only a single value can be selected. The lstWhereClause is a list box that contains the "Filters To Apply" to the data. The buttons are used to add or remove statements to the where clause list box or to add or remove parentheses to the where clause.

Because this control is going to use AJAX to post back to the server to load the drop-down or list box with the values, an UpdatePanel control must be used. The controls must reside inside the UpdatePanel control in order for them to be AJAX enabled.

The next three member variables are specific to an AJAX control called the ModalPopupExtender. This control is found in the ASP.NET AJAX Control Toolkit at www.ASP.net. This control enables you to hook to a panel control that will be displayed modally to the user. As long as the panel is displayed modally, users will not be able to click on any other controls on the form. When the AJAX call is complete, the modal panel is hidden. Normally the ModalPopupExtender control uses a TargetControl such as a button to trigger the panel to be shown, but in this control any drop-down list or button can trigger a postback, so JavaScript will be added to control the modal panel. The _hiddendDummyField is simply a dummy field on the form that is set to the ModalPopupExtender control's TargetControl property because it is a required field. It will never be used. The _pleaseWaitPanel is the panel control that will be shown to the user during postback, and the _mde variable is the ModalPopupExtender control. When the screen posts back using AJAX, it will look like Figure 10-2.

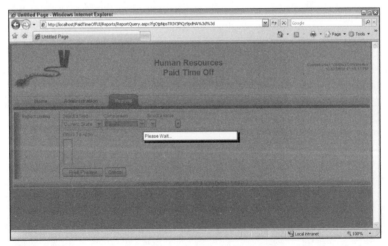

Figure 10-2

Next, add the list of constants that represents the text for the comparison operator drop-down list.

```
private const string COMPARISON_EQUALS = "Equals";
private const string COMPARISON_NOT_EQUALS = "Is Not Equal To";
private const string COMPARISON_IN = "Is In List";
private const string COMPARISON_NOT_IN = "Is Not In List";
private const string COMPARISON_IS_BLANK = "Is Blank";
```

```
private const string COMPARISON_IS_NOT_BLANK = "Is Not Blank";
private const string COMPARISON_IS_GREATER_THAN = "Is Greater Than";
private const string COMPARISON_IS_GREATER_THAN_EQUAL = "Is Greater Than Or Equal
                                                         To";
private const string COMPARISON_IS_LESS_THAN = "Is Less Than";
private const string COMPARISON_IS_LESS_THAN_OR_EQUAL = "Is Less Than Or Equal To";
```

Now you can add the only two properties for this control. The first property, QueryObjectName, must be set to the fully qualified name of the business class. In the preceding example, this is ReportPTORequests:

```
public string QueryObjectName { get; set; }
```

The second property persists the list of query fields returned from the GetCustomAttributes method in the business class to the ViewState. These fields are used to load the drop-down lists and build the where clause behind the scenes:

```
public object[] QueryFields
{
  get
  {
    return (object[])ViewState["QueryFields"];
  }

  set
  {
    ViewState["QueryFields"] = value;
  }
}
```

The next step is to override the CreateChildControls method. This method is used to instantiate the controls and add them to the Controls collection of the custom control:

```
protected override void CreateChildControls()
{
  _updatePanel = new UpdatePanel();

  CreateDropDowns();

  CreateWhereList();

  Controls.Add(_updatePanel);

  CreatePleaseWait();

  base.CreateChildControls();
}
```

This method instantiates the UpdatePanel control and then calls private methods to create all the other controls. These will be added to the UpdatePanel's ContentTemplateContainer.Controls collection. The UpdatePanel is then added to the Controls collection of this control. The Please Wait panel and ModalPopupExtender controls are created outside of the UpdatePanel and simply added to the server control's Controls collection.

The `CreateDropDowns` method creates a `Table` object that contains the drop-downs, the list box, and the button controls. The code is as follows:

```
private void CreateDropDowns()
{
    //Create the table that contains the dropdown lists
    Table tblDropDowns = new Table();
    tblDropDowns.BorderWidth = 1;
    tblDropDowns.CellPadding = 1;
    tblDropDowns.CellSpacing = 1;

    //Add header that contains the text for each column.
    TableRow trHeader = new TableRow();
    TableCell tcField = new TableCell();
    tcField.Text = "Select a field";
    trHeader.Cells.Add(tcField);

    TableCell tcComparison = new TableCell();
    tcComparison.Text = "Comparison";
    trHeader.Cells.Add(tcComparison);

    TableCell tcValue = new TableCell();
    tcValue.Text = "Select a value";
    trHeader.Cells.Add(tcValue);
    tblDropDowns.Rows.Add(trHeader);

    //Add drop down controls to each column
    TableRow tr = new TableRow();
    tr.VerticalAlign = VerticalAlign.Top;

    TableCell tc1 = new TableCell();
    _ddlFields = new DropDownList();
    _ddlFields.ID = "ddlFields";
    _ddlFields.AutoPostBack = true;
```

Because the _ddlFields control posts back to the server, you have to hook an event handler to the `SelectedIndexChanged` event:

```
    _ddlFields.SelectedIndexChanged += new
        EventHandler(_ddlFields_SelectedIndexChanged);

    tc1.Controls.Add(_ddlFields);
    tr.Cells.Add(tc1);

    TableCell tc2 = new TableCell();
    _ddlComparison = new DropDownList();
    _ddlComparison.ID = "ddlComparison";
    _ddlComparison.AutoPostBack = true;
    _ddlComparison.SelectedIndexChanged += new
        EventHandler(_ddlComparison_SelectedIndexChanged);

    tc2.Controls.Add(_ddlComparison);
    tr.Cells.Add(tc2);
```

```
        TableCell tc3 = new TableCell();
        _ddlValues = new DropDownList();
        _ddlValues.ID = "ddlValues";
        tc3.Controls.Add(_ddlValues);

        _lstValues = new ListBox();
        _lstValues.ID = "lstValues";
        _lstValues.Visible = false;
        _lstValues.SelectionMode = ListSelectionMode.Multiple;
        _lstValues.Rows = 10;
        tc3.Controls.Add(_lstValues);

        tr.Cells.Add(tc3);

        CreateButtons(tr);

        tblDropDowns.Rows.Add(tr);

        _updatePanel.ContentTemplateContainer.Controls.Add(tblDropDowns);
    }
```

This method calls another private method called `CreateButtons` that will add the buttons to the row in the table. Each button is added and hooked to an event handler to handle the button click event:

```
private void CreateButtons(TableRow tr)
{
  //Create the buttons
  TableCell tc1 = new TableCell();
  _btnAdd = new Button();
  _btnAdd.ID = "btnAdd";
  _btnAdd.Text = "+";
  _btnAdd.ToolTip = "Add to filter";
  _btnAdd.Click += new EventHandler(_btnAdd_Click);
  tc1.Controls.Add(_btnAdd);
  tr.Cells.Add(tc1);

  TableCell tc2 = new TableCell();
  _btnAddAnd = new Button();
  _btnAddAnd.ID = "btnAddAnd";
  _btnAddAnd.Text = "And";
  _btnAddAnd.ToolTip = "Add And Clause";
  _btnAddAnd.Visible = false;
  _btnAddAnd.Click += new EventHandler(_btnAddAnd_Click);
  tc2.Controls.Add(_btnAddAnd);
  tr.Cells.Add(tc2);

  TableCell tc3 = new TableCell();
  _btnAddOr = new Button();
  _btnAddOr.ID = "btnAddOr";
  _btnAddOr.Text = "Or";
  _btnAddOr.ToolTip = "Add Or Clause";
  _btnAddOr.Visible = false;
  _btnAddOr.Click += new EventHandler(_btnAddOr_Click);
  tc3.Controls.Add(_btnAddOr);
```

```
        tr.Cells.Add(tc3);

        TableCell tc4 = new TableCell();
        _btnRemoveLine = new Button();
        _btnRemoveLine.ID = "btnRemoveLine";
        _btnRemoveLine.Text = "-";
        _btnRemoveLine.ToolTip = "Remove Line";
        _btnRemoveLine.Visible = false;
        _btnRemoveLine.Click += new EventHandler(_btnRemoveLine_Click);
        tc4.Controls.Add(_btnRemoveLine);
        tr.Cells.Add(tc4);

        TableCell tc5 = new TableCell();
        _btnLeftParen = new Button();
        _btnLeftParen.ID = "btnLeftParen";
        _btnLeftParen.Text = "(";
        _btnLeftParen.ToolTip = "Add Left Parenthesis";
        _btnLeftParen.Visible = false;
        _btnLeftParen.Click += new EventHandler(_btnLeftParen_Click);
        tc5.Controls.Add(_btnLeftParen);
        tr.Cells.Add(tc5);

        TableCell tc6 = new TableCell();
        _btnRightParen = new Button();
        _btnRightParen.ID = "btnRightParen";
        _btnRightParen.Text = ")";
        _btnRightParen.ToolTip = "Add Right Parenthesis";
        _btnRightParen.Visible = false;
        _btnRightParen.Click += new EventHandler(_btnRightParen_Click);
        tc6.Controls.Add(_btnRightParen);
        tr.Cells.Add(tc6);

        TableCell tc7 = new TableCell();
        _btnRemoveLeftParen = new Button();
        _btnRemoveLeftParen.ID = "btnRemoveLeftParen";
        _btnRemoveLeftParen.Text = "(-";
        _btnRemoveLeftParen.ToolTip = "Remove Left Parenthesis";
        _btnRemoveLeftParen.Visible = false;
        _btnRemoveLeftParen.Click += new EventHandler(_btnRemoveLeftParen_Click);
        tc7.Controls.Add(_btnRemoveLeftParen);
        tr.Cells.Add(tc7);

        TableCell tc8 = new TableCell();
        _btnRemoveRightParen = new Button();
        _btnRemoveRightParen.ID = "btnRemoveRightParen";
        _btnRemoveRightParen.Text = ")-";
        _btnRemoveRightParen.ToolTip = "Remove Right Parenthesis";
        _btnRemoveRightParen.Visible = false;
        _btnRemoveRightParen.Click += new EventHandler(_btnRemoveRightParen_Click);
        tc8.Controls.Add(_btnRemoveRightParen);
        tr.Cells.Add(tc8);

    }
```

The CreateChildControls method also calls the CreateWhereList method, which creates the list box that contains the where clause:

```
private void CreateWhereList()
{
    Table tbl = new Table();
    tbl.BorderWidth = 1;

    TableRow tr1 = new TableRow();
    TableCell tc1 = new TableCell();
    tc1.Text = "Filters To Apply";
    tr1.Cells.Add(tc1);
    tbl.Rows.Add(tr1);

    TableRow tr2 = new TableRow();
    TableCell tc2 = new TableCell();
    _lstWhereClause = new ListBox();
    _lstWhereClause.ID = "lstWhereClause";

    tc2.Controls.Add(_lstWhereClause);
    tr2.Cells.Add(tc2);
    tbl.Rows.Add(tr2);

    _updatePanel.ContentTemplateContainer.Controls.Add(tbl);
}
```

CreateChildControls also creates the controls for the Please Wait div to be shown modally in the CreatePleaseWait method:

```
private void CreatePleaseWait()
{
    //Add the please wait panel
    _pleaseWaitPanel = new Panel();
    _pleaseWaitPanel.ID = "pnlPleaseWait";
    _pleaseWaitPanel.Style.Add("display", "none");
    _pleaseWaitPanel.CssClass = "modalPopup";
    _pleaseWaitPanel.Controls.Add(new LiteralControl("Please Wait…"));

    Controls.Add(_pleaseWaitPanel);

    //Add a dummy control for the popup extender
    _hidDummyField = new HiddenField();
    _hidDummyField.ID = "hidDummyField";

    Controls.Add(_hidDummyField);

    //Add the pop up extender.
    _mde = new ModalPopupExtender();
    _mde.ID = "mdePleaseWait";
    _mde.PopupControlID = _pleaseWaitPanel.ID;
    _mde.TargetControlID = _hidDummyField.ID;
    _mde.DropShadow = true;
```

```
    _mde.BackgroundCssClass = "modalBackground";

    Controls.Add(_mde);
}
```

The `_pleaseWaitPanel` uses a style sheet class called `modalPopup` and the `ModalPopupExtender` object sets its background to a style sheet class called `modalBackground`. These two styles are defined as inline styles in the `RenderContents` method:

```
protected override void  RenderContents(HtmlTextWriter writer)
{
    //Add the style
    StringBuilder sb = new StringBuilder();
    sb.Append("<style type='text/css'>" + Environment.NewLine);
    sb.Append(".modalBackground {" + Environment.NewLine);
     sb.Append("    background-color:Gray;" + Environment.NewLine);
     sb.Append("    filter:alpha(opacity=70);" + Environment.NewLine);
     sb.Append("    opacity:0.7;" + Environment.NewLine);
    sb.Append("}" + Environment.NewLine);
    sb.Append(Environment.NewLine);
    sb.Append(".modalPopup {" + Environment.NewLine);
     sb.Append("    background-color:#ffffdd;" + Environment.NewLine);
     sb.Append("    border-width:3px;" + Environment.NewLine);
     sb.Append("    border-style:solid;" + Environment.NewLine);
     sb.Append("    border-color:Gray;" + Environment.NewLine);
     sb.Append("    padding:3px;" + Environment.NewLine);
     sb.Append("    width:250px;" + Environment.NewLine);
    sb.Append("}" + Environment.NewLine);
    sb.Append("</style>");

    writer.Write(sb.ToString());

    base.RenderContents(writer);
}
```

The next step is to override the `OnPreRender` method to create the JavaScript that handles displaying the modal pop-up panel when the screen is posting back:

```
protected override void OnPreRender(EventArgs e)
{
    EnsureChildControls();

    //Add custom java script
    if (Page.ClientScript.IsClientScriptBlockRegistered("PleaseWait") == false)
    {
        StringBuilder sb1 = new StringBuilder();

        sb1.Append("function pageLoad(sender, args){" + Environment.NewLine);
        sb1.Append("Sys.WebForms.PageRequestManager.getInstance().add_beginRequest(
                    beginRequest);" + Environment.NewLine);
        sb1.Append("Sys.WebForms.PageRequestManager.getInstance().add_endRequest(
                    endRequest);" + Environment.NewLine);
        sb1.Append("} " + Environment.NewLine);
        sb1.Append(Environment.NewLine);
        sb1.Append("function beginRequest(sender, args){" + Environment.NewLine);
```

```
            sb1.Append("    var modalPopupBehavior = $find('" + _mde.ClientID + "');" +
                    Environment.NewLine);
            sb1.Append("    modalPopupBehavior.show();" + Environment.NewLine);
            sb1.Append("}" + Environment.NewLine);
            sb1.Append(Environment.NewLine);
            sb1.Append("function endRequest(sender, args) {" + Environment.NewLine);
            sb1.Append("    var modalPopupBehavior = $find('" + _mde.ClientID + "');" +
                    Environment.NewLine);
            sb1.Append("    modalPopupBehavior.hide();" + Environment.NewLine);
            sb1.Append("}" + Environment.NewLine);

            Page.ClientScript.RegisterClientScriptBlock(typeof(Page), "PleaseWait",
                                            sb1.ToString(), true);
        }

        base.OnPreRender(e);
    }
```

When this script is rendered it looks like the following, which is easier to explain:

```
function pageLoad(sender, args){
    Sys.WebForms.PageRequestManager.getInstance().add_beginRequest(beginRequest);
    Sys.WebForms.PageRequestManager.getInstance().add_endRequest(endRequest);
}

function beginRequest(sender, args){
    var modalPopupBehavior = $find('ctl00_ContentPlaceHolder1_mdePleaseWait');
    modalPopupBehavior.show();
}

function endRequest(sender, args) {
    var modalPopupBehavior = $find('ctl00_ContentPlaceHolder1_mdePleaseWait');
    modalPopupBehavior.hide();
}
```

The pageLoad JavaScript hooks the beginRequest and endRequest functions to the ScriptManager control's begin and end request methods. Because this control uses AJAX, a ScriptManager control must exist on the page. When the ScriptManager posts back to the server, the beginRequest function is called. The beginRequest finds the ModalPopupExtender control and calls its show method. This will display the Please Wait panel and disable the form. When the AJAX call is complete, the endRequest function is called, which finds the ModalPopuExtender control and calls its hide method. This hides the Please Wait panel and enables the form again.

The next step is to override the control's OnLoad event. The OnLoad event takes care of creating an instance of the business object this control is hooked to and calls the GetCustomAttributes method on the business object. The custom attributes are set to the QueryFields property, which actually stores them in the page's ViewState. These fields are then added to the _ddlFields drop-down list:

```
protected override void OnLoad(EventArgs e)
{
    EnsureChildControls();
    base.OnLoad(e);

    if (!Page.IsPostBack)
```

```
        {
            Type objectType = Type.GetType(QueryObjectName);
            object listObject = Activator.CreateInstance(objectType);

            //Call the method to load the object
            QueryFields = (object[])objectType.InvokeMember("GetCustomAttributes",
                BindingFlags.InvokeMethod, null, listObject, new object[] { });

            foreach (object attribute in QueryFields)
            {
                if (attribute is QueryFieldAttribute)
                {
                    QueryFieldAttribute qfa = (QueryFieldAttribute)attribute;

                    _ddlFields.Items.Add(new ListItem(qfa.FriendlyFieldName,
                                        qfa.FieldName));
                }
            }

            _ddlFields.Items.Insert(0, "");
        }
    }
```

The next step is to handle all the events that the drop-down lists and buttons are firing. The first event to handle is the _ddlFields event. This should look at the field type that is selected and change the items in the Comparison drop-down list:

```
void _ddlFields_SelectedIndexChanged(object sender, EventArgs e)
{
  if (_ddlFields.SelectedIndex > 0)
  {
    _ddlComparison.Visible = true;
    _ddlComparison.Items.Clear();

    _ddlValues.Items.Clear();
    _ddlValues.Visible = true;
    _lstValues.Items.Clear();
    _lstValues.Visible = false;

    //Get the field name
    string friendlyFieldName = _ddlFields.SelectedItem.Text;
    QueryFieldAttribute.QueryFieldTypeEnum queryFieldType =
        QueryFieldAttribute.QueryFieldTypeEnum.NotSet;

    foreach (object attribute in QueryFields)
    {
      if (attribute is QueryFieldAttribute)
      {
        QueryFieldAttribute qfa = (QueryFieldAttribute)attribute;

        if (qfa.FriendlyFieldName == friendlyFieldName)
        {
          queryFieldType = qfa.FieldType;
        }
```

```
        }
    }

    switch (queryFieldType)
    {
        case QueryFieldAttribute.QueryFieldTypeEnum.NotSet:
            //hide drop downs
            _ddlComparison.Visible = false;
            break;
        case QueryFieldAttribute.QueryFieldTypeEnum.Boolean:
            _ddlComparison.Items.Add(COMPARISON_EQUALS);
            _ddlComparison.Items.Add(COMPARISON_NOT_EQUALS);
            break;
        case QueryFieldAttribute.QueryFieldTypeEnum.String:
        case QueryFieldAttribute.QueryFieldTypeEnum.Lookup:
            _ddlComparison.Items.Add(COMPARISON_EQUALS);
            _ddlComparison.Items.Add(COMPARISON_NOT_EQUALS);
            _ddlComparison.Items.Add(COMPARISON_IN);
            _ddlComparison.Items.Add(COMPARISON_NOT_IN);
            _ddlComparison.Items.Add(COMPARISON_IS_BLANK);
            _ddlComparison.Items.Add(COMPARISON_IS_NOT_BLANK);
            break;
        case QueryFieldAttribute.QueryFieldTypeEnum.Date:
        case QueryFieldAttribute.QueryFieldTypeEnum.Number:
            _ddlComparison.Items.Add(COMPARISON_EQUALS);
            _ddlComparison.Items.Add(COMPARISON_NOT_EQUALS);
            _ddlComparison.Items.Add(COMPARISON_IN);
            _ddlComparison.Items.Add(COMPARISON_NOT_IN);
            _ddlComparison.Items.Add(COMPARISON_IS_GREATER_THEN);
            _ddlComparison.Items.Add(COMPARISON_IS_GREATER_THEN_EQUAL);
            _ddlComparison.Items.Add(COMPARISON_IS_LESS_THEN);
            _ddlComparison.Items.Add(COMPARISON_IS_LESS_THEN_OR_EQUAL);
            _ddlComparison.Items.Add(COMPARISON_IS_BLANK);
            _ddlComparison.Items.Add(COMPARISON_IS_NOT_BLANK);
            break;
    }

    _ddlComparison.Items.Insert(0, "");
}
else
{
    _ddlComparison.Visible = false;
}
}
```

The next event handler to add is the Comparison drop-down list's `SelectedIndexChanged` event. When the user selects an item in this list the page will postback and display either the Values dropdown list or the list box. The one that is displayed will be populated with data from the query:

```
void _ddlComparison_SelectedIndexChanged(object sender, EventArgs e)
{
    if (_ddlComparison.SelectedIndex > 0)
    {
        //Get the field name
```

```
        string valueFieldName = _ddlFields.SelectedValue;
        string lookupFieldName = "";

        //Get the values for this field in the database.
        foreach (object attribute in QueryFields)
        {
          if (attribute is QueryFieldAttribute)
          {
            QueryFieldAttribute qfa = (QueryFieldAttribute)attribute;

            if (qfa.FieldName == valueFieldName)
            {
              if (qfa.LookupFieldName == null)
              {
                lookupFieldName = valueFieldName;
              }
              else
              {
                lookupFieldName = qfa.LookupFieldName;
              }
            }
          }
        }

        Type objectType = Type.GetType(QueryObjectName);
        object listObject = Activator.CreateInstance(objectType);
        List<LookupData> data = (List<LookupData>)objectType.InvokeMember("GetLookup",
            BindingFlags.InvokeMethod, null, listObject, new object[] {
                                                        lookupFieldName,
                                                        valueFieldName });

        switch (_ddlComparison.SelectedItem.Text)
        {
          case COMPARISON_EQUALS:
          case COMPARISON_NOT_EQUALS:
          case COMPARISON_IS_GREATER_THEN:
          case COMPARISON_IS_GREATER_THEN_EQUAL:
          case COMPARISON_IS_LESS_THEN:
          case COMPARISON_IS_LESS_THEN_OR_EQUAL:
            _ddlValues.Visible = true;
            _lstValues.Visible = false;
            _ddlValues.DataSource = data;
            _ddlValues.DataTextField = "Text";
            _ddlValues.DataValueField = "Value";
            _ddlValues.DataBind();
            break;

          case COMPARISON_IN:
          case COMPARISON_NOT_IN:
            _ddlValues.Visible = false;
            _lstValues.Visible = true;
            _lstValues.DataSource = data;
            _lstValues.DataTextField = "Text";
```

```
        _lstValues.DataValueField = "Value";
        _lstValues.DataBind();
        break;

    case COMPARISON_IS_BLANK:
    case COMPARISON_IS_NOT_BLANK:
      _ddlValues.Visible = false;
      _lstValues.Visible = false;
      break;
  }
 }
}
```

Now add the event handlers for the Add, AddAnd, and AddOr buttons:

```
void _btnAdd_Click(object sender, EventArgs e)
{
    AddWhereSQL("");

    if (_lstWhereClause.Items.Count > 0)
    {
      _btnAdd.Visible = false;
      _btnAddAnd.Visible = true;
      _btnAddOr.Visible = true;
      _btnRemoveLine.Visible = true;
      _btnLeftParen.Visible = true;
      _btnRightParen.Visible = true;
      _btnRemoveLeftParen.Visible = true;
      _btnRemoveRightParen.Visible = true;
    }
}

void _btnAddOr_Click(object sender, EventArgs e)
{
    AddWhereSQL(" OR ");
}

void _btnAddAnd_Click(object sender, EventArgs e)
{
    AddWhereSQL(" AND ");
}
```

These all call one common method called AddWhereSQL that adds the text to the WhereClause list box:

```
private void AddWhereSQL(string andOr)
{
  //The field, comparison, and value must have a value selected
  if (_ddlFields.SelectedIndex > 0)
  {
    if (_ddlComparison.SelectedIndex > 0)
    {
```

The `friendlyText` variable holds the text that will be displayed to the user in the list box. This is just a concatenation of the drop-down boxes:

```
string friendlyText = andOr + " " + _ddlFields.SelectedItem.Text + " " +
                        _ddlComparison.SelectedItem.Text + " ";

string sqlValue = "";
string friendlyValue = "";
string comparison = "";
string beginParen = "";
string endParen = "";
```

The `GetValueText` method determines whether the field is a string and surrounds it with single quotes. If the value is a date, it formats it as a date. Because the application is using dynamic SQL, text and dates must be handled differently than when using a stored procedure:

```
GetValueText(ref friendlyValue, ref sqlValue);

//Translate the comparison operator to the correct SQL syntax.
if (sqlValue.Length > 0)
{
  switch (_ddlComparison.SelectedItem.Text)
  {
    case COMPARISON_EQUALS:
      comparison = " = ";
      break;
    case COMPARISON_NOT_EQUALS:
      comparison = " <> ";
      break;
    case COMPARISON_IN:
      comparison = " IN ";
      beginParen = "(";
      endParen = ")";
      break;
    case COMPARISON_NOT_IN:
      comparison = " NOT IN ";
      beginParen = "(";
      endParen = ")";
      break;
    case COMPARISON_IS_BLANK:
      comparison = " IS ";
      break;
    case COMPARISON_IS_NOT_BLANK:
      comparison = " IS NOT ";
      break;
    case COMPARISON_IS_GREATER_THEN:
      comparison = " > ";
      break;
    case COMPARISON_IS_GREATER_THEN_EQUAL:
      comparison = " >= ";
      break;
    case COMPARISON_IS_LESS_THEN:
      comparison = " < ";
```

```
        break;
    case COMPARISON_IS_LESS_THEN_OR_EQUAL:
      comparison = " <= ";
      break;
    }
```

This adds the friendly text to the `lstWhereClause` list box and sets the item's value to the real SQL syntax for this line:

```
        friendlyText += beginParen + friendlyValue + endParen;
        _lstWhereClause.Items.Add(new ListItem(friendlyText, andOr +
                          _ddlFields.SelectedValue + comparison +
                          beginParen + sqlValue + endParen));

        if (_lstWhereClause.Items.Count > 1)
        {
          _lstWhereClause.Rows = _lstWhereClause.Items.Count;
        }
      }
    }
  }
}
```

Here is the code for the `GetValueText` method:

```
private void GetValueText(ref string friendlyValue, ref string sqlValue)
{
  //The comparison type will determine which list is displayed
  switch (_ddlComparison.SelectedItem.Text)
  {
    case COMPARISON_EQUALS:
    case COMPARISON_NOT_EQUALS:
    case COMPARISON_IS_GREATER_THEN:
    case COMPARISON_IS_GREATER_THEN_EQUAL:
    case COMPARISON_IS_LESS_THEN:
    case COMPARISON_IS_LESS_THEN_OR_EQUAL:
      friendlyValue = _ddlValues.SelectedItem.Text;
```

Format the value in the drop-down list using SQL syntax:

```
      sqlValue = FormatValue(_ddlValues.SelectedValue);
      break;

    case COMPARISON_IN:
    case COMPARISON_NOT_IN:
      string tempValue = "";
      string tempFriendlyValue = "";
      foreach (ListItem li in _lstValues.Items)
      {
        if (li.Selected)
        {
          tempFriendlyValue += li.Text + ", ";
```

Format the value in the list item using SQL syntax:

```
            tempValue += FormatValue(li.Value) + ", ";
        }
    }

    if (tempValue.Length > 0)
    {
      //Trim off the last space and comma.
      friendlyValue = tempFriendlyValue.Substring(0, tempFriendlyValue.Length -
                                                    2);
      sqlValue = tempValue.Substring(0, tempValue.Length - 2);
    }
    else
    {
      friendlyValue = tempFriendlyValue;
      sqlValue = tempValue;
    }
    break;

  case COMPARISON_IS_BLANK:
  case COMPARISON_IS_NOT_BLANK:
    sqlValue = " NULL ";
    friendlyValue = "";
    break;

  default:
    sqlValue = "";
    friendlyValue = "";
    break;
  }
}
```

This method calls the `FormatValue` method, which surrounds a string with single quotes and replaces single quotes with repeated single quotes. Dates are also surrounded by single quotes:

```
private string FormatValue(string value)
{
  //Get the field name
  string valueFieldName = _ddlFields.SelectedValue;

  //Get the values for this field in the database.
  foreach (object attribute in QueryFields)
  {
    if (attribute is QueryFieldAttribute)
    {
      QueryFieldAttribute qfa = (QueryFieldAttribute)attribute;

      if (qfa.FieldName == valueFieldName)
      {
        switch (qfa.FieldType)
        {
          case QueryFieldAttribute.QueryFieldTypeEnum.String:
```

```
            return "'" + value.Replace("'", "''") + "'";

         case QueryFieldAttribute.QueryFieldTypeEnum.Date:
            return "'" + value + "'";

         case QueryFieldAttribute.QueryFieldTypeEnum.Boolean:
         case QueryFieldAttribute.QueryFieldTypeEnum.Lookup:
         case QueryFieldAttribute.QueryFieldTypeEnum.Number:
            return value;
      }
    }
  }
 }
 return value;
}
```

The button with the "-" is used to remove the selected line in the WhereClause list box. The code for this event is as follows:

```
void _btnRemoveLine_Click(object sender, EventArgs e)
{
  if (_lstWhereClause.SelectedIndex > -1)
  {
    bool firstLineRemoved = (_lstWhereClause.SelectedIndex == 0);

    _lstWhereClause.Items.RemoveAt(_lstWhereClause.SelectedIndex);

    if (_lstWhereClause.Items.Count == 0)
    {
      _btnAdd.Visible = true;
      _btnAddAnd.Visible = false;
      _btnAddOr.Visible = false;
      _btnRemoveLine.Visible = false;
      _btnLeftParen.Visible = false;
      _btnRightParen.Visible = false;
      _btnRemoveLeftParen.Visible = false;
      _btnRemoveRightParen.Visible = false;
    }
    else
    {
      if (firstLineRemoved)
      {
        //Remove the and/or from the new first line.
        if (_lstWhereClause.Items[0].Text.Trim().Substring(0, 3) == "AND")
        {
          _lstWhereClause.Items[0].Text =
              _lstWhereClause.Items[0].Text.Substring(4);
          _lstWhereClause.Items[0].Value =
              _lstWhereClause.Items[0].Value.Substring(4);
        }
        else
        {
          _lstWhereClause.Items[0].Text =
```

```
                    _lstWhereClause.Items[0].Text.Substring(3);
                _lstWhereClause.Items[0].Value =
                    _lstWhereClause.Items[0].Value.Substring(3);
            }
        }
    }
  }
}
```

The "(" button inserts a left parenthesis on the currently selected line in the WhereClause list box:

```
void _btnLeftParen_Click(object sender, EventArgs e)
{
  if (_lstWhereClause.SelectedIndex > -1)
  {
    int insertParenIndex;

    //if this is the first line then just add the paren to the beginning.
    if (_lstWhereClause.SelectedIndex == 0)
    {
      insertParenIndex = 0;
    }
    else
    {
      //Check if this is an AND statement
      if (_lstWhereClause.SelectedItem.Text.Trim().Substring(0, 3) == "AND")
      {
        insertParenIndex = 5;
      }
      else
      {
        //Must be an OR clause
        insertParenIndex = 4;
      }
    }

    ListItem li = _lstWhereClause.SelectedItem;
    li.Text = li.Text.Insert(insertParenIndex, "(");
    li.Value = li.Value.Insert(insertParenIndex, "(");
  }
}
```

The button with the ")" adds a right parenthesis to the currently selected line in the WhereClause list box:

```
void _btnRightParen_Click(object sender, EventArgs e)
{
  if (_lstWhereClause.SelectedIndex > -1)
  {
    _lstWhereClause.Items[_lstWhereClause.SelectedIndex].Text =
        _lstWhereClause.SelectedItem.Text + ")";

    _lstWhereClause.Items[_lstWhereClause.SelectedIndex].Value =
        _lstWhereClause.SelectedItem.Value + ")";
  }
}
```

The "(-" button removes the leftmost parenthesis from the currently selected line in the WhereClause list box:

```
void _btnRemoveLeftParen_Click(object sender, EventArgs e)
{
  if (_lstWhereClause.SelectedIndex > -1)
  {
    int lengthOfPrefix = -1;

    //Check if this is the first item
    if (_lstWhereClause.SelectedIndex == 0)
    {
      if (_lstWhereClause.SelectedItem.Text.Trim().StartsWith("("))
      {
        lengthOfPrefix = 0;
      }
    }
    else
    {
      //Check if this is an AND statement
      if (_lstWhereClause.SelectedItem.Text.Trim().Substring(0, 3) == "AND")
      {
        if (_lstWhereClause.SelectedItem.Text.Substring(5, 1) == "(")
        {
          lengthOfPrefix = 5;
        }
      }
      else
      {
        //OR
        if (_lstWhereClause.SelectedItem.Text.Substring(4, 1) == "(")
        {
          lengthOfPrefix = 4;
        }
      }
    }

    if (lengthOfPrefix > -1)
    {
      ListItem li = _lstWhereClause.SelectedItem;
      li.Text = li.Text.Substring(0, lengthOfPrefix) +
          _lstWhereClause.SelectedItem.Text.Substring(lengthOfPrefix + 1);
      li.Value = li.Value.Substring(0, lengthOfPrefix) +
          _lstWhereClause.SelectedItem.Value.Substring(lengthOfPrefix + 1);
    }
  }
}
```

Finally, the ")-" button removes the rightmost parenthesis in the currently selected line in the WhereClause list box:

```
void _btnRemoveRightParen_Click(object sender, EventArgs e)
{
  if (_lstWhereClause.SelectedIndex > -1)
  {
```

```
          if (_lstWhereClause.SelectedItem.Text.EndsWith(")"))
          {
            _lstWhereClause.SelectedItem.Text =
                _lstWhereClause.SelectedItem.Text.Substring(0,
                _lstWhereClause.SelectedItem.Text.Length - 1);

            _lstWhereClause.SelectedItem.Value =
                _lstWhereClause.SelectedItem.Value.Substring(0,
                _lstWhereClause.SelectedItem.Value.Length - 1);
          }
        }
      }
    }
```

The last step is to add a public method that can be called to return the where clause that the control has built. This creates a string that can be passed to the data layer. This method must validate that the parentheses are set up correctly. It does this by simply counting the number of left and right parentheses and making sure they are equal. The method will also append any required where clauses that were defined by the custom attributes in the data class:

```
public bool GetWhereClause(ref string whereClause, ref ENTValidationErrors
    validationErrors)
{
  //The left and right parens must equal each other.
  int leftParenCount = 0;
  int rightParenCount = 0;

  whereClause = "";

  //Append any required where clauses
  foreach (object attribute in QueryFields)
  {
    if (attribute is RequiredQueryFieldAttribute)
    {
      if (whereClause == "") whereClause = " WHERE ";

      whereClause += ((RequiredQueryFieldAttribute)attribute).Clause + " AND ";
    }
  }

  //If there were any required where clauses then the rest of the query must be
  //surrounded by parens (  )
  bool requiredWhereClauseExists = (whereClause != "");

  if (requiredWhereClauseExists)
  {
    whereClause += "( ";
  }

  //Add a line for each item in the list box.
  if (_lstWhereClause.Items.Count > 0)
  {
```

```
      if (whereClause == "") whereClause = " WHERE ";

      foreach (ListItem li in _lstWhereClause.Items)
      {
        leftParenCount += CountParens('(', li.Value);
        rightParenCount += CountParens(')', li.Value);

        whereClause += li.Value;
      }
    }

    //Close out the parenthesis if a required where clause existed.
    if (requiredWhereClauseExists)
    {
      whereClause += ")";
    }

    //Validate that the left and right parens were equal.
    if (leftParenCount == rightParenCount)
    {
      return true;
    }
    else
    {
      validationErrors.Add("Error In Filter: The nubmer of left and right parenthesis
                      must match");
      return false;
    }
}
```

This method calls a helper function called CountParens. This returns the number of parentheses in the specified string:

```
private int CountParens(char paren, string text)
{
  int tempCount = text.Split(new char[] { paren }).Count();

  if (tempCount > 1)
  {
    return (tempCount - 1);
  }
  else
  {
    return 0;
  }
}
```

You now have a fully functioning query builder control. The next section will implement this control on a new screen that enables users to run reports and create their own "filter" before displaying the data on the screen.

Solution

Remember Mary? She asked for three reports that would enable her to view the list of outstanding requests, the list by current owner, and the list of approved requests. These are all the same report but with different filters. The solution section will show you how to incorporate the query builder control in the `PaidTimeOffSolution` and create the pattern for generic reporting. Two new pages will be added to the application: one that displays the list of reports and a second that enables users to apply a filter to a report and preview it in PDF. The first screen looks like Figure 10-3.

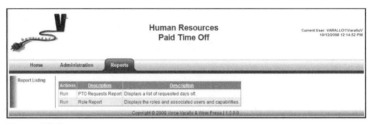

Figure 10-3

This is very similar to the grid pages developed in the previous chapters. It uses the custom `GridView` control and when the user clicks the Run button, it displays the second page (refer to Figure 10-1).

To build this functionality you first need to create the menu item for the Report Listing link and the capabilities associated with the report. The capabilities will be at the report level so that users can control access for each report.

Add the following record to the `ENTMenuItem` table:

MenuItemName	Url	ParentENT MenuItemId	Display Sequence	IsAlways Enabled
Report Listing	Reports/ReportList.aspx	Reports (ID)	1	False

Now add the following capabilities to the `ENTCapability` table:

CapabilityName	ENTMenuItemId	AccessType
PTO Requests Report	Report Listing ID	1
Role Report	Report Listing ID	1

A new table called `ENTReport` must be added that contains the list of available reports. The structure for this table is as follows:

ENTReport			
	Column Name	Data Type	Allow Nulls
🔑	ENTReportId	int	☐
	ReportName	varchar(50)	☐
	FileName	varchar(255)	☐
	ObjectName	varchar(255)	☐
	Description	varchar(255)	☐
	SubReportObjectName	varchar(255)	☑
	SubReportMethodName	varchar(50)	☑
	InsertDate	datetime	☐
	InsertENTUserAccountId	int	☐
	UpdateDate	datetime	☐
	UpdateENTUserAccountId	int	☐
	Version	timestamp	☐
			☐

Figure 10-4

The `ReportName` field contains the user-friendly name of the report. The `FileName` contains the Crystal Reports file that you create in Visual Studio. The `ObjectName` field contains the business object's fully qualified name, and contains the logic to populate the report. The `Description` field contains the description of the report. The `SubReportObjectName` and `SubReportMethodName` fields contain the object name and method that should be called on the object to retrieve the data for the subreport. Remember that the Role report created in the previous chapter uses a subreport to display the list of users in the role.

Next, create the five standard stored procedures for this table:

```
CREATE PROCEDURE ENTReportDelete
(
    @ENTReportId int
)
AS
    SET NOCOUNT ON

    DELETE
      FROM ENTReport
     WHERE ENTReportId = @ENTReportId

    RETURN
```

```
CREATE PROCEDURE ENTReportInsert
(
    @ENTReportId  int OUTPUT,
    @ReportName  varchar(50),
    @FileName  varchar(255),
    @ObjectName  varchar(255),
    @Description  varchar(255),
    @SubReportObjectName  varchar(255),
    @SubReportMethodName  varchar(50),
    @InsertENTUserAccountId  int
)
```

```
AS
    SET NOCOUNT ON

    INSERT INTO ENTReport (ReportName, FileName, ObjectName, Description,
                           SubReportObjectName, SubReportMethodName, InsertDate,
                           InsertENTUserAccountId, UpdateDate,
                           UpdateENTUserAccountId)
        VALUES (
                @ReportName,
                @FileName,
                @ObjectName,
                @Description,
                @SubReportObjectName,
                @SubReportMethodName,
                GetDate(),
                @InsertENTUserAccountId,
                GetDate(),
                @InsertENTUserAccountId
                )
    SET @ENTReportId = Scope_Identity()

    RETURN
```

```
CREATE PROCEDURE ENTReportSelectAll
AS
    SET NOCOUNT ON

    SELECT ENTReportId, ReportName, FileName, ObjectName, Description,
           SubReportObjectName, SubReportMethodName, InsertDate,
           InsertENTUserAccountId,      UpdateDate, UpdateENTUserAccountId, Version
      FROM ENTReport

    RETURN
```

```
CREATE PROCEDURE ENTReportSelectById
(
    @ENTReportId int
)
AS
    SET NOCOUNT ON

    SELECT ENTReportId, ReportName, FileName, ObjectName, Description,
           SubReportObjectName, SubReportMethodName, InsertDate,
           InsertENTUserAccountId, UpdateDate, UpdateENTUserAccountId, Version
      FROM ENTReport
     WHERE ENTReportId = @ENTReportId

    RETURN
```

```
CREATE PROCEDURE ENTReportUpdate
(
    @ENTReportId  int,
    @ReportName  varchar(50),
    @FileName  varchar(255),
    @ObjectName  varchar(255),
```

```
       @Description  varchar(255),
       @SubReportObjectName  varchar(255),
       @SubReportMethodName  varchar(50),
       @UpdateENTUserAccountId  int,
       @Version  timestamp
)
AS
    SET NOCOUNT ON

    UPDATE ENTReport
       SET
            ReportName = @ReportName,
            FileName = @FileName,
            ObjectName = @ObjectName,
            Description = @Description,
            SubReportObjectName = @SubReportObjectName,
            SubReportMethodName = @SubReportMethodName,
            UpdateDate = GetDate(),
            UpdateENTUserAccountId = @UpdateENTUserAccountId
       WHERE ENTReportId = @ENTReportId
         AND Version = @Version

    RETURN @@ROWCOUNT
```

Now you can create the entity object using the ORM Designer and add the stored procedures to the Methods pane as you have done in the previous chapters. Then add the class declaration for the entity class to the CustomizedEntities class:

```
public partial class ENTReport : IENTBaseEntity { }
```

Now you can add the Data class. Add a new class to the Framework\Reports folder in the V2.Paid TimeOffDAL project. This class should inherit from the ENTBaseData class and implement the Select, Delete, Insert, and Update methods using the same pattern defined in Chapter 2.

Next, add the business class to the Framework\Reports folder in the V2.PaidTimeOffBLL project. This class should be called ENTReportBO and inherit from the ENTBaseBO object. The code for this class uses the same pattern defined in Chapter 3:

```
[Serializable()]
public class ENTReportBO : ENTBaseBO
{
    public string ReportName { get; set; }
    public string FileName { get; set; }
    public string ObjectName { get; set; }
    public string Description { get; set; }
    public string SubReportObjectName { get; set; }
    public string SubReportMethodName { get; set; }

    public override bool Load(int id)
    {
        //Get the entity object from the DAL.
        ENTReport eNTReport = new ENTReportData().Select(id);
        MapEntityToProperties(eNTReport);
```

```
        return eNTReport != null;
      }

    protected override void MapEntityToCustomProperties(IENTBaseEntity entity)
    {
      ENTReport eNTReport = (ENTReport)entity;

      ID = eNTReport.ENTReportId;
      ReportName = eNTReport.ReportName;
      FileName = eNTReport.FileName;
      ObjectName = eNTReport.ObjectName;
      Description = eNTReport.Description;
      SubReportObjectName = eNTReport.SubReportObjectName;
      SubReportMethodName = eNTReport.SubReportMethodName;
    }

    protected override string GetDisplayText()
    {
      return ReportName;
    }
  }
}
```

Now add the `List` class to this file. This also uses the pattern defined in Chapter 3:

```
[Serializable()]
public class ENTReportBOList : ENTBaseBOList<ENTReportBO>
{
  public override void Load()
  {
    LoadFromList(new ENTReportData().Select());
  }

  private void LoadFromList(List<ENTReport> eNTReports)
  {
    if (eNTReports.Count > 0)
    {
      foreach (ENTReport eNTReport in eNTReports)
      {
        ENTReportBO newENTReportBO = new ENTReportBO();
        newENTReportBO.MapEntityToProperties(eNTReport);
        this.Add(newENTReportBO);
      }
    }
  }
}
```

Now you're ready to add the page to the user interface. Add a new Web Form to the `Reports` folder in the `PaidTimeOffUI` project and name the file `ReportList.aspx`. This page should use the `PaidTimeOff EditGrid.master` page and inherit from the `BasePage` class. Drag a `CustomGridView` control on this page and name it `cgvReports`. Create an event handler for the `OnRowDataBound` event by clicking on the lightning bolt in the Properties window and double-clicking on the `OnRowDataBound` event.

Open the code-behind file and add the following `using` statements:

```
using V2.PaidTimeOffBLL.Framework.Reports;
using V2.PaidTimeOffBLL.Framework;
using System.Collections.Generic;
```

Add the code to the `Page_Load` event that hides the Add button, as this screen will not allow users to add new reports. The `Page_Load` event must also set the class name for the CustomGridView control and set its columns:

```
protected void Page_Load(object sender, EventArgs e)
{
  Master.btnAddNewRef().Visible = false;

  if (!IsPostBack)
  {
    //Tell the control what class to create and what method to call to load the
    //class.
    cgvReports.ListClassName = typeof(ENTReportBOList).AssemblyQualifiedName;
    cgvReports.LoadMethodName = "Load";

    //Action column-Contains the Run link
    cgvReports.AddBoundField("", "Actions", "");

    cgvReports.AddBoundField("ReportName", "Description", "ReportName");
    cgvReports.AddBoundField("Description", "Description", "Description");

    cgvReports.DataBind();
  }
}
```

Because this page inherits from the `BasePage` class, you must implement the `MenuItemName` and `CapabilityNames` methods. The `MenuItemName` method simply returns the menu item that should be highlighted when this page is displayed:

```
public override string MenuItemName()
{
    return "Report Listing";
}
```

The `CapabilityNames` method must be implemented in a different way than all the other screens. Because security for the reports is at the individual report level, a list of all the capabilities associated with the ReportListing menu item must be returned. If a user has access to at least one report, he or she should have access to this screen:

```
public override string[] CapabilityNames()
{
  IEnumerable<ENTCapabilityBO> capabilities =
      Globals.GetCapabilities(this.Cache).GetByMenuItemId(
      Globals.GetMenuItems(this.Cache).GetByMenuItemName(MenuItemName()).ID);;
```

```
    string[] capabilityNames = new string[capabilities.Count()];

    for (int i = 0; i < capabilities.Count(); i++)
    {
      capabilityNames[i] = capabilities.ElementAt(i).CapabilityName;
    }

    return capabilityNames;
}
```

This page contains multiple capabilities, so the NoAccessToPage method in the BasePage class must be overridden because the default functionality expects one capability. Overriding the NoAccessToPage method simply turns off the default functionality and enables you to create custom logic for this page to enable or disable controls on the screen based on the capabilities. Because this page only lists the reports, no special logic is needed in this method. Simply override the method without any implementation:

```
protected override void NoAccessToPage(string capabilityName)
{
  //This page has a capability associated with each report so override the default
  //functionalit in the BasePage class so an error does not get thrown if the user
  //does not have access to all the reports.
}
```

The last step for this page is to implement the RowDataBound event handler. This is where the system determines whether a user has access to the specific report and shows or hides the row accordingly:

```
protected void cgvReports_RowDataBound(object sender, GridViewRowEventArgs e)
{
  if (e.Row.RowType == DataControlRowType.DataRow)
  {
    e.Row.Visible = false;

    //A capabilty must exist for this report in order for it to appear in the list.
    //The capability name must match the report name.
    ENTCapabilityBOList capabilities = Globals.GetCapabilities(this.Cache);
    ENTCapabilityBO capability =
        capabilities.GetByName(((ENTReportBO)e.Row.DataItem).ReportName);

    if (capability != null)
    {
      ENTRoleEOList roles = Globals.GetRoles(this.Cache);
      int currentUserId = CurrentUser.ID;

      foreach (ENTRoleEO role in roles)
      {
        if (role.RoleUserAccounts.IsUserInRole(currentUserId))
        {
          ENTRoleCapabilityEO roleCapability =
              role.RoleCapabilities.GetByCapabilityID(capability.ID);

          if ((roleCapability != null) && (roleCapability.AccessFlag !=
              ENTRoleCapabilityEO.CapabiiltyAccessFlagEnum.None))
          {
            //Add the Run link to the action column.
```

```
                         HyperLink runLink = new HyperLink();
                         runLink.Text = "Run";

                         runLink.NavigateUrl = "ReportQuery.aspx" + EncryptQueryString("id=" +
                             ((ENTReportBO)e.Row.DataItem).ID.ToString());

                         e.Row.Cells[COL_INDEX_ACTION].Controls.Add(runLink);

                         e.Row.Visible = true;
                    }
                }
            }
        }
    }
}
```

That's all the code that is needed to create the report list page with the appropriate security for the reports. The next step is to create the page that enables users to filter the report and preview it. This is the page the system navigates to when the user clicks the Run link in the report list screen.

Add a new Web Form to the `Reports` folder in the `PaidTimeOffUI` project. Using the `PaidTimeOff` `.master` page, name the class `ReportQuery.aspx` and inherit from the `BasePage` class. This page uses the new `QueryBuilder` control built earlier, so it needs to support AJAX functionality. Any page that uses AJAX must contain the AJAX `ScriptManager` control, so drag and drop this control onto the form from the Toolbox. Drag the `QueryBuilder` control from the Toolbox to below the `ScriptManager` control on the form. Now add two buttons below the `QueryBuilder` control for Preview and Cancel. The buttons should be in a HTML table so they are positioned nicely:

```
<asp:ScriptManager ID="ScriptManager1" runat="server">
</asp:ScriptManager>
<cc1:QueryBuilder ID="QueryBuilder1" runat="server" />
<table>
    <tr>
        <td>
            <asp:Button ID="btnPreview" runat="server" Text="Print Preview"
                onclick="btnPreview_Click" />
        </td>
        <td>
            <asp:Button ID="btnCancel" runat="server" Text="Cancel"
                onclick="btnCancel_Click" style="height: 26px" />
        </td>
    </tr>
</table>
```

Open the code-behind and add the following `using` statements:

```
using System.Collections.Specialized;
using V2.PaidTimeOffBLL.Framework;
using V2.PaidTimeOffBLL.Framework.Reports;
using V2.PaidTimeOffBLL.Reports;
using CrystalDecisions.CrystalReports.Engine;
using CrystalDecisions.Shared;
using System.Reflection;
```

This page will generate the reports, so it needs to reference the Crystal Reports namespaces and all the custom objects that are used to process reports.

The Preview button should open the report in a new window, so it must use the JavaScript built in Chapter 9. The GetPrintButtonScript is in the BasePage class:

```
protected void Page_Load(object sender, EventArgs e)
{
    btnPreview.Attributes.Add("onclick", GetPrintButtonScript(btnPreview));
}
```

Now override the MenuItemName and CapabilityNames methods:

```
public override string MenuItemName()
{
    return "Report Listing";
}

public override string[] CapabilityNames()
{
    SetCurrentReport();
    return new string[] { CurrentReport.ReportName };
}
```

The CapabilityNames method calls a new method, SetCurrentReport, which creates an instance of the ENTReportBO object based on the ID passed in the queryString. This object is then serialized and stored in the ViewState so it can be used for subsequent postbacks:

```
private void SetCurrentReport()
{
    //Decrypt the query string
    NameValueCollection queryString =
        DecryptQueryString(Request.QueryString.ToString());

    if (queryString != null)
    {
        //Check if the id was passed in.
        string id = queryString["id"];

        if ((id != null) && (id != "0"))
        {
            //Get the report object
            ENTReportBO report = new ENTReportBO();
            report.Load(Convert.ToInt32(id));

            QueryBuilder1.QueryObjectName = report.ObjectName;

            CurrentReport = report;
        }
    }
}
```

```
private ENTReportBO CurrentReport
{
  get
  {
    return (ENTReportBO)ViewState["Report"];
  }
  set
  {
    ViewState["Report"] = value;
  }
}
```

Next, add the code to handle the Cancel button's click event. This simply returns the user to the Report List page:

```
protected void btnCancel_Click(object sender, EventArgs e)
{
    Response.Redirect("ReportList.aspx");
}
```

The last step is to handle the Preview button's click event. This event will retrieve the Where clause from the QueryBuilder control, create an instance of the business object associated with this report, call its Select method, and then create the report and export it to PDF:

```
protected void btnPreview_Click(object sender, EventArgs e)
{
  string whereClause = "";
  ENTValidationErrors validationErrors = new ENTValidationErrors();
```

Get the Where clause from the QueryBuilder control. If the query has errors, they will be returned in the validationErrors list:

```
  if (QueryBuilder1.GetWhereClause(ref whereClause, ref validationErrors))
  {
    ENTReportBO currentReport = CurrentReport;
```

Create an instance of the Crystal Report based on the filename for this report:

```
    ReportDocument report = new ReportDocument();
    report.Load(Server.MapPath(currentReport.FileName));
```

This object must inherit from the ENTBaseQueryBO object so it is guaranteed to have the Select method. This code creates the business object and calls the Select method, passing in the Where clause:

```
    Type objectType = Type.GetType(currentReport.ObjectName);
    object listObject = Activator.CreateInstance(objectType);
    object[] data = (object[])objectType.InvokeMember("Select",
        BindingFlags.InvokeMethod, null, listObject, new object[] { whereClause });

    //Set the data
    report.SetDataSource(data);
```

If there is a subreport, then retrieve the data for the subreport. The code supports only one subreport:

```
//Check if there is a sub report
if (report.Subreports.Count > 0)
{
  //Only support 1 subreport
  //Get the object that can retrieve the data for the subreport
  Type objectType1 = Type.GetType(currentReport.SubReportObjectName);

  //The methods must be static for this data.
  object[] subreportData =
      (object[])objectType1.InvokeMember(currentReport.SubReportMethodName,
        BindingFlags.InvokeMethod, null, objectType1, new object[] { });

  report.Subreports[0].SetDataSource(subreportData);
}
```

Export the report to PDF and send it to the browser:

```
report.ExportToHttpResponse(ExportFormatType.PortableDocFormat, Response,
    false, "");
}
else
{
```

If it got here, then there was an error in the query. Show any errors to the user:

```
Response.Clear();
foreach(ENTValidationError ve in validationErrors)
{
    Response.Write(ve.ErrorMessage + "<br>" + Environment.NewLine);
}
Response.End();
}
}
```

Now you have a page that will list all the reports in the system that support querying, and a page that enables you to filter the report and preview it. Add a record to the ENTReport table for the PTO Requests report. Use the following values for each field:

- ❑ **ReportName:** PTO Requests Report
- ❑ **FileName:** MyPTORequests.rpt
- ❑ **ObjectName:** V2.PaidTimeOffBLL.Reports.ReportPTORequests, V2.PaidTimeOffBLL, Version=1.0.0.0, Culture=neutral, PublicKeyToken=null
- ❑ **Description:** Displays a list of requested days off.
- ❑ Leave the subreports null.

Now run the project and give yourself permission to this report using the Roles screen. You can now navigate to the Report List screen and run this report. Try playing with the query control and previewing the report. If you create a filter for "Current Status Equals Approved," then you have created the Approved Requests report simply by changing the filter and not creating a new report.

Summary

This chapter showed you how to create a query builder control that can be used for filtering reports, HTML tables, or even exports. It also provided an example of a server-side control that supports AJAX functionality and used the ASP.NET AJAX Control Toolkit found on www.asp.net. Custom attributes were also used to define the fields that can be queried by the control. This control can save plenty of development time, especially when it comes to reports.

The steps to create an object that supports querying capabilities are as follows:

❑ Create a data class that inherits from ENTBaseQueryData.

❑ Implement the SelectClause and FromClause methods in the data class.

❑ The data class must pass in a generic class that will be passed back to the business layer; this is always an entity class. To create this entity class you can take the Select and From clauses and create a stored procedure and then use the ORM Designer to automatically generate the entity class by dragging the stored procedure to the Methods pane. Once the entity class is created, you can delete the stored procedure from the database.

❑ Add the appropriate QueryField and RequiredQueryField attributes to the top of the data class.

❑ Create a business object class that inherits from ENTBaseQueryBO. There is nothing to implement in this class if you use its default functionality.

❑ Create a Web Form and add the AJAX ScriptManager and QueryBuilder controls.

❑ Set the QueryBuilder control's QueryObjectName property to the business object.

❑ In the event handler that needs to retrieve the data from the database, call the GetWhereClause method of the QueryBuilder control and pass it to the business class.

I went back to Mary to show her the new report screen and the query builder control. Her eyes lit up when she found out that she wouldn't have to keep coming back to me for each report she wanted because she could do it herself. After explaining to Mary how to access the Reports screen and run the report she was quite happy. Unfortunately, a client's happiness only lasts a few minutes before they think of their next request. Now she wants to be able to see this data without having to go through all the motions of clicking on the reports and building the query.

This is where dashboards can help her. A *dashboard* means different things to different people, but for this application the dashboard is a series of Web Parts that Mary can view on her home page that contain important information about the data in the requests in her system. The data can be displayed as a graph, an HTML table, or even just a link to another screen in the application. Microsoft provides a great framework for building dashboards into your application, and the next chapter will walk you through a step-by-step example that demonstrates how to create a home page in the PaidTimeOffUI project with dashboard functionality.

11

The Dashboard

One of the big buzzwords these days is "dashboard." This is one of those words that seems to have made its way into the vernacular of executive management. "I want to see a high-level snapshot off all activity in all my divisions, by department, by business unit, by person." A *dashboard* is a web page that contains critical information displayed as graphs, links, speedometers, reports, and many other forms. The goal of the dashboard is to give users a high-level view of the data collected in the application. The concept is similar to the dashboard in your car. You see the fuel gauge, your speed, the battery charge, the RPMs, and so on, in one place, which enables you to quickly make decisions based on the information provided.

Many vendors are more than willing to sell you their out-of-the-box solutions and tools to create these dashboards. They usually include a demo with pie charts, line graphs, or speedometers that are used to show you the health of your organization. These demos may throw in some other buzz phrases like *key performance indicators,* and they make it look very easy with the staged data in the demo database. Yes, these tools can be useful and make an application look professional.

Problem

I'm here to let you know that you can forget about all those high-priced third-party tools and save your company a lot of money by building your own dashboard using the free web part controls included with Visual Studio. The web part controls were released with Visual Studio 2005 and are pretty much the same in Visual Studio 2008. Why change them when they work great? The web part controls enable you to create a dashboard in your application that has customizable "parts" that users can choose to include or not include on their page. These web parts can contain the same graphs as the third-party tools. The page containing the web parts can even enable users to change the position of the web parts on the page with minimal programming.

The web parts included with Visual Studio are actually a framework to which you have to add meaningful content for your application. The framework comes with a database that "talks" to the web parts and stores the customized settings for each user, so all of the plumbing is taken care of for you. You can get a lot of mileage from the web parts with little code and effort, but don't tell the user that!

This chapter adds a home page to the `PaidTimeOffUI` project that will contain the web part controls to create the dashboard. The dashboard will contain three web parts: one that shows pending requests that the current user should approve or deny, one that shows the current user's requests in an HTML table, and one that uses the calendar control to show the current user's requests on the calendar. The home page will also enable users to close any web parts or rearrange them on the page.

Design

Figure 11-1 shows a screen shot of the home page for the `PaidTimeOff` solution. The home page acts as the dashboard for the system.

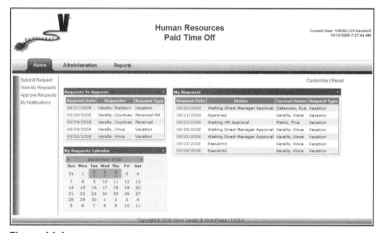

Figure 11-1

This page contains three web parts: Request To Approve, My Requests, and My Requests Calendar. Each web part has a title bar with a menu that enables the user to minimize or close the web part, as shown in Figure 11-2.

Figure 11-2

This enables the user to either minimize the web part so only the title bar is displayed or close the web part entirely. Behind the scenes, the web part framework keeps track of all of these settings on a user-by-user basis, so the next time a user navigates to this page the application retains these settings.

Note two important links in the top right-hand corner of the screen. The first is the Customize link, which enables the user to move the web parts around on the page. For example, this page uses a table to control its layout. The table contains two columns, so selecting Customize enables users to move the web parts from column to column. They can also move them above or below one another. The Customize link also enables users to add web parts to pages that have been closed or are not displayed by default. For example, if you close the Requests To Approve web part and then want to add it back to the page, you could click the Customize link and the screen shown in Figure 11-3 would appear.

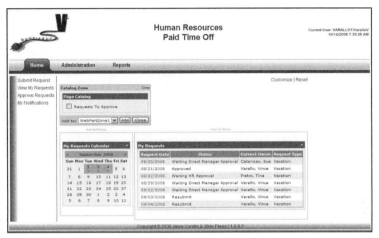

Figure 11-3

The `CatalogZone` is a web part control included with Visual Studio. The Requests To Approve web part appears in the Page Catalog, and users can add it back to the page by selecting which web part zone to add it to and then clicking the Add button. While in customize mode, users can also drag and drop the web parts around on the page by clicking on the title of the web part. Figure 11-4 shows the page as the My Requests Calendar web part is dragged from the first zone to the second zone.

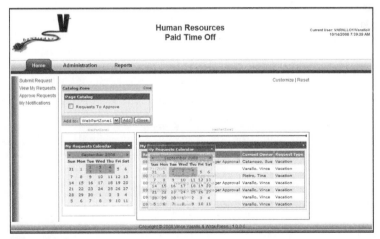

Figure 11-4

After dropping the web part in the second zone, the page looks like Figure 11-5.

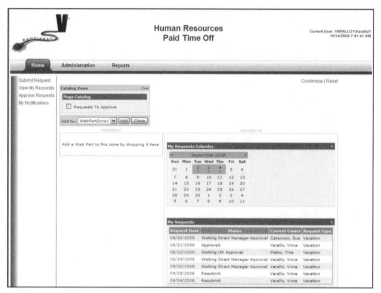

Figure 11-5

To exit out of the customize mode, you simply click the Close button in the Catalog Zone. If you need to get back to the original layout, simply click the Reset link at the top of the page. The page will then appear with the controls in the position you placed them when designing the page.

As you can see, you can create user-friendly pages that can be very useful to users, and you might be surprised by how little custom code is needed to enable this functionality.

The Web Part Controls

Open Visual Studio 2008 and load the `PaidTimeOffSolution`. Add a new Web Form called `TestWebParts.aspx` to the `PaidTimeOffUI` project. This page doesn't have to use a master page or inherit from any other class because it will be used for discussion purposes only. Open the page in design view so the toolbox appears. All the web part controls are found in the toolbox on a tab called WebParts.

Drag a `WebPartManager` control onto the page. The `WebPartManager` control is needed for any page that uses web parts. This is similar to the `ScriptManager` control for the ASP.NET AJAX controls. You only need to drop it on the form in order for the functionality to work. Switch to source view and add an HTML table to the form that will act as a placeholder for the other web part controls. The table should simply contain three empty columns. The HTML should look similar to this:

```
<form id="form1" runat="server">
    <div>
        <asp:WebPartManager ID="WebPartManager1" runat="server">
        </asp:WebPartManager>

        <table>
            <tr>
```

```
                    <td></td>
                    <td></td>
                    <td></td>
                </tr>
            </table>
        </div>
    </form>
```

The first two columns will be used to enable users to view and move web parts around. The third column will be used to display the `PageCatalogPart`, which controls adding new web parts to the page when in customize mode. Drag a `WebPartZone` control into the first column and then do the same for the second column:

```
    <tr>
        <td>
            <asp:WebPartZone ID="WebPartZone1" runat="server">
            </asp:WebPartZone>
        </td>
        <td>
            <asp:WebPartZone ID="WebPartZone2" runat="server">
            </asp:WebPartZone>
        </td>
        <td></td>
    </tr>
```

The `WebPartZone` control is a container control that enables you to set up placeholders on the page where web parts can be positioned. Change the view of the web page to design view and drag a `Button` control into the first web part zone, drag a `Label` control to the second web part zone, and then drag a `TextBox` control to the first web part zone. Notice that each control appears in its own box with a title and menu, as shown in Figure 11-6.

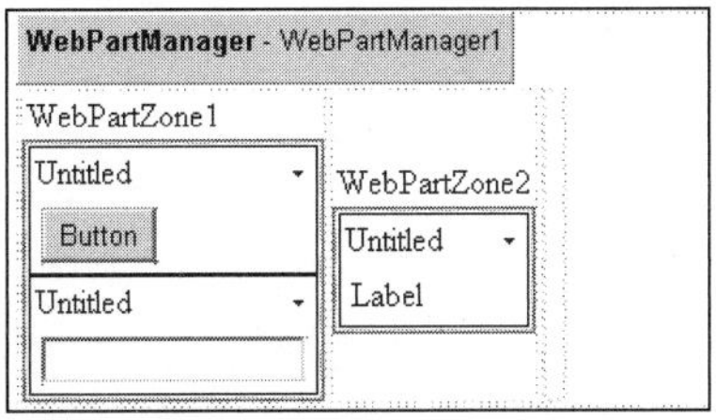

Figure 11-6

If you change back to source view you'll notice that the controls were added between `ZoneTemplate` tags, which were automatically added to the HTML by the designer. Each control placed in the `ZoneTemplate` tags will have its own web part title and menu displayed on the page:

```
    <tr>
        <td>
            <asp:WebPartZone ID="WebPartZone1" runat="server">
                <ZoneTemplate>
                    <asp:Button ID="Button1" runat="server" Text="Button" />
                    <asp:TextBox ID="TextBox1" runat="server"></asp:TextBox>
                </ZoneTemplate>
```

```
                </asp:WebPartZone>
        </td>
        <td>
            <asp:WebPartZone ID="WebPartZone2" runat="server">
                <ZoneTemplate>
                    <asp:Label ID="Label1" runat="server" Text="Label"></asp:Label>
                </ZoneTemplate>
            </asp:WebPartZone>
        </td>
        <td></td>
    </tr>
```

To change the title from Untitled to something meaningful, simply add the `Title` attribute to your control. Add the `Title` attribute to the `Button` control and set its value to "Button Web Part." Do the same for the `TextBox` and `Label` controls. If you switch back to design view, the title of the web part should be changed to the title of the control (see Figure 11-7).

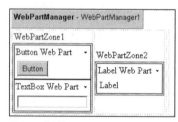

Figure 11-7

The appearance of the web parts is controlled by the properties of the `WebPartZone`. If you hover your mouse over WebPartZone1's title, you should see a button with an arrow. Click the button to display the WebPartZone Tasks menu, and then click Auto Format. This enables you to format the control, similar to how a `GridView` can be formatted with built-in schemes. Choose the Professional scheme and click OK. The page should now look like the one shown in Figure 11-8.

Figure 11-8

Switch to the source view to see what actually happened. The `WebPartZone` control has many properties that enable you to control the look of the web parts contained in it:

```
<asp:WebPartZone ID="WebPartZone1" runat="server" BorderColor="#CCCCCC"
    Font-Names="Verdana" Padding="6">
    <EmptyZoneTextStyle Font-Size="0.8em" />
```

```
        <PartStyle Font-Size="0.8em" ForeColor="#333333" />
        <TitleBarVerbStyle Font-Size="0.6em" Font-Underline="False" ForeColor="White" />
        <MenuLabelHoverStyle ForeColor="#E2DED6" />
        <MenuPopupStyle BackColor="#5D7B9D" BorderColor="#CCCCCC" BorderWidth="1px"
            Font-Names="Verdana" Font-Size="0.6em" />
        <MenuVerbStyle BorderColor="#5D7B9D" BorderStyle="Solid" BorderWidth="1px"
            ForeColor="White" />
        <PartTitleStyle BackColor="#5D7B9D" Font-Bold="True" Font-Size="0.8em"
            ForeColor="White" />
        <ZoneTemplate>
            <asp:Button ID="Button1" runat="server" Text="Button" Title="Button Web
                Part" />
            <asp:TextBox ID="TextBox1" runat="server" Title="Textbox Web
                Part"></asp:TextBox>
        </ZoneTemplate>
        <MenuVerbHoverStyle BackColor="#F7F6F3" BorderColor="#CCCCCC"
            BorderStyle="Solid" BorderWidth="1px" ForeColor="#333333" />
        <PartChromeStyle BackColor="#F7F6F3" BorderColor="#E2DED6" Font-Names="Verdana"
            ForeColor="White" />
        <HeaderStyle Font-Size="0.7em" ForeColor="#CCCCCC" HorizontalAlign="Center" />
        <MenuLabelStyle ForeColor="White" />
    </asp:WebPartZone>
```

If you click on WebPartZone1 and view the Properties window, you'll see all of the available properties for the control. Switch back to design view before continuing.

Next, drag a CatalogZone control to the third column. The CatalogZone control is another placeholder control but this doesn't display web parts; instead, it displays controls that enable users to customize the page. Drag a PageCatalogPart into the CatalogZone. The PageCatalogPart is the control that knows which controls are available for placement on this page, and enables users to add controls to the WebPart Zones defined on the page. The screen should now look like the one shown in Figure 11-9.

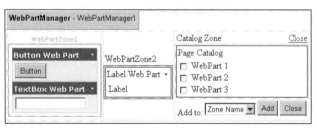

Figure 11-9

Set this page as the Start Page and the project as the StartUp project and run the solution. The page should appear and display all three web parts, but the catalog is not displayed because you have to add this functionality yourself. I know, they really make this tough — we have to add one line of code. Stop the running solution and add a button to the top of the page and set its Text property to Customize. Double-click on the button to create the click event handler. Add the following code to the event handler:

```
WebPartManager1.DisplayMode = WebPartManager.CatalogDisplayMode;
```

Run the project again. This time close the TextBox web part by clicking on the menu and selecting Close. The web part should disappear from the page. Now click the Customize button. The page should show the Catalog Zone and the Page Catalog web part (see Figure 11-10).

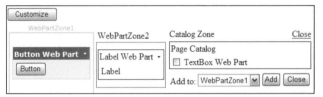

Figure 11-10

Because the TextBox web part was closed it now appears as an available web part to add to the page. Check the box next to Textbox Web Part and then add it to WebPartZone2. The Textbox web part is now added to WebPartZone2. Notice that is looks like the Label web part control now instead of the Button web part control because this zone was not formatted the same way. While in customize mode, you can also drag and drop any web part to another position in the zone or into another zone. Drag the TextBox web part so it appears above the Button web part in WebPartZone1. It will now look like the Button web part. Click the Close button on the Catalog Zone control. The page should now look like Figure 11-11.

Figure 11-11

Close the browser and relaunch the project. The page somehow retained the customization, like magic. Well, not really. What actually happened, unbeknownst to you, is that a database was added to your project the first time you ran this page. Close the browser again and refresh the App_Data folder in the PaidTimeOffUI project. There is now a database file called ASPNETDB.MDF. This database contains all the personalization settings used for any pages that use web parts in this project. If you double-click on the file and expand the Tables node, you'll be able to see its table structure in the Server Explorer window (see Figure 11-12).

If you open the aspnet_Users table, you should see a record in this table with your user name. Open the aspnet_PersonalizationPerUser table, which will have a record with your user ID. The Page Settings field contains your customized settings for this page. The PathId field points to a record in the aspnet_Paths table, which contains a record for any page that has a web part on it, so you can create multiple pages in the same project with this functionality. Of course, you wouldn't want to use this database in production because this is an SQL Express DB. You can create an SQL Server database by running a command-line tool that comes with Visual Studio.

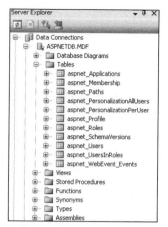

Figure 11-12

Create a new SQL Server database and call it PTOPersonalization. Add to this database a user who has permissions to create tables and add, update, and delete data. Open the Visual Studio 2008 Command Prompt and navigate to the c:\Windows\Microsoft.NET\Framework\v2.0.50727 directory. There should be an executable named aspnet_regsql.exe in this directory. Run this program in the command line without passing any parameters. This will bring up a wizard that helps you configure the database (see Figure 11-13).

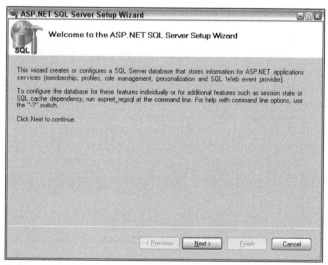

Figure 11-13

Click the Next button. Choose "Configure SQL Server for application services" and click the Next button, as shown in Figure 11-14.

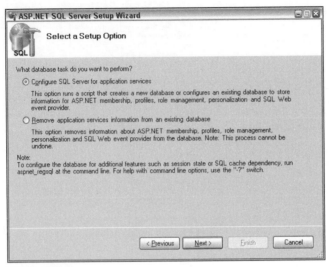

Figure 11-14

Enter the name of your server and the PTOPersonalization database and click the Next button, as shown in Figure 11-15.

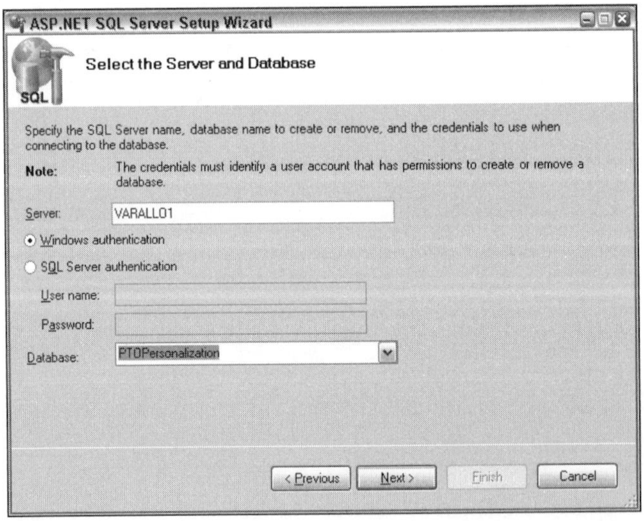

Figure 11-15

A summary page will appear with your settings. Click the Next button to create the database. The last page of the wizard will remind you to configure your application to use this database. Click the Finish button to close the wizard. If you open SQL Server and expand the tables in the PTOPersonalization database, you will see all the new tables created by the wizard.

The next step is to use this database in the PTO application. By default, the application looks in the `machine.config` file for the personalization database if none exists in the `web.config` file. The setting in the `web.config` file is as follows:

```
<connectionStrings>
  <add name="LocalSqlServer" connectionString="data source=.\SQLEXPRESS;Integrated
      Security=SSPI;AttachDBFilename=|DataDirectory|aspnetdb.mdf;User
      Instance=true" providerName="System.Data.SqlClient"/>
</connectionStrings>
```

The `machine.config` file is used by all applications. You want to change the setting just for your application, so you need to add a new connection string to `web.config`. Simply name it `LocalSqlServer` and set the `connectionString` attribute to the new personalization database you just created. If you get an error that this is a duplicate entry, you have to add a `remove` tag before the `add` tag in the `connectionString` section:

```
<remove name="LocalSqlServer"/>
<add name="LocalSqlServer" connectionString="Data Source=VARALLO1;Initial
    Catalog=PTOPersonalization;User ID=V2Application;Password=wrox" />
```

Solution

Now you have an idea of what web parts are and how they can be used. Microsoft made this very simple and I can tell you from experience it works on a large scale and doesn't affect performance. Getting back to Mary's application, the goal of the home page is to act as a dashboard into the PTO application. Three web parts will be added to the dashboard: one for the current user's requests, one that displays any requests the current user is supposed to approve, and one that displays the current user's requests as a calendar. Refer to Figure 11-1 to see how the dashboard will look.

Add a new page to the project called `Home.aspx` and have it use the `PaidTimeOff.master` page and inherit from `BasePage`. Implement the two `BasePage` abstract methods as follows:

```
public override string MenuItemName()
{
    return "Home";
}

public override string[] CapabilityNames()
{
    return new string[] { "Home" };
}
```

In order for this page to work, you need to create a record in the `ENTMenuItem` table. The only difference between this page and the other records is that the `IsAlwaysEnabled` field should be set to True. This is the home page, so everyone will have access to it. In addition, because no capabilities are associated with this page, the "Capability Check" functionality in the base page should be turned off. To do this, override the `OnInit` method in the `Home.aspx` page:

```
protected override void OnInit(EventArgs e)
{
    IgnoreCapabilityCheck = true;
    base.OnInit(e);
}
```

Now switch back to the source view of the page. The layout of the page with all the controls is as follows:

	Customize | Reset
Catalog Zone	
Web Part Zone 1 Requests To Approve Web Part My Request Calendar Web Part	Web Part Zone 2 My Requests Web Part

Add an HTML table to the page with three rows. The first and second rows should have one column that spans two columns. The third row should contain two columns that are vertically aligned at the top. The HTML should look as follows:

```
<table>
    <tr>
        <td colspan="2" align="right">
        </td>
    </tr>
    <tr>
        <td colspan="2">
        </td>
    </tr>
    <tr>
        <td valign="top">
        </td>
        <td valign="top">
        </td>
    </tr>
</table>
```

Add a `WebPartManager` control to the page by dragging it from the Toolbox to above the `table` tag. The first row in the table should contain two link buttons: The first one enables users to customize the page, and the second one is for resetting the page to the original layout. Drag two Link Button controls from the Toolbox to the first row and separate the buttons by a pipe (|). Change the name of the first link button to `lbtnCustomize` and change its text to "Customize." Change the name of the second link button to `lbtnReset` and change its text to "Reset." Double-click on the Customize link to create its click event handler. Add the following code to the event handler:

```
protected void lbtnCustomize_Click(object sender, EventArgs e)
{
    WebPartManager1.DisplayMode = WebPartManager.CatalogDisplayMode;
}
```

Double-click on the Reset link button to create its click event handler and add the following code:

```
protected void lbtnReset_Click(object sender, EventArgs e)
{
    WebPartManager1.Personalization.ResetPersonalizationState();
}
```

The next step is to add the Catalog Zone control. Simply drag the Catalog Zone control from the Toolbox to the second row. Now drag a PageCatalogPart from the Toolbox to the Catalog Zone. Now you need to format the web part. Hover the mouse pointer over the Catalog Zone's title and click the button with the arrow. Then click the Auto Format link. The AutoFormat dialog will appear. Select the Professional scheme and click OK. The page should look like Figure 11-16 in design mode.

Figure 11-16

Next, add the two web part zone controls to each column. Drag a `WebPartZone` control from the Toolbox to each column in the third row. Format both zones to use the Professional scheme that the Catalog Zone is using.

The web parts that are to be placed in the web part zones must exist as controls. They can be any of the standard controls that come with Visual Studio, a user control, or a custom server control. The three controls that must be created for this application will be developed as user controls. These controls aren't reusable in other projects so they don't need to be server controls. The first control to build is the PTO requests control. This control will display either the current user's requests or the current user's requests to approve. A property of the control will determine which is to be displayed.

Add a new folder to the `PaidTimeOffUI` project called `Controls`. Right-click on this folder and select Add New Item. Select Web User Control from the list of templates and name the file `PTORequests.ascx`. Note that the extension for controls is .ascx and the extension for pages is .aspx. Think of user controls as include files in the classic ASP world. These are controls that can be added to any page in the current project.

Open the code-behind for the control and add an enumeration for the "types" of data this control will display. For now, this control will only be able to display the current user's requests or the current user's requests to approve:

```
public enum FilterEnum
{
    MyRequests,
    RequestsToApprove
}
```

Now add a property to this control. When you create a property on a user control it is displayed in the Properties window in Visual Studio when a user adds the control to a form:

```
public FilterEnum Filter { get; set; }
```

The `Page_Load` event should check the `Filter` property and load the grid with the correct information. Since other pages already display this information, you can reuse the business objects that already exist. Add the following code to the `Page_Load` event:

```
CustomGridView cgvPTORequests = new CustomGridView();

cgvPTORequests.ListClassName = typeof(PTORequestEOList).AssemblyQualifiedName;

cgvPTORequests.AddBoundField("", "Request Date", "");

//Check the filter type
switch (Filter)
{
    case FilterEnum.RequestsToApprove:
        //Get request to approve
        cgvPTORequests.LoadMethodName = "LoadByCurrentOwnerId";
        cgvPTORequests.LoadMethodParameters.Add(((BasePage)Page).CurrentUser.ID);

        //Add the requestor column.
        cgvPTORequests.AddBoundField("", "Requestor", "");
        break;
    default:
        //Default to my request if the developer forgot to set the filter property
        cgvPTORequests.LoadMethodName = "LoadByENTUserAccountId";
        cgvPTORequests.LoadMethodParameters.Add(((BasePage)Page).CurrentUser.ID);

        //Add status and current owner
        cgvPTORequests.AddBoundField("", "Status", "");
        cgvPTORequests.AddBoundField("", "Current Owner", "");
        break;
}

cgvPTORequests.AddBoundField("RequestTypeString", "Request Type", "");

cgvPTORequests.RowDataBound += new
    GridViewRowEventHandler(cgvPTORequests_RowDataBound);

//Default the sort to the request date
cgvPTORequests.SortExpressionLast = "RequestDate";

cgvPTORequests.DataBind();

Controls.Add(cgvPTORequests);
```

This code creates a new custom `GridView` control at runtime and binds the `PTORequestEOList` object to the grid. Depending on the `Filter` property, either the `LoadByCurrentOwnerId` method or the `LoadByENTUserAccountId` method will be called to display the data. If the control is set to display requests to approve, the requestor column is added to the grid. If the control is set to display the current user's requests, the status and current owner columns are added to the grid. Since this control is added on-the-fly, the `RowDataBound` event handler must be hooked to the control dynamically. The is what the `cgvPTORequests.RowDataBound += new GridViewRowEventHandler(cgvPTOReques ts_RowDataBound);` command does. The last line adds the custom `GridView` to the `Controls` collection of this control.

Now you need to handle the `RowDataBound` event. This method displays the request date as a link that navigates to the `PTORequest` page. It also resolves the ID of the requestor to first name and last name:

```
protected void cgvPTORequests_RowDataBound(object sender, GridViewRowEventArgs e)
{
  if (e.Row.RowType == DataControlRowType.DataRow)
  {
    //Add the data link to the first column.
    HyperLink editLink = new HyperLink();
    PTORequestEO request = (PTORequestEO)e.Row.DataItem;
    editLink.Text = request.RequestDateString;

    if (Filter == FilterEnum.RequestsToApprove)
    {
      editLink.NavigateUrl = BasePage.RootPath(Context) + "PTORequest.aspx" +
          BasePage.EncryptQueryString("id=" + request.ID.ToString() +
          "&Approving=true");
    }
    else
    {
      editLink.NavigateUrl = BasePage.RootPath(Context) + "PTORequest.aspx" +
          BasePage.EncryptQueryString("id=" + request.ID.ToString());
    }

    e.Row.Cells[COL_INDEX_REQUESTDATE].Controls.Add(editLink);

    if (Filter == FilterEnum.RequestsToApprove)
    {
      //Show the requestor
      e.Row.Cells[COL_INDEX_REQUESTOR].Text =
          Globals.GetUsers(Page.Cache).GetByID(request.ENTUserAccountId).DisplayText;
    }
    else
    {
      //Must be showing my requests.
      e.Row.Cells[COL_INDEX_STATUS].Text = request.CurrentState.StateName;

      e.Row.Cells[COL_INDEX_CURRENT_OWNER].Text = request.CurrentOwnerUserName;
    }
  }
}
```

This method uses constants for the columns that should be added to the top of the code-behind page:

```
private const int COL_INDEX_REQUESTDATE = 0;
private const int COL_INDEX_REQUESTOR = 1;
private const int COL_INDEX_STATUS = 1;
private const int COL_INDEX_CURRENT_OWNER = 2;
```

That's all there is to do for this control. You can add it to the home page by switching to design view on the home page and dragging the control from the Solution Explorer window to the Web Part Zone. For this page, drag a PTORequests control into WebPartZone1 and WebPartZone2. Click on the control in WebPartZone1 and view the Properties window. Note for the Filter property that the options are limited to the enumeration you defined for this control. Set this control's filter to RequestsToApprove. Click on the control in WebPartZone2 and set its Filter property to MyRequests. Now view the HTML for these controls and add the title attribute to each one. The first should have a title of "Requests To Approve" and the second should be "My Requests." Your page should now look like the one shown in Figure 11-17.

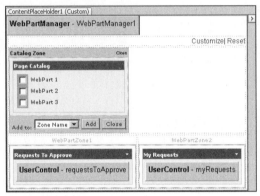

Figure 11-17

Now create the My Requests Calendar control. Add a new Web User control to the Controls folder and name it PTORequestsCalendar.ascx. Drag a Calendar control from the Toolbox to the design surface. This control will display the current user's requests in blue in the calendar. The user's requests will be loaded into a List object in the Page_Load and then the calendar's DayRender method will determine whether the day should be displayed in blue.

Add a member variable to hold the list of requests:

```
private PTORequestEOList _requests = new PTORequestEOList();
```

Now add code to the Page_Load event to load this list:

```
protected void Page_Load(object sender, EventArgs e)
{
    _requests.LoadByENTUserAccountId(((BasePage)Page).CurrentUser.ID);
}
```

Create the DayRender event for the Calendar control by viewing its properties and click the lightning bolt button. This displays the events for this control. Double-click on the DayRender event and add the following code to the event handler. This will set the color of the day cell. If a request is denied or cancelled, it should be ignored:

```
protected void Calendar1_DayRender(object sender, DayRenderEventArgs e)
{
    List<PTORequestEO> todaysRequests = _requests.GetByRequestDate(e.Day.Date);
```

```
        foreach (PTORequestEO ptoRequest in todaysRequests)
        {
            if ((ptoRequest.CurrentState.StateName != "Cancelled") &&
                (ptoRequest.CurrentState.StateName != "Denied"))
            {
                SetPTORequestCellText(e, ptoRequest.PTORequestTypeId,
                                        ptoRequest.PTODayTypeId);
            }
        }
    }
```

This method calls a private method that sets the background color:

```
private void SetPTORequestCellText(DayRenderEventArgs e,
    PTORequestTypeBO.PTORequestTypeEnum requestType, PTODayTypeBO.PTODayTypeEnum
    dayType)
{
    string text;

    switch (requestType)
    {
        case PTORequestTypeBO.PTORequestTypeEnum.Vacation:
            text = "V";
            break;
        case PTORequestTypeBO.PTORequestTypeEnum.Personal:
            text = "P";
            break;
        case PTORequestTypeBO.PTORequestTypeEnum.Unpaid:
            text = "U";
            break;
        default:
            throw new Exception("Unknown request type.");
    }

    switch (dayType)
    {
        case PTODayTypeBO.PTODayTypeEnum.AM:
            text += "-AM";
            e.Day.IsSelectable = true;
            break;
        case PTODayTypeBO.PTODayTypeEnum.PM:
            text += "-PM";
            e.Day.IsSelectable = true;
            break;
        case PTODayTypeBO.PTODayTypeEnum.Full:
            e.Day.IsSelectable = false;
            break;
        default:
            throw new Exception("Unknown day type.");
    }

    Label lbl = new Label();
    lbl.Text = text;
    lbl.Font.Size = 6;
```

```
        e.Cell.Controls.Add(new LiteralControl("<br />"));
        e.Cell.Controls.Add(lbl);

        e.Cell.BackColor = Color.LightSkyBlue;
    }
```

That's all that is needed for this control. You can now drag it to the `WebZonePart1` control on the home page. Change its title to "My Requests Calendar" and now you are good to go. Set `Home.aspx` as the Start Page and run the project. You should see the custom controls on the screen and you can customize or reset the page back to its original state. There really isn't a lot of coding to do for this functionality. The Web Part framework enables you to concentrate on creating the controls to display the relevant data for your application; the framework handles the rest. These types of pages are quite handy to users and "sell" systems when demonstrated. You can get fancy by adding graphs or even reports to the home page to complete your "dashboard" and greatly impress the user.

Summary

This chapter focused on building the dashboard for the Paid Time Off application. As shown in the chapter, the bulk of the functionality for creating a customizable screen that gives user a peek at important system information is handled by the web part controls that are included with Visual Studio. As the developer, you simply have to determine what information you want to display and in what format. This is a slam dunk for you, and you should be able to get a lot of mileage out of the web parts' functionality.

The steps required to create a page with customizable web parts are as follows:

❑   Add a Web Form to your project and add a `WebPartManager` control to the page.

❑   Create an HTML table or `DIV` tags to determine the positioning of the controls on the screen.

❑   Add a `CatalogZone` control and then add a `PageCatalogPart` control to the Catalog Zone.

❑   Add a button that enables users to customize the page and a button that enables users to reset the page to the default view.

❑   Add code to the button click events to customize the page or reset the page.

❑   The code to customize a page is `WebPartManager1.DisplayMode = WebPartManager.CatalogDisplayMode;`

❑   The code to reset a page is `WebPartManager1.Personalization.ResetPersonalizationState();`

❑   Add `WebPartZone` controls to the page where you would like to add the web parts.

❑   Use standard controls or create your own user or server controls and add them to the `WebPartZone` controls. The formatted properties of the `WebPartZone` control determine the format of the controls in that zone.

❑   Use the default SQL Express database generated by Visual Studio to manage the personalization state management or create an SQL Server database using the `aspnet_regsql.exe` command-line utility to manage this functionality.

I went back to Mary to show her the dashboard functionality and she was quite happy again, but she still has one last itch to scratch. She would like to know when anyone changes a request, who changed it, and the old and new value for the changed data. She essentially wants an audit trail in the system. Once again she is in luck because the framework being built in this book has a pattern for an audit trail that captures the exact information she is asking for. The next chapter will walk you through the audit trail pattern and create a report that uses Crystal Reports for .NET and the query builder control to enable Mary to view the audit trail.

12

Auditing

Building a solid audit trail is critical in many of today's enterprise-level applications, not to mention it can get you out of a heap of trouble when people start asking questions about missing data. Wouldn't it be great if you could produce a nice, fancy report that indicates whenever anyone adds, updates, or deletes a record? Not only is an audit trail good for covering your butt, but an increasing number of regulations mandate that system activity be traceable.

Audit trails are another one of those features that never seem to make it into the first round of requirements. "Oh, we'll get to that later after we figure out what we want" is a common refrain. Well, it's much easier to take care of auditing up front, rather than after the fact; and with the pattern that has been defined in this book already, it is easy to slip in an audit trail without refactoring the entire project.

Problem

The key features of the audit trail for the Paid Time Off solution are as follows:

❑ It enables users to track additions, updates, and deletion of data.

❑ It enables users to configure how much detail to capture. If they don't care about updates to certain tables, then they can turn the audit trail off so the database does not become bloated.

❑ The audit trail captures the before-and-after picture of each field when it is updated, which makes tracing changes easy.

There are many patterns out there for audit trails. Some use database triggers that are deployed in the database itself; others add the code only in the data access layer; and still others implement the code in the business layer. A decision also needs to be made regarding how much data is captured. Some systems have a duplicate table structure for every table and when a record is updated in the main table, a copy of the original record — including all its fields — are added to the audit table. Other patterns use a single audit table that keeps track of only those changes made at the field level, as well as additions and deletions. There is no right or wrong way to create an audit trail, as long as the solution you implement meets the user's and/or auditor's requirements.

This chapter will implement auditing in the business layer and use a single table to track all the additions, changes, and deletions of records. Discussed in detail are the requirements of the audit trail for the Paid Time Off solution and how it can be implemented in the business logic layer.

Design

Before getting into the design of the audit trail for the Paid Time Off solution, let's review the requirements defined by Mary:

❑   Anytime a record is added to the system, the user and date/time must be tracked by the system.

❑   Anytime a record is deleted from the system, the user, date/time, and ID of the record being deleted must be tracked by the system.

❑   Anytime a record is updated in the system, the before and after values for each field must be tracked by the system, as well as the user and date/time when the update occurred.

❑   To avoid excess data in the database, the system must enable users to turn off auditing of specific data.

❑   The system must enable users to run a report and filter by date, user, record, or type of change.

This is a fairly straightforward list of requirements for an audit trail in most enterprise-level applications. Three main areas need to be developed: The first is the capability to customize the audit trail by enabling users to select what is audited. Second, the audit trail needs to be implemented in the existing business objects. Third, the report that enables users to see the audit trail needs to be created. "The Design" section of this chapter will review the setup of the audit trail and "The Solution" section covers implementation and reporting of the audit trail.

Customizing the Audit Trail

Figure 12-1 shows how users will be able to turn on the audit trail to track changes of an object.

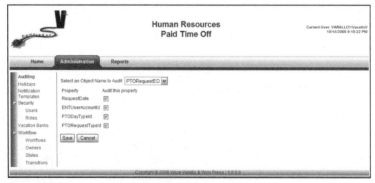

Figure 12-1

Notice that for auditing purposes, users are given a list of classes, not tables, that reside in the business layer. This is because the audit trail will be implemented in the business layer for any EditObject class. Only EditObjects classes can be added, updated, or deleted, so they are the only items that can be audited. This screen enables the user to turn on auditing changes for any EditObject class and to pick which fields should be audited.

Two new tables need to be added to the database to support this functionality (see Figure 12-2).

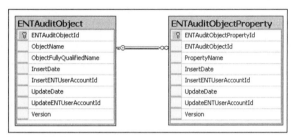

Figure 12-2

The ENTAuditObject table contains the "friendly" name of the business object that is displayed to the user and the fully qualified name of the object. The system uses the fully qualified name and reflection to determine the available properties for the object. The ENTAuditObjectProperty table contains all the properties that should be audited. There is a one-to-many relationship between the ENTAuditObject and the ENTAuditObjectProperty table.

The standard five stored procedures should be added for each table, along with three custom stored procedures. The first is the ENTAuditObjectSelectByObjectName procedure. This procedure will select a record by object name, rather than ID:

```
CREATE PROCEDURE ENTAuditObjectSelectByObjectName
(
    @ObjectName varchar(255)
)
AS
    SET NOCOUNT ON

    SELECT ENTAuditObjectId, ObjectName, ObjectFullyQualifiedName, InsertDate,
           InsertENTUserAccountId, UpdateDate, UpdateENTUserAccountId, Version
      FROM ENTAuditObject
     WHERE ObjectName = @ObjectName

    RETURN
```

The second custom stored procedure selects all the ENTAuditObjectProperty records based on the ENTAuditObjectId. This is used when loading the EditObject class:

```
CREATE PROCEDURE ENTAuditObjectPropertySelectByENTAuditObjectId
(
    @ENTAuditObjectId int
)
AS
```

```
    SET NOCOUNT ON

    SELECT ENTAuditObjectPropertyId, ENTAuditObjectId, PropertyName, InsertDate,
           InsertENTUserAccountId, UpdateDate, UpdateENTUserAccountId, Version
      FROM ENTAuditObjectProperty
     WHERE ENTAuditObjectId = @ENTAuditObjectId

    RETURN
```

The third custom stored procedure deletes all the ENTAuditObjectProperty records based on the
ENTAuditObjectId. When the user clicks the Save button (refer to Figure 12-1), all the child records
are deleted and re-added based on what has been selected using the checkboxes:

```
CREATE PROCEDURE ENTAuditObjectPropertyDeleteByENTAuditObjectId
(
    @ENTAuditObjectId int
)
AS
    SET NOCOUNT ON

    DELETE
      FROM ENTAuditObjectProperty
     WHERE ENTAuditObjectId = @ENTAuditObjectId

    RETURN
```

The Chapter12Auditing.sql file contains the DDL to create these tables and stored procedures.

Once the database is set up, you need to add the tables and stored procedures to the DataContext
object as you've done before. Remember to add the partial class declarations in the Customized
Entities.cs file:

```
public partial class ENTAuditObject : IENTBaseEntity { }

public partial class ENTAuditObjectProperty : IENTBaseEntity { }
```

Now that the DataContext is set up, you can add the Data classes to the Framework folder in the DAL
project. This should all be familiar so far, as each class follows the same pattern that has been used
throughout the rest of the book:

```
public class ENTAuditObjectData : ENTBaseData<ENTAuditObject>
{
  public override List<ENTAuditObject> Select()
  {
    using (HRPaidTimeOffDataContext db = new
           HRPaidTimeOffDataContext(DBHelper.GetHRPaidTimeOffConnectionString()))
    {
      return db.ENTAuditObjectSelectAll().ToList();
    }
  }

  public override ENTAuditObject Select(int id)
  {
    using (HRPaidTimeOffDataContext db = new
```

```
                      HRPaidTimeOffDataContext(DBHelper.GetHRPaidTimeOffConnectionString()))
    {
      return db.ENTAuditObjectSelectById(id).SingleOrDefault();
    }
}

public override void Delete(HRPaidTimeOffDataContext db, int id)
{
    db.ENTAuditObjectDelete(id);
}

public int Insert(string connectionString, string objectName, string
    objectFullyQualifiedName, int insertENTUserAccountId)
{
    using (HRPaidTimeOffDataContext db = new
          HRPaidTimeOffDataContext(connectionString))
    {
      return Insert(db, objectName, objectFullyQualifiedName,
                    insertENTUserAccountId);
    }
}

public int Insert(HRPaidTimeOffDataContext db, string objectName, string
                  objectFullyQualifiedName, int insertENTUserAccountId)
{
    Nullable<int> eNTAuditObjectId = 0;

    db.ENTAuditObjectInsert(ref eNTAuditObjectId, objectName,
                          objectFullyQualifiedName, insertENTUserAccountId);

    return Convert.ToInt32(eNTAuditObjectId);
}

public bool Update(string connectionString, int eNTAuditObjectId, string
    objectName, string objectFullyQualifiedName, int updateENTUserAccountId, Binary
    version)
{
    using (HRPaidTimeOffDataContext db = new
          HRPaidTimeOffDataContext(connectionString))
    {
      return Update(db, eNTAuditObjectId, objectName, objectFullyQualifiedName,
                    updateENTUserAccountId, version);
    }
}

public bool Update(HRPaidTimeOffDataContext db, int eNTAuditObjectId, string
    objectName, string objectFullyQualifiedName, int updateENTUserAccountId, Binary
    version)
{
    int rowsAffected = db.ENTAuditObjectUpdate(eNTAuditObjectId, objectName,
      objectFullyQualifiedName, updateENTUserAccountId, version);

    return rowsAffected == 1;
}
```

```
    public ENTAuditObject Select(HRPaidTimeOffDataContext db, string objectName)
    {
      return db.ENTAuditObjectSelectByObjectName(objectName).SingleOrDefault();
    }
}
```

The `ENTAuditObjectPropertyData` class is omitted for brevity's sake but can be found in the solution that comes with the book.

The next step it to build the business classes. Keep a few things in mind:

❑ New classes should be added to the `Framework` folder in the BLL project for the two new tables.

❑ The classes should be called `ENTAuditObjectEO`, `ENTAuditObjectEOList`, `ENTAuditObjectPropertyEO`, and `ENTAuditObjectProperyEOList`.

❑ They should inherit from the `ENTBaseEO` and `ENTBaseEOList` classes.

❑ Only a few customizations to the classes deviate from the standard pattern.

Add a property in the `ENTAuditObjectEO` class to reflect the relationship between the two tables:

```
private ENTAuditObjectPropertyEOList _properties = new
    ENTAuditObjectPropertyEOList();

public ENTAuditObjectPropertyEOList Properties
{
    get { return _properties; }
}
```

The `Load` method should be customized to load this object:

```
public override bool Load(int id)
{
    //Get the entity object from the DAL.
    ENTAuditObject eNTAuditObject = new ENTAuditObjectData().Select(id);
    MapEntityToProperties(eNTAuditObject);
    _properties.Load(ID);
    return eNTAuditObject != null;
}
```

The `Save` method needs to be customized to save all the child records in the same transaction when the parent record is being saved:

```
public override bool Save(HRPaidTimeOffDataContext db, ref ENTValidationErrors
    validationErrors, int userAccountId)
{
  if (DBAction == DBActionEnum.Save)
  {
    //Validate the object
    Validate(db, ref validationErrors);

    //Check if there were any validation errors
    if (validationErrors.Count == 0)
    {
```

```
              if (IsNewRecord())
              {
                //Add
                ID = new ENTAuditObjectData().Insert(db, ObjectName,
                          ObjectFullyQualifiedName,  userAccountId);

                //Add the ID to all the property objects
                foreach (ENTAuditObjectPropertyEO property in _properties)
                {
                  property.ENTAuditObjectId = ID;
                }
              }
              else
              {
                //Update
                if (!new ENTAuditObjectData().Update(db, ID, ObjectName,
                  ObjectFullyQualifiedName, userAccountId, Version))
                {
                  UpdateFailed(ref validationErrors);
                  return false;
                }
                else
                {
                  //Delete the existing records for this object
                  _properties.Delete(db, ID);
                }
              }

              //Save the new settings
              _properties.Save(db, ref validationErrors, userAccountId);

              return true;

          }
          else
          {
            //Didn't pass validation.
            return false;
          }
      }
      else
      {
        throw new Exception("DBAction not Save.");
      }
  }
```

Add two overloaded Load custom methods that enable users to load this object by the object name, rather than the Id:

```
    internal bool Load(string objectName)
    {
        using (HRPaidTimeOffDataContext db = new HRPaidTimeOffDataContext())
        {
            return Load(db, objectName);
        }
```

```
    }

    internal bool Load(HRPaidTimeOffDataContext db, string objectName)
    {
        //Get the entity object from the DAL.
        ENTAuditObject eNTAuditObject = new ENTAuditObjectData().Select(db, objectName);
        MapEntityToProperties(eNTAuditObject);
        _properties.Load(db, ID);
        return eNTAuditObject != null;
    }
```

That's it for the ENTAuditObjectEO class. Only one custom method should be added to the ENTAudit ObjectEOList class and that is a method that searches the current instance for the object by name:

```
public ENTAuditObjectEO GetByObjectName(string objectName)
{
    return this.SingleOrDefault(a => a.ObjectName == objectName);
}
```

The ENTAuditObjectPropertyEO class has no customization but the ENTAuditObjectPropertyEOList object has four custom methods. The first deletes all the records in the ENTAuditObjectProperty table based on the ENTAuditObjectId. This is called from the Save method defined earlier:

```
internal void Delete(HRPaidTimeOffDataContext db, int entAuditObjectID)
{
    new ENTAuditObjectPropertyData().DeleteByENTAuditObjectId(db, entAuditObjectID);
}
```

The second custom method searches the current instance and returns the object in the list that matches the property name:

```
public ENTAuditObjectPropertyEO GetByPropertyName(string propertyName)
{
    return this.SingleOrDefault(p => p.PropertyName == propertyName);
}
```

The third and fourth custom methods are overloaded methods that load the current instance with all child records for the ENTAuditObjectId:

```
internal void Load(int entAuditObjectId)
{
    using (HRPaidTimeOffDataContext db = new HRPaidTimeOffDataContext())
    {
        Load(db, entAuditObjectId);
    }
}

internal void Load(HRPaidTimeOffDataContext db, int entAuditObjectId)
{
    LoadFromList(new ENTAuditObjectPropertyData().SelectByENTAuditObjectId(db,
        entAuditObjectId));
}
```

Creating the User Interface

As usual, you need to add the ENTMenuItem and ENTCapability records to the database and give
yourself access to the pages we are creating. Two new pages will be added: one that displays the list of
all objects being audited and one that enables users to edit the record. This follows the exact same pattern defined in all the other chapters.

Add a new Web Form to the Administration folder and name it AuditObjects.aspx. This page should
use the PaidTimeOffEditGrid.master page and inherit from the BasePage class. The page should
only contain the custom grid control, which will be used to display the list of objects being audited:

```
<%@ Register Assembly="V2.FrameworkControls" Namespace="V2.FrameworkControls"
    TagPrefix="cc1" %>
<%@ MasterType virtualPath="~/PaidTimeOffEditGrid.master"%>

<asp:Content ID="Content1" ContentPlaceHolderID="ContentPlaceHolder3"
            Runat="Server">
    <cc1:CustomGridView ID="cgvAuditObjects" runat="server"
        onrowdatabound="cgvAuditObjects_RowDataBound" >
    </cc1:CustomGridView>
</asp:Content>
```

The code-behind simply loads the grid, following the same pattern defined before. It also enables users
to delete a record. Here is the code for the Page_Load, which specifies the columns that should be displayed in the grid control:

```
private const int COL_INDEX_ACTION = 0;
private const int COL_INDEX_OBJECT_NAME = 1;

protected void Page_Load(object sender, EventArgs e)
{
  Master.AddButton_Click += new
    PaidTimeOffEditGrid.ButtonClickedHandler(Master_AddButton_Click);

  if (!IsPostBack)
  {
    //Tell the control what class to create and what method to call to load the
    //class.
    cgvAuditObjects.ListClassName =
      typeof(ENTAuditObjectEOList).AssemblyQualifiedName;
    cgvAuditObjects.LoadMethodName = "Load";

    //Action column-Contains the Edit link
    cgvAuditObjects.AddBoundField("", "Actions", "");

    //Name
    cgvAuditObjects.AddBoundField("DisplayText", "Name", "DisplayText");

    cgvAuditObjects.DataBind();
  }
  else
  {
    string eventTarget = Page.Request.Form["__EVENTTARGET"].ToString();
```

```
         if (eventTarget.IndexOf("lbtnDelete") > -1)
         {
           //Rebind the grid so the delete event is captured.
           cgvAuditObjects.DataBind();
         }
      }
   }
```

The Add button on the master page should navigate the user to the edit page:

```
void Master_AddButton_Click(object sender, EventArgs e)
{
  Response.Redirect("AuditObject.aspx" + EncryptQueryString("id=0"));
}
```

The Delete button deletes the record from the database and reloads the grid:

```
void lbtnDelete_Command(object sender, CommandEventArgs e)
{
  ENTValidationErrors validationErrors = new ENTValidationErrors();
  ENTAuditObjectEO auditObject = new ENTAuditObjectEO();
  auditObject.DBAction = ENTBaseEO.DBActionEnum.Delete;
  auditObject.ID = Convert.ToInt32(e.CommandArgument);
  auditObject.Delete(ref validationErrors, CurrentUser.ID);

  Master.ValidationErrors = validationErrors;

  cgvAuditObjects.DataBind();
}
```

The menu item name and the capability name are both "Auditing":

```
public override string MenuItemName()
{
  return "Auditing";
}
public override string[] CapabilityNames()
{
  return new string[] { "Auditing" };
}
```

Finally, the cgvAuditObjects_RowDataBound event adds the Edit and Delete links dynamically as each row is created in the grid:

```
protected void cgvAuditObjects_RowDataBound(object sender, GridViewRowEventArgs e)
{
  if (e.Row.RowType == DataControlRowType.DataRow)
  {
    //Add the edit link to the action column.
    HyperLink editLink = new HyperLink();
    if (ReadOnly)
    {
      editLink.Text = "View";
    }
    else
```

```
        {
            editLink.Text = "Edit";
        }
        editLink.NavigateUrl = "AuditObject.aspx" + EncryptQueryString("id=" +
            ((ENTAuditObjectEO)e.Row.DataItem).ID.ToString());

        e.Row.Cells[COL_INDEX_ACTION].Controls.Add(editLink);

        //If the user has read only access then do not show this Delete link.
        if (ReadOnly == false)
        {
            //Add a pipe between the Edit and Delete links
            LiteralControl lc = new LiteralControl(" | ");
            e.Row.Cells[COL_INDEX_ACTION].Controls.Add(lc);

            //Add the Delete link
            LinkButton lbtnDelete = new LinkButton();
            lbtnDelete.ID = "lbtnDelete" +
                ((ENTAuditObjectEO)e.Row.DataItem).ID.ToString();
            lbtnDelete.Text = "Delete";
            lbtnDelete.CommandArgument =
                ((ENTAuditObjectEO)e.Row.DataItem).ID.ToString();
            lbtnDelete.OnClientClick = "return ConfirmDelete();";
            lbtnDelete.Command += new CommandEventHandler(lbtnDelete_Command);
            e.Row.Cells[COL_INDEX_ACTION].Controls.Add(lbtnDelete);
        }
    }
}
```

The next step is to create the `AuditObject` page that enables users to add or edit an existing
`ENTAuditObject` record. This is the page that is displayed in Figure 12-1. Add a new Web Form to
the `Administration` folder and name it `AuditObject.aspx`. This page should use the `PaidTimeOff`
`EditPage` master page and inherit from the `BaseEditPage` class. This page displays a drop-down list
of all the objects in the business layer that inherit from the `ENTBaseEO` class. Since only `EditObject`
classes can add, update, or delete records, you only need to display these objects. The one tricky part to
the page is that when the user selects an object name from the drop-down list, the page should display
all the public properties that have a `set` accessor. Only properties that can be changed by the user have
a `set` accessor, which is why they are displayed.

Add the following HTML to the `AuditObject` page:

```
<%@ MasterType virtualPath="~/PaidTimeOffEditPage.master"%>

<asp:Content ID="Content1" ContentPlaceHolderID="ContentPlaceHolder3"
    Runat="Server">

    <table>
        <tr>
            <td>Select an Object Name to Audit:</td>
            <td><asp:DropDownList ID="ddlObjectName" runat="server"
                    AutoPostBack="True"
                    onselectedindexchanged="ddlObjectName_SelectedIndexChanged">
                </asp:DropDownList>
            </td>
        </tr>
```

```
        <tr>
            <td colspan="2"><asp:Table runat="server" ID="tblProperties">
                            </asp:Table>
            </td>
        </tr>
    </table>

</asp:Content>
```

As usual, the page contains a `MasterType` directive that enables you to have IntelliSense in the code-behind file for the master page. A two-column HTML table is used to position the controls on the page. The first row contains the drop-down list that contains the object names. The second row contains a nested HTML table that is dynamically created when the user selects an object from the drop-down list.

Now open the code-behind file for this page. The `Page_Load` event handler should hook the Save and Cancel button click events to the event handlers in this page and then load the properties table:

```
protected void Page_Load(object sender, EventArgs e)
{
    Master.SaveButton_Click += new
        PaidTimeOffEditPage.ButtonClickedHandler(Master_SaveButton_Click);
    Master.CancelButton_Click += new
        PaidTimeOffEditPage.ButtonClickedHandler(Master_CancelButton_Click);

    LoadPropertiesTable();
}
```

Notice that the `LoadPropertiesTable` method is always called, even if this is a postback. That's because the properties are loaded dynamically when the user selects an object from the list, and on a second post-back the HTML table must be rebuilt to retain the value of the checkboxes that are checked. Here is the `LoadPropertiesTable` method:

```
private void LoadPropertiesTable()
{
  if (ddlObjectName.SelectedValue != "")
  {
    //Add header
    TableRow trHeader = new TableRow();
    TableCell tc1 = new TableCell();
    tc1.Text = "Property";
    trHeader.Cells.Add(tc1);

    TableCell tc2 = new TableCell();
    tc2.Text = "Audit this property";
    trHeader.Cells.Add(tc2);

    tblProperties.Rows.Add(trHeader);

    //Create an instance of the type.
    PropertyInfo[] properties =
        Type.GetType(ddlObjectName.SelectedValue).GetProperties(BindingFlags.Instance
          | BindingFlags.DeclaredOnly | BindingFlags.Public);

    //Populate the table with all the fields.
```

```
foreach (PropertyInfo prop in properties)
{
    //Only show properties the have a public set property.
    MethodInfo[] methodInfo = prop.GetAccessors();

    //Get the set method
    IEnumerable<MethodInfo> set =
        from m in methodInfo
        where m.Name.StartsWith("set")
        select m;

    if (set.Count() > 0)
    {
        if (set.Single<MethodInfo>().IsPublic)
        {
            ENTWFStatePropertyEO entWFStateProperty = new ENTWFStatePropertyEO();

            TableRow tr = new TableRow();

            //Name of property
            TableCell tcName = new TableCell();
            tcName.Text = prop.Name;
            tr.Cells.Add(tcName);

            //Checkbox
            TableCell tcAudit = new TableCell();
            CheckBox chkAudit = new CheckBox();
            chkAudit.Enabled = !ReadOnly;
            chkAudit.ID = "chk" + prop.Name;
            tcAudit.Controls.Add(chkAudit);
            tr.Cells.Add(tcAudit);

            tblProperties.Rows.Add(tr);
        }
    }
}
else
{
    tblProperties.Rows.Clear();
}
}
```

This method creates a two-column table. The first column displays the name of the property and the second column displays a checkbox that enables users to designate that this property should be audited. Notice that this method uses reflection to get the properties for the object and then uses a LINQ expression to return only the list of set accessors:

```
//Get the set method
IEnumerable<MethodInfo> set =
    from m in methodInfo
    where m.Name.StartsWith("set")
    select m;
```

The method simply loops around this list and adds a row to the table and adds the two columns to the row.

The next method to implement is the `LoadControls` method. This method should load the drop-down list with all the objects in the BLL that inherit from the `ENTBaseEO` class. When a user is adding a new record using this screen, all of the `EditObject` classes that are not already being audited will be displayed in the list. If the user is editing an existing record, then only the object name will be displayed in the list. This logic is handled in the `LoadScreenFromObject` method. Here is the code that loads the Object Name drop-down list:

```
protected override void LoadControls()
{
  if (base.GetId() == 0)
  {
    //Load the list of object that inherit from the EO object
    Assembly assembly = Assembly.Load("V2.PaidTimeOffBLL");

    Type[] types = assembly.GetTypes();

    //Load the list of objects already being audited
    ENTAuditObjectEOList auditObjects = new ENTAuditObjectEOList();
    auditObjects.Load();

    foreach (Type t in types)
    {
      if ((t.IsClass) && (t.IsSubclassOf(typeof(ENTBaseEO))))
      {
        //Do not include any items in the list that already are being audited.
        if (auditObjects.GetByObjectName(t.Name) == null)
        {
          ddlObjectName.Items.Add(new ListItem(t.Name, t.AssemblyQualifiedName));
        }
      }
    }

    ddlObjectName.Items.Insert(0, new ListItem("", ""));
  }
}
```

Here is the code for the `LoadScreenFromObject`, which not only adds the object name to the drop-down list when editing a record, but also sets the value of the checkboxes for each property being audited:

```
protected override void LoadScreenFromObject(ENTAuditObjectEO baseEO)
{
  ENTAuditObjectEO auditObject = (ENTAuditObjectEO)baseEO;

  if (auditObject.ObjectName != null)
  {
    ddlObjectName.Items.Add(new ListItem(auditObject.ObjectName,
                                  auditObject.ObjectFullyQualifiedName));
    ddlObjectName.SelectedIndex = 0;

    //Load the properties table for this object
    LoadPropertiesTable();

    //Set the checkboxes for the properties that are selected to audit.
    if (tblProperties.Rows.Count > 1)
    {
```

```
      //skip the header
      for (int row = 1; row < tblProperties.Rows.Count; row++)
      {
        TableRow tr = tblProperties.Rows[row];

        string propertyName = tr.Cells[0].Text;

        //Try to find the item in the properties list
        if (auditObject.Properties.GetByPropertyName(propertyName) != null)
        {
          ((CheckBox)tr.Cells[1].Controls[0]).Checked = true;
        }
      }
    }
  }
}

  ViewState[VIEW_STATE_KEY_AUDIT_OBJECT] = baseEO;
}
```

The next method to implement is the LoadObjectFromScreen method, which is used to scrape the values of the controls on the screen and load them in the object before saving the record:

```
protected override void LoadObjectFromScreen(ENTAuditObjectEO baseEO)
{
  baseEO.ObjectName = ddlObjectName.SelectedItem.Text;
  baseEO.ObjectFullyQualifiedName = ddlObjectName.SelectedValue;

  //Set the values for the properties that are checked to audit.
  baseEO.Properties.Clear();

  //Load the properties
  if (tblProperties.Rows.Count > 1)
  {
    //skip the header
    for (int row = 1; row < tblProperties.Rows.Count; row++)
    {
      TableRow tr = tblProperties.Rows[row];

      string propertyName = tr.Cells[0].Text;

      if (((CheckBox)tr.Cells[1].Controls[0]).Checked)
      {
        baseEO.Properties.Add(new ENTAuditObjectPropertyEO
          {
            ENTAuditObjectId = baseEO.ID,
            PropertyName = propertyName
          });
      }
    }
  }
}
```

This method will add an object to the Properties property of the ENTAuditObject object for any row that has the checkbox checked in the Properties table.

Next, implement the event handler for the Object Name drop-down list. When the user changes the drop-down list, the page should refresh and display all the properties for the object. Set the control's `AutoPostBack` property to true and add the `SelectedIndexChanged` event handler:

```
protected void ddlObjectName_SelectedIndexChanged(object sender, EventArgs e)
{
    tblProperties.Rows.Clear();
    LoadPropertiesTable();
}
```

The rest of the code follows the same pattern defined in all the other pages. Implement the event handlers for the Cancel and Save buttons and set the menu item name and capability name for this page:

```
protected override void GoToGridPage()
{
    Response.Redirect("AuditObjects.aspx");
}

public override string MenuItemName()
{
    return "Auditing";
}

public override string[] CapabilityNames()
{
    return new string[] { "Auditing" };
}

void Master_CancelButton_Click(object sender, EventArgs e)
{
    GoToGridPage();
}

void Master_SaveButton_Click(object sender, EventArgs e)
{
    ENTValidationErrors validationErrors = new ENTValidationErrors();
    ENTAuditObjectEO auditObject =
        (ENTAuditObjectEO)ViewState[VIEW_STATE_KEY_AUDIT_OBJECT];
    LoadObjectFromScreen(auditObject);

    if (!auditObject.Save(ref validationErrors, CurrentUser.ID))
    {
        Master.ValidationErrors = validationErrors;
    }
    else
    {
        GoToGridPage();
    }
}
```

Run the project and add some records to this table using the interface. The sample code in the next section will implement the audit trail in the `PTORequestEO` object, so be sure to add this as an object to be audited.

Solution

Now the system has a way for the user to set up auditing, but it has to be implemented in the business layer. Luckily, the only classes that can be audited in the Paid Time Off solution are the `EditObject` classes, and there is a base class that can handle the majority of the logic needed to audit the object without having to completely overhaul the existing objects. Some custom code is needed in each object but it is minimal.

The first thing to consider is where the audit data will be stored. The requirements state that the system must store the user, date/time, before value, after value, and type of action that occurred, such as add, update, or delete. All of this data will be stored in one table called `ENTAudit`. The table structure is shown in Figure 12-3. The field names are straightforward.

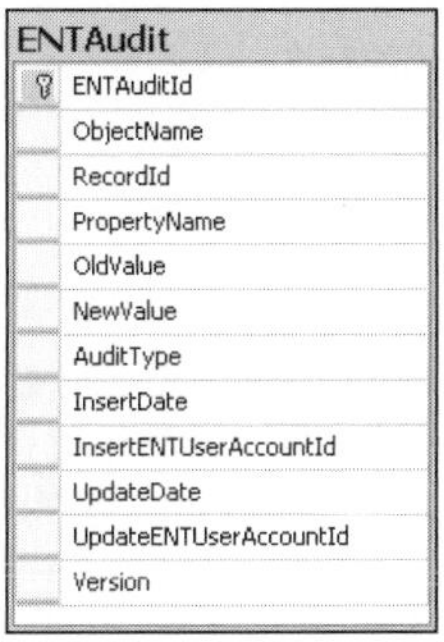

ENTAudit
🔑 ENTAuditId
ObjectName
RecordId
PropertyName
OldValue
NewValue
AuditType
InsertDate
InsertENTUserAccountId
UpdateDate
UpdateENTUserAccountId
Version

Figure 12-3

The `Chapter12Auditing.sql` script contains the DDL to create this table and the stored procedures associated with it. The standard five stored procedures can be created for this table without any customization. Once the table is created, add the table and the stored procedures to the `DataContext` object as you've done before using the ORM Designer. Again, remember to add the partial class to the `CustomizedEntities.cs` file for this table. Also add the `ENTAuditData` class to the `Framework` folder in the DAL project.

Now you can add the business classes: `ENTAuditEO` and `ENTAuditEOList`. These use the exact same pattern defined previously. Only one extra feature is needed in the `ENTAuditEO` class: an enumeration that specifies the type of audit. When creating the `AuditType` property, it should be declared as the `AuditTypeEnum` type:

```
public enum AuditTypeEnum
{
    Add,
    Update,
    Delete
}
```

That takes care of where the audit results will be stored. The next step is to implement the audit trail in the EditObject class. Adding and deleting are the easiest functionality to add to the class. When a record is added or deleted, a record should be added to the `ENTAudit` table with the ID of the record being added or deleted. Two new methods will be added to the `ENTBaseEO` object. The first takes care of adding the "Add" audit record:

```
public void AuditAdd(HRPaidTimeOffDataContext db, ref ENTValidationErrors
    validationErrors, int userAccountId)
{
    //Check if the object is being audited
    ENTAuditObjectEO auditObject = new ENTAuditObjectEO();
    if (auditObject.Load(db, this.GetType().Name))
    {
        ENTAuditEO audit = new ENTAuditEO();

        audit.ObjectName = this.GetType().Name;
        audit.RecordId = ID;
        audit.AuditType = ENTAuditEO.AuditTypeEnum.Add;

        audit.Save(db, ref validationErrors, userAccountId);
    }
}
```

This code must be called within the transaction of the calling `EditObject` class, so the `DataContext` must always be passed in. As with all the other methods that save to the database, the validation errors and user account ID must be passed in also. The method creates an instance of the `ENTAuditEO` object, sets its ObjectName and RecordId, and sets the audit type to Add and then adds the record to the audit trail. Unfortunately, this code cannot be automatically called without modifying the inheriting class. For this example, the `PTORequestEO` class will be used to track changes to its data. Add a line to the `Save` method in the `PTORequestEO` class to call this method after the record has been added:

```
if (isNewRecord)
{
  //Add
  ID = new PTORequestData().Insert(db, ENTUserAccountId, RequestDate,
    Convert.ToInt32(PTODayTypeId), Convert.ToInt32(PTORequestTypeId),
    userAccountId);

  AuditAdd(db, ref validationErrors, userAccountId);
}
```

The next step is to add the method that audits when records are deleted. This method is added to the `ENTBaseEO` class also:

```
public void AuditDelete(HRPaidTimeOffDataContext db, ref ENTValidationErrors
    validationErrors, int userAccountId)
{
  ENTAuditObjectEO auditObject = new ENTAuditObjectEO();
  if (auditObject.Load(db, this.GetType().Name))
  {
    ENTAuditEO audit = new ENTAuditEO();

    audit.ObjectName = this.GetType().Name;
    audit.RecordId = ID;
    audit.AuditType = ENTAuditEO.AuditTypeEnum.Delete;
```

```
    audit.Save(db, ref validationErrors, userAccountId);
  }
}
```

This method should be called whenever a record is deleted by the business layer. What's nice here is that by default the `Delete` method is implemented in the `ENTBaseEO` class, so each inheriting class does not have to be changed to implement this functionality. You simply add a line to the `Delete` method in this class:

```
internal virtual bool Delete(HRPaidTimeOffDataContext db, ref ENTValidationErrors
    validationErrors, int userAccountId)
{
  if (DBAction == DBActionEnum.Delete)
  {
    //Check if this record can be deleted.  There may be referential integrity
    //rules preventing it from being deleted
    ValidateDelete(db, ref validationErrors);

    if (validationErrors.Count == 0)
    {
      this.DeleteForReal(db);

      //Chapter 12-Auditing
      AuditDelete(db, ref validationErrors, userAccountId);
      return true;
    }
    else
    {
      //The record can not be deleted.
      return false;
    }
  }
  else
  {
    throw new Exception("DBAction not delete.");
  }
}
```

Finally, create the functionality that will do a property-by-property comparison when a record is updated and add a record for each property that changed. To do this, a helper class is needed that stores the name of the property and the value of the property when the record is loaded in the object. The new class is called `ENTProperty` and a companion list class should be created:

```
[Serializable]
internal class ENTProperty
{
    public string Name { get; set; }
    public object Value { get; set; }
}

[Serializable]
internal class ENTPropertyList : List<ENTProperty>
{

}
```

The ENTBaseEO object needs to be changed so that each object has a place to save the list of property values before updating the object's data. To do this, add a member variable to the ENTBaseEO class:

```
private ENTPropertyList _originalPropertyValues;
```

Now add to the base class a method that can enumerate through the current object's properties and store their values. This method is added to the ENTBaseEO class but it needs to be called in the inheriting class's Load method:

```
protected void StorePropertyValues()
{
  //Check if this object is being audited.
  ENTAuditObjectEO auditObject = new ENTAuditObjectEO();
  if (auditObject.Load(this.GetType().Name))
  {
    _originalPropertyValues = new ENTPropertyList();

    //Store the property values to an internal list
    //Create an instance of the type.
    PropertyInfo[] properties = this.GetType().GetProperties(BindingFlags.Instance
      | BindingFlags.DeclaredOnly | BindingFlags.Public);

    //Add an object to the list for each property and store it's current value.
    foreach (ENTAuditObjectPropertyEO auditObjectProperty in
            auditObject.Properties)
    {
      //Name of property
      _originalPropertyValues.Add(new ENTProperty
        {
          Name = auditObjectProperty.PropertyName,
          Value = this.GetType().GetProperty(auditObjectProperty.PropertyName)
                .GetValue(this, null)
        });
    }
  }
}
```

Change the Load method of the PTORequestEO object to call this method:

```
public override bool Load(int id)
{
    //Get the entity object from the DAL.
    PTORequest pTORequest = new PTORequestData().Select(id);
    MapEntityToProperties(pTORequest);

    //Chapter 12
    StorePropertyValues();
    return true;
}
```

Now that there is a place to store the existing values for the object, add a method to the `ENTBaseEO` class that can enumerate through the current properties after the user has made his or her changes, and add a record to the `ENTAudit` table for any property that changed and is being audited:

```
public void AuditUpdate(HRPaidTimeOffDataContext db, ref ENTValidationErrors
    validationErrors, int userAccountId)
{
  foreach (ENTProperty property in _originalPropertyValues)
  {
    object value = this.GetType().GetProperty(property.Name).GetValue(this, null);

    if (((value != null) && (property.Value != null)) &&
        (Convert.ToString(value) != Convert.ToString(property.Value)))
    {
      ENTAuditEO audit = new ENTAuditEO();
      audit.ObjectName = this.GetType().Name;
      audit.RecordId = ID;
      audit.PropertyName = property.Name;
      audit.OldValue = (property.Value == null ? null :
                        Convert.ToString(property.Value));
      audit.NewValue = (value == null ? null : Convert.ToString(value));
      audit.AuditType = ENTAuditEO.AuditTypeEnum.Update;
      audit.Save(db, ref validationErrors, userAccountId);
    }
  }
}
```

This method loops around any property being stored in the `_originalPropertyValues` list and retrieves the same property's value on the current instance of the object using reflection. If the value is different, then it adds a record to the `ENTAudit` table.

The last step is to call this method in the `PTORequest`'s `Save` method. This should be called after the update is successful:

```
//Update
if (!new PTORequestData().Update(db, ID, ENTUserAccountId, RequestDate,
    Convert.ToInt32(PTODayTypeId), Convert.ToInt32(PTORequestTypeId),
    userAccountId, Version))
{
  UpdateFailed(ref validationErrors);
  if (isNewRecord) ID = 0;
  return false;
}
else
{
  AuditUpdate(db, ref validationErrors, userAccountId);
}
```

Now the `PTORequest` object has full auditing capabilities. If you run the application and start adding and updating records, you'll see the `ENTAudit` table start to fill up. Be sure to turn on the auditing capabilities of this object using the "Auditing" screen created earlier in "The Design" section of this chapter.

Creating the Audit Report

It's great that the auditing capabilities now work in the application but you don't want users looking directly in the database to see the audit trail. Instead, using the pattern defined in Chapters 10 and 11, a report will be created that enables users to use the query control to filter the report data. Audit trails tend to get quite large, so it is important to enable users to filter out exactly what they are looking for in the report. The report will be quite simple. It is just a dump of the table data with the exception that the user ID will be resolved to the user's first and last name. The report is shown in Figure 12-4.

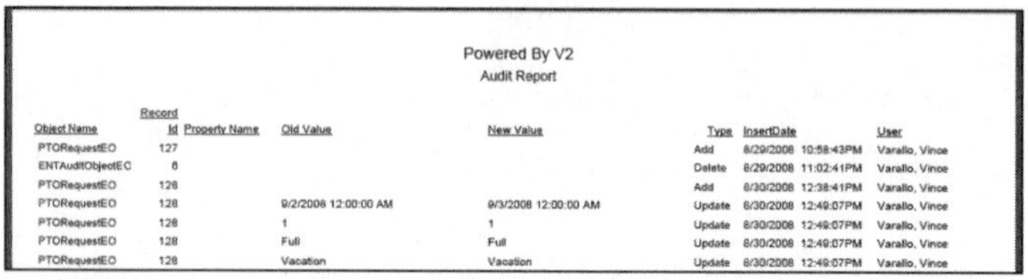
Powered By V2
Audit Report

Object Name	Record Id	Property Name	Old Value	New Value	Type	InsertDate	User
PTORequestEO	127				Add	8/29/2008 10:58:43PM	Varallo, Vince
ENTAuditObjectEO	6				Delete	8/29/2008 11:02:41PM	Varallo, Vince
PTORequestEO	128				Add	8/30/2008 12:38:41PM	Varallo, Vince
PTORequestEO	128		9/2/2008 12:00:00 AM	9/3/2008 12:00:00 AM	Update	8/30/2008 12:49:07PM	Varallo, Vince
PTORequestEO	128		1	1	Update	8/30/2008 12:49:07PM	Varallo, Vince
PTORequestEO	128		Full	Full	Update	8/30/2008 12:49:07PM	Varallo, Vince
PTORequestEO	128		Vacation	Vacation	Update	8/30/2008 12:49:07PM	Varallo, Vince

Figure 12-4

Use the following steps to create this report:

1. Add a new `DataSet` to the `Report\Schemas` folder in the user interface project.
2. Name the `DataSet ReportAudit.xsd`.
3. Drag a `TableAdapter` from the Toolbox onto the design surface of the `DataSet`. The TableAdapter Configuration Wizard will appear.
4. If you already added the `HRPaidTimeOff` database to the Server Explorer, then it should appear in the drop-down list of available databases. If it isn't in the list, then click the New Connection button and add the appropriate setting to connect to the database.
5. Select the `HRPaidTimeOff` database from the list and click the Next button.
6. The next screen asks whether you want to save the connection string to the configuration file. Uncheck the box and click the Next button because the connection string already exists in the configuration file.
7. The next screen asks which type of command you want to use to populate the `DataSet`. Choose Use SQL Statements. Remember that for reports, the schema file is simply used by the Report Builder so it knows what the data structure will look like; the `DataSet` will not be populated.
8. Click the Next button. This displays a screen where you can enter an SQL statement that will be used to automatically generate the columns in the schema file. You can either use the Query Builder screen or enter the following SQL statement in the text box:

```
    SELECT ENTAuditId, ObjectName, RecordId, PropertyName, OldValue,
           NewValue, AuditType, ENTAudit.InsertDate, FirstName, LastName
      FROM ENTAudit
INNER JOIN ENTUserAccount
        ON ENTAudit.InsertENTUserAccountId = ENTUserAccount.ENTUserAccountId
```

   This joins to the `ENTUserAccount` table, so the user's name is displayed instead of the ID.

9. Click the Next button.

10. The next screen asks whether you want to add any methods to the `DataSet`. Uncheck the two boxes and click the Next button.

11. A warning will appear stating that the data access logic will not be created. Click OK to this message because you don't need this functionality. The DAL will do this.

12. Click the Finish button and the `DataSet` should be generated for you (see Figure 12-5).

Figure 12-5

Now you can create the classes in the DAL that will serve up the data in this format. Since LINQ to SQL is being used to retrieve the data, an entity object must be created in the `DataContext` that contains the fields for this query. To make this easier, you can add a new stored procedure to the database and copy the SQL statement into the stored procedure. Then you can drag the stored procedure to the Methods pane of the `DataContext` to automatically generate the entity class. The stored procedure will never be used but it makes it easier to create the entity class. The sample code has a stored procedure named `ReportAudit` and the entity object is called `ReportAuditResult`.

The next step is to add the `Data` class. Since this report will enable users to filter the data using the `QueryBuilder` control, the `Data` class should inherit from the `ENTBaseQueryData` class and implement the `SelectClause` and `FromClause` methods. Call the new class `ReportAuditQueryData` and add it to the `Framework\Reports` folder in the DAL project:

```
public class ReportAuditQueryData : ENTBaseQueryData<ReportAuditResult>
{
  protected override string SelectClause()
  {
    return "SELECT ENTAuditId, ObjectName, RecordId, PropertyName, OldValue, " +
               "NewValue, AuditType, ENTAudit.InsertDate, FirstName, LastName ";
  }

  protected override string FromClause()
  {
  return "FROM ENTAudit " +
   "INNER JOIN ENTUserAccount " +
       "ON ENTAudit.InsertENTUserAccountId = ENTUserAccount.ENTUserAccountId ";
  }
}
```

Now add to this class the attributes that you want to expose to the `QueryBuilder` control. These are the fields users will be able to filter the report by:

```
[QueryField("ObjectName", "Object Name",
```

```
        QueryFieldAttribute.QueryFieldTypeEnum.String)]

    [QueryField("RecordId", "Record Id",
     QueryFieldAttribute.QueryFieldTypeEnum.Number)]

    [QueryField("PropertyName", "Property Name",
     QueryFieldAttribute.QueryFieldTypeEnum.String)]

    [QueryField("AuditType", "AuditType",
     QueryFieldAttribute.QueryFieldTypeEnum.Number)]

    [QueryField("CAST(ENTAudit.InsertDate AS smalldatetime)" , "Audit Date",
     QueryFieldAttribute.QueryFieldTypeEnum.Date)]

    [QueryField("ENTAudit.LastName + ', ' + ENTAudit.FirstName", "User",
     QueryFieldAttribute.QueryFieldTypeEnum.String)]
```

These attributes should be added above the class declaration in the `ReportAuditQueryData` class.

Now you can add the business class. Add a new class to the `Framework\Reports` folder in the BLL project and name the file `ReportAudit`. Shown here, the class should inherit from `ENTBaseQueryBO`:

```
    public class ReportAudit : ENTBaseQueryBO<ReportAuditQueryData, ReportAuditResult>
    {
    }
```

All of the methods that are needed for the report to work are in the base class, so you don't need to implement any methods.

Now you can move on to the report. Add a new Crystal Reports file named `Audit.rpt` to the `Reports` folder in the user interface project. Use the Report Designer Wizard to connect to the `ReportAudit` schema file. Follow the instructions in Chapter 9 to create a report that looks like the one shown in Figure 12-6. Change the report's orientation to Landscape instead of Portrait.

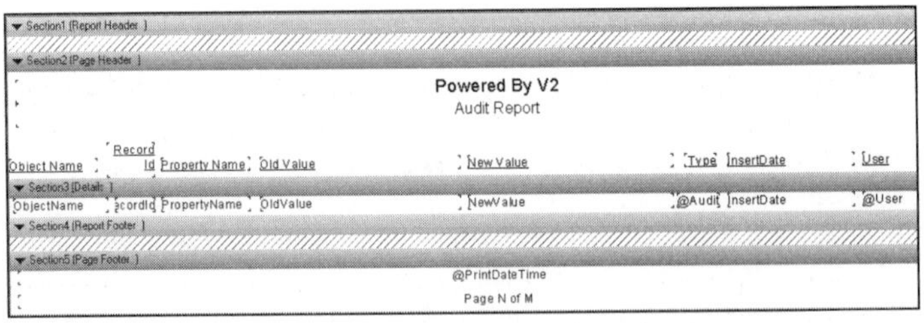

Figure 12-6

You need to add two formulas to the report — one to resolve the audit type and one to concatenate the user name. Add a new formula and name it @AuditType. The code for this formula is as follows:

```
    if {DataTable1.AuditType} = 0 then
        "Add"
    else
```

```
if {DataTable1.AuditType} = 1 then
    "Update"
else
    "Delete"
```

Add a second formula to the report and name it @User. The code for this formula is as follows:

```
{DataTable1.LastName} + ", " + {DataTable1.FirstName}
```

Once you've completed the report's design, you need to add a record to the ENTReport table and give yourself access to the report so you can run it. The record in the ENTReport table should be as follows.

ReportName	FileName	ObjectName	Description	SubReport ObjectName	SubReport MethodName
Audit Report	Audit.rpt	V2.PaidTimeOffBLL. Framework.Reports. ReportAudit, V2.PaidTimeOffBLL, Version=1.0.0.0, Culture=neutral, PublicKeyToken=null	Displays the list of records added, updated, and deleted	NULL	NULL

Launch the application and navigate to the Role screen. Give yourself access to this report by selecting the Read Only option next to the Audit Report (see Figure 12-7).

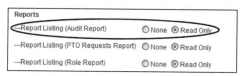

Figure 12-7

Click the Reports tab on the top menu in the application and then click the Run link next to the Audit report. The report screen should appear with the QueryBuilder control, and you should see the list of names defined in the custom attributes of the Data class in the Select a Field drop-down list. Add some criteria to the filters and then run the report. The Audit report should display as a PDF file onscreen (see Figure 12-8).

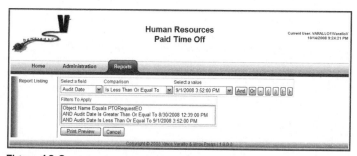

Figure 12-8

Summary

The audit trail is now complete and meets all of Mary's requirements. Even though this was added last, it is still quite trivial to implement the audit trail in the existing objects. The steps needed to implement the audit trail in an EditObject class are as follows:

❑ Modify the Save method in the EditObject class to call the AuditAdd method after a record has been inserted.

❑ Modify the Save method in the EditObject class to call the AuditUpdate method after a record has been updated.

❑ Turn the audit trail on for the EditObject class using the Auditing screen in the Administration section of the application.

The ENTBaseEO object and the ENTAudit objects handle the rest of the work.

Mary now has her fully functioning enterprise-level application, which she can use to track everyone's paid time off requests. After showing her all of the functionality of the workflow, the reports, the automated e-mails, the filtering capabilities on the reports, the security, and the audit trail, she is ecstatic. She has already submitted a request to upper management to give you a raise. The application included more functionality than she asked for or even knew to ask for, and her manager already has a wish list for other applications with similar functionality. You're going to become quite popular soon.

The only thing left to do now is find a way to automate all of this redundant code for building the stored procedures, data classes, and business classes. As you've probably noticed, most of the code is exactly the same for every table. Of course, there will be exceptions, but 80 to 90 percent of the time the code is boilerplate from the templates defined in the first three chapters.

The next chapter creates a code-generation tool that you can use to generate all of the mundane code, enabling you to concentrate on the business rules of the application. The code-generation tool makes building applications a snap, although I recommend that you understand the pattern before using the automation tool. When you know what's going on behind the scenes, you're in a good position to customize the pattern to meet your own needs or standards.

13

Code Generator

If you have made it this far in the book, then you probably realize that about 80 percent of the code in each chapter is repeated. The stored procedures all look the same and have the same five standard procedures for select all, select by ID, insert, update, and delete. The `Data` classes all look exactly the same because they implement the same base class and implement the same abstract methods. The editable business classes inherit from either the `BaseEO` or `BaseEOList` object and implement the same standard methods. Most of the customization to each of the classes varies according to the fields in the table the classes are managing.

Problem

As a developer, you are supposed to create systems to make business processes more efficient. Well, now it's time to help yourself out by writing a code generator that can handle up to 80 percent of the repetitive code needed for the stored procedures, data classes, and business classes. Once you have a code generator in place, you can concentrate on more important things — like playing golf or creating your own blog. If you're really lucky, you work in a shop that measures performance by the number of lines of code you write. You could be making ten times your current salary by the end of the year with a code generator!

This chapter builds a code generator that can be accessed through the Add New Item menu option in the Solutions Explorer. The code generator will enable you to choose a table and generate an SQL file for the stored procedures, a data class, an edit object class, and an edit object list class. I can tell you from experience that code generators save you a tremendous amount of time, and it is worth investing some time into creating your own code generator even if you don't use the pattern in this book.

Design

Before getting into the code-behind, this section will step through the process of using the code generator. It's a trivial process but it is easier to understand the code if you see it in action. The goal is to enable you to create your stored procedures and standard class files without leaving Visual Studio. Let's assume you need to generate the code for the ENTRole table. The first step after the table has been added to the database is to create the stored procedures. The code generator will enable you to use the Add New Item menu to generate the DDL statements to create the standard procedures and then you can execute these against the database. The Add New Item dialog displays the wizard shown in Figure 13-1.

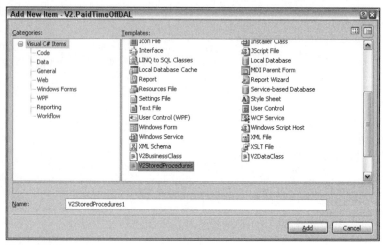

Figure 13-1

Notice you can pick from three new templates: V2BusinessClass, V2DataClass, and V2StoredProcedures. If you click on the V2StoredProcedures template and click the Add button, the window shown in Figure 13-2 will appear.

Figure 13-2

The Select a Connection list displays the names of the connection strings in any project in the current solution. When you select the connection, the screen will automatically populate the Select a Table drop-down list with all the tables in that database. Click OK to create a new file called TABLENameSP.sql and add it to the project. If you selected the ENTRole table, the file would be called ENTRoleSP.sql and the content would be as follows:

```sql
CREATE PROCEDURE ENTRoleSelectAll
AS
    SET NOCOUNT ON

    SELECT ENTRoleId, RoleName, InsertDate, InsertENTUserAccountId, UpdateDate,
           UpdateENTUserAccountId, Version
      FROM ENTRole

    RETURN
GO

CREATE PROCEDURE ENTRoleSelectById
(
    @ENTRoleId int
)
AS
    SET NOCOUNT ON

    SELECT ENTRoleId, RoleName, InsertDate, InsertENTUserAccountId, UpdateDate,
           UpdateENTUserAccountId, Version
      FROM ENTRole
     WHERE ENTRoleId = @ENTRoleId

    RETURN
GO

CREATE PROCEDURE ENTRoleDelete
(
    @ENTRoleId int
)
AS
    SET NOCOUNT ON

    DELETE
      FROM ENTRole
     WHERE ENTRoleId = @ENTRoleId

    RETURN

GO

CREATE PROCEDURE ENTRoleInsert
(
    @ENTRoleId  int OUTPUT,
    @RoleName  varchar(50),
    @InsertENTUserAccountId  int
)
```

```
AS
    SET NOCOUNT ON

    INSERT INTO ENTRole (RoleName, InsertDate, InsertENTUserAccountId, UpdateDate,
                         UpdateENTUserAccountId)
        VALUES (
                @RoleName,
                GetDate(),
                @InsertENTUserAccountId,
                GetDate(),
                @InsertENTUserAccountId
                )
    SET @ENTRoleId = Scope_Identity()

    RETURN

GO

CREATE PROCEDURE ENTRoleUpdate
(
    @ENTRoleId   int,
    @RoleName    varchar(50),
    @UpdateENTUserAccountId   int,
    @Version   timestamp
)
AS
    SET NOCOUNT ON

    UPDATE ENTRole
       SET
           RoleName = @RoleName,
           UpdateDate = GetDate(),
           UpdateENTUserAccountId = @UpdateENTUserAccountId
     WHERE ENTRoleId = @ENTRoleId
       AND Version = @Version

    RETURN @@ROWCOUNT

GO
```

Data and Business Classes

The same concept applies to the data and business classes. If you were to click the Add New Item menu and select V2DataClass, you would be presented with the same dialog. When you click the OK button, the system adds a new class to the project and names it TABLENAMEData.cs. Using the ENTRole table as the example again would create a file called ENTRoleData.cs, and the code would look as follows:

```
using System;
using System.Collections.Generic;
using System.Linq;
using System.Data.Linq;
using System.Text;
using V2.PaidTimeOffDAL.Framework;
```

```
namespace V2.PaidTimeOffDAL
{
    public class ENTRoleData : ENTBaseData<ENTRole>
    {
        #region Overrides

        public override List<ENTRole> Select()
        {
            using (HRPaidTimeOffDataContext db = new
             HRPaidTimeOffDataContext(DBHelper.GetHRPaidTimeOffConnectionString()))
            {
                return db.ENTRoleSelectAll().ToList();
            }
        }

        public override ENTRole Select(int id)
        {
            using (HRPaidTimeOffDataContext db = new
             HRPaidTimeOffDataContext(DBHelper.GetHRPaidTimeOffConnectionString()))
            {
                return db.ENTRoleSelectById(id).SingleOrDefault();
            }
        }

        public override void Delete(HRPaidTimeOffDataContext db, int id)
        {
            db.ENTRoleDelete(id);
        }

        #endregion Overrides

        #region Insert

        public int Insert(string connectionString, string roleName, int
                        insertENTUserAccountId)
        {
            using (HRPaidTimeOffDataContext db = new
                HRPaidTimeOffDataContext(connectionString))
            {
                return Insert(db, roleName, insertENTUserAccountId);
            }
        }

        public int Insert(HRPaidTimeOffDataContext db, string roleName, int
                        insertENTUserAccountId)
        {
            Nullable<int> eNTRoleId = 0;

            db.ENTRoleInsert(ref eNTRoleId, roleName, insertENTUserAccountId);

            return Convert.ToInt32(eNTRoleId);
        }

        #endregion Insert
```

```
            #region Update

            public bool Update(string connectionString, int eNTRoleId, string roleName,
                            int updateENTUserAccountId, Binary version)
            {
                using (HRPaidTimeOffDataContext db = new
                        HRPaidTimeOffDataContext(connectionString))
                {
                    return Update(db, eNTRoleId, roleName, updateENTUserAccountId,
                                version);
                }
            }

            public bool Update(HRPaidTimeOffDataContext db, int eNTRoleId, string
                            roleName, int updateENTUserAccountId, Binary version)
            {
                int rowsAffected = db.ENTRoleUpdate(eNTRoleId, roleName,
                                updateENTUserAccountId, version);
                return rowsAffected == 1;
            }

            #endregion Update
        }
    }
```

The data class assumes you are inheriting from the ENTBaseData class, and you would create the entity class using the LINQ to SQL Designer, just as you have done in the previous chapters. The code generator creates the methods that can be used to call the methods on the DataContext object that calls the stored procedures.

Adding a new business class is just as easy. If you click the Add New Item menu and select V2BusinessClass, the same dialog appears, from which you can select the connection and table for which you want to create the classes. Clicking the Add button adds a file called TABLENAMEEO.cs to the project and the code would be as follows (both the EO and EOList classes are in this same file):

```
using System;
using System.Collections.Generic;
using System.Linq;
using System.Text;
using V2.PaidTimeOffDAL.Framework;
using V2.PaidTimeOffDAL;
using V2.PaidTimeOffBLL.Framework;

namespace V2.PaidTimeOffBLL
{
    #region ENTRoleEO

    [Serializable()]
    public class ENTRoleEO : ENTBaseEO
    {
        #region Properties

        public string RoleName { get; set; }
```

```
#endregion Properties

#region Overrides

public override bool Load(int id)
{
    //Get the entity object from the DAL.
    ENTRole eNTRole = new ENTRoleData().Select(id);
    MapEntityToProperties(eNTRole);
    return eNTRole != null;
}

protected override void MapEntityToCustomProperties(IENTBaseEntity entity)
{
    ENTRole eNTRole = (ENTRole)entity;

    ID = eNTRole.ENTRoleId;
    RoleName = eNTRole.RoleName;
}

public override bool Save(HRPaidTimeOffDataContext db, ref
    ENTValidationErrors validationErrors, int userAccountId)
{
    if (DBAction == DBActionEnum.Save)
    {
        //Validate the object
        Validate(db, ref validationErrors);

        //Check if there were any validation errors
        if (validationErrors.Count == 0)
        {
            if (IsNewRecord())
            {
                //Add
                ID = new ENTRoleData().Insert(db, RoleName, userAccountId);

            }
            else
            {
                //Update
                if (!new ENTRoleData().Update(db, ID, RoleName,
                                             userAccountId, Version))
                {
                    UpdateFailed(ref validationErrors);
                    return false;
                }
            }

            return true;

        }
        else
        {
            //Didn't pass validation.
```

```
                            return false;
                }
            }
            else
            {
                throw new Exception("DBAction not Save.");
            }
        }

        protected override void Validate(HRPaidTimeOffDataContext db, ref
                                    ENTValidationErrors validationErrors)
        {
            throw new NotImplementedException();
        }

        protected override void DeleteForReal(HRPaidTimeOffDataContext db)
        {
            if (DBAction == DBActionEnum.Delete)
            {
                new ENTRoleData().Delete(db, ID);
            }
            else
            {
                throw new Exception("DBAction not delete.");
            }
        }

        protected override void ValidateDelete(HRPaidTimeOffDataContext db, ref
            ENTValidationErrors validationErrors)
        {
            throw new NotImplementedException();
        }

        public override void Init()
        {
            throw new NotImplementedException();
        }

        protected override string GetDisplayText()
        {
            throw new NotImplementedException();
        }

        #endregion Overrides
}

#endregion ENTRoleEO

#region ENTRoleEOList

[Serializable()]
public class ENTRoleEOList : ENTBaseEOList<ENTRoleEO>
{
    #region Overrides
```

```
        public override void Load()
        {
            LoadFromList(new ENTRoleData().Select());
        }

        #endregion Overrides

        #region Private Methods

        private void LoadFromList(List<ENTRole> eNTRoles)
        {
            if (eNTRoles.Count > 0)
            {
                foreach (ENTRole eNTRole in eNTRoles)
                {
                    ENTRoleEO newENTRoleEO = new ENTRoleEO();
                    newENTRoleEO.MapEntityToProperties(eNTRole);
                    this.Add(newENTRoleEO);
                }
            }
        }

        #endregion Private Methods

        #region Internal Methods

        #endregion Internal Methods
    }

    #endregion ENTRoleEOList
}
```

As you can see, most of the grunt work is done for you. Once the business class is created you can add the validation rules to the `Validate` method or make any customizations needed to represent relationships. This truly saves you a tremendous amount of time.

Solution

Now that you've seen the code generator in action, you will see how it works behind the scenes in this section. To add your own custom "wizards" to the Add New Item dialog in Visual Studio, you create a new Class Library project and add a class that implements the `IDTWizard` interface. The full definition of the `IDTWizard` interface can be found at `http://msdn.microsoft.com/en-us/library/envdte .idtwizard.execute.aspx`.

The `IDTWizard` interface is in the `EnvDTE` namespace, which is an assembly wrapped COM library containing the objects that enable you to manipulate the Visual Studio Design Time Environment. The interface has only one method, `Execute`, which is called when the wizard is launched using the Add New Item or Add New Project menu items. The method signature for the `Execute` method is as follows:

```
public void Execute(object Application, int hwndOwner, ref object[] ContextParams,
                    ref object[] CustomParams, ref wizardResult retval)
```

The parameters are defined as follows:

❑ **Application:** A dispatch pointer to the highest-level automation object for the Visual Studio environment

❑ **hwndOwner:** The hWnd handle for the parent of the wizard's window

❑ **ContextParams:** An array of elements that varies according to whether your wizard is launched from the Add Items or the New Project dialog. The following table describes which options are available depending on which type of wizard you are creating.

Wizard Type	Parameters Used
New Project	WizardType, ProjectName, LocalDirector, InstallationDirectory, FExclusive, SolutionName, Silent
AddSubProject	WizardType, ProjectName, ProjectItems, LocalDirectory, ItemName, InstallationDirectory, Silent
AddItem	WizardType, ProjectName, ProjectItems, LocalDirectory, ItemName, InstallationDirectory, Silent

❑ **CustomParams:** An array of user-defined parameters, determined by the param= statements in the wizard's .vsz file. You can use the parameters passed in this array to customize a wizard's behavior and role.

❑ **retval:** A wizardResult constant specifying the results of the wizard

The Execute method contains the logic to display the form, generate the new code modules, and add them to the project.

You also need to create a file with an extension of .vsz and drop it into the c:\Program Files\ Microsoft Visual Studio 9.0\VC#\CSharpProjectItems folder. The filename is what is displayed in the Add New Item dialog. The first line of the file is VSWizard 7.0. The second line in the file tells the development environment which object should be created for this wizard. This should be the name of the class that implements the IDTWizard interface — for example: Wizard=MyNewWizard .Class1. The third line starts a list of custom parameters that you can pass to the Execute method in the CustomParams parameter array. You simply start the line with the word Param and set the value using an equals sign — for example, Param=Data. Each parameter must be on its own line in the file.

You also need to ensure that you add an extra linefeed after the last parameter; otherwise, you get an error when the wizard is launched. The following example represents a wizard that will create the MyNewWizard.Class1 and pass a parameter of 1 to the execute method:

```
VSWizard 7.0
Wizard=MyNewWizard.Class1
Param=1
```

To create the code generator project, open the PaidTimeOff solution in Visual Studio 2008 and add a new Class Library project. Name the project V2.CodeGenerator. Right-click on the Class1.cs file that was created and rename it ENTCodeGen.cs. The class should be changed to ENTCodeGen for you automatically. Two references need to be added to this project so you can programmatically interact with the design-time environment. Add a reference to the EnvDTE and EnvDTE80 components and add the following using directives to the top of the ENTCodeGen class:

```
using EnvDTE;
using EnvDTE80;
using System.IO;
using System.Data;
```

The System.IO and System.Data classes will be used to write the class files and retrieve the table's schema from the database.

Change the class declaration so that it implements the IDTWizard interface and instruct Visual Studio to automatically implement the interface:

```
public class ENTCodeGen : IDTWizard
{
    #region IDTWizard Members

    public void Execute(object Application, int hwndOwner, ref object[]
        ContextParams, ref object[] CustomParams, ref wizardResult retval)
    {
        throw new NotImplementedException();
    }

    #endregion
}
```

The Execute method is called when users add a new item to their project. This method should be changed so that it displays the form that enables the user to select a connection string and the table for which the developer wants to generate the code. Before changing this method, you must first add the form to the project. Right-click on the project file and select Add New Item. The Add New Item dialog will appear. Click on the Visual C# Items\Windows Forms node in the tree on the left-hand side. This will display all the Windows Forms templates that can be added. Select the Windows Form template and name it DatabaseSelector.cs. This is the form that will display the drop-down list of all connection strings in this solution, and the tables associated with the selected connection string. Add to the form two Label controls, two ComboBox controls, and two Button controls. It should look like the form shown in Figure 13-3.

Figure 13-3

Name the first ComboBox **cboConnectionString** and name the second **cboTable**. Rename the buttons to **btnOK** and **btnCancel**. The DatabaseSelector_Load event will populate the first ComboBox with all the connection strings in the current solution. In order to do this the form must be made aware of the current solution that is open in Visual Studio. Therefore, add a property to the form that the ENTCodeGen's Execute method will set. Remember that the first parameter to the Execute method is a reference to the design-time environment. Add the following using statements to the DatabaseSelector form:

```
using EnvDTE;
using EnvDTE80;
```

Next, add a property that references the design-time environment:

```
public DTE2 Designer { get; set; }
```

Now change the DatabaseSelector_Load event to use this property to load the connection string ComboBox:

```
private void DatabaseSelector_Load(object sender, EventArgs e)
{
    //List all the connection strings in the config file
    foreach (Project p in Designer.Solution.Projects)
    {
        //Check if this is a web project.
        if (p.Name.StartsWith("http"))
        {
            //Open the web.config file to retrieve the connection strings settings.
            System.Configuration.Configuration webConfig =
                System.Web.Configuration.WebConfigurationManager.OpenWebConfiguration(
                p.Name.Substring(p.Name.IndexOf("localhost") + 9));

            foreach (ConnectionStringSettings css in
                    webConfig.ConnectionStrings.ConnectionStrings)
            {
                //Check if this has already been loaded.
                if (cboConnectionString.Items.Contains(css) == false)
                {
                    //Add the connection string.
                    cboConnectionString.Items.Add(css);
                }
            }
        }
    }

    cboConnectionString.DisplayMember = "Name";
    cboConnectionString.ValueMember = "ConnectionString";
}
```

You must also add a reference to the System.Configuration and System.Web components in order for this code to work. The event handler loops around each project in the Designer.Solution.Projects collection. If the project name starts with http, then it is a website and you want to read all the connection strings from the web.config file. It then adds an item to the ComboBox for each unique connection string found in the web.config file.

The next event to handle is the cboConnectionString_SelectedIndexChanged event for the connection string ComboBox. When the user selects an item from the list, the "Tables" ComboBox should be populated with all the tables in the database:

```csharp
private void cboConnectionString_SelectedIndexChanged(object sender, EventArgs e)
{
    if (cboConnectionString.SelectedItem.ToString() != "")
    {
        //Get the tables from the selected database.
        SqlConnection cn = new
            SqlConnection(cboConnectionString.SelectedItem.ToString());

        cn.Open();
        DataTable dt = cn.GetSchema("Tables");

        cboTable.DataSource = dt;
        cboTable.DisplayMember = "TABLE_NAME";
    }
}
```

This uses the GetSchema method from the connection object that returns the table definition in the database. The schema is returned as a DataTable and then bound to the ComboBox. You need to add a using statement to reference the System.Data.SqlClient namespace for this code in order to recognize the SqlConnection class.

Now you can add the code for the OK and Cancel buttons. The OK button should ensure that the user selected a table from the list and then hide the form. It also must let the wizard know that the user clicked the OK button. To do this, a property will be added to the form and set to true when the user clicks the OK button. The Cancel button should just hide the form:

```csharp
//Property to signal the caller that the OK button was clicked
public bool OKClicked { get; set; }

private void btnOK_Click(object sender, EventArgs e)
{
    if (cboTable.SelectedItem == null)
    {
        MessageBox.Show("Please select a table.");
    }
    else
    {
        OKClicked = true;
        Hide();
    }
}

private void btnCancel_Click(object sender, EventArgs e)
{
    OKClicked = false;
    Hide();
}
```

The last step is to expose a method on the form that enables the wizard to retrieve the table schema from the table the user selected in the ComboBox. This method returns the table name and the DataTable containing the schema:

```
public void GetTableInfo(ref string tableName, ref DataTable schema)
{
    SqlConnection cn = new
        SqlConnection(cboConnectionString.SelectedItem.ToString());

    cn.Open();

    tableName = ((DataRowView)cboTable.SelectedItem)["TABLE_NAME"].ToString();

    SqlCommand cmd = new SqlCommand("SELECT * FROM " + tableName, cn);

    schema = cmd.ExecuteReader(CommandBehavior.CloseConnection).GetSchemaTable();
}
```

That's all the code for the form. Now you can implement the Execute method in the ENTCodeGen class. The first thing to do in this method is create an instance of the form, set its Designer property, and then show the form as a modal dialog:

```
DatabaseSelector dbSelector = new DatabaseSelector();
dbSelector.Designer = (DTE2)Application;
dbSelector.ShowDialog();
```

Execution will pause at the ShowDialog line until control returns back from the form. After control returns, you must check whether the user clicked the OK button. If so, you can retrieve the information to write the new file:

```
//Check if the user clicked the OK button.
if (dbSelector.OKClicked)
{
    //Get the project items from the parameters.
    ProjectItems projectItems = (ProjectItems)ContextParams[2];
    string newItemDir = (string)ContextParams[3];

    //This string will contain the code that will be written to the file.
    string code = "";
    string fileName = "";

    //Get the default namespace for the curren projectc.
    string defaultNamespace =
        projectItems.ContainingProject.Properties.Item("DefaultNamespace").
        Value.ToString();

    //Retrieve the table name and schema from the form.
    string tableName = "";
    DataTable schema = new DataTable(); ;

    dbSelector.GetTableInfo(ref tableName, ref schema);
```

The `ProjectItems` collection contains the information about the selected project in the design-time environment and is passed into the `Execute` method in the `ContextParams` parameter. You can use this collection to add new items or retrieve information about the project. The `newItemDir` is a string that contains the path to the directory where the item should be saved. This is also passed into the `Execute` method in the `ContextParams` parameter. The `code` variable is a string that will be appended to the code that should be written to the file. The `fileName` variable will be set according to which type of file you are creating — either an SQL file, a data class, or a business object class. The next few lines retrieve the default namespace from the current project. This is used when creating the data or business object classes. The next three lines simply retrieve the table name and schema from the form shown to the user. This can now be used to create the code for the type of file you are creating.

The Code Module

This section generates the code module, adds it to the project, and opens the file in the design-time environment:

```
//Check if the user is creating a data or business class.
switch (CustomParams[0].ToString())
{
    case "Data":
        code = CreateDataClass(tableName, defaultNamespace, schema);
        fileName = tableName + "Data.cs";
        break;
    case "Business":
        code = CreateBusinessClass(tableName, defaultNamespace, schema);
        fileName = tableName + "EO.cs";
        break;
    case "StoredProcedures":
        code = CreateStoredProcedures(tableName, schema);
        fileName = tableName + "SP.sql";
        break;
}

//Write the file to disk.
StreamWriter sw = new StreamWriter(newItemDir + fileName);
sw.Write(code);
sw.Close();

//Add the file to the project.
ProjectItem newfile = projectItems.AddFromFile(newItemDir + fileName);

// Open file so that the user can start editing it
dbSelector.Designer.ExecuteCommand("File.OpenFile", "\"" + newItemDir + fileName +
                                   "\"");
```

The `CustomParams` are passed in via the .vsz file that you will be creating. Three .vsz files are created: one for the stored procedures, one for the data class, and one for the business class. Each .vsz file will create this same object but it will pass in a different parameter to signal which file should be created. The `switch` statement is used to determine which type of file should be created and then it calls another method to generate the string that should be saved in the file. After the code has been written to the string, it is persisted to the disk using the StreamWriter object and then added to the current project using the AddFromFile method on the ProjectItems. The last line opens the file in the design-time environment.

The CreateDataClass, CreateBusinessClass, and CreateStoredProcedure methods all use a StringBuilder object to create the appropriate code. This section won't go over all the code in these methods but it will get you started. The complete code can be found in the solution available on the Wrox website. Most of it is repetitive:

```
private string CreateDataClass(string tableName, string defaultNamespace,
    DataTable schema)
{
    StringBuilder sb = new StringBuilder();

    string camelCaseName = CamelCase(tableName);

    //Using statements.
    sb.Append("using System;" + Environment.NewLine);
    sb.Append("using System.Collections.Generic;" + Environment.NewLine);
    sb.Append("using System.Linq;" + Environment.NewLine);
    sb.Append("using System.Data.Linq;" + Environment.NewLine);
    sb.Append("using System.Text;" + Environment.NewLine);
    sb.Append("using V2.PaidTimeOffDAL.Framework;" + Environment.NewLine);

    //Declare the namespace.
    sb.Append(Environment.NewLine);
    sb.Append("namespace " + defaultNamespace + Environment.NewLine);
    sb.Append("{" + Environment.NewLine);

    //Declare the class.
    sb.Append("    public class " + tableName + "Data : ENTBaseData<" + tableName +
            ">" + Environment.NewLine);
    sb.Append("    {" + Environment.NewLine);
    sb.Append("        #region Overrides" + Environment.NewLine);
    sb.Append(Environment.NewLine);

    //Select method 1.
    sb.Append("        public override List<" + tableName + "> Select()" +
            Environment.NewLine);
    sb.Append("        {" + Environment.NewLine);
    sb.Append("            using (HRPaidTimeOffDataContext db = new HRPaidTimeOffDa
taContext(DBHelper.GetHRPaidTimeOffConnectionString()))" + Environment.NewLine);
    sb.Append("            {" + Environment.NewLine);
    sb.Append("                return db." + tableName + "SelectAll().ToList();" +
            Environment.NewLine);
    sb.Append("            }" + Environment.NewLine);
    sb.Append("        }" + Environment.NewLine);
    sb.Append(Environment.NewLine);
```

As you can see, the method is simply mimicking the code in the data class and replacing the custom logic where the namespace or table-specific information should be written. The Insert methods are worth mentioning because they need to take in the list of fields as parameters to the method. The `Insert` methods are as follows:

```
//Insert method 1.
sb.Append("          public int Insert(string connectionString, ");

//Create the parameters for the insert method.
CreateParameterDeclarationForInsert(ref sb, schema, tableName);

sb.Length = sb.Length - 2;
sb.Append(")" + Environment.NewLine);
sb.Append("          {" + Environment.NewLine);
sb.Append("              using (HRPaidTimeOffDataContext db = new HRPaidTimeOffDataCo
ntext(connectionString))" + Environment.NewLine);
sb.Append("              {" + Environment.NewLine);
sb.Append("                  return Insert(db, ");

//Call the overloaded Insert method by passing in all the parameters.
CreateParametersForInsert(ref sb, schema, tableName);

sb.Length = sb.Length - 2;
sb.Append(");" + Environment.NewLine);

sb.Append("              }" + Environment.NewLine);
sb.Append("          }" + Environment.NewLine);
sb.Append(Environment.NewLine);

//Insert method 2.
sb.Append("          public int Insert(HRPaidTimeOffDataContext db, ");

//Create the parameters for the insert method.
CreateParameterDeclarationForInsert(ref sb, schema, tableName);

sb.Length = sb.Length - 2;
sb.Append(")" + Environment.NewLine);
sb.Append("          {" + Environment.NewLine);
sb.Append("              Nullable<int> " + camelCaseName + "Id = 0;" + Environment.
NewLine);
sb.Append(Environment.NewLine);
sb.Append("              db." + tableName + "Insert(ref " + camelCaseName + "Id, ");

//Call the overloaded Insert method by passing in all the parameters.
CreateParametersForInsert(ref sb, schema, tableName);

sb.Length = sb.Length - 2;
sb.Append(");" + Environment.NewLine);
sb.Append(Environment.NewLine);
sb.Append("              return Convert.ToInt32(" + camelCaseName + "Id);" +
Environment.NewLine);
sb.Append("          }" + Environment.NewLine);
sb.Append(Environment.NewLine);
sb.Append("          #endregion Insert" + Environment.NewLine);
```

The string that is generated for the `Insert` method looks like this in the data class:

```
public int Insert(string connectionString, string roleName, int
                  insertENTUserAccountId)
{
    using (HRPaidTimeOffDataContext db = new
            HRPaidTimeOffDataContext(connectionString))
    {
        return Insert(db, roleName, insertENTUserAccountId);
    }
}

public int Insert(HRPaidTimeOffDataContext db, string roleName, int
                  insertENTUserAccountId)
{
    Nullable<int> eNTRoleId = 0;

    db.ENTRoleInsert(ref eNTRoleId, roleName, insertENTUserAccountId);

    return Convert.ToInt32(eNTRoleId);
}
```

As you can see, the fields in the table are written in the parameter lists. To create this code, a helper method called `CreateParameterDeclarationsForInsert` is called:

```
private void CreateParameterDeclarationForInsert(ref StringBuilder sb, DataTable
    schema, string tableName)
{
    foreach (DataRow dr in schema.Rows)
    {
        if ((dr["ColumnName"].ToString() != tableName + "Id") &&
            (dr["ColumnName"].ToString() != "InsertDate") &&
            (dr["ColumnName"].ToString() != "UpdateDate") &&
            (dr["ColumnName"].ToString() != "UpdateENTUserAccountId") &&
            (dr["ColumnName"].ToString() != "Version"))
        {
            sb.Append(GetCSharpType(dr) + " " +
                    CamelCase(dr["ColumnName"].ToString()) + ", ");
        }
    }
}
```

This method will loop around each field in the table, get the equivalent C# type based on the column's data type, and camel case the variable name. The `GetCSharpType` method is as follows:

```
private string GetCSharpType(DataRow dr)
{
    bool isNullable = Convert.ToBoolean(dr["AllowDBNull"]);

    switch (dr["DataType"].ToString())
    {
        case "System.Int16":
            if (isNullable)
            {
```

```
                    return "Nullable<short>";
            }
            else
            {
                    return "short";
            }
        case "System.Int32":
            if (isNullable)
            {
                    return "Nullable<int>";
            }
            else
            {
                    return "int";
            }
        case "System.String":
            return "string";
        case "System.DateTime":
            return "DateTime";
        case "System.Byte":
            if (isNullable)
            {
                    return "Nullable<byte>";
            }
            else
            {
                    return "byte";
            }
        case "System.Byte[]":
            return "Binary";
        case "System.Boolean":
            return "bool";
        default:
            throw new Exception("Type not known");
    }
}
```

The `CamelCase` method simply takes a string and lowercases the first letter:

```
private string CamelCase(string s)
{
    return s.ToLower()[0].ToString() + s.Substring(1);
}
```

The rest of the code repeats this familiar pattern that simply builds a string to look like the code module. Look at the sample code to copy and paste the code if you are following along.

Once you have the code created to generate the files, you need to create the three .vsz files that tell Visual Studio that the code generator exists. Open Notepad and enter the following text:

```
VSWizard 7.0
Wizard=V2.CodeGenerator.ENTCodeGen
Param=StoredProcedures
```

Be sure to add at least two extra linefeeds after the `Param` line, which tells the `Execute` method to create the `StoredProcedure` file. Save this file to the `c:\Program Files\Microsoft Visual Studio 9.0\ VC#\CSharpProjectItems` folder and name the file `V2StoredProcedures.vsz`. Create the other two files and name them `V2DataClass.vsz` and `V2BusinessClass.vsz`. In each file, change the `Param` line to `Param=Data` and `Param=Business`. You can leave the first two lines unchanged.

Once you save the files, they should appear in the Add New Item dialog when you select the Add New Item menu from any project file. If you click on the template in the Add New Item dialog, you may get an error stating "Invalid at the top level of the document." This error message is misleading; to fix the error, you need to change the build options on the CodeGenerator project to be registered for COM interop. To do this, right-click on the `V2.CodeGenerator` project and select Properties. Select the Build tab and check the box that says "Register for COM interop." Next, change a line in the `AssemblyInfo.cs` file that is located in the `Properties` folder in the `V2.CodeGenerator` project. The `ComVisible` attribute should be set to true:

```
[assembly: ComVisible(true)]
```

Now you can rebuild the DAL and it should work correctly. You may need to close Visual Studio and open it again in order for it to work properly.

Summary

Code generators are great investments in time that will save you countless hours of tedious work. You can follow the pattern defined in this chapter to create any number of templates, not just the ones shown as examples in this chapter. You'll more than likely need to customize the code to meet your company's standards, but this should give you a big head start. Once you start using the generated code, you'll never have to write another class again with 30 properties for all 30 fields in a table.

Now the entire project is complete. Mary is happy and so is her boss. You have successfully restored her faith in IT by building her an enterprise-level application that she can use to manage the entire company's paid time off schedules. You also have a framework for future applications that will more than likely have similar features for security, reporting, querying, workflow, and auditing. You also have a tool that will generate 80 percent of the code for you, but you might want to keep that bit of information to yourself.

I hope that you have enjoyed reading through this book and have benefited from the samples in each chapter. Visual Studio 2008 has some great new features such as LINQ, the ORM Designer, extension methods, automatic parameterized constructors, and many more features. It also offers numerous features that were not covered in this book, including Silverlight, the WCF, the Entity Framework, and much more, but you'll have to wait for the second edition of this book for all of those goodies. For now, happy programming — and I hope you enjoy your experience with Visual Studio 2008.

Index

Link Button controls